Creating Costumes for Devised Theatre

Creating Costumes for Devised Theatre combines perspectives from a variety of theatre practitioners to guide artists through the journey of creating costumes for devised work.

Devised theatre can take a number of different forms, and it can be a challenge for the costume department to plan, organize, and assemble things for performers to wear while the entire shape of the piece is constantly changing. This book provides practical resources to guide the theatre artist through the journey of designing costumes as the characters are created. It addresses a wide range of questions, including how to adapt traditional methods of costume design to non-traditional practices, how to effectively collaborate with a team, and how to adapt costume technology practices to meet the needs of devising. Stories and photographs from performers, designers, technicians, directors, writers, educators, students, and activists working in the realm of devised theatre around the world are contextualized through the author's own involvement in unscripted, partially scripted, and otherwise dynamic drama, dance, and physical theatre to offer tangible solutions to streamline costume design and construction processes.

This book is an invaluable guide for both experienced and novice costume designers, costume technicians, students, teachers, directors, managers, and theatre artists who exist in the spaces where all these roles overlap.

Kyla Kazuschyk is Associate Professor of Costume Technology at Louisiana State University. Kyla holds a Bachelor of Arts degree in Theatre from the University of Central Florida and a Master of Fine Arts degree in Costume Technology from Ohio University. She has created costumes for the Santa Fe Opera, the Washington National Opera, the Florida Grand Opera, the Colorado Shakespeare Festival, and the Texas Shakespeare Festival, as well as uniforms for the dance teams of the professional basketball teams Orlando Magic and Detroit Pistons. Professional costume design credits include *Airline Highway*, *Disgraced*, and *The Mountaintop* at Louisiana's Swine Palace Theatre in addition to several devised adventures.

Creating Costumes for Devised Theatre

Kyla Kazuschyk

Designed cover image: Photo courtesy of Andy Phillipson-Livewireimage.com

First published 2023
by Routledge
605 Third Avenue, New York, NY 10158

and by Routledge
4 Park Square, Milton Park, Abingdon, Oxon, OX14 4RN

Routledge is an imprint of the Taylor & Francis Group, an informa business

© 2023 Kyla Kazuschyk

The right of Kyla Kazuschyk to be identified as author of this work has been asserted in accordance with sections 77 and 78 of the Copyright, Designs and Patents Act 1988.

All rights reserved. No part of this book may be reprinted or reproduced or utilised in any form or by any electronic, mechanical, or other means, now known or hereafter invented, including photocopying and recording, or in any information storage or retrieval system, without permission in writing from the publishers.

Trademark notice: Product or corporate names may be trademarks or registered trademarks, and are used only for identification and explanation without intent to infringe.

Library of Congress Cataloging-in-Publication Data
Names: Kazuschyk, Kyla, author.
Title: Creating costumes for devised theatre / Kyla Kazuschyk.
Description: New York, NY : Routledge, 2023. | Includes index.
Identifiers: LCCN 2022032531 (print) | LCCN 2022032532 (ebook) |
 ISBN 9781032019598 (hardback) | ISBN 9781032019529 (paperback) |
 ISBN 9781003181170 (ebook)
Subjects: LCSH: Costume. | Theater.
Classification: LCC PN2067 .K39 2023 (print) | LCC PN2067 (ebook) | DDC 792.02/6--dc23/eng/20220908
LC record available at https://lccn.loc.gov/2022032531
LC ebook record available at https://lccn.loc.gov/2022032532

ISBN: 978-1-032-01959-8 (hbk)
ISBN: 978-1-032-01952-9 (pbk)
ISBN: 978-1-003-18117-0 (ebk)

DOI: 10.4324/9781003181170

Typeset in GillSansStd-Light
by SPi Technologies India Pvt Ltd (Straive)

To my brother, Edmund

CONTENTS

Acknowledgments   ix

CHAPTER 1   INTRODUCTION   1

CHAPTER 2   ORGANIZE!   7

CHAPTER 3   COMMUNICATE!   35

CHAPTER 4   KNOW YOUR RESOURCES   67

CHAPTER 5   "SHARE YOUR BABY OFTEN"   105

CHAPTER 6   GET INVOLVED!   119

CHAPTER 7   PAPERWORK   157

CHAPTER 8   BEYOND THEATRE   179

Appendix   221
Index   235

ACKNOWLEDGMENTS

I extend my deepest gratitude to Emma Arends Montes, Rachel Baranski, Adanma Onyedike Barton, Carrie Bellew, Suellen Coelho, Gina Sandí Díaz, Siouxsie Easter, Rachel Engstrom, Nick Erickson, Kain Gill, Tonya Hays, Rowen Haigh, Mikaela Herrera, Kendra Johnson, Andréa Iza Morales, Maggie McGurn, Camilla Morrison, Carrigan O'Brian, Kendra Rai, Rhiannon Reese, Emilio Rodriguez, Pamela Rodríguez-Montero, Lena Sands, Bryan Scott, Sara Osi Scott, Alan White, Val Winkleman, and Nathan Ynacay.

Portions of this book originally appeared in the article "Embracing the Chaos: Creating Costumes for Devised Work" in *Theatre Symposium 2018*, Volume 26, a publication of the University of Alabama Press.

CHAPTER 1

INTRODUCTION

WHAT IS DEVISED THEATRE?

Devised theatre is difficult to define because it can be many things! It can be a performance that is entirely improvised. It can be a performance that starts with the framework of a script or some sort of written words. It can be a performance practice that works towards an end result of a finished script, or it can be a performance that starts and ends its process without ever having a written script or even an audience!

A group of dancers on a stage move in response to the movement of each other's bodies. A single performer standing on stage tells a story as a memoir. Actors use lines of written poetry to communicate new ideas to each other. Audiences walk through a haunted house where performers adjust their work to each individual. A team of artists meets with a community and listens to their stories, then acts out those stories on a stage or on a computer screen. All of these examples can be considered devised work.

It can be a challenge for the costume department to plan, organize, and assemble things for performers to wear as the entire shape of the piece is constantly changing. The ways in which we create costumes can adapt to suit all kinds of situations. As theatre artists, we generally practice a process that follows a linear timeline. Typically, crucial aspects of successfully creating costume designs and producing realized versions of those designs for theatrical practice include in-depth script analysis, careful study of characters, and detailed planning of materials and labor budgets. However, when tasked with designing and creating costumes for a project that begins with no script, no characters, and sometimes even an amorphous cast, the wisest course of action to take is to embrace the chaos.

The absence of familiar structures can feel scary, but the disassembling of old structures makes way for new ideas. New methods can be more inclusive and equitable than the way things have been in the past.

Numerous sources offer guidance on how to create costumes for characters that have already been defined in a script, yet few resources are available to guide the theatre artist through the journey of creating costumes as the characters are simultaneously created. I hope that this guide can be helpful to you as you embark on adventures in the world of devising and beyond. I have included ideas I've developed through my own experiences as well as conversations with technicians, designers, directors, performers, writers, students, and teachers who share suggestions from their perspectives.

In traditional theatre, the production process usually starts with a team of people assembling around a script that specifies the plot, setting, and characters of the piece. Design meetings are often hierarchical, with the director at the top and all other collaborators working to serve the director's vision. In devised theatre, a team assembles to start the process, yet they often start with no written text to use as a blueprint to guide the production journey, and the lineup of the team can change throughout the process. The responsibilities of people on the team can be more or less structured and shared. In some cases of devised theatre, there is written text, yet that text does not assign lines of dialogue to specific characters, or define who the characters are, or where they are, or what they are doing.

Although tried and true procedures work for many productions, when creating costumes for devised theatre, one must be open to unusual practices and procedures. These productions sometimes call for entirely new frameworks, or familiar frameworks plus additions from unexpected places. A brave costumer must enter into this process being unafraid to try new things, ready to accept ideas from new sources, experiment with techniques never tried before, and maintain calm as chaos creeps into the equation. This can be especially difficult for those of us accustomed to the standard production process, yet, if we truly embrace the chaos, the results can be exponentially fulfilling.

All theatre is collaborative art, and devised theatre could be explained as art that is ultra-collaborative. In an ideal world, a devised theatre company is formed as a sort of intentional community, members joining based on their particular skills, with the understanding that the work and the artists will grow in concert. In reality, there are a number of possible variations on this model, particularly in regard to how costumes are designed and created.

The first set of possible variables involves how many people are contributing to the project. In some instances, the costume department is an entire team of people, and on other productions costumes are provided by the director, the cast, or one person wearing many hats. There might be one person holding the title of costume designer, and that person may have one or more assistants. There could be a separate person responsible for managing the costume shop, and any number of people filling out the roles of cutter/draper, first hand, stitcher, crafts artisan, dyer/painter, and shopper. In my experiences, I was the designer, shop manager, cutter/draper, crafts artisan, dyer/painter, and shopper. Working in educational theatre, I had students of various skill levels to train as assistants, first hands, and stitchers. Each scenario has its own set of pros and cons. Many hands make light the work, yet make heavy the amount of necessary clear communication. Fewer hands means a heavier workload, but less of a need to spend time and energy sharing information.

The second set of possible variables surrounds the existence or non-existence of a script. Some works of devised theatre begin with a finalized script. Other forms bring a costumer into the process as the script is being developed. In some dance and movement pieces, there will never be a script. In other situations, there is a script; however, the script does not specify characters and/or settings. Such was the case in two of the projects I have worked on.

FIGURE 1.1 Savage/Love *at the Edinburgh International Fringe Festival (photo courtesy of Andy Phillipson—Livewireimage.com)*

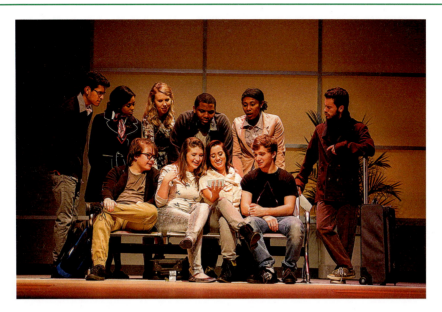

FIGURE 1.2 *Love and Information* at Louisiana State University

As costume designer, cutter/draper, and costume shop manager for Sam Shepard and Joseph Chakin's *Savage/Love* and Carol Churchill's *Love and Information*, I was able to participate in all aspects of the theatrical costume process, from inventing underlying meanings to ensuring that costume pieces appropriately fit the performers' bodies. *Savage/Love* is a series of poems about love and loss and connection. This work became a multimedia, multidisciplinary performance piece that evolved over the course of several months. *Love and Information* is a non-linear collection of over 50 scenes about connections and missed connections in the modern world, written to be performed by an unspecified number of people, portraying an unspecified number of characters, in an unnamed setting. Over the eight-week production period within the academic calendar of Louisiana State University's 2016–17 season, this production eventually became ten actors playing over one hundred different characters, in an airport.

After *Savage/Love*, I collaborated with physical theatre performers on *Dream Logos*, a project that went down similar dance and multimedia pathways, yet it began with no script or text at all and it continued to evolve and change throughout the run of the show.

IN WHAT WAYS DOES DEVISED WORK HOLD POWER AND POSSIBILITY?

The process of creating and sharing devised work contains incredible potential for changing the current landscape of the theatre. Solo performance, installation art, and abstract, non-linear forms are propelling us all toward gender parity and toward a myriad of other intersectional goals. Works of devised theatre can be created quickly and in response to specific instances of injustice or broader societal problems. They can be created with communities to address issues facing those communities. Creating and presenting the work is also creating space to question, to raise awareness, and to learn and grow.

One example of devised theatre is the thesis project for the graduate degree in performance at Louisiana State University, where students create a one-person show. Students are responsible for the entire piece—from choosing a concept and developing a script to directing, performing, and assembling design elements. Stories can be personal, creative, historical, or a combination of these. This type of autonomous and independent storytelling allows each person to find and share their voice, and trains them in a variety of skills useful in the world beyond university.

The worlds of dance, physical theatre, interactive and immersive installation art, and loosely scripted or non-scripted theatre provide opportunities for truly collaborative environments, where everyone's voices can be heard. Through the lens of a variety of experiences in roles including writer, director, performer, dramaturg, costume designer, costume shop manager, and cutter/draper on several recent devised works, this book will share concrete strategies for overcoming fear, diving into the unknown, and emerging as a driving force toward a more balanced and equal world.

FIGURE I.3 *Experimenting with costumes as projection surfaces in rehearsal for* Dream Logos

FIGURE 1.4 Dream Logos *at the Edinburgh International Fringe Festival (photo courtesy of Andy Phillipson—Livewireimage.com)*

As artists and craftspersons, we dwell in a world of possibility. We can work together each and every day to build environments where we can support, encourage, and inspire one another. We can all actively create and support positive environments within the microcosms of our specific disciplines. From the costume shop to the rehearsal room, the choices we make and the actions we take can contribute bit by bit to creating an equitable world. How can we nourish inclusive spaces where people with all sorts of identities can feel welcome? What can we learn from structures of spaces unfamiliar to our own? What can we bring to situations in which we have varying degrees of agency? In what specific ways can we listen to and amplify each other's voices?

CHAPTER 2

ORGANIZE!

PRODUCTION MANAGE YOUR OWN DEPARTMENT

Devising projects often begin with no scheduled production calendar. I have worked on projects where the calendar is created and then distributed, and it is the responsibility of each contributor to fill their own department's deadlines into the existing calendar. Sometimes directors and performers enter into a piece without thinking about having to make decisions regarding costumes. Identify where you have agency and where you do not. Some things are going to be within your ability to control, and others will not. Maybe you have a say in when all the deadlines will be. Maybe you have signed on to a project that has an opening date set in stone. If there are no existing deadlines, make your own. When drafting a schedule for costumes, look at your own calendar and create timelines with deadlines that are realistic and achievable. Share your proposed calendar with the entire team. Be as clear and specific as possible with regard to what you will deliver and what you will need. Invite feedback, make adjustments, and then get the entire team on board with it.

As a costume shop manager, I create a timeline for every show, working backwards from opening night and filling in relevant milestones from there. On a devised project, you might want to include all these deadlines plus even more.

When I was first approached by director/choreographer Nick Erickson and asked to create costumes for the "summer abroad show" which would eventually become *Savage/Love*, there were too many unknowns for me to make a responsible commitment to the project. I sent an email to him and the rest of the production team, proposing a more concrete timeline with deadlines to be mutually agreed upon. I broke it down into a sequence of design meetings, first discussing the concept, then reviewing research images, reviewing preliminary designs, and finally approving final designs. All this was combined with the clear directive that in order for production to be completed on time, work would need to happen concurrently along these deadlines. Flexibility within boundaries is key.

For example, here is the email I sent out committing to the *Savage/Love* project:

Hi, Nick!

As classes are winding down, I have finally had time to sit down and look at the spring calendar and come up with a possible plan for the Edinburgh project. It does sound like an exciting opportunity, and I would like to design and construct costumes for it, with a student as my assistant. Here is my proposed timeline:

January 15—First design meeting—designers, assistants, and director (team) discuss initial concept

February 1—Design Meeting 2—team goes over visual research images

February 15—Design meeting 3—Preliminary costume renderings are due—feedback from director

February 29—Design meeting 4—Final costume designs are approved

Week of March 7—Costume build process begins in costume shop

Week of April 4—Performers are called to the shop for first fittings

April 11—Production meeting—team gets together to touch base, discuss progress

Week of April 18—Performers are called to the shop for second fittings

Week of May 2—Performers are called to the shop for FINAL fittings, final alterations and adjustments are completed

May 6—Finished costumes are turned over to the director.

Meeting dates could be shifted a day forward or back to accommodate everyone's schedules.

What do you think? Does this sound like a workable time frame for the costume element? I know it is on top of many other events and projects. Looking at my schedule and other commitments, I believe that this timeline allows for the best possible outcome.

Thank you!

—Kyla

I have used this example many times with students to illustrate what setting boundaries can look like. For the director or choreographer who is working on only one project, it makes sense that they might expect a significant time commitment from their collaborators. As designers and technicians, we are often working on multiple projects simultaneously, and it is not sustainable or sometimes even possible to give the same amount of time and energy that a director or choreographer is giving. So, as a designer/technician, look at your own schedule, take stock of all the projects that are on your plate, and think about what a feasible schedule will look like. Exactly how many hours per week can you spend on a certain project? What are you capable of accomplishing in that time? (More on this in the section on knowing your resources.) At what points will you need concrete decisions from collaborators in order to move forward? How much can stay flexible? Your own personal answers to all these questions are what can inform how you create your calendar.

Some aspects of the calendar might be put in place by others. Maybe there is a production manager involved in the process, and maybe not. At different theatres and in different theatre companies, the responsibilities of a production manager can vary. For example, in university theatre, a production manager often wears several more hats in addition to production manager. The responsibilities and level of involvement of directors and choreographers can vary as well.

Opening dates might be on the books, or perhaps the goal for a process is the process itself, without working toward a specific opening night at all.

Artist Alan White describes an extended devising process that they participated in:

We were using a space at one of the members' place of work, which was an arts organization, so we had unlimited access. We weren't paying for the rehearsal space, and so we had unlimited access to it. So we spent probably over a year, maybe two, just playing and devising, and always going back to the beginning and starting over and bringing new things in, before we were like maybe we should actually create something. Like, do we want to share this with an audience, or do we just want to keep playing forever?

It wasn't that one was better than the other, it was like, Okay we need to decide what we want. Because we could just keep, we referred to it as training, we could just keep training and just keep doing this. We just needed to decide: Is this what we're going to do? Or do we want to have something that we're going to share publicly? Most artists I know who have worked in devised spaces, who like it, would be thrilled to have a group that they could meet with every week or twice a month and just play without care.

If there's no opening night in sight or any financial commitments, artists can keep exploring their creativity and costumes can stay as the equivalent of rehearsal pieces indefinitely.

We are afraid of things we do not yet understand. It is natural that a completely unfamiliar process or framework will be scary. The traditional design process is so deeply ingrained in our training. We are accustomed to starting with a script, analyzing it, and designing costumes for characters as defined in the text, in harmony with a director's vision.

For designers trained in this text-based method, shaking up the process can be frightening. For actors and directors as well, beginning without a clear blueprint may feel scary. Chaos can seem threatening to a system that thrives on order, though sometimes the strongest ideas emerge from this chaos. When the needs of the costumes for the characters are not dictated by an outside source, there exists the freedom for the costumes to be born as the characters are born, to develop alongside the characters, and ultimately be more steeped in connection to the characters than costumes that are added on top of existing characters.

Rachel Sullivan, of the Honest Accomplice Theatre, addressed the puzzle of designing costumes for devised work by saying, "As a designer, you need a lot of adrenaline to work with a devising project." This is because nothing is ever solid, things are always changing, and the entire process is chaotic. Perhaps this chaos and the mentality that adrenaline is imperative stem from the inherent goal of some forms of theatre to present questions and ideas rather than solutions. Live theatre has the power to incite ideas by presenting multiple points of view simultaneously. Audience members can see parts of themselves in different characters and are hence more inclined to think about different sides of the story than they might be if the story was just dictated to them from one perspective. Some works of theatre tell a story and tie the ending together neatly, delivering solutions that may not inspire much further thought. Devised theatre almost always strives to offer questions rather than answers. Costumes can only stay in the questioning phase for so long though; eventually some solid decisions must be made and costumes must be created. "You can whip together a scripted play in a couple weeks," Sullivan attests, but creating a new devised piece takes much longer, sometimes nine months or more. In some forms of devised theatre, the process is actually of greater importance than the product. This emphasis on process allows designers and technicians to be more involved with the whole creation of meaning and the expression of the themes in the piece than there is space for in traditional theatre.

"Production manage your own department" means focus on what you *can* control and learn how to let go of the things you cannot. (This applies to more than just our work, of course.) Some aspects will be beyond what you have power to change. I encourage you to accept the necessary chaos, embrace it. Reassure yourself that you have managed the chaos that is able to be managed, and follow the winding path to where the rest of it leads you.

DEVELOP A PLAN

The first questions to ask yourself when embarking upon a devising project include: How many collaborators are involved? What are their roles? What is your role? How can you continue to set and hold healthy boundaries?

Designer/Shop Manager/Draper/Shopper roles often overlap. If you have teammates, what will they contribute? How much of the labor falls on your shoulders? How much can be delegated? In educational theatre, another consideration to keep in mind is student experiences. Is it possible to give students more responsibility? If we are not trusting students and giving them opportunities, what is the point?

Weigh what is necessary versus what is possible. This is a huge question, and it can and should be applied to scripted work as well. Dream big, and then edit down to what is achievable within the parameters of the project. How much time do you have? How much skilled labor do you have? How much money do you have for this project? Start drafting a budget as early as possible. Begin with a plan of rough estimates and check in with it and adjust as time passes and decisions get made. How much could you afford to spend on materials, on costume pieces? Could you save time by spending money on labor? Could you save money by doing more of the labor yourself? What costume elements are absolutely essential to help tell the story?

For *Savage/Love*, costumes had to fit to accommodate performers on aerial silks. Each performer has specific needs

FIGURE 2.1 *Aerial artist at work in the student devised show* Dream Logos

and preferences. Some aerial artists prefer to have skintight fabric covering their legs, particularly behind their knees, while others are more comfortable in short garments, with no fabric between their legs and the aerial equipment at all. Communicate with performers about what they need.

To get rolling on *Savage/Love* before themes, characters, and plots were set, the plan I developed and then carried out was this:

Step 1: Order a range of sizes and styles of dyeable stretch knitwear pieces.
Step 2: Fit the undyed garments on the performers, communicating with them about their comfort level and preferences.
Step 3: As the scenes and characters took shape, I dyed and painted the garments using various techniques to make each character distinctive.

The plan can look different on every project. Because devised work exists on a spectrum, it is not possible to use one specific formula to suit every project. However, it is possible to approach each project with a flexible toolkit, to take what might work and try it and adapt with the project as it takes shape.

CONSIDER THE CAST

Maybe the cast list is set in stone … but most likely it is not. Plus, what is ever really set in stone anyways? Everything can always change.

FIGURE 2.2 *The rack of possible costumes for* Savage/Love *undyed, before characters were determined, and then dyed and painted, as the show developed*

Often production and purchasing for a devised piece must begin before the cast is finalized. Such was the case on *Savage/Love*. Initially introduced as a summer abroad project, the cast for the piece was contingent on students who could go on the summer study abroad trip. Work on the piece would begin in Baton Rouge, Louisiana; it would then travel to France where additional cast members would join the production, and finally the piece would be performed at the Edinburgh International Fringe Festival. The initial cast was a list of students who had expressed interest in the project. Over the course of several months, some ensemble members dropped out and others joined. In a perfect world, I would have waited until the cast was completely finalized before starting to purchase, build, and fit costume pieces. However, in this instance, if I had waited, there would not have been enough time left to get anything done. I moved forward as early as possible by purchasing a variety of dyeable garments in a range of sizes. As performers came in for the first round of fittings, I fit the plain white garments to their bodies, and then later added dye and paint treatments to indicate character, as the characters and stories developed. This flexibility allowed the ensemble to continue to experiment with blocking throughout the rehearsal process. Characters who grew to be connected to each other had designs painted on their garments that connected together when they were blocked to stand together or embrace. Because I waited until later in the process to complete the dye and paint treatments, the ensemble was able to make changes that could later be enhanced by costume details. These details are what give audiences clues as to who the characters are.

Prepare more than you need so that you have options. If the cast changes, be ready to fit a costume on someone else.

Keep the rack of pieces you pulled, the range of options for each character. On *Airline Highway*, which was a scripted show, the cast unexpectedly changed drastically multiple times during the run, and costumes had to adapt. Our designs can feel so precious, but in reality our designs can exist as a range of options. Specificity is important, but so is flexibility.

FIGURE 2.3 *A dress rehearsal for Swine Palace's Airline Highway*

When fitting and finalizing costumes, consider sizes and shapes of the cast. What is crucial to the telling of the story? Is it a silhouette? A certain detail? What works and what conveys the character on that particular performer?

Costume designer Kendra Rai suggests, "As scary as it is to us costumers to bring actors in from day one, try to bring them in at research point, because they're the ones wearing the clothes." If we think about talking to actors in fittings about what they are wearing instead of talking them into what to wear, we can arrive at a costume that an actor feels comfortable and safe in. It can be something that we create together.

Start talking about hair right away. Ask performers what they would be comfortable doing with their hair, what they would be okay with changing and what they would not be okay with changing, what styles they could create on their own and what they could create with assistance, what products they will need. You can start this conversation even before characters are determined, and then as things get more solidified, hopefully you will have established a relationship where a performer feels comfortable speaking up.

Similarly with understructure garments—start having the conversation about silhouette and comfort level as early as possible, with performers and with directors. Are corsets essential to this piece? Would boned bodices without corsets be enough to show structure? And even regardless of the time period the piece ends up being set in, would performers feel more comfortable or less comfortable in shapewear undergarments? If the answer is more comfortable, it is imperative to get those undergarments for performers to wear, and build the rest of the costumes on top of whatever shapes they create.

STAY FLEXIBLE!

It is okay for things to change, slightly or completely. If we approach a project not with an empty mind but definitely with an open mind, our ideas can grow exponentially. Stay open to change. Stay open to letting anything go, as well as inviting anything in.

FIGURE 2.4 Students performing in Cajun Christmas on the Bayou, *an original piece presented to a live audience as a radio play, using only live folio and costume pieces to establish characters. During intermission, alumni were pulled from the audience to draw numbers and were given scripts to perform as the characters that were assigned that number (alumni were not aware that this was going to happen) (photo courtesy of Carrie Bellew)*

There are multiple possibilities. *Love and Information* started with a script, but a script that did not specify characters. Some projects start with a cast and no script.

Always ask yourself, how can costumes help tell this story?

ARTIST SPOTLIGHT: CARRIE BELLEW

As a high school teacher, Carrie Bellew understands the importance of staying flexible. Here she discusses the advantages of creating devised work with students.

CARRIE BELLEW: My definition of devised theatre is an exploration of creativity that levels the playing field for everyone involved in a project. It's like learning to create and capture a story in singular moments that when you weave together, like a tapestry, every single fiber is a part of the story.

KYLA KAZUSCHYK: I love the metaphor of a tapestry. I can see that continuing in a lot of ways, like every participant is a different fiber, every idea is a fiber, and you weave them together to create a beautiful tapestry that's more than just a bunch of disparate threads.

CARRIE BELLEW: Yes, that's kind of how I see it. Especially utilizing the moment work from Tectonic theatre. I don't think that most of us realize that we're already doing devised theatre. And some aspects, if you think about design work that's exactly what you're doing: you're devising something to tell a story. You're one little small piece of a bigger picture. But the devised work captures or focuses in on those small moments to create the story. Which is an interesting aspect, to go completely reverse and backwards and just start literally from nothing but a blank canvas and then you just start painting. When I learned about moment work, I realized I had been doing devised theatre without even knowing I was doing it.

In our monologue shows, I just give the students a title and say write what you think. What does this make you feel, how do you feel about this title? And create a story. Create your own story using that one word or something that inspires you from the title and then they come up with these amazing monologues and then we do it as a show. So that's baby scale of course, that's not creating a full complete show from start to finish. It was really interesting to watch my students evolve and take charge. That was cool.

KYLA KAZUSCHYK: I think that's an advantage of devised work, that it's scalable. It doesn't have to be a fully realized production. You could take the principles of it and apply them to teaching in the classroom.

CARRIE BELLEW: And you never know, one monologue that a student creates could become a whole new story. Scenes, plays, weaving those together, it becomes a play. It's a devised piece of work from a title, a topic, anything. You could do so much with just one simple focus.

In my advanced classes, I always challenge them with choosing a play that they have to write a critical analysis on, but they have to analyze it first. And then I also task them with coming up with a children's piece.

So, think about the age bracket, the group that we're pushing this towards, and then go from there. What lessons do you want these kids to learn? What should they think about? One girl came up with "Stinky and Marmalade" which the title alone is just too cute. It's a bear and a fox and the bear doesn't know how to make a sandwich. That was it, that was the whole thing: a bear and a fox and the bear is hungry and doesn't know how to make a sandwich. Well now, using that little jump-off point, my theatre students have absorbed the characters and they're writing one about learning how to not judge a book by its cover and how you should respect and play with everyone and so it's evolved into a social experiment for younger kids to see this. And I think they've come up with a raccoon. Nobody wants to play with the raccoon because it is a raccoon. So they're taking a political stance, so to speak, for social justice, but geared towards children. It is showing an experience and letting the kids experience it and still learn something from it. I'm really proud of them.

What are the advantages to devised theatre? It places the story in everyone's hands. Equity! Everyone is equal. Everyone is important. Every opinion matters. Every little, teeny tiny facet matters. Opportunity! Devising allows one to play with theatrical elements that they never had been able to do before. Investment! Everyone's invested in the project because everyone gets a slice of the pie. Topics vary and the body of work is original: no royalties. You don't have to get licensing permission! And you create this original body of work that you can be proud of.

One of the opportunities that I always relished was originating a role. Being the first person to design the show, those opportunities don't come around all the time for students, especially an undergraduate or even in high school that just doesn't happen. So that is a big big plus of being the original producer, designer, actor, director, whatever of this work. It just means more, I think, in some aspects, I won't say all of it, but it's just really cool.

I don't think students honestly comprehend sometimes how impactful that can be. Because we've done original works. I've written a few things here and there. I'm not a playwright, by any means, but I've written some things specifically for my students, because we are strapped budget wise and the first time I wrote something, those students did not appreciate it, and so we didn't do it, but I gave everyone the opportunity to actually read it.

And then several years later, the students who had been in my theatre class joined my advanced class and they begged me to do one of the pieces that I wrote. We did it as a radio show. And it was one of the most successful shows we ever had. And some of the students that were originally in that class actually came to see it. At intermission I had them draw numbers, and then they had to get on stage. I put the audience on stage in the roles. Some of them actually drew the roles that were originally written for them, which was hilarious. They had costume pieces that were pulled specifically by the stage manager/costume designer for them to wear while they were reading. It was so funny.

KYLA KAZUSCHYK: I love the idea that it can be nimble. It can be flexible, it can start right now, like: put on this hat you're this person.

CARRIE BELLEW: I think the other advantage of doing devised theatre is you can use it as a teachable moment. We have all heard, over and over again "trust the process." In devised theatre you really do have to trust the process to get from point A to point B, and if you don't then you're going to hit some roadblocks and speed bumps. I think devised theatre offers extreme process work for creativity, design work, writing.

Just the spontaneity alone kind of hearkens back to commedia, where you have these characters but you don't know what situation they're going to be put in, or you know the situation, and you have the stock characters and then they just go for it.

It really does offer the opportunity to evolve as a true team. I miss production meetings, coming to the table and bringing your ideas and then hearing the banter and everyone else. I do try to have the same type of production meetings with my students but some of them are just so green, and they don't quite comprehend everything, so it's not quite the same. But there are moments where you see the light bulbs go on and you're just like yeah we're on the same page.

I do try to let them design, when they're ready, or even if they're not ready! More and more I try to place more responsibility on them and see where they go.

KYLA KAZUSCHYK: I am so impressed by that, how you have them design, even when they're not ready. Why not figure it out on the go!

CARRIE BELLEW: Well, and you can only learn so much about theatre from a book. You just have to get up and do it, and if it works, great, if it doesn't, you say, Oh okay, and you make it work. And we do that because we're the problem solvers.

I make sure that they know that I make mistakes too. There's always something more. When you look back at a piece of work, and think, well that could have been better. We have postmortems after our shows, every show, doesn't matter what it is, monologue show, everything. We sit here and we talk about it. We hash it out. It's all a learning process, and if you don't make mistakes or go in a wrong direction you're never going to find where you're supposed to go. It's all about making mistakes and recovering. You've got to be truthful because if you're not, nothing's ever going to change or get fixed, so you have to be honest.

I try to be mindful of that and when doing devised theatre, especially one piece, there were a couple of moments where there was some friction there between the girls, and of course we had to step back and talk about it and work through it to come to a solution, and they did. They did work through it, and they came to a solution. Being truthful to what you're doing and trying to work together is tough when some people are really strong willed, but I think with devised theatre, since nothing is set in stone, you can ask students to step back and look at what they are creating as they are creating it, what is working and what is not working.

KYLA KAZUSCHYK: I'm so impressed that you're creating a culture of honesty, being honest about your own mistakes and being honest and direct about when students are making mistakes. And that probably makes it easier for them to listen to you and respect you and be honest with themselves and be able to admit when they're making mistakes.

CARRIE BELLEW: I hope so. I always tell them: this is an inclusive program not exclusive.

KYLA KAZUSCHYK: This idea of community circles back to devised theatre and how if everyone's on the same playing field, everyone has to figure out how to set whatever differences aside to create something, figure out how to work with each other and listen to each other to create something.

CARRIE BELLEW: Yes, and everyone has a valid opinion. And it may or may not work. But you at least have to try. That's really, really important, you have to try. That's with any production.

KYLA KAZUSCHYK: How do you approach creating costumes?

CARRIE BELLEW: If you've already chosen your basic topic of what you are going to do for a show, say for example we were going to do a show based on the 1800s and the potato famine. I mean there's your starting point right there, but you don't have anything else to go off of. Are you going to go from the English perspective, the Irish perspective, the perspective of the American having to deal with this influx of immigration, like where are you going to go with it? Then you have to figure out what direction are we going to go in. And then that kind of does drive the costuming. But if you're just placing a whole bunch of stuff on stage, like all sorts of costume pieces, you could pick up a hat, you could pick up a fan, a coat, a scarf, a tie, and just ask who would wear these? Who would this be? Where would they be?

There's an infinite number of possibilities just with costuming because costumes define and enhance who the characters are and there's no getting away from that.

When we did *The Trojan Women*, I took it and I placed it in the Bosnian war crisis. We had to do a lot of research. During the Bosnian war crisis, there were towns that were completely decimated, not a single man was left alive. Similar to the Trojan war, not a single man was left alive. Even male children were murdered. Women were enslaved and stuck in these brothel type hotels, which is horrific.

The show was very successful, and it all stemmed from just that one thing, just taking it out and plopping it into another time period. That helped evolve everything from the set looking like a burned-out building, with dead trees everywhere, to the women wearing the wraps around their heads. At the moment when they bring out the son that had just been murdered, all the women stand around him, and I had them take off their head wraps and cover him with their head wraps.

And it was just something that came to me because I didn't want him completely exposed, I needed him to be covered, but I thought, wow, how impactful that would be because women always had their hair covered, for them to just give that up and literally lay it to rest, right with the body of the small child.

It was a very moving experience, and it was all from costuming and location. It wouldn't have been successful without it. The costumes can really drive a show. You can have the most simple set and the costumes just make everything flow because they make the characters.

FIGURE 2.5 The Trojan Women *"Although we utilized the script from Euripides, it was placed in the Bosnian war crisis and students had to do research on the crisis and what the women went through during this time period"* —Carrie Bellew (photo courtesy of Carrie Bellew)

KYLA KAZUSCHYK: When you're devising, how do you handle delegating? Do you have just one person take on the role of costume designer or does everyone figure out well my character would wear this or my character would wear that?

CARRIE BELLEW: I feel like you should put it in the hands of the actors, what they feel their character would wear. Because I think having them take ownership completely of the character, with the costuming, it makes them more comfortable, because they've made that choice for the character, because they are the character. But that doesn't mean that you can't have a full-on costume designer, scenic designer, and all that, but I think everybody should have a stake, have a claim. All costume designers work with their actors anyway, to make sure that they're comfortable. Boundaries are there, and you just have to figure out what yours are, what everyone else's are, and kind of work together to build a bridge.

KYLA KAZUSCHYK: Do you think that working in devised theatre helps you to be more flexible, even when you're doing scripted work?

CARRIE BELLEW: Oh, without a doubt. When we do Shakespeare or Greek pieces, I want to make sure that they understand and know what they're saying, so for one entire rehearsal they have to put it in their own words.

I do use devised theatre in my rehearsals, which, number one is sort of a stress relief. When you're telling them to put it in your own words, because even if you're doing something that's a dramatic piece, you're going to laugh. They're going to say something and they're going to crack up laughing and laughter is the best stress reliever. There's nothing else like it.

Using those moments and using play is so helpful. They need to play, and devised theatre is playing.

I forget a lot of times because we're so driven. And normally, pre-Covid, we do like eight shows a year, and then the after-school theatre program. There's one each semester and I've done a lot of devised theatre with them to save money. And I've just given them the theme and they write monologues. There's little vignettes and scenes and then they do it.

KYLA KAZUSCHYK: And you find play is important there too?

CARRIE BELLEW: Oh, without a doubt. Without a doubt, because that after school theatre program is made up of students who want to do theatre, but they just don't have time to fit it into their schedule or they're involved in band or choir or some other sport like soccer or cross-country. It's just an amalgamation of different people that just want to try theatre, and so the advanced class become the designers and they design the costumes and everything else for the production.

KYLA KAZUSCHYK: What advice do you have for people approaching devised theatre?

CARRIE BELLEW: Allow for as much play time as possible, that is for sure.

Make sure you write down what's working and what didn't work, because just because something doesn't work in one piece, does not mean that it might not work in another. Keeping a log or a journal while you're doing the process is very beneficial because, again, not everything is going to make the cut. But it could be utilized in some other space or time or even a show that is not devised. You could look back and go yeah this moment could work. And since I am working with younger students, I like to put them in the driver's seat. I want to give them as much responsibility as possible. And sometimes that doesn't always work out as well.

I think that's one thing that theatre has always given me is that the deadline was always looming and I could see, well if I got this done now, I could focus more on this. As soon as you get the script, start learning your lines because you're going to have to be off book in two weeks. You know the set has to be painted by this date, because this is when the photographer is coming in. Costumes have to be finished. It just goes on and on and on.

There's a lot to do, and it is a big job, no matter what area you're in, so I think making sure the students understand that this is not going to happen unless you do your job, they have to know that, and they have to realize that they're the ones that are in charge of the piece.

Everybody has to be invested. Everybody has a stake in it, and so, making sure that the students or anyone involved, they're the drivers. They're picking the destination, they're putting the gas in the tank, and they're the ones driving. They have a job to do and everybody else has to keep it going. If we're in a locomotive, a steam engine, somebody's got to put the coal in!

I think starting small, especially for beginners, gives you a better understanding of where it could go. They always say dream big, start small. So just getting your feet wet in a specific area, just choosing some random topic and saying here, we want to write this, this is what our show is going to be about.

Choosing a topic for them to do helps because sometimes that's the hardest part, not knowing where to start. If you start small and give them a starting point, then the doors open to various possibilities. Devised theatre could be anything, it could be about a kid who thinks the moon is actually cheese, or a beautiful fairy walking through a field of tulips.

It could be anything. It could be about the George Floyd trial, it could be about the GOP and what's going on right now on the Senate floor, it could be anything, anything you want it to be.

KYLA KAZUSCHYK: And it can be a way to start conversations about those things, too. Whatever you are thinking about it, if you're trying to have a framework of a conversation, theatre can absolutely be a vehicle for all of that.

CARRIE BELLEW: Oh hands down. One of the things I send home to my students' parents or guardians is sort of like: theatre is a reflection of life and some of the conversations we have are sometimes difficult to have.

The piece that I picked out for dramatic criticism this year is by Angelina Weld Grimké. It was written in 1916. It is called *Rachel* and she was an African American woman who wrote this piece, and I did pick it specifically. I didn't tell my students exactly what it was about, but I did send a disclaimer home saying this is the piece that I have selected this year and there's some really heavy topics, heavy situations, this was written in the 1900s. I gave them the title, I gave them the playwright's name. And I said, there are certain words that are mentioned in this play, we will not be saying them out loud in my classroom, but I wanted you to be aware.

That was it. The students read it, they could have gone and looked it up, but they didn't. And so when we sat down to read it, they were reading it reading it reading it. And then we get to a certain point, we get to the part where the mother is revealing how their half-brother and their father were lynched. This entire time before we got to that point, they thought it was a white family. They assumed it was a white family. They had not done their homework. They hadn't looked up that the playwright was an African American woman, and presumably a lesbian as well.

I usually do a deep dive myself on the piece, which I did, but I didn't write anything down this time. I thought you know what I'm actually going to let them really teach me about this piece. I read the play; I love the play. It's totally relevant today, even though it's set way back when. It's a really good piece. I let them drive it. I let them do the information heavy research.

Our midterm is usually where they give me their thesis, we have a roundtable discussion. For some reason every year I've picked a play, there's always a meal in the play, so normally for midterms we'd have a meal, like the family in the play. We couldn't this year because of Covid. But we have a roundtable discussion. They give me their thesis, what they're going to write

FIGURE 2.6 Letters to a Lady, *written by students as a devised theatre project using letters from children to Eleanor Roosevelt during the Great Depression (photo courtesy of Carrie Bellew)*

about what they found analyzing the script. And it's really cool. It's one of my favorite lessons to do throughout the entire year.

One of my students who is transgender really did a deep dive on this person, the playwright, and brought to light a whole slew of things and I was like this is really amazing.

KYLA KAZUSCHYK: They were probably so excited to do it, to have the opportunity to do it.

CARRIE BELLEW: Very, very excited and some of the theses were really, really well done. I think they get confused, which I have to stress all the time, yes I'm teaching you how to analyze a script but you are going to write a critical analysis on the script so you have to have a thesis.

I think responsibility is the big thing, really, and being open, being open to the experiences, knowing that mistakes are going to happen and that's okay. Being willing to learn from those mistakes, rather than pouting about them or getting angry. All of this stuff is so important, outside of theatre. I mean, because again, theatre is life. It's a reflection of life.

What's going to move the story? Because it's not about you, it's not even about your ideas, it's about the story. And this goes back to designing: how are you going to tell the story? How are you going to support what the messages are? What does it mean to you to be a part of this story? And not you in the story, you know there's so many egos. And it is so disappointing sometimes to see some people that are so talented but they are so eaten alive, like they're stuck. It is really sad.

I think, realizing that from the get-go, and making sure that the focus is the story is super super important. If you focus on the story, then it just kind of naturally evolves in the direction you want to go with it anyway.

And again going back to stories, nobody knows the origins of storytelling. It probably started around a campfire, people just sharing stories, and so by nature that's who we are, we are the storytellers. To be able to create a story from the ground up just kind of even takes you back to that time of when your parents were in school, walking 10 miles through the snow. I think everybody's parents use that no matter how far south you are. Getting to the heart of it like, how do you want to tell it, where's the focus? How are you going to drive this story? What do you ultimately want to say?

And I know everybody always goes back to Aristotle, and the poetics and the framework of writing a story, but with devised theatre there's no framework. You could just think of one idea and then just go with it and see where it takes you.

KYLA KAZUSCHYK: And still the question of what is the story, and why tell this story now? Why?

CARRIE BELLEW: I think, being able to answer those questions, you better have answers, you have to justify every single choice you made, why you feel this way, why you made that choice. You have to, because if you can't, then, what are you doing? I know sometimes people just have good instincts about certain things, especially some actors just have really good instincts, but some don't.

And there are times when you see a piece or read a piece, and you see it all in your head so clearly, the design is already there you just have to get it out on paper. But you still have to be able to answer why. You can't just say, Oh well, I saw it all in my head. It has to be rooted in something.

KYLA KAZUSCHYK: And it has to be communicated to other people. That's how you get it out of your head and express it to someone else.

ARTIST SPOTLIGHT: TONYA HAYES

Tonya Hayes is a director, facilitator, writer, and professor who collaborated with her students and with Carrie Bellew and her students to create a collection of devised performances shown at the Southeastern Theatre Conference (SETC) convention in 2020. They found the book, *Moment Work: Tectonic Theater Project's Process of Devising Theater*, by Moises Kaufman and Barbara Pitts McAdams to be a valuable resource in developing their own practices.

TONYA HAYS: To me devised theatre is really based in moment work because that is where I really got into it. I took a devised theatre workshop at SETC a few years ago, where we started with a myth that everybody knew and we divided into groups, and we were assigned to tell a portion of the saga, and that was really fun. That was kind of my first toe dipping into it. I did a little bit of that exercise work with kids when I was working with a nonprofit theatre program. My big baptism by fire into the whole devised theatre thing was through moment work through the *Tectonic Theater* book.

I think devised theatre is creating theatre based on a hunch. I think that you have to start with a question. We're working on a project—I submitted a grant to our state arts organization and the question that I want to work with to devise the project is called "Who Gets to Be an American?" A really good friend of mine is a superintendent of a school and it made national news—a few years ago they did these big raids on a chicken processing place and they picked up, I don't know like 600 people, a lot of people. So, the superintendent and all her teachers had to deal with all these kids that were left with no parents, you know? And she's agreed to do interviews. I create devised theatre to really examine something that I think has a lot of sides and a lot of issues. I'm really passionate about that so that's what it means to me.

KYLA KAZUSCHYK: I think that that's vital. What are the advantages to devised theatre? Why do devised instead of doing scripted work?

TONYA HAYS: I think the big answer to that is ownership. Because if you've got a group of people collaborating on a script and the creation of it, however, you do it through elements, through story, whatever, they feel so powerful that they own it. And it's not easy, and I think everybody's super proud of it because it's a work that was born out of all of them, finding a way to work together towards an end.

KYLA KAZUSCHYK: Absolutely and you're not just saying someone else's words, it can be your own.

TONYA HAYS: I direct a lot, so I get so excited about the piece I'm directing. I work on all this research and have all this stuff that I bring to the table. But the actors, they just want to do a play. They'll tie into some of it if it's something really special. We did a production where they got to meet the playwright, and she talked with them about why she wrote the piece. It was really cool; it was a really cool thing that happened. Most of the time it's just they want to learn the lines, it's not like they're so invested passionately in the piece. Sometimes they are. Most of the time, not so much. They're not going to get nearly as excited about your research as you are. In devised theatre they are.

KYLA KAZUSCHYK: It's a different level of investment. On the projects that you've worked on, how did you approach creating costumes for them?

TONYA HAYS: My biggest project was the one I did for SETC and that was about a veteran who kind of went down the wrong path because he came back from a war injury, and he got hooked on opioids. I was working with high school kids for that project, and we just asked who has what. We needed a lab coat; I went and found a lab coat from a doctor that I knew. It was basically just them bringing in things. I have a small costume morgue, but nothing extensive. One of the boys was an ROTC kid, a marine, so he had a really nice dress uniform and I made sure as the play progressed it didn't look quite as good and was a little sloppier in the way it was presented. We wanted to express the idea of a hero falling apart, so that's what we did, through the uniform.

KYLA KAZUSCHYK: As it becomes more disheveled you see that he's falling apart further.

TONYA HAYS: Right.

KYLA KAZUSCHYK: How do you approach making decisions and dividing up roles? Especially if you're working with students, who decides yeah that's what the character is going to wear, or yes, this works, no this doesn't work?

TONYA HAYS: Well, I think everything is collaborative. You are not really the director as much as you are the facilitator and the mentor. Kids would bring in things and we would all look at it together. That was a pretty small project, we only had like five in the cast and so it was pretty simple, everybody kind of looked at everything. Of course, as the teacher mentor facilitator, I had rights of refusal. Like no that doesn't work, that doesn't look like a housewife, you know? I'm somebody in that age group that would have a son that age, go with something a little bit more, older. I did have some things like that, but it was kind of like a group thing. People would bring things in, and we'd all look at it.

KYLA KAZUSCHYK: Do you have visions for future projects? What other devised work do you want to create?

TONYA HAYS: The one "Who Gets to Be an American?" is my next passion project. I like that question because that question is huge. It's not just about kids at the border trying to get into the US. It's about what happens when you split up families. My ancestors came in from Ellis Island. I found my great-great grandfather's name on the roster that he came in from Ukraine. So just knowing that my people came in that route into the country, and they were accepted, they weren't turned away. And then I have a few Jewish friends I'm really close to and knowing that there was a boat full of Jewish people trying to escape the Holocaust that were turned away. A lot of those people died. I think "Who Gets to Be an American?" is huge and it's timeless. And I especially think it's something we should examine.

I went through hurricane Katrina, and I will tell you that our area would not have been rebuilt without the immigrants that came in from Mexico. I also grew up in New Mexico where it was 3 to 1 Native Americans and Latinx compared to white, so I grew up in a really diverse like rainbow culture. In the end, that was so enriching. The diversity was so enriching. So, I have strong feelings about it. It's important. That's what America is, we're this melting pot of all these rich traditions and cultures.

KYLA KAZUSCHYK: It really does encompass a lot. Do you have plans for community involvement? Do you think that you'll take a company of people and just create it, or will you work with communities to tell their stories?

TONYA HAYS: Part of my idea is that I take the students that I'm working with, and we go to the school district that had the ICE raids. And then I think it would be really cool because we're not very far from the Choctaw, Choctaw well I guess it's called the reservation, but then the Mississippi Choctaw story is another really cool story. And in going in to talk with them, because they got citizenship, state citizenship, they were the first Indigenous people to get citizenship. And then of course Mississippi is 45 to 50% African American and at what point you can go back and look racially at slaves, at what point did that enter into them getting to be an American? I think there's so many paths this could take and that's why I like the topic.

KYLA KAZUSCHYK: America really has a complex history. Thinking about the Choctaw community, I wonder what their perspective is on who gets to be an American and who decides who gets to be an American.

TONYA HAYS: Right. We have several students that come to school here because we're not far from the Choctaw lands and I'm getting to know some of them. They've gotten involved in our program a little bit more.

I think having source material is great, it also saves a lot of time if everybody's worked with the same source material before the start of the piece. What I'd like to do next is do a class on devised theatre. And as a class project we'd be working on this piece, not that we couldn't welcome other students and community members. The grant was written as a community engagement project, where we would talk to citizens of our town and get other people's opinions, asking who gets to be an American, what's your answer to that. It was written to engage community.

KYLA KAZUSCHYK: That would be so interesting to hear the diversity of viewpoints. I bet you could talk to 20 people and get 20 different answers. Do you have a proposed timeline for this project? Do you see it taking a whole semester, do you see it expanding beyond the semester? And in general, how do you create timelines for devised theatre?

TONYA HAYS: I think when we did the piece for SETC we didn't get the initial funding that we had asked for just because it took a while to get the whole project together and get everybody's approval on it. So we didn't know for sure if we were going to get to do it, but right before the holiday break I ordered all the books. The students went home with *Dreamland*, the Sam Kinonas book, and I had the moment work book to go through. Everybody was supposed to have read the book, most of them did.

For additional source material we brought in a couple of people that we did interviews with. One was a woman who had lost her significant other to an opioid alcohol combination situation. Another person was a student whose mom had continued to struggle. So they had other source material besides just the book, and that was really powerful. That timeline was, I think we came back to school in January, and then we took it to SETC, it was early last year, right before Covid hit. Thank God we all got to go to SETC. But it was the very end of February, so we came back January sixth. We probably didn't start it that first week, so it was like four or five weeks. And it was a short piece, but we were also in rehearsal for *Hairspray*. So we weren't working every day on it or anything and it wasn't a class, but I think if you have a class instead of just a private group of students rehearsing because it does take time, so in the class, you can also require that they read certain materials and source materials and stuff. So we're looking at, I think we start right after MLK day and then we go to end of April, early May so I'm thinking that it'll be pretty much the whole semester.

KYLA KAZUSCHYK: That makes sense to use the structure of a class to give structure to the project.

TONYA HAYS: And that project was really cool because we were all communicating, and we all ended up going a little different way with the performances. That was a really cool project. And this was before Covid, so we're introducing each other, through little video clips we're doing all this stuff, I don't think I'd ever used Zoom before and it was fun for the students to know that another group was working on it. That was really fun. And then they all met at SETC when we put it together, and they developed this amazing camaraderie.

The value of moment work is that you look at things a lot differently after you worked with it. You explore a lot more of the theatrical storytelling, the spectacle. There's so many things that you can show, and you don't have to tell. I think moment work benefits everybody: playwrights, actors, directors, technicians, I think it's beautiful.

KYLA KAZUSCHYK: How do you think that technicians can use moment work?

TONYA HAYS: Well, I think as a costumer, for example, there's an exercise in the book where there's a wedding dress on a chair. And the actors went in and did different things with the wedding dress. Like one of course, the automatic thing is, a young girl walks in and just holds it up to her like it's her wedding dress and moves with it. And then there was a man that entered and picked up the wedding dress and it was like somebody had died in that dress. It was just, how do you relate to costume pieces? I thought that was really beautiful.

When we talk about the moments in theatre, some of them are really simple and they're more related to elements. For example, that scarf just floating in the wind in *Finding Neverland* when the woman dies, that was so beautiful. There's so many things that can be explored easily that are powerful as far as the technical elements of theatre.

KYLA KAZUSCHYK: It's so true to think about the moments that stick with you. It seems more of a challenge to think about how to nail stuff down, like when do you decide this is what the moment will be this is what we need for this moment this is what we need to go forward.

TONYA HAYS: Right, that's probably the hardest part because you fall in love with these moments, and then they don't really work. Or you start putting it together with the narrative and well this was really cool but doesn't really help tell the story. So the questions are, does it advance the story and does it really matter. When we were doing *Diary of Anne Frank*, our wonderful sound designer had this sound of flapping birds because Anne Frank talks about the sound of flapping birds, but it sounded like a salsa beat or something, and it was just so distracting and he was really hanging on to it, but it was distracting, so I said, it just doesn't sound like flapping birds, I know what you're going for but it's not working.

KYLA KAZUSCHYK: And that's the question for every production: what is serving the story, what is not serving the story, is this really helping to communicate our ideas or how do we let go of it? Do you have any words of advice, things that you would want to pass on to other artists that are creating devised work? What are the most important things to keep in mind?

TONYA HAYS: I think it's a lot easier if you have source material, instead of just saying we're going to do a devised piece and what do you guys want to do. That's so hard and it takes a lot more time if you don't give people some kind of foundation, so I think that would be really important. I think allow yourself time. It is always going to take more time than you think it will.

And somebody like me from a directing background, just backs off. You have to just back off and let it happen. You can't control things. You have to really respect the collaborative process, because if you want to direct a play, you're not directing a play, you have to get that out of your head. This is a totally different thing, you know? So those would be the big things, I think.

And when you're choosing your hunch or your source material, make sure it's something that people are going to engage with and care about that all your actors are invested in.

KYLA KAZUSCHYK: So you have that buy in and that ownership, from the beginning. Do you think that it's a different skill set between directing and facilitating or is it just adjusting?

TONYA HAYS: I think it's adjusting. Well, I guess it depends on what kind of director you are. I'm a very collaborative director, but I know that some people aren't, that's not their thing. My daughter got a theatre degree, she went to the Vassar apprenticeship program as an actress and she said there was a director there that just directed every single element of the production, she said mom it's like he's telling us when to breathe, we're all so done with him, and I said well it's just a different style. You've got to work with different kinds of directors. I have definite ideas, and I of course pre-block and do my prep work, but if an actor comes in and says, you know, I'm always interested in them too, like if they say can I try this and I'll tell them before we even start, if you have ideas, I'm open to them you're not going to hurt my feelings. If something's not working for you, you want to try something, please be verbal. I think those kind of directors, collaborative directors, probably do better with devised, but even me, and I'm super collaborative, I have to take my hands off and let them do it.

KYLA KAZUSCHYK: It's hard to do. I think that applies to teaching and mentoring too. I do a lot of mentoring of student designers and I struggle with the same thing: how do I not just tell them what to do and let them figure it out on their own. It's hard to figure out, but that's key: they have to figure it out on their own. That seems to be part of the point of devised theatre is that it's everyone's voices, not just one director's vision.

ARTIST SPOTLIGHT: KAIN GILL

Kain Gill is a multifaceted artist who is skilled in costume design and costume technology for film and theatre as well as in arts administration. Here he discusses his experience on director Anthony Doyle's undergraduate honors thesis project, *Upgrade*, and more.

KYLA KAZUSCHYK: Could you tell me more about your experience on *Upgrade* or if there's other devised projects you've worked on?

KAIN GILL: I worked on Anthony's thesis and not necessarily devised theatre per se but devised film where we just come together in a room and just make something, bouncing ideas off of each other, and that same sort of realm. Anthony was much more involved, which was really fun, because as a costumer and as an administrator I've never been in the room with the director or the writer and just seeing like how their creative process works, it was a lot of talking about the topics that we want to cover and then seeing how that could be translated into movement, into speech, into art, into other physical elements. It was really interesting to see that side of theatre because I'm used to just saying here's a script, go from the script, you know, there's a time period, go from the time period. But creating something out of nothing and watching it come to life is just absolutely inspiring.

KYLA KAZUSCHYK: It's like a totally different experience.

KAIN GILL: Yeah absolutely it's nothing that I thought I was going to get going to get in college and I was very pleasantly surprised with it.

KYLA KAZUSCHYK: How did the team form? Did Anthony reach out to you, did he hire you as the costume person, how did that work?

KAIN GILL: So he was observing all of our work at school and, of course, being his friend, he asked me if I wanted to do costuming and I said yes, so he hired me on as a costumer. I also helped a little bit with administrative stuff like helping him get the budget ready and helping him get stuff together for the grant that he wrote. So that was fun and I was in charge of doing all the costumes for the show and working together with the whole team to see how we could make it happen. It was really interesting hearing everyone's input.

KYLA KAZUSCHYK: What were other roles of the people on the team? Was it like arts and administrators and then actors were separate?

KAIN GILL: Oh, I think everybody did a little bit of something. It was a really small team. We had our props person, Crystal Hayner, and I think they also did scenic. Then Zoey was sound, and I think she also did lights, which was really interesting for her. Anthony did everything that's happening, he was mostly the administrative side, he always asked us if we needed questions and Dr. Walsh was the mentor. Kayla was the stage manager so that administrative aspect was really nice to have someone there holding us together like glue. And then the actors, of course, the actors were really fun, to watch them become their characters in front of us, watching them come together and seeing what they create and also their inputs on what they feel like costuming would look like and their makeup and all the other elements. Everyone had a seat at the table, so to speak, when it came to the story's progression or just art and the art of the show in general.

KYLA KAZUSCHYK: How did you develop a timeline? Was everyone present for rehearsals or did y'all have meetings before rehearsals?

KAIN GILL: We had weekly meetings, sometimes they were pretty informal so like just like a quick check in and sometimes there were actual production meetings, or we debriefed on a previous run or a previous draft of the script. Those happened weekly and biweekly. Then rehearsals were open so anybody can come in and watch and be a part and just take in what the devised work was which is really cool. I think rehearsals happened after the production meetings, because they happened every day, or every other day.

KYLA KAZUSCHYK: Did you end up going to a lot of rehearsals? Did you find that helpful to inform the costumes?

KAIN GILL: I went to three to five just normal rehearsals, and then, of course, I went to all of the designer runs and the read throughs from script changes which was really fun. They did inform the costumes a lot because of how they were playing the characters not just how I saw them, how they brought them to life. They added a new element. It was more nuanced as the show went on.

KYLA KAZUSCHYK: So in typical theatre we have a timeline where like you said, we have a script, we do the script analysis and we design things for all the characters. But if the costumes in the script are being developed, how do you set deadlines for yourself, how do you keep yourself on a schedule, how do you get things accomplished?

KAIN GILL: I think that the training in normal theatre really helped with that, with deadlines and timelines, I was used to those so I made them for myself. Did I stick to them that well? mmm But I did have them. So I had when I needed to have final designs and when wigs to be styled and brought to set, when I needed my fabrics picked out, and when I needed pieces at least cut, when all of that had to happen, but I was very flexible when things change because you have to be, just being ready for anything and being ready to make split decisions and go with how the art is going. I's just like, you make a mistake, you go with it, you know? Something changes, go with it.

KYLA KAZUSCHYK: Did you find that like more scary or more empowering? I think it's both.

KAIN GILL: I would agree. I was truly so scared. I was like I don't know how this is going to work, I don't know what's happening anymore I'm just sewing, I'm just putting these costumes together, I'm just going. But then it was also really fun because it's nothing, but you make it what it is. There's nothing telling you what it needs to be. And that's always fun. I love when the process needs to be made up as you go, and when you have a little bit of structure. But you don't need too much to facilitate art.

KYLA KAZUSCHYK: I remember talking to you about that before, finding that balance of structure and flexibility. And you have to find that on every project, whether it's devised or not, there's still got to be room for flexibility and there's got to be some semblance of structure and so it's always a question of how do you decide where to draw those lines.

KAIN GILL: That was always a hard point to get to because I don't want to be like "this is this and that's it now" because it's not. Things change, they have to change, you have to be flexible. Of course, some things, like if we are running out of money, maybe not. If buying materials is the issue it's like well it is what it is, but we can tweak nip tuck whatever we need to do to make it a little different, to make it more in line with our newer vision. The vision was always changing. I thought that was really interesting too.

KYLA KAZUSCHYK: Can you tell me more about the story? How did y'all come up with it? Was it all Anthony's idea and y'all just contributed to it? And what was the idea, what did it become?

KAIN GILL: It was a very long process, I know it was very long on Anthony's end, because he had to do this for a while. First, he started with his meetings with Dr. Walsh and was talking about what he wanted it to be, because he needed to have just a fully realized production from start to finish with funding and all the administrative stuff taken care of. But when it came down to creating the piece itself, we started with all his ideas written down on the board. And then we discussed our relatability to each of the topics and what we know the topics to be, and then we played a couple of games where we tried to make pictures with our bodies, just very fun, very out of the box. Anthony's thesis focused on a lot. There were robots, there were single frames, it was the idea of a picture frame and what you see and what you don't see. I remember that there were some things that we didn't have, so there were ghosts and diners were a thing, I don't remember where those came in and left. And then it got to ACA [the Affordable Care Act] and political division too and his piece ended up becoming a two-track story. You could see Milo and the Milo side of the story, and the Carvel side, which is like the politician and then the people being affected by all changes that the political people don't care about which I thought was very interesting. You could see where he's coming from, Carvel, because we got to see a little bit of his backstory. It's just a little bit you're like, Oh, I guess he's like trying to do good but he's getting lost in his own vision. And then you see Milo and his struggles, like him and his sister going together and watching their community not collapse, but become empowered. It was so interesting to watch them have their own struggles and watching them have their … what was the question again?

KYLA KAZUSCHYK: How did y'all come up with the idea for the show, and what was the idea for the show?

KAIN GILL: Oh that's right. Yeah it encompassed a lot of themes. Whittling it down to a cohesive vision was hard, but I feel like towards the end it had a more unified and more streamlined idea of where we wanted the show to go.

KYLA KAZUSCHYK: And wasn't it about technology too?

KAIN GILL: Yeah advancement in technology and how that's replacing, well, oh yeah that's right the robotics. How that came into play was the decision about disabilities and how for many, ACA is no longer there, but the people that can't afford it are still disabled. Milo was in a wheelchair for most of the show until his sister stole the legs that he needed which gives them the ability to walk which was interesting in the fact that they had to show all the struggle for the people that have disabilities and how the government just doesn't care, which I thought was very interesting. It played on those themes of the minority not being enough for the majority to care about. That's present now because we see it with like AIDS research and how like yeah "a couple people have it" is what they think so why put so much money towards it. And you can compare that to the Covid research, where a lot of people were getting it and it was a pandemic. Like AIDS isn't a pandemic that was widespread? So you see how much funding went towards that and how quickly that developed and how you can see a minority, with the right funding and treatment and help could become part of the majority or part of the greater good. I don't know if that's the right words for it, but like you know the not marginalized population.

KYLA KAZUSCHYK: Everyone can succeed. There's room for everyone. We just make it so there's not room for some people.

KAIN GILL: Yeah and then profits apparently matter more than people's lives because that was also something that was in the show. It was a lot of encompassing current worldviews and current world issues, at least in America. And moving at a little bit forward in the future. So if ACA is no longer needed, because we have all these advancements in technology, what about the people that can't afford it? Does insurance cover it? How does that keep going? And why are we not helping the people that don't have the money for it? Why do we need to persecute them for just doing what they need to do to get by in the world?

KYLA KAZUSCHYK: It is a lot. It sounds like the model of devised theatre can be praxis for a lot of the themes in the show. You talked about how everyone had a seat at the table, you proved that it's possible to create something when everyone has a seat at the table. Do you see a parallel there?

KAIN GILL: Yeah absolutely there there's always room for everybody. I don't understand why people say there's not because there always is. You can make the room. Everyone should have a voice and it doesn't necessarily mean everyone's literally sitting at tables together, but as long as you have their voices heard and you're listening to their input and valuing the input that's what's important. It's not black and white. Everybody can do it; everybody can be a part of the process.

KYLA KAZUSCHYK: I have so much hope for the structure of devised theatre and that the things that are not working, that the things that are harming people about the way we practice traditional theatre, we could adjust them and practice them in the ways that we practice devised theatre, why not?

KAIN GILL: I don't see why not. It's literally perfect. Take the good. I don't understand why people think the bad stuff is necessary. It's not always necessary, it's probably never necessary. I don't know, I didn't do a study on it, yet, but I can tell you right now devised theatre is where it's at right now for me. I love that process.

KYLA KAZUSCHYK: To circle it back to costumes, how did you use costumes to tell the story? In what ways did costumes reflect the story that you were telling?

KAIN GILL: So a lot of the costuming, because it was futuristic, it was set 50 to 100 years in the future. To me it reminded me of *Hunger Games*. Very, very dystopian, very run down, ragged, you get what you have, you know? My idea for the poor characters was that all their clothes were discrete, not necessarily seen by others. I tried to keep it in line with layers and making sure that they don't leave fingerprints and some very smuggler type. But that's just the sister, opposed to Milo who was the one who was like, I believe change can happen through nonviolence, through not illegal ways, through changes in law and changing people's hearts. So his costume was a little different. It was still run down, but it was not as I would say off the radar as his sister. As opposed to the people that were rich and had the robotic enhancements they had. We were trying to figure out the best way to do robotic limbs. We got a couple contacts. I don't know why I didn't think of it sooner, I had a glove for a robotic hand when we could have just spray painted the hand. They did that at one of the runs and I was like yeah does that make sense, it looks completely real. So it was just like making it very obvious that they are different and that their stuff is supposed to be more extreme. The rich people were more extreme. They wore nicer clothes, more vibrant clothes, insane hair, insane makeup.

I had little things for people who had special eyes. They had this little thing that was like a radio, their social media, all their connection to the World Wide Web essentially. It looked like it was implanted. The integration of the robotic pieces into some of the characters, that was something that I was really interested in. Daja was playing the boyfriend or the girlfriend of Theo's character and they had a fake hand and they always wore a glove to cover it because they don't like it, they don't want to be shown. I always thought that was so interesting because it's like, well it's not really shameful, it's not wrong to need these enhancements, but you don't want to give power to the system that's oppressing you. I thought that was so interesting. There's a lot of things with costuming that I would like to revisit if we ever did the show again, maybe, or the next installment of the show.

KYLA KAZUSCHYK: It sounds like y'all really created a whole universe.

KAIN GILL: Absolutely, there was so much attention to detail. The way Anthony led us was very helpful. There was so much that went into the staging and lighting and the props. The props were gorgeous, The way that the props just really transformed the space, it was just so exciting to see them, to see the world build around us. It's very like I assume early theatre was, very like wow we can actually do this and it's not cut and dry.

KYLA KAZUSCHYK: How did you communicate ideas about the costumes? Did you create a stack of renderings and show the actors look this drawing is going to be you or did you use other means of communication?

KAIN GILL: Because I had 20 something hours, everything was time sensitive, I did not have enough time to get those renderings out. I did do a few sketches. I don't think I have them anymore, but I did mostly do a collage of what I wanted them to look at. And then we had a design meeting and I showed it to them, because we all showed each other everything, and then we talked about the designs and how they could be more like the character, or just everyone's input on the designs and just seeing how they felt about it it's really interesting to see.

KYLA KAZUSCHYK: So you got input from the performers about what they thought the characters would be?

KAIN GILL: And that was really fun. I love that. That's like my favorite part of costuming is that while I'm not playing the character, I'm making the character and they're playing the character. So bringing a little bit of their rendition and our rendition together, it makes this beautiful, well-rounded character. Because it's not, I mean like I can give you a costume and just say wear this and if you don't feel good in it like oh well. But that's not that's not collaborative, that's not what theatre is. Sometimes costumes hurt, yeah sure, but that doesn't mean you should be uncomfortable.

KYLA KAZUSCHYK: I completely agree and not every costume designer approaches it that way. Some costume designers do think, my work is art, that's that, you just wear it. But you're right that the work suffers, because if an actor feels uncomfortable, they're not going to be able to portray the character to the fullest embodiment of that character.

KAIN GILL: That's the thing I've always had in mind. Because I'm not playing the character, I'm helping the character come to life through the clothing, and through hair makeup whatever else I need to give. So their input is just as valuable as my input, if not more so, because I need to understand what they're thinking, how they're playing this character, what are the motivations, is there a certain tic, maybe they wear long sleeves for a certain reason, you know? I need to know more about the character from how they see it, so I can make a better, more informed choice.

KYLA KAZUSCHYK: And using collage for efficient communication, I think, is another great idea because you're right sometimes you don't have time to create fully realized renderings. And sometimes a collage can express everything, can say whatever you need to say, and it can be more malleable, and you can make more changes to it, and it can be clearer. I think that collage is a great idea. (More on visual communication and collage in Chapter 3.)

KAIN GILL: I use collage a lot because my drawing skills have not improved too much. I mean, that's not entirely true, I'm pretty good. I just find collage being so much more helpful because sometimes directors have a harder time seeing what I'm saying so if I can find specific reference images, like this silhouette for this shirt, and this for the pants but like maybe from the side it looks a little different. Getting reference images is more important. At least having those in addition to what you want the show to look like. I think the combination of references and renderings and collages, that's peak.

KYLA KAZUSCHYK: I feel the same way. I don't feel super strong with my sketching abilities and I'm certainly not that fast. But with collage you can pull together so quickly, you can assemble the images you want to get. I mean maybe some people are really fast at sketching but I'm not.

KAIN GILL: Same.

KYLA KAZUSCHYK: Well, and it doesn't have to be. I think that's another place where costume designers get tripped up is in thinking that the rendering is the art. The piece on stage is the art. The rendering is a communication tool to get there.

KAIN GILL: Oh, I also did another devised show, kind of, it's called *Plastic Drastic*. Do you remember *Plastic Drastic*, with Eric Meyer Garcia?

KYLA KAZUSCHYK: Yes, of course. Tell us more about that. What was that show about?

KAIN GILL: It was, so they made a lot of script changes. It was like this idea of a script that they had and they got a script and it was about this boy or girl going on an adventure and going and getting all this trash and stuff. But we changed the script so many times. So essentially, we all had input on everything that happened, where the story went, where the costuming went. That was really fun, especially when I had a budget of like nothing, so I was just making things out of nothing. That's what was important, and I thought they looked great. I would think that was like my first taste. Because when I was working on *Upgrade* it really reminded me a lot of *Plastic Drastic* and how I was like wow, we all need to put input into like where the story is going and then comparison of like I need to make this world come to life and I can't necessarily do that with just what is in the script because there wasn't much direction, it was like lines only, which is cool.

KYLA KAZUSCHYK: That's so interesting to me too, that devised theatre really exists on a spectrum. Sometimes there's a bit of a script, sometimes there is source material, sometimes it's nothing, it can be so many different things.

KAIN GILL: That was really fun. I want to see more devised theatre on the stage, and I want to see more devised theatre in collegiate theatre because that's where we have the time to learn and develop our skills. It doesn't necessarily need to be the main thing, but it needs to be a part of it, because if we just do the classics over and over how are we developing new art? We need to keep going, keep progressing, and I don't see another way to do it at this point. Like, just put it in the curriculum.

KYLA KAZUSCHYK: I'm for it! You mentioned budget, and you mentioned comparing *Plastic Drastic* to *Upgrade*. How do you approach a budget for costumes if you have it, or if you don't? When we're doing scripted theatre it's like okay ten characters, $100, each character has $10 for their costume. But in devised you don't often know how many characters there are. So how do you plan your budget?

KAIN GILL: That's so hard. When I start, I'm like, Okay, this is all the money I have, we will make it work. I immediately start asking any of the performers involved, what does your wardrobe look like, can I see your pictures? And sometimes I know who they are beforehand so I'm like, Okay, they have these kinds of clothing items and like this is their style so I can incorporate a little bit of that. And so, what they have and then add in some choice pieces and then like layer. It's always a lot of just, I don't want to say waiting, but like, once the idea of character starts to come true, starts to come to fruition, I like to start sourcing material of like, Oh, so it looks like this world to me, this world is what I'm seeing. And from there, I start sourcing materials, shirts and clothing items that look in that same realm. And I'm like, Okay, so my budget needs to look a little bit like this just based on how I want the world to look not necessarily anything else other than that. I don't know how many characters there are yet, but I'm like if I need a shirt for this many people, I'm like, Okay we'll go from there. Because we sometimes know around a rough estimate of how many people we want, but you can never be too sure. I always just put a rough estimate number. I think eight is a pretty good number to costume for. I'm like, Okay, if I had eight people this this this and this.

KYLA KAZUSCHYK: Can you tell me more about how you stay organized? Do you create other paperwork templates? Do you do a scene breakdown, do you do dressing lists?

KAIN GILL: Yes, I do, that's the only way to stay sane at this point. Every time I see no paperwork for costuming, I'm like oh get out of here. But I did a tracking sheet of like ok, so we have this, when I start is like days, how many days are there in the show or they're doing, is one scene, one day, do we go to multiple days in the scene, what are we seeing? From there, I break down how many days we have, then I see how many characters we have and then it's always a running list, it never stays the same, so it's always going to be like a Google sheet or something, something that people can see it updated live. Because everyone needs to be able to see where I'm going, and if it's not updated, they can let me know. I always stay up to date on the dressing sheet, the tracking sheet, just making sure that I understand what I'm looking at, because if I get confused at any point, I need something to fall back on and be like, Oh yes, this is what I was thinking. And writing everything down, just taking notes all the time being like, Oh yes, an idea or Oh yes, let me get this down from Anthony.

Or sometimes even Zoey had something crazy about costumes and I was like, oh my God you're absolutely right, add that to my paperwork. It was really fun.

KYLA KAZUSCHYK: I was going to ask you for advice, but you've already given so much good advice. Take notes of everything and be open to ideas from everywhere. Why not! Zoey is in the process with you, just because she's not in the role of costume designer, she might have something to add that could spark something else. And if you make yourself siloed and closed off to that, then you're going to miss out on that.

KAIN GILL: And that's something that I've always not enjoyed. It is like why isn't everyone talking about this? We all have a voice on this. We are producing this together and what we see on the stage and we hear on the stage is what we are ultimately presenting together. Why shouldn't you have a voice? If you think it's wrong or if you think something cool could come up, it doesn't even need to be like a grand big like, hey I have something to tell you guys, it could just be like a pull to the side and say, hey, what do you think about this, should we bring it up. It doesn't have to be very right or wrong, it could be simple conversations too.

KYLA KAZUSCHYK: I think so much of that depends on the culture that's created by the people that have power. That's what I've seen in my experience. If the director is exerting all the power and saying what I say goes and nobody else can have a say, no one is going to feel comfortable speaking up. But it sounds like directors you've worked with have been interested in creating environments and setting it up like starting out by playing a game, starting out by inviting everybody, so that everyone feels more comfortable speaking up.

KAIN GILL: I like the even playing field that's created because we're all collaborators. There's no hierarchy and there shouldn't be a hierarchy, because once again it's a collaborative effort. Just like no idea is a bad idea, listen to everyone's ideas you know? I like the idea of someone unifying our visions together, but not being tyrannical. It doesn't need to be like iron fisted, it could just be a gentle nudge towards this beautiful thing that we're making.

KYLA KAZUSCHYK: It can be healthier.

KAIN GILL: Yes.

KYLA KAZUSCHYK: And thinking about this idea of being open, being open to other ideas, you mentioned keeping track of your paperwork on Google sheets. That's such a great idea. I want to start doing that for regular shows because, why not! Then if I'm out sick, the wardrobe supervisor can just log on to Google and get it. It's in a central location.

KAIN GILL: Yes, we've been doing that for *Grits*. Other paperwork that wasn't wardrobe paperwork we've been doing that so we can see everyone's process as long as everyone has access to it. I'm always seeing what the camera team is doing, or what the props team is doing, just being open and just seeing what everyone's doing. If they have reference images, I very often went to Hayner's reference images saying, like oh this is what they think the world looks like let me see, let me how can I incorporate some of that into my stuff. Yes, I love Google, I love Google sheets, I love Google drive, that's a must.

KYLA KAZUSCHYK: And then everything is saved, and everything is flexible, you can make changes to it easily and it is saved. You're passionate about how we should be teaching devising in college, and we do a little bit, but I think there's room for more of it everywhere. Can you tell me more about why you think that's important? What's the advantage to teaching devising in college?

KAIN GILL: College theatre needs to be a place to learn, we need to feel and be in a place where we can just be creative and expressive. It needs to be more freeing; it needs to not be so rigid and structured all the time. There needs to be places where we can be creative and fun. Because we are artists, we have to keep that creativity going. I think there's just not enough of it. I do like the structure because of course traditional theatre has a structure, we should learn about it and learn the good parts of it and learn what has worked in the past, but we also need to think about moving forward, how can we keep the theatre going? Devising is how you create new pieces of work. Why isn't that done more? In collegiate theatre, you should not be afraid to fail. You're supposed to fail, that's how you learn. Devising theatre, that should be its own class. Honestly, just fail. Just fail. You'll learn so much. I fail all the time. I've learned so many things. You don't need to be mean and that's the thing too. It needs to be a place to learn without fear and you need people who are not going to belittle you for the art that you do make. Those two things together, solid art. Solid artists, solid progression. We can see good pacing and where we want to go in our theatre, where we want to go as artists.

KYLA KAZUSCHYK: I think that some of the reasoning behind why we don't do more devising is that it's not preparing students for what they're going to see in the quote unquote real world, like there's not that much of it out there. But like you talk about creating the next generation, creating the future of theatre, that's going to be up to younger artists that are creating what they want to create, right?

KAIN GILL: Why do we have playwrights still? We should all be writing theatre. We have theatre, we have plays to produce now, so we need new things. I get the preparing for the future, but things need to grow. That is definitely growth that could be explored, it should at least be explored. I don't see why that's a no no area, but also, I guess, budget and trying to make money. I noticed that that's a pretty big determining factor, or at least for collegiate theatre like are we going to make money on this and I'm like, Okay sure, but we could also be making really good art. It shouldn't always be about money.

If it went to more facilitating of fun and explorative art, then I'd be like sure let's have Shakespeare for the fiftieth time if we can get to a new devised show. But we need to try something new. I think we need to stop worrying about money, if it's going to make money and worry about also what do kids want to produce? What do audiences now want to see? How do we feed the need, the new needs for the new art that we will make, the art that needs to be made?

KYLA KAZUSCHYK: And I think another thing that you've touched on too, this idea of making mistakes. That's going to serve you, no matter what. You make mistakes and you keep going. That's what we can learn in devised theatre is that, like you said, no idea is a bad idea. You can have ideas, you can make mistakes, you can try things, and you can build up resilience.

KAIN GILL: Yes, and when you fail in something that has low stakes, and you don't have people criticizing you, you feel much more confident to try in the future and keep experimenting until you get to the point where you are like, Oh I've done this enough, so I know that this is how I want to do it, and you're able to make those changes as the process goes along because you've been in those situations. I don't think I've had enough of that experience. I've definitely failed a lot and I've grown a lot in the costume shop. You guys have corrected me a lot and it's so nice and I didn't feel intimidated. Literally just being able to accept failure and take criticism and all that stuff is so important as you grow just, not even as an artist, but just as a person coming into this world in general.

KYLA KAZUSCHYK: Absolutely. You said you worked on semi devised films, tell me more about that.

KAIN GILL: So Horribly Short, which is the little film festival, those are basically always devised because it's like you have 48 hours to make this whole show, this is your budget, if you have a budget, this is your team of people, go. When I was doing it, I was the producer, Zoey was the director, we had a director of photography who was like cameras and lights, we have makeup costume like artsy people. But when we were starting, we were all together in the room, we're all talking about where the ideas could go. We had people who specifically wanted to write, but we all had ideas of where the story could go. And we gave the writer the freedom because they want to experiment with where they want to go. We all had ideas. We shared our ideas. We felt heard. The writer went and did their thing and made it very fun. I don't remember what the story was, I think it was just ridiculous, but I loved it. It was fun. It was hard. And also, knowing necessarily what their job specifically was gave us the time to explore different ways of doing things because we don't know where we're going, we're just having fun, we're just learning how to write, how to costume, how to use equipment. We find the mistakes that we've made and where to pick up next time. And doing it in the essence of film is really interesting because film is really tight, because you have to create everything, shoot everything, and then put it together. I wouldn't say it's easier than theatre, but you can cut out the things that you don't want to see. In the theatre you can't do that. If a mistake happens, it's on stage, it is there, we can all see it. In film mistakes might also be on screen too, but you can cut it. Film is already in its essence kind of devised, especially like short films and like smaller projects. And theatre is less like that.

KYLA KAZUSCHYK: I'm so glad you brought that up because I hadn't thought about that at all. I've watched Horribly Short, but I've never made the connection. The way you described it, that's exactly what a devising process is: everyone gets in a room, you have the constraints of time, everyone has to collaborate together and then create something. So that's totally devising.

KAIN GILL: When you think about it like that, also any of those school projects that we did, like for theatre history, all those little like performances we had to do, we had to devise something on the spot. We were like go, you have to do this, read the lines go go go who's going to read the lines who is going to do this, does it need to be like this can it be really fun, you know stuff like that. I guess we had a little bit of devising but it's never like here, this is your class to make a play, let's make a play, let's make a point, let's talk about what our writers room looks like, let's talk about collaborating together and how the different artists work simultaneously and together.

KYLA KAZUSCHYK: Art is created in conjunction and concurrently. Did you design for dance while you were here?

KAIN GILL: No but I loved watching the process, watching Suellen do all her designs and watching them on stage

I was like this is really, really cool. I feel like dance is kind of also devised because it, I mean it literally in itself is devised, because you create the piece right there. There you go, everything is devised it feels like, except for like traditional theatre.

KYLA KAZUSCHYK: Exactly, everything is devised, film is devised, school projects are devised, why not.

KAIN GILL: Now dance that's cool I didn't think about that. You have to create while it's being created. That's the only way to do it at this point. You have to go with it, and any changes that happen have to happen. It also is a good example of like, you have to listen to the performers. You can't just say, well, you have to wear this. Because the whole point is what they are wearing has to suit the movement.

KYLA KAZUSCHYK: Why not, if we're creating collective art, why not always be working as a collective? I found that it is possible to do that in classes. I'm interested in figuring out more ways to do that. Do you have any more advice for artists approaching devised work? What advice would you say to collaborators and maybe specifically costume people, what do you need to know to go into devising?

KAIN GILL: Don't sell yourself short. Don't get overwhelmed. If you get overwhelmed, take a step back, take a breath, think about everything, and don't overthink. Because it feels like you have to do so much to make a world when really just small things like, why do we drive on one side of the road? Maybe that's just one thing you know, just bite size pieces. Because creating a whole world is hard but it doesn't have to be. Just bite size and don't worry about getting overwhelmed. It's always going to be overwhelming, just, you know, just small bites.

KYLA KAZUSCHYK: I think part of the antidote to being overwhelmed is leaning on your teammates and not feeling like you have to do everything yourself, being comfortable being vulnerable and asking for help when you need it.

KAIN GILL: That's a very important skill, especially in devised theatre, because your team is there to help you. They don't want to see you fail, they don't want the show to fail. Asking for help is always something that people find hard. Always ask for help. Just ask for help. There's nothing wrong with it. Honestly, asking for help is more powerful than doing it on your own because it shows that you have strength to know when something is going wrong, and when you need help. And then recognize when you need someone to lean on, you need someone to support you up. That's actually pretty big, for life in general, not just devised theatre, but especially for devised theatre.

KYLA KAZUSCHYK: Absolutely, and this is oppression, that we're taught to be individuals, we are taught that we have to be self-reliant. We don't have to be, that's not actually human to be self-reliant. Humans are made to rely on each other.

KAIN GILL: It takes a village, that's a real thing. Is a country made with one person? Absolutely not. One person didn't make the country, so why would one person make the show? That's not how that works. Definitely collaborate. Just don't be afraid. Everybody needs to help each other. Lift each other up because there's no reason to watch someone sink while you're flying.

KYLA KAZUSCHYK: And what you said about selling yourself short is so paramount too because we're taught that as well, we're taught to be insecure and to not value our own voices and to not trust ourselves. But if we do, if we do start trusting our intuition and trusting our vision, we can create incredible things.

KAIN GILL: Absolutely. Always always always say: this is a hard thing to do and I'm doing it right now. Remember where you're at and remember how much work you're putting into it. Literally never sell yourself short. That is so good. And remember how much value you put into everything you do just by being there and by being yourself.

ARTIST SPOTLIGHT: ROWEN HAIGH

Rowen Haigh is a freelance director, deviser, producer, and educator as well as an activist and organizer for gender parity in the theatre. She loves devising because it is so alive. They point to "the excitement of discovering what you know and what you believe as it comes into being."

In devising you are not interpreting, not mining a text for clues ... which I enjoy, but it is really different from being with other people and mining your humanity together, your experiences, your intuition, subtle resonances, and intuition. There is something really exciting about learning where a piece wants to go. As a deviser, that's one of the ways I approach scripted theatre. Other people don't like that, it freaks them out, they look at me like I'm not prepared. I'm prepared, I just don't think that me predetermining the direction we should go is the best choice.

Devising can be collaborative, investigative, messy, playful, and what makes it all work is that collaborators trust each other. "You're not trying to get something right, you're not trying to achieve something, you're exploring, and allowing the work to evolve."

To create timelines, work backwards from a performance deadline. There can be a time period of exploration and development, then a draft of script, then a performance for an

Organize! 29

FIGURE 2.7 This for That, *a collaboration with artists in Pune, India (photo courtesy of Rowen Haigh)*

FIGURE 2.8 *Performers on stage in* The Bear Loves Honey *(photo courtesy of ©2013 Bruce F. Press Photography)*

FIGURE 2.9 *Devised scenic and costume elements in* The Bear Loves Honey *(photo courtesy of ©2013 Bruce F. Press Photography)*

FIGURE 2.10 *Costumes for* The Bear Loves Honey *included a dress that had to be cut apart on stage each night (photo courtesy of ©2013 Bruce F. Press Photography)*

invited audience. Feedback from the audience is critical to the development of a piece.

The idea for Rowen's work, The Bear Loves Honey, came from a news story she read online about a Russian grave robber.

One cool thing about devising is that

it goes so fast that you don't have time to second guess yourself. You do it and if it works it works, if it doesn't you try something else. You don't have time to prevaricate. Because it is a collective process, I can bring something imperfect to my team for them to adapt. I don't have the pressure of it having to be perfect. Sharing it with the audience as an original devised work, within that there is a freedom of saying to an audience: this is raw, this is imperfect, it is going to continue developing and you're part of it. I've always been really interested in audience dynamic.

For The Bear Loves Honey, "part of our development process was doing a performance art installation, as part of the development process for the set, something that was going to become a touring show." They cut up boxes of children's books to create a fluttering, textured flock of book pages and covered the floors with sawdust. China cups suspended from the ceiling also contributed to the atmosphere of a macabre children's tea party.

After an initial performance, they would talk with audiences about what resonated with them and then take that into developing the psychological world of the play and the development of the characters. It is a sort of experiential dramaturgical research.

On The Bear Loves Honey, there were two codirectors, three actors, and a set designer who designed sets that everyone helped execute. Costuming happened by taking the cast to thrift stores and having them try different things. There were some practical considerations. In one scene, the grave robber character cuts a dress off of one of the girls, so they needed a fabric that would bear being cut and restitched nightly. They ended up going with a patterned dress of stretch fabric, which they cut along the same seam each show.

Sets, props, and costumes were all developed by the team working together. They went to a flea market together and selected objects they felt drawn to. The visual vocabulary evolved from the practical needs of the play. Everything was based on the intuition of the whole group and the evolving needs of the script. "I love that I don't remember whose idea what thing was for the most part. We just started creating the work and then integrating the tools that were needed to make it happen."

FIGURE 2.11 *Performers on stage in* The Bear Loves Honey *(photo courtesy of ©2013 Bruce F. Press Photography)*

FIGURE 2.12 Costumes devised by performers in Our Weddings. Pictured, left to right: Hannah Mayer, Sasha Wright, Ash Alter, Kaitlyn Reiersen, Sophia Hoffer Perkins (photo courtesy of Rowen Haigh)

Other projects Rowen has worked on have been more autobiographical. A piece called *Our Weddings* was about contemporaries getting married. "I didn't really understand the wedding industry, and the heteronormativity of the industry. What if you don't want to get married? What if you don't see yourself in this narrative? How do people who don't see themselves in that frame find the language to articulate their perspective?" So, Rowen found people who were interested in working on that, and they started playing and experimenting. The visual vocabulary was in part inspired by birthday party decorations. They used plastic tablecloths and ribbon to make huge poufy wedding-style dresses. Everyone wore their own clothes as a base costume and played around with adding all sorts of things on top, including dollar store polyester lace curtains. Silhouettes can be altered just by tying and draping materials in different ways. The content came from that group's personal experiences and, depending on where they presented it, they used the venue to inform the composition as well. "It is so helpful to be adaptable, and to trust that it might not work." The practice is based in exploration and curiosity, experimenting without trying to achieve a particular end, like going shopping for yourself without looking for the perfect outfit.

Rowen cites the skills developed in devising as being helpful in producing, marketing, and crowd funding. It can make you so much more prepared to be adaptable. Even written, scripted projects can be created in a very collaborative devised spirit. "I actually get confused in processes where the design folks are siloed. I'm not used to that. I'm used to folks being able to weigh in, across production teams, and including the actors." Humans, characters, and costumes all exist in close relation to one another.

This was a collaboration with an ensemble of artists in Pune, India, for Pukaar, Pune's first English-language theatre festival. The collaboration came about because one of the festival organizers was Hina Siddiqui, a theatre maker I'd met a few years previously at an international conference for artists who work in youth and community contexts ("Contacting the World" held in Manchester, England). Hina initially contacted me about bringing a show to the festival. That was going to be cost-prohibitive and logistically too complex, so my counterproposal was to travel to Pune with my (then) creative partner and devise a show there with local actors. We came in with the idea of creating a show about money and our

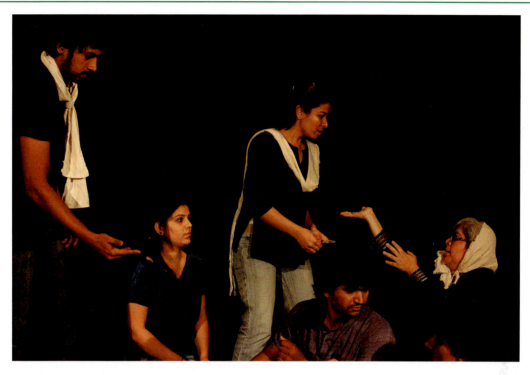

FIGURE 2.13 *Performers in devised costumes on stage in* This for That *(photo courtesy of Rowen Haigh)*

relationships to money because that felt like both a pertinent and, in truth, kind of scary thing to bring into the light—particularly in terms of the relative affluence and poverty of America and India.

We spent ten days in Pune. The first day we just got settled in, and then on day 2 we started full day devising sessions with our team of actors (a group that Hina secured and coordinated). They ranged in age from late twenties to late fifties and were an incredibly talented and committed group. All in all we spent about seven days in the rehearsal room developing, structuring, and refining content. We got costumes and props from "found" sources—notably, we used the blankets from our plane journey (which we had kept because, well, we're theatre people and you never know when you're going to need things!), torn into strips and used as kind of a visual connective tissue that showed up as scarves, shawls, headscarves, and other costume accents. We also got some empty burlap grain sacks from local merchants. The actors wore their own clothes as base costumes.

One of the best parts of the whole experience was also spending time with the cast outside of rehearsal. They took us around the city to show us different parts throughout the process. So, while that wasn't an explicit part of the content, that community-building and exchange of experiences and cultures was nonetheless a major part of the foundation of the whole work.

In the end, we created a show that was around 50 minutes long. It was loosely structured on the evolution of the "this for that" model that gave birth to the use of money. So, starting with bartering one good/service for another, moving into physical money as a representation of a thing's value, then into cards/electronic "money" down the line. In addition to those pieces of the story, the actors also developed content around "value" as a concept as well—the value of health, food, and human connection, and how, at the end of the day, money is secondary to those things. Some sections were dialogue-based, some were purely physical. It was an incredible show sand an incredible experience all around!

CHAPTER 3

COMMUNICATE!

VISUAL COMMUNICATION

Near the beginning of the process for *Love and Information*, I tried to follow the standard method of script analysis that a costume designer practices. The second time I read the script, I began to discover the futility of trying to answer questions like "How many people are in this scene?" "Is the person speaking male or female?" and "Where does this conversation take place?" Because the script does not specify who speaks which line, it was impossible to create a typical scene and character breakdown. So, instead, I made a list of over 100 evocative symbols and ideas contained in the text. This list included red flowers, small snails, celebrity couples, diseased chicken entrails, binary code sequences, microscopic images of heart and brain cells from people suffering from schizophrenia and Alzheimer's disease, Jackson Pollack paintings, rollercoasters, and stars. I collected images of these things by doing an image search online. I printed all the images out and kept them in a folder so that I could bring them to design meetings and table rehearsals, to share them with the director and the performers. Having images printed and cut apart allows you to move things around, group things together, and easily remove images that emerge as less instrumental to the developing story.

A trusted resource for the creation of costumes is *The Costume Technician's Handbook*, by Rosemary Ingham and Liz Covey. I, and many other educators, use this as a textbook for costume construction classes. In it, Ingham and Covey outline the steps involved in creating a theatrical costume, describing 26 steps that follow examining the design sketch with the designer. This process is built around the idea that, by the time the designer has created that sketch, the director has signed off on the design and production may proceed, subject only to minor adjustments near the end of the process. In the world of devised theatre, this process must be almost entirely revised. As a designer, it is impossible to draw design sketches at the beginning of the process because there is not yet any content to inform what those sketches should be. The traditional process cannot be followed, and designers must be open to a rollercoaster of new experiences and ideas instead of a tried-and-true set of questions that may be answered. The chaotic process of creating costumes for devised theatre involves visual communication early on, designer presence in rehearsal, and the ability to be extremely flexible while preplanning as much as possible.

Any time artists come together to collaborate and create theatre, whether they are working from a traditional script or on a devised piece, clarity in all forms of communication is extremely important. We must be as precise as possible with verbal communication, and we must understand that exact precision with verbal communication might actually never be possible. There is no way to really be sure through talking or writing that the images in your head are the same as the images in another person's head. This is why we must transition to visual communication early and often in the production process. When Shakespeare's Richard III says, "My kingdom for a horse," the director might picture a healthy, noble, muscular steed. If the costume designer is reading that same line and envisioning a gnarly black skeleton of a horse, their perspectives on the world of the play will be vastly at odds. Even

FIGURE 3.1 *Printed out research images for* Love and Information, *cut apart and spread out over a cutting table in the costume shop*

colors can vary—what I see as red might not be what you see as red. My idea of "romantic" might be a Taylor Swift music video, and yours might be late 18th- and early 19th-century Europe.

By sharing research images as you discuss the design concept for the show, you can ensure that the costumes reflect a coherent vision for the play. When showing research images, initial sketches, or color renderings to the team, every designer has an opportunity to shape the growth of the piece. Perhaps the director didn't initially imagine the world being created on stage to be a certain way, but when presented with compelling pictures, the direction of the piece could shift.

What I have found to be most effective in terms of visual communication is collaged research images. This collection of images could be photographs, paintings, objects, or digitally created images. They could be clippings from magazines or newspapers, printed photographs, or digital files stored on a computer. An advantage to collaged images is that they can be evocative, specific, and fairly easy to edit. A savvy costumer can start with many images, and then distill that collection down to the most vital. As the shape of the production evolves, some images will stand out as more relevant to the production's theme, and others can be left behind.

The advantage to analog is you can spread your images out over the table, and collaborators can respond. You can shuffle the images, group them together in different ways, eliminate those that are not helping us go in the direction we desire. Start large and funnel or distill. Start with a wide range of images and together narrow them down to the most vital.

The poetic text for *Savage/Love* does not denote specific characters or settings, yet it does invoke underlying themes of love, connection, euphoria, longing, heartbreak, and anguish. I began as a designer would in a traditional process, by finding

Communicate! 37

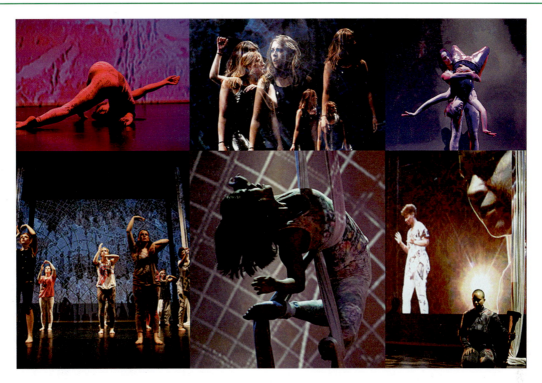

FIGURE 3.2 *Scenes from Savage/Love (photos courtesy of Andy Phillipson–Livewireimage.com)*

FIGURE 3.3 *Renderings for Savage/Love*

FIGURE 3.4 Dream Logos *on stage (photo courtesy of Andy Phillipson–Livewireimage.com)*

and loss. Initial rehearsals with the cast involved reading parts of the script and taking measurements, as well as discussing personal experiences and perspectives on love and relationships. While a costume designer is usually closely connected to actors through drawing pictures of them, planning garments for them to wear, and talking to them about their characters in fittings, it is unusual to be as intimately connected as this. Since characters do not exist before the costume designer is involved, the costume designer's input, in the form of ideas communicated through visual images, can influence who the characters become.

VERBAL COMMUNICATION

Keep the lines of communication open, between everybody. This includes directors, performers, other designers, technicians, stage managers, everyone involved in the project.

Maybe there are designated times and spaces, like production meetings, or maybe there are not. When some members of the team are together and some are remote (as is often the case in 2020–21 pandemic times), seek opportunities to connect with others whenever possible.

Pay attention to each individual's preferred communication style and use it. Email, in-person, telephone, text message, zoom meeting—each has pros and cons. Text messages can get quick answers to questions, but they can lack the clarity of tone that can be conveyed in-person.

Check for understanding when speaking. Use phrases like "What I'm hearing is (fill in the blank), is that right?" and "Is there more?"

In group situations, like production meetings or classes, it is not a bad idea to establish community agreements at the start of every meeting. These can vary depending on the needs and desires of each group. My favorite shared agreement is connected to the easy to remember acronym "W.A.I.T." I have participated in many workshops and conference meetings where this one is employed. It stands for both "Why Am I Talking?" and also "Why Aren't I Talking?" So, "W.A.I.T" before you speak up. If you find that you have been talking a lot, practice some self-awareness and yield the floor to someone else. If you have an idea that you haven't brought up yet, speak up, introduce your idea to the group.

Carrigan O'Brian, of the Eugene O'Neil Theater Center advises, "If you're talking/generating ideas more than everyone else, take a back seat and ask one of the quieter collaborators if they need help or have any ideas." This can make a tremendous difference to the dynamic of a room. A collaborator who naturally feels more shy to speak up may feel more welcome if they are directly asked for their input.

images that visually represented my emotional response to the piece. In this case, the images were a mix of anatomical drawings of human hearts, photocopies of torn up love letters, surrealist collages depicting flowers growing out of hearts, medical images of blood vessels and veins, horror movie style disembodied hearts dripping with blood, and cheery valentine style candy hearts. These images represented the themes contained in the text. When designing for a scripted show with specified characters, the initial emotional response images often end up being reflected subtly in the color palette or texture of the finished costumes. When I showed these images to director/choreographer Nick Erickson, before rehearsals had started, he was so inspired by the evocative nature of the images, together we brainstormed that the costumes could include more literal representations of these images. Nick's vision for the piece was that it would include a mixture of dance, aerial performance, live acting, and projected recordings, all coming together to express both the ideas contained in the script as well as the performers' own views of love

FIGURE 3.5 *One way to visually represent the themes of heartbreak and anguish started with finding images of microscopic views of diseased heart cells. I experimented with different dye and paint techniques, eventually using watercolor pencils heat set into cotton blend fabrics*

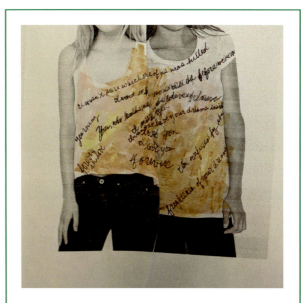

FIGURE 3.7 *As one section of Savage/Love developed into a dance duet with voiceover spoken word of love letters and breakup letters, I imagined this concept where the dancers' costumes look like weathered pages with the words written to each other scrawled across each others' bodies*

FIGURE 3.6 *Diseased heart cell painted fabric in action in Savage/Love*

FIGURE 3.8 *Savage/Love on stage at Louisiana State University*

Everyone is different. Directors and designers might offer more ideas or fewer ideas. Each project or company develops its own culture. Some designers feel comfortable sharing ideas about topics beyond their disciplines, and some do not. Assistant designers, who are often students or emerging artists, sometimes feel confident using their voice. Sometimes they feel less confident, but could feel more comfortable speaking up with a little encouragement and support.

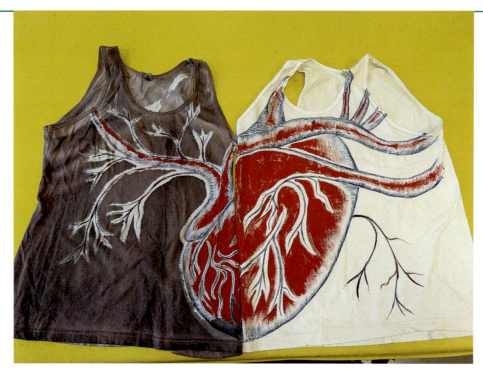

FIGURE 3.9 Another paint treatment for Savage/Love, an anatomical heart in acrylic paint becomes whole when choreography and blocking has this performer press against another performer wearing the other half

FIGURE 3.10 Juxtaposed with the anatomical hearts are cheerful valentine candy hearts, created by printing from an inkjet printer onto photo transfer fabric

There are pros and cons to how many people you have on your costume team. In our world, we are often a party of one. If you are the designer and shop manager and draper and first hand and stitcher, then you do not need to express your ideas to anybody, but you've got to work quickly and efficiently.

Relationships are delicate, and respectful communication is essential.

If you are the designer and you are working with a separate shop manager or cutter/draper, it is helpful to employ visual and verbal means of communicating your design. The more, the better! Research images, line drawings, color renderings, pencil sketches—as much as possible!

When communicating with fellow designers, be open. Maybe your perspectives can inspire them, and vice versa.

With performers, be gentle and open.

Be honest about what you know, and, more importantly, about what you don't. If you have experience performing, call upon that memory to have compassion. It is ultimately their body on stage in front of an audience telling the story. The clothes costumers provide can help boost confidence or

FIGURE 3.11 *Maja Dupas and Rio Jsanea on stage in Savage/Love (photo courtesy of Andy Phillipson—Livewireimage.com)*

FIGURE 3.12 *Experimenting with resist dye techniques, many types of paints, and printer transfer paper to create more dichotomies between darkness and light*

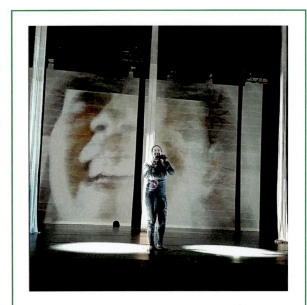

FIGURE 3.13 *Savage/Love on stage in 2016*

FIGURE 3.15 *After fitting each performer in a solid white dyeable stretch outfit, I waited as long as I could before beginning painting, while performers were still devising who was in each scene. Some of the connections never ended up happening on stage, but many did*

FIGURE 3.14 *Hearts and arteries created with direct dye application and acrylic paint*

heighten vulnerability. Have conversations with performers as early and as often as possible (more on this in Chapter 6).

Cultural humility is paramount as we create new worlds. The problem with the ideal of "cultural competency" is that we can never be completely competent in another culture. Especially because things are always changing/evolving/shifting. As costume creators, we have a responsibility to do as much research as possible to be as accurate and specific as possible when depicting characters from cultures beyond our own. And we must evolve and update our ideas when we learn new information.

Costume designer and educator Kendra Johnson has lots of useful suggestions for how to approach research and how to design in a way that is respectful to all cultures. Costume design will always depend on the cast and can change depending on what the performers are bringing to it. This requires us as designers to ask actors what is important to them and to listen to students when they call us out. Johnson suggests utilizing social media to be constantly broadening our worldview and doing what we can to immerse ourselves in things that are not of our culture. There are fantastic social media accounts in all sorts of areas, from Afropunk to Chinese street fashion to historical reenactors of color. If we are saving images always, even in between projects, we will have a collection of images to pull from when we have a specific topic to research.

While I recommend coming in at the beginning with lots of ideas and images, you might find that for you and with your collaborators, taking a different approach is more effective. Kendra Johnson says, "I don't show anything at the first meeting. I just want to listen and take notes." Ask a lot of questions. Ask for the why behind every choice.

FIGURE 3.16 Savage/Love on stage at the Edinburgh International Fringe Festival (photo courtesy of Andy Phillipson–Livewireimage.com)

FIGURE 3.17 Jesus In Vitro Panthera Onca (photo courtesy of Gina Sandí Díaz)

ARTIST SPOTLIGHT: GINA SANDÍ DÍAZ

GINA SANDÍ DÍAZ: I'm a theatre director specializing in devised theatre and acting and directing in general and I'm located in Fresno. Right now, I teach at Fresno state. So why devised theatre? I went to school in Costa Rica, which is where I'm from. There is a strong collective creation history in Latin America. Latin American theatre is very tied up to political issues; it's never just for entertainment. There's not a big industry for theatre for entertainment. Theatre is more linked to the social change drive and to political issues. So, when I was in college, that was the type of theatre I was exposed to. A lot of my professors specialized in collective creation and that's what they did, and so that's what we would do in our classes. A lot of that is how I was taught to make theatre, always with collaboration at the center and always this idea that you are constantly negotiating and balancing with everybody else who is involved in the process.

Not to say that there's no formal theatre in Costa Rica—there's obviously also some very formal theatre companies that are sponsored by the state and that produce Ibsen and Shakespeare, and you know, same old stuff as we do here. Those exist as well, but it's not a huge industry.

When I made the transition to the US, it was hard for me because I noticed that the way of making theatre inside the institution, because I was in a university, was very hierarchical and I wasn't accustomed to that. As an actor, I was accustomed to my input being asked and incorporated into the process. I was accustomed to having some freedom as a creator, as an actor creator, into how I view that character and bringing my own input to it, and that was not a part of the training here and not a part of the theatre-making experience.

And then there was also the added conflict of me being a foreigner, which has an impact when you're trying to be an actor, you know? I wasn't offered many roles. I was offered only certain types of roles, typical roles where Latinas are placed, as housekeepers and maids and that kind of stuff. And it's not that there's anything wrong with that, but if you are a professional actor, and you have training and you have experience, you know that you can do more, and you want to see yourself doing more. It came to the point where I wasn't really doing anything, I wasn't doing theatre. I wanted to do theatre, but I wasn't a part of any company. I wasn't being called by anybody; nothing was really happening for me. So, I just kind of started doing my own thing and using the tools that I knew, which are collective creation. I started doing little projects and that's what I've been doing since I arrived in the US. I permanently moved here in 2013. And you know, just doing little devised theatre projects here and there and then kind of shaping that as my professional aesthetic, I guess. It's kind of my thing.

KYLA KAZUSCHYK: What has been the response of people that you bring in to collaborate with? Is there a learning curve for explaining your process?

GINA SANDÍ DÍAZ: Oh absolutely, yes, great question. Another thing that I have to mention is that in Costa Rica a lot of my professional experience was in the area of applied theatre, which is working with people that are not in the theatre industry. I have a lot of experience and I enjoy working with non-actors. And so that's a very huge learning curve for people that have zero acting experience coming in and doing something like this. But what I've discovered is that what's really valuable about devised theatre is the process. Of course we come up with a product and the audience enjoys that product and that product can be transformative but really the people that are transformed by the process are the people that are participating in the process.

I think that there are a lot of learning curves. But usually, even if there are non-actors, people become really really engaged, because they have ownership of whatever is happening there—it's theirs. And that's a huge learning experience, in whatever way you want to look at it—for self empowerment, for discovering things about yourself, for learning to collaborate with other people, communication, etc., etc., etc.

KYLA KAZUSCHYK: How do you approach dividing responsibilities on a project? Are you a part of a company where there's a costume designer and a director and actors or is everybody on the same level?

GINA SANDÍ DÍAZ: In my experience in Costa Rica, we don't have any resources or any money or even any infrastructure. In that case, when I was there, I had a company with my friends—it's not a company, it was a group, a collective. And we called ourselves Las Anates, which is a type of bird, you know that black bird that appears everywhere, I don't know what it's called in English. It was a group of four of us, four actors. We divided the chores, so we all did everything. I had a little bit of experience when I was in college with lighting. I'm not a designer or anything like that, and I have zero training on it, but I was the lighting operator at this little theatre in San Jose for two years, and so I learned how to operate the equipment. I can change one of those pan lights, I can change a gel, I can put a gobo in, those kinds of things. So, I was in charge of kind of thinking about lights. And then another of my colleagues, who had more experience in the visual arts, he would take on the set and costume ideas. But we would all collaborate, so we didn't necessarily have people in specific roles. We all kind of bring to the table, and then we might have like coordinators.

Then over here in the US when I'm working with non-actors, I kind of coordinate the whole thing, like I'm the center, I'm the director. I try to identify what people are good at and passionate about and then make them my go-to for that area.

And then in school I teach a devised theatre class and the way that I like to do it, because designers come into the class as well, is I like to do like Area Coordinators. And then the students, they're all in the class together and they can belong to two or three areas. And each of those areas has a coordinator, and so we divide time in class for the areas to kind of meet together, discuss what's going on. They're all in class so they are seeing what's happening on stage, so we're all kind of working together at the same time.

So that's how I've been exploring it. I don't have a particular model or way of working, it kind of also depends on who I'm working with and what they bring to the table, and then we come up with a way of making it work.

KYLA KAZUSCHYK: This is one of the things that's so exciting but also challenging: that it's not possible for there to be a formula. Because no matter what, it's going to be different, no matter who the people involved are, or whatever the subject matter is, or what the context and the parameters, how are we going to develop a formula for devised theatre?

GINA SANDÍ DÍAZ: I think it requires flexibility, right? If you are a person that works well in structures and cannot see yourself outside of structure, you are probably going to struggle a lot. And I do have those experiences as well. Sometimes students in the class are very lost, and they cannot find their way through whatever it is that we're doing, because of the lack of structure. It scares them or takes them off balance, but not everybody. Some other people thrive in those environments, because it takes the pressure off of getting it right or doing things to please whoever's in charge. I like it, I think everybody eventually takes something from the experience. And I don't think that traditional theatre making necessarily does that. I've been involved in many productions where there was nothing I took from that experience and there's nothing that I think like wow, being in that production really spoke to me and stuff. But I can remember every single devised theatre experience that I've been a part of because I have had some level of ownership over it.

KYLA KAZUSCHYK: You can be more connected to it, there's much more room for that. Part of what I'm trying to figure out is developing a formula for something where there can be no formula. And I think part of a way I can do this is by sharing examples. So if I was to explain to someone how to create costumes for devised work, I can say well, here's one way that it worked, here's another example of how it worked. In your experiences, how did you approach creating costumes for some of the projects you've worked on?

GINA SANDÍ DÍAZ: In that case, we have to wait until we are at a part of the process where we know the theme that we're dealing with and what do we want out of that theme. So usually, like when we begin a devised theatre process, depending on the setting, we might have something in mind, or we might not have something in mind.

If it's a class, a devised theatre class, I start from zero. I don't know what's going to be. It's going to come from the students, what are they interested in and then eventually we'll have a theme and we'll say okay—"oh okay we're dealing with violence" or "we're dealing with communication" and that's the theme, perfect.

So once we have the theme, so that takes a while, I like to think, also in devised theatre, as you know, it has three big processes. The first process is exploration, and then structuring and polishing, and then sharing it with the audience.

So that exploration phase, we still don't know what it's going to be, and it could be very frustrating for designers who need something to work with, but it's just different. So devised theatre, I would say that designers have to be invited to that process, that first exploration process. And they don't have to necessarily be there all the time, but they should regularly visit to see what's happening and what shape this is getting. And then, once we have a concept and a theme and more specificity about that, then I absolutely share that with the team. If it's one designer, but usually in my devised theatre experience the participants are the ones that are designing, so it's a lot more fluid than if somebody is on the outside, going to be coming in and out, coming in and out.

One thing that I appreciate about devised theatre is that the level of collaboration is different. Usually everybody is in the room, always. I've never had an experience that I think might be your experience of creating devised theatre and bringing designers from outside. That has not been my experience, yet. Although I'm sure I will come to that because I'm trying to build a devised theatre program that can do a production every two or three years, have a devised theatre production and so that's going to involve bringing in our designers one way or another. And so I'm also curious about that—I would like to hear you talk about how you manage that, when it's a more structured role that is just collaborating to create the costumes and it's not necessarily fully involved in the day to day of the devising process.

KYLA KAZUSCHYK: It's different levels of experience and participation. The roles can be almost the same, like when you're talking about it's a group of friends and someone has a little more experience in lighting, so they do more lighting, someone has more experience in visuals, then they do more visuals. But then on top of that you're also acting and developing the show together. And in my experience, coming into a project as costume designer, I'm not acting, I'm not participating in the acting things, but I'm bringing lots of experience designing costumes. So, it's maybe bringing more experience than someone else would have but also less experience in acting and performing. And then beyond that it's just figuring out how to manage time, like how much time can be devoted on top of everything else, which is like the question of the ages, how do we balance everything that we're doing teaching classes and designing shows and building shows.

GINA SANDÍ DÍAZ: So when you're doing that, do you come in once a week or how does it work for a designer?

KYLA KAZUSCHYK: It's always different. If it's physical theatre, I'm so lucky that the costume shop is right across the hall from the movement studio so I'm there every day. If they're working on stuff and I'm in here working on stuff I might as well be in *there* working on stuff. But if it's a show where they're rehearsing somewhere else, it's not as in proximity to the costume shop—then yeah more like once a week, not every night.

GINA SANDÍ DÍAZ: Cool. That's really interesting how each social group is going to find their own way of making it work.

KYLA KAZUSCHYK: It's so true and it's so interesting to look at a company as a social group and the cast or the assembled team, for whatever project, they're always going to develop their own culture and their own methods of communication and you have to learn that whenever you embark on a project. There's a million ways to do it.

You were telling me about how you're developing this devised theatre program. Will it also have an applied theatre focus? I'm curious more about the connections between devised and applied.

GINA SANDÍ DÍAZ: For me they go hand in hand. I'm not sure. It's still very green in my head, but I think that it should, I think that they should connect.

In Costa Rica, I was at the national university for a while, before I moved to the US. When I was there I formed an applied theatre program and so that program still exists and it's still working and they do specifically applied theatre. They're doing devised theatre in communities always, outside of the city and outside of the university. I like that idea. I think that would be really cool. It's a way of merging the two things. I am in a place in the country where that is very needed. I'm in California Central Valley, which is incredibly diverse. This is home to many refugee communities, so we have a lot of work to do in bringing cultures together and understanding different points of view. And then also, just how much is produced in the Central Valley—this is the biggest agricultural area in the whole country.

I think applied theatre would be wonderful here, because there are a lot of working-class communities that are surviving and are being affected very strongly right now with the pandemic and everything, so creating those spaces for self-empowerment and stuff, it would be significant. I am doing that with other organizations in the central valley, but not with the university.

And you know, sometimes it can be difficult with the universities. So I'm still kind of trying to find my way and see how much support I might have for something like that or not, but I think internally my department is more interested in making devised theatre for entertainment, for the university theatre and something that could sell us, for students who want to come here. I don't think they necessarily want me to add a social justice component to it, but I can't divorce that from my work—that is who I am as an artist as well. I would love for that to take off, like a merging of the two.

KYLA KAZUSCHYK: It's possible. There are possibilities there, and you talk about the need and community and how that can be at odds with the desire of the university, but universities have so many resources. I look at my own university that way too, like what's the point of just doing another show that everyone's seen before? With our space and time and money and people and energy, we could be telling other stories.

GINA SANDÍ DÍAZ: And reaching other people. When I'm thinking of productions, I don't think about the audience that we already have. My colleagues are making theatre for them. I'm making theatre for something else, for someone else. And I'm hoping to bring those people to the theatre to come and see it. I'm building a Latinx theatre program, that's why I'm here, so all of the plays I've directed have been by Latinx playwrights. And the response has been wonderful. All of my students are Latino so their parents are Latinos and their uncles and aunts and their grandparents, and they're all coming to the theatre, so I think that's wonderful.

KYLA KAZUSCHYK: That is wonderful and that's so exciting to think about sustainability and the future. Why create art for the people that already have access to art? Let's create art and communicate and tell stories and engage audiences that aren't the existing audience.

GINA SANDÍ DÍAZ: Build new audiences for the future.

KYLA KAZUSCHYK: Exactly. What advice do you have for artists approaching devised work?

GINA SANDÍ DÍAZ: Go for it! I think you know and it's part of the training, because I think we should open it up. I think devised theatre like that should be taught in all of the programs, a little bit of it should be taught. I think it's really significant. I kind of work against the industry, because I have to be realistic. I could never even dream of making it in the industry, that was never my dream and I'm glad that it was not because I would probably have been very disappointed. And so I don't want to break my students' hearts by telling them like that you're not going to make it, right? I'm not going to do that. What I want to do is give them, show them all the opportunities of what you can do with a degree in theatre and then go for it. You know, you are an artist, go make yourself a space, find a space. If we just sit and wait for theatres to call us, the dream evaporates, it just goes away. Very few people make it and I'm not saying that some of my students can't make it. I'm sure they can but it's just, I don't want to feed into that false narrative and then it also kind of leaves artists with no outlet to work. And I think that theatre is just so needed in our society. There are so many applications of it.

But we don't teach our students in our programs that they can do other things. We just prepare them to go to Broadway and that's just not, at least where I am right now, that's kind of like the dream they are dreaming to do and I feel heartbroken because I'm like we're in Fresno, California, you guys, like, why are we feeding our students that dream? It's just not realistic.

KYLA KAZUSCHYK: Absolutely, I deal with that at my school too. The reality of it is there's only so many opportunities for designers at regional theatres, for performers at regional theatres, for performers and designers on Broadway. Like that's great and like you said yeah some of our students can do that, but if we're going to have students every year, there aren't that many spots.

GINA SANDÍ DÍAZ: No. You have to teach them what else they can do. So right now, one of the things I'm doing is, in my acting class I did a collaboration with social work. The professor of social work wanted his students to have the opportunity to have like a fake session with a client to try on their social worker skills. And so we did that. The social work students came up with profiles of character, so they gave us like the given circumstances of who those characters were and then I took those profiles with my students and we created private moments, they created these private moments to kind of get into the shoes of those characters and then we had a few improv sessions about those characters and then we paired them up in a zoom meeting and they had little interviews and it was fantastic. The social workers discovered a lot of things that they need to work on and things that work out really well and my students discovered that their job has applications for other people, that they could be of service in other areas.

And then, they also learned that they have so much power. Because, since they were actors and they were prepared to step into these shoes and into this role, they completely dominated those interviews. The social work students were so much more vulnerable in those situations, and so they discovered how powerful it is and I think that those lessons are important. I'm sure not a lot of teachers would agree with me, but they are important. If you value theatre and the arts and you want to make a living out of it, those lessons are important.

KYLA KAZUSCHYK: Absolutely! Empowerment is so valuable and knowing possibilities of what else is out there and that's so cool that you were able to apply it to zoom too. That's something that so many of my students are struggling with, having that narrow-minded focus that, like, I just want to be on a stage on Broadway, that's it. That's not going to be it. The pandemic has taught us that there's going to be so many different things. Even when we can get back in person there's going to be so many other applications of theatre.

GINA SANDÍ DÍAZ: Exactly and for the majority of us who don't have the support of a regional theatre like a big institution that is going to give us money to produce art, we have to make ourselves and that's what I wanted my students to leave this program with. Don't graduate and just forget about theatre because you couldn't make it into any theatre. If this is what you want to do you have to go do it. And eventually you'll find a little home, even if it's like we have this little theatre company that we get together on the weekends and if that's what it is that's what it is, but don't let your dream just fall off because the industry is savage.

KYLA KAZUSCHYK: It really is savage, but it will change. It has to change. There's a lot of movement going on and people that are traditionally theatre patrons aren't all going to live forever. Our students now are going to grow up to be theatre patrons or not.

GINA SANDÍ DÍAZ: Right. How is the demographics, where you are? Where I am is incredibly diverse, incredibly diverse. So that gives us hope also that in the future, the audiences that we're attracting are going to be a lot more diverse and that's going to force us into more diverse stories and more diverse forms of storytelling and et cetera et cetera et cetera yeah that's exciting.

KYLA KAZUSCHYK: I'm curious, do you have any involvement, or have you had any involvement with community theatres?

GINA SANDÍ DÍAZ: In the US, no not yet I have not.

KYLA KAZUSCHYK: I grew up in community theatre and the community theatre in my town would be like we're going to put on a big musical and all the kids can be in the chorus and that's that. And when I went to college, I was trained on like, no community theatre—that's for amateurs—you don't want to be involved in that, no, you want to do professional theatre not community theatre.

But actually, in the past few years, being involved with the Southeastern Theatre Conference and seeing their connection to the community theatre festivals, now I think community theatre is an untapped resource for potential, where you could get together and create something and it doesn't have to be what it's always been, and it doesn't have to be looked down upon either.

GINA SANDÍ DÍAZ: I agree. I tried to incorporate those things into my classroom, not denigrating any form of theatre art or whatever because at the end of the day, exactly, we're all trying to make it, we're all trying to live out of this. We all want to make theatre so let's find our space. I think that's great. And you know what since I have you here, let me ask you, because I don't really understand the difference, like, I know the category of like a regional theatre. But then why do community theatres also do entertainment like consumer theatre? I thought that, you know in Latin America our idea of community theatre is a lot more grassroots and so I'm surprised that our community theatre here will also put on a musical, for example.

KYLA KAZUSCHYK: Well, I think, part of it, what you mentioned too, is that you said in Costa Rica there are State-sponsored theatres? I've never been involved in a theatre that gets money from the State. So it's the sustainability model of like we've got to do a big musical to sell tickets to get butts on seats to do other things that we want to do. With theatres I've been involved in that are independent, they don't have any State funding, so to keep going, they have to do something that's going to sell tickets.

GINA SANDÍ DÍAZ: So, but then the difference, like in the community it just means that anybody can audition and anybody can participate—it's not like equity actors?

KYLA KAZUSCHYK: That right. I'm excited to talk about it because, like so many things, we're taught that the industry is like this because it has to be, but that's not true, it doesn't have to be like that, it could be something different. It's possible to reimagine it.

GINA SANDÍ DÍAZ: Absolutely and there's a lot of resources.

KYLA KAZUSCHYK: You mentioned work you did in a women's prison; can you tell me more about that?

GINA SANDÍ DÍAZ: There is a women's prison in San Jose Costa Rica it's called El Buen Pastor and it's the only one in the country, so every woman prisoner is located there. My friend Ophelia Leon, who was our choreographer and dancer, passed away already, but she initiated this program and she was going there weekly and she had developed a group of women there. And then she became big. It became a big thing, they wanted to do stuff and the prison was into it. She was getting help so she brought some people in and one of those persons with me. And I was in charge of helping her with the theatre directing, because she was more of a choreographer, so I was doing more like the theatre portion, like the acting part. And then we had another collaborator that was also a choreographer who was doing all of the dance portion of it. And this went on for three years. So what we started, it was a process of developing self-love in the inmates, so that they could accept themselves. It was a process of peacemaking, but like individual peacemaking with themselves, and we were using expressivity, language, a lot of dancing. And then that led into storytelling. We started with dancing but then it turned into storytelling and they were creating their own little sketches that they wanted to share with the women in the group, and these were private moments as well, so some of them were sharing.

One that stuck in my head is she was like spending the night at a cemetery with her boyfriend because they were homeless and on drugs. And so they were sharing this type of stories and putting them in sketches and then we had a whole bunch of material and we were like—what do we do with this? There was all kinds of stuff going on, but it was a lot of experiences of people that were living on the streets.

Eventually we brought in this other collaborator who is a writer, and he has a book called Los Pejor, that is, it means "the worst," and so it's about precisely homeless people living on the street. And there's one character in this book that he's smarter, he's very wise and he speaks differently than everybody, but he's just, there's so many meanings in the things that he's saying, he's just so wise. And everybody else looks at him as lower than them but he's bigger than all of them, in a spirit anyway. He had that book, and so what we did was, how about we adapt this book because it's about people from the streets, and we can incorporate the stories of our women into it. And instead of Los Pejor it became Las Pejor because it's women—language in Spanish has that gendered form. And he was a part of it, so he gave us the rights to do this, and he participated in it and stuff. So anyway, we kept some of these main characters that appear in that book as a way to tie everything together, but then we added the little stories of the women into it and that became our show. And the way that we were doing that is, we were entering the prison once a week every Tuesday in the mornings for like three hours—I think we did like from 8 o'clock to 11, every Tuesday morning and it took us three years to get to a point where we were like Okay, we have something here that we can show.

For costumes and things like that, it was only like whatever the women had. We couldn't bring anything in or anything but they created it all, the women, they came up with it. They just really wanted to express themselves. So they got T-shirts and cut them up and so, you know, they had like a hole here or their shoulder, so you know things like that. And then they used a lot of things in their hair. It was very crazy like there wasn't any idea that was tying everything together, but it was because the goal was for self-expression. We wanted them to express themselves and to feel like they were at peace with each other. It was really wonderful. It really touched my heart in many, many different ways. And this was right before I came here like 2012, 2013. We were getting attention from newspapers and things like that, and we got like the Ministry of Security, I guess, in Costa Rica, or something to allow us to take the prisoners to the national theatre to do a performance. It was filmed and everything, it was in the newspaper. TV news were there, and it was huge. It was really, really big and their families came to see them and because they were out of the prison, they were allowed like five minutes to like hug with their families, it was really beautiful, it was amazing.

But then it was in the newspapers all over the place of what had happened. And then the following week when we got to the prison, they told us that we weren't allowed anymore, and they were shutting down the program like—thank you very much for your service, goodbye, and that was it, no explanation. Nothing else, they just shut us down like that. It was very disappointing and hard to process, but many months later, I realized that there was actually power in that—that they had shut it down because it had achieved its goal and I'm very grateful for those 14 women that were involved in there. I'm still in touch with two of them—I don't know where the other 12 are, but yeah it was it was transformative to say the least.

FIGURE 3.18 Las Peor. *Inspired by the novel* Los Peor *by Fernando Contreras. Devised theatre piece created in 2013 by Signos Teatro Danza with a group of incarcerated women in the prison of El Buen Pastor in San José, Costa Rica. Directed by Ofir León, Assistant Directors Gina Sandí Díaz and Valentina Marenco (photo courtesy of Gina Sandí Díaz)*

KYLA KAZUSCHYK: It sounds fantastic, and it sounds like such a good example of process being of more value than the product. You weren't in it to sell tickets; the goal is self-expression and the goal is the transformative journey that the participants are going on. And that's so cool that they had the freedom to create their own costumes. I bet even that was very empowering for them.

GINA SANDÍ DÍAZ: Oh, my God, yes, absolutely and they would help each other out and the makeup that they came up with because they were really bright and colorful and helping each other out, because you had this and I had that other thing and like, just kind of, resources. They didn't have much, but they made it work. And that's exactly how we work as theatre artists, I think, right? The same principle: we work with what we have.

KYLA KAZUSCHYK: That's such a great example of collaboration too, that even when you don't have much, it is possible to share what you have with someone else or to listen to someone else.

GINA SANDÍ DÍAZ: There was a trans man in the group. I can't remember his name now, but his biological name was a woman and so he was in the women's prison, but everybody respected his identity and called him by his male name. And his scene was precisely, it was this gorgeous monologue that he wrote about the rejection from his family. His mother had rejected him the moment that he had announced his change and kicked him out of the house and all of that, so he had this really powerful monologue about talking to his mom when she was pregnant with him, expecting him. And the whole monologue was like, you are so excited about having this girl and what this girl was going to mean to you in your life and stuff and then it turned out to be a boy. And he chose to undress and share his transformation like that, so he was wearing a dress underneath. He had his male clothes, and then he's undressing and ends up dressed as a woman. It was incredibly powerful, very, very powerful and all of those things were processes. Initially they weren't necessarily comfortable sharing but eventually they open up to sharing it and then the collective of the group empowers them to add more to it, to become even more vulnerable, and at the end we had these amazing moments.

These are women that were like 18 years old, 18 to 20. The majority of them are there because they smuggled drugs into other prisons to take to their fathers or to their boyfriends or to their you know. That was usually the case, that was the most common thing and then there were a lot of foreigners also, foreigners that are caught in Costa Rica smuggling drugs. There was a woman from Italy in my group, there was a woman from England in my group. They learned to speak Spanish in prison. Imagine. Imagine! These life stories are just incredible.

KYLA KAZUSCHYK: Have you thought about working with incarcerated people here?

GINA SANDÍ DÍAZ: It's very draining, emotionally draining for me. I don't think I want to do it anymore. And you know that might sound a little selfish, but I just feel like I'm in a different moment of my life right now. But yeah, it was very draining. I did that, and I also did a project in a psychiatric hospital, which was incredibly draining. It affected me a lot what I saw there and the humanity of the people and gosh it's just so horrible.

KYLA KAZUSCHYK: Yeah you have to think about how you want to use your energy and how you want to protect your energy.

GINA SANDÍ DÍAZ: Yeah, but it's needed, it is absolutely needed and I think, maybe, at another time of my life, I will have the strength to do it. I think we also find that sometimes we might be ready for something like that, and some other times, we are not.

KYLA KAZUSCHYK: Totally, it ebbs and flows like anything else. Do you have ideas for other future devised works? You said that you want to do devised works at your university, do you have visions for what they're going to be?

GINA SANDÍ DÍAZ: No, no, no, no, I never I never come up with a vision for any of my projects. It has to come from the participants, whatever they want it to be that's what it becomes. Unless it's a project that the starting point is a book. I've done several of those. I like Gabriel García Márquez short stories and so I've done a lot of theatrical adaptations of those short stories. And they are devised processes, but they have a starting point. It's a little bit different when it's like that. Yes, I have a starting point and I can share some ideas, even before we get started, but usually from a good old devised project I come in with a blank page.

KYLA KAZUSCHYK: I bet the students love to work with you. I bet the students really appreciate that. Have you gotten feedback from the students that they value that?

GINA SANDÍ DÍAZ: Oh, they love it, they love the devised theatre class. I only taught this class once, I'm going to teach it again next semester. But it was incredibly successful, and we had to finish it at home because the pandemic hit. We ended up with three products, we had three different devised theatre projects that were born out of all of the stuff that they created that semester. We turned it into three different videos. It started in the classroom and we had a whole show going in the classroom and all of that fell to pieces. And we went home and then we were able to rescue some things and like do it in a virtual format, but most of it was brand new material and they just created it from home. What I did was I would throw prompts; I would send them a prompt and they had to create little videos based on those prompts. And they could use anything, light, objects, themselves, other people in their houses, etc. They would send in clips and stuff and then we try to organize those clips into stories and some of them kind of work and some others they were just like a fun video to watch. But I mean for a pandemic that was pretty cool.

KYLA KAZUSCHYK: I think this is interesting about devising too, that not everything has to have a story, it doesn't have to have the arc of beginning, middle and end.

GINA SANDÍ DÍAZ: Some of them had written texts, like monologues that they had written and stuff. One of the videos was just one actor sort of reading the monologue or performing that monologue. And then we just had images that other people had captured, footage that other people had captured and brought in. And we organized it so it's still a devised piece because it's created from pieces from everybody. But yeah, it's just going to take so many shapes and forms, so it didn't matter. Another of my students, he just wanted to do a film, so he just did his own film. There was a lot going on.

KYLA KAZUSCHYK: I have found that to be the best thing to do in teaching in a pandemic, like what do you have to bring, what do you have to give, okay do that, because the pandemic is so taxing, do whatever.

GINA SANDÍ DÍAZ: And you know what, that's how we work in Costa Rica anyway, because we don't have any resources, we don't have any money. It's always—work with what you got. I have four actors and let's make it work. It doesn't matter what they look like, what race they are, it's just, you work with what you got.

ARTIST SPOTLIGHT: ALAN WHITE

Alan White is an artist and educator who has devised, written, performed in, and created costumes for shows on a wide range of topics. Here, they share their perspectives on communicating ideas about history, racism, technology, cosplay, and more.

KYLA KAZUSCHYK: How would you define devised theatre? What does it mean to you?

ALAN WHITE: That is such a hard question. I know what I do and what I've seen other people do and I think, to me, devising theatre means, however you think of the writing process, the performance comes first, or the performance

FIGURE 3.19 *Artist Alan White at work, using puppets and props in their devising process (photo courtesy of Alan White)*

is the first stage of the writing. So that the performative acts are the first draft before you write text on paper. And that that doesn't preclude, like a text can still be your source, but generally for it to be devised, for me that text should not be a theatrical script. Such as, for example, taking a book or a news article or something as a source and then devising it, you may even use the text verbatim from that in the creation, but the first step of your writing your creative piece, or the artist writing their creative piece, is through some medium of performance before putting pen to paper or fingers to the keyboard.

KYLA KAZUSCHYK: So you're moving before writing.

ALAN WHITE: Moving, speaking, juggling, puppeteering, going through the physical act of whatever your performance medium is before going through the act of actually writing text on that document.

KYLA KAZUSCHYK: What are the advantages to creating devised work? Why do it?

ALAN WHITE: There are several practical advantages to creating devised work. One is that with devised work you're creating original work, so you're creating work about something that hopefully you care about. A huge advantage to devising work is that casting is not a factor in devising work, because you're starting your work from the people who are involved in it, so you're creating the work for the artists that you're working with. Devising work is the most inclusive form of theatre there could be because everyone who's in the room is a part of the production. There's no elimination of anyone because they're not right for something. There are advantages to devising work too in that the act of creation is a collaborative act. With performance, where you have your ensemble that you rely on, you have that reliance on your ensemble from the creation of the piece, so you have different points of view and different brainstorming ideas and different thoughts coming into it. So, as opposed to a solo creation, and there are solo forms of devising as well, but I'm just thinking in terms of devising as an ensemble. No one ensemble member has the full burden of coming up with the ideas. They can rely on other people and help can be asked for and given at that point.

KYLA KAZUSCHYK: It's truly collaborative. How would you approach creating costumes for devised work? Or how have you approached it, if there's projects you've worked on that are examples?

ALAN WHITE: In the work that I've done with devising work and costumes, when devising work, and again this depends on your tradition, but doing work with companies like Double Edged Theater and Sandglass Theater and even working with Leigh and her moment work, the costume becomes even more of an active participant in creating the work. When you're devising work the costume can transform from a garment that a character wears to the character's partner in a scene, or an object that the character uses. It can become something other than literally what it is.

I'm thinking of a piece that I worked on, with a group that I was devising with in Boston before I came down here. One of our costume pieces was a muslin bag, but we wore it as a hood. And we could pass this hood from person to person and shine lights in it and shadows on it, and this one costume piece could go from being as small as a hat on a character's head to being a world that we could project into and create these small microcosms of worlds and entire communities could live on this one costume piece. In creating costumes for devised work, often, not being a costume designer, or working with people who maybe have limited costume building skills, on one hand we might have been limited by what we could find for costumes, like if we could purchase things from thrift stores or things like that. But on the other hand, bringing costumes in to devising works allows the costumes to be so much more than the garments that the character wears. And they're still all of the things, the factors that go into the costume design, like what does this color say about the character, what does this cut say about the character? What does having the character wear a collared shirt or a non-collared shirt say about the character? But then there's also the element of what happens when the character takes that shirt off? And what if they roll it into a tube shape, or what if they fold it into a block shape, you know? What can I turn this costume piece into? And then that becomes part of the language of the performance. Does it ever turn back into the garment again, or does it remain something else forever?

KYLA KAZUSCHYK: It's so interesting that all the lines become blurry. Beyond just the lines between collaborators, but the lines between what's a costume, what's a prop, what's a set piece? We can blur all of that together, everything can overlap.

ALAN WHITE: Things not overlapping is kind of the death of devising. One of the things of devising is that you need that willingness for things to overlap, you need that willingness to take things beyond, as opposed to a well-made play where you can clearly have the performance, the costumes, the props, the set, the lights. Particularly at the creation stage of devising, if you put things into those silos and try to label them that way it can hamper the creative process. And it really fuels the creative process and fuels the creation of the piece to allow things to overlap and to take things and let those lines blur without trying to put things in a box of saying, Well, this is a prop so I can use this, and this is a costume so I can wear this. A lot of that attitude comes from companies that work with object theatre. Everything is an object in object theatre because an object can do all these different things. An object can be your partner, an object can be used or be worn, it can be given. So they're freed from the role of costume. They can move. An object can move through all of those roles. They're freed from the role of prop or the role of set. An object can serve all those functions, it can be in all those roles and move through all those lines.

When I worked with Sandglass theatre, which is a puppet theatre, we were doing a show titled *Babylon: Journey of Refugees* that was sort of devised and created based on the stories of different refugees who would come to the United States from Syria, Burundi, Afghanistan, and El Salvador. And all the refugees were puppets. They were these large wooden three-person manipulated puppets that we did so that none of the cast members were ever playing refugees. We might narrate their story, we might give voice to them, but the actual refugees were represented by puppets so that we never had an American-born artist playing the role of the refugee. And we worked a lot with, when did we treat the puppet like a person versus when did we treat the puppet like a puppet or an object. It was a way of enacting or staging the violence or inhumanity that can be done to refugees. By treating the puppet like what it actually was, a puppet, an object, versus showing humanity toward them. An example of that would be if I had a puppet that I was responsible for, if I was treating her like a person I would carefully make sure to put the puppet's—like if I had to leave the puppet behind, I would carefully make sure to place the puppet's feet on the ground in such a way that they look like she was doing it herself and carefully put the puppet in a sitting position, maybe fold her arms and make sure the puppet was stable in such a way that she'd stay in that position and not fall over before I took my hands off of her. Versus, for example, when we were treating a different puppet like a puppet, we just tossed the puppet through the air from person to person. So that's sort of an example of how an object can move through different roles and become different things, whether it's a puppet or a costume piece or a prop or a set piece, those are all possible.

KYLA KAZUSCHYK: That's so powerful, the thing with the puppets because it must have forced the audience to question, how do we treat other people and how do we decide who we treat with respect, and who we don't.

ALAN WHITE: Yeah it was, it was a very powerful thing because it would be like if you're throwing this puppet around after an audience has come to imbue it or personify it as a person there's a lot of anxiety they feel about that. They're concerned about harm coming to that because to them it's a person.

KYLA KAZUSCHYK: Theatre is so powerful. I have another question about how you have approached creating a timeline. In devised theatre so many things are malleable, so many things are flexible, how do you decide when things are finalized, or when things can still change?

ALAN WHITE: That's difficult. Sometimes it comes down to booking your show before you've made it so that you force yourself to have a deadline. Other times, it may come down to sort of needing to choose or elect a person to sort of be a producer or to be sort of the artistic voice who is going to put the brakes on. Because you can get caught up in devising, especially if you don't have a set timeline and you have a space that you can use for an unlimited amount of time that you're not paying money for, you don't have any budget constraints, you can get caught up in the creative process forever and just keep playing and playing and playing and playing. There is a level of discipline that you just need for that.

And sometimes that might mean, for example, what some companies will do is, if they're taking a theme or a topic where they're starting from a book or something, they will assign each member of their ensemble to create an etude, which is like a short performance piece. Often they don't have words but they may. They may have dialogue, they may not. An etude may be like a five-minute performance that tells a story. If an ensemble is working from a book, for example, they may choose particular chapters from the book that they feel were really powerful and they'll have different members of the ensemble create an etude of the major events with a major theme of those chapters. They will also do solo work and then they'll present their etudes to each other and then, from the ideas that may have been sparked from those etudes, they may create an entirely new story, or they may create some version of that original text that they started working from, taking ideas from the various different etudes that they had and incorporating them in different ways. They might choose a particular director for those individual etudes or they might choose someone to be like, Okay it's your turn, you're going to be the artistic director for the show, you're going to be the one who's going to say, Okay here's what we're going to keep, here's what we're going to lose, here's what we're going to try to put together—you're going to be the person to say, Okay we've reached the point where we need to reproduce something over and over again so that we can share it with an audience.

KYLA KAZUSCHYK: It can still be a grey line between creating and performing but that idea of starting to reproduce, starting to rehearse and then adjustments can come after that.

ALAN WHITE: You're reaching a point where you're sort of refining it, where you feel like you know what it is that you're making and now you're trying to improve it, refine it, clarify the message that's in it.

The group that I was working with in Boston, we were using a space at one of the members' places of work, which was an arts organization, so we had unlimited access, other than maybe giving it up for the students who are actually there. We weren't paying for the rehearsal space, and so we had unlimited access to it, so we spent probably over a year, maybe two just playing and devising, and always going back to the beginning and starting over and bringing new things in, before we were like maybe we should actually create something. Do we want to share this with an audience, or do we just want to keep playing forever?

KYLA KAZUSCHYK: But that has value too. And that's so interesting to me too, that maybe it is just playing forever. Maybe it doesn't become performance, maybe the value really is in the process.

ALAN WHITE: Yes. Which was why we, that group, we had to have that conversation. It wasn't that one was better than the other, it was like, Okay, we need to decide what we want. Because we could just keep—we referred to it as training—and we were like, we could just keep training and just keep doing this, we just needed to decide is this what we're going to do? Or do we want to have something that we're going to share publicly? Most artists I know who have worked in devised spaces, who like it would be thrilled to have a group that they could meet with every week or twice a month and just play without care, without opening night in sight, without it being a financial commitment that they have to make, something that they have to budget in, just something where they could just explore their creativity, over and over and over again.

KYLA KAZUSCHYK: What did your group in Boston decide to do, did you all decide to have a performance?

ALAN WHITE: We did and unfortunately the pandemic happened. I came down to Louisiana before we got to the performance. We picked a text based on a folk tale about how the ravens stole the moon and used that as a starting point to start creating a more crystallized performance. And then they were continuing to work on that when I came down to Louisiana and then the pandemic happened so it hasn't had a public performance yet.

KYLA KAZUSCHYK: But it still could.

ALAN WHITE: That's the idea. There has still been work continuing to happen on it with the people who are still in Boston since I've been down here.

KYLA KAZUSCHYK: Do you consider your thesis project devised theatre or do you think of that as something that you wrote?

ALAN WHITE: I think of my thesis as something that I wrote. Because really my thesis started from a text that I started writing first. There are devised elements to it. There are some physical theatre elements to it, but really, I don't consider it a devised piece, because it really started from a message that I wanted to say, and a text that I started writing. And then later I sort of created physical elements to match the text that I was writing. So I don't really think of it as a devised piece. The closest to something similar to the devising process came when I had the opportunity to do some rehearsals in the studio theatre with the actual set pieces that I had, and I had all of my props and then I started to make some discoveries as I was going through it.

And so some things changed based on the discoveries that I made. Like, Oh, I can use these set pieces in different ways, and I can create more levels, I can actually do this with this prop. But I would say, those were more my devising instincts coming into a piece that I was doing that I wouldn't necessarily consider a devised piece.

If I had, for example, decided to do the piece from say, one of the characters, Alexander Dumois' autobiography and I decided I was going to do his autobiography and I read it, and then started performing it before writing it—that would have felt more like a devised piece to me than the process that I went through for that piece.

KYLA KAZUSCHYK: That is really interesting because I think that other MFA students have approached it differently. I think sometimes they do approach it more as they're going to start performing before they have anything written. But it seems like a lot of your classmates this year decided to write it entirely and then get on their feet.

ALAN WHITE: I don't know if that would have been the case if not for the pandemic and the changes. Because I was definitely like, in my first brainstorming of ideas for it, for this piece, I know that I was thinking like I had three three different sort of major ideas of playing to play with, including a piece that sort of explored the ideas of transhumanism and what does it mean to be human versus a cyborg versus somehow artificially augmented, and does a cyborg still strictly fit into sort of the science fiction idea that technology has to be physically a part of you, or are we in some way cybernetic in general. And when I was sort of just brainstorming that piece, I had a number of just sort of idea inspirations for ways of bringing devised content into that. And I really thought that I would possibly approach that piece more from the performance first, or at least even aspects of it from the performance first and then go through writing the text versus the other way around. Ultimately, that idea is interesting to me, but I didn't feel a personal connection to it.

I thought, Oh, that would be really fun and that'd be a really cool idea, but when it came down to it, part of the reason that I wanted to do that idea was, I wanted to end the show wearing one of those LED light-up masks that respond to music around it. But also, because that idea is about transhumanism and technology, I wanted to have full support for projections and lights. It's an idea that I want to explore in the future, when it can be explored on a stage with projections potentially with augmented reality, apps as part of the brain.

I was talking with some people from acting programs at other universities and they were talking about how people have been using apps and phones to sort of create theatrical experiences. And so a lot of my work obviously centers around the question of race and experiences and things like that. And I want a show, an experience, where the audience goes in and they see a character of color, who through the plot of the show is going through something every day, trying to get a job or going to their job or going through life, and throughout the course of the production this character encounters people who, say, commit different microaggressions or micro invalidations or things like that. And then through the augmented reality app, if the audience raises their phone they can see the impact of that micro aggression, because they will see a character who's not physically on stage from the main characters past who's done the same thing or see all the characters who've done the same thing, so they can see how the psychic damage of these experiences adds up on someone. They can see triggering happen, basically, because they see the character's memory. There are two physical actors on stage and one says something that's racist or sexist or whatever, and then through the app they see all the people who have said something similar because they're seeing the characters memory.

KYLA KAZUSCHYK: But if you're not looking at the app you're just like yeah what was the big deal.

ALAN WHITE: Exactly. So it's kind of like the app lets you see into the character's head and see the character's history and see how those things follow you. And then when someone says something that they think is harmless or don't think about at all, it sparks all of those experiences again.

KYLA KAZUSCHYK: That sounds so cool. That'd be so interesting to see. Do you think that you're going to pursue it?

ALAN WHITE: Oh yeah I'm going to pursue that. I feel like virtual theatre has just blown the world of possibilities wide open and I think, yes we're all tired of zoom plays and we're all looking forward to when we don't watch another play on zoom. But at the same time, it's like Okay, but there's no reason we should go back to where we were before. We have these technologies, we've seen what they can do and now it's time for us to break them, you know? It's time for us to go like, how do we push this to the boundary even more when we come back to the theatre? How does this help us, what can we do with this, what can we create? What illusions can we give to our audience?

KYLA KAZUSCHYK: And with that too, like yeah we broke them open, but I think we've also really just scratched the surface of what's possible because we still have to be distanced. But if we can have everything, if we can be in the room with each other and have our phones and our computers, then what? I think there's a lot more possibilities there. If you were going to pursue the cyborg idea versus your other idea, why would principles of devising be more applicable to that than something else?

ALAN WHITE: The principles of devising aren't necessarily more applicable than another, it's a matter of choosing one good or another good. Both could work. One of the reasons that I didn't choose to use devising principles on the show that I did create for my thesis was because I was playing historical characters who really existed, I felt a responsibility to try to portray them as true to those actual people as I knew them. I did take a little bit of liberties and part of the theme of the show was fantasy and comic books, I took dramatic license wherever I wanted to, to sort of, added to them for the sake of my geek joy and fun and hopefully to be interesting for the audience. But that's just the approach that I take whenever I'm dealing with historic persons is to do a lot of research on who they were and then to try to craft a text appropriate for them. Whereas the cyborg show, the transhuman show, would have been, I would have sort of read the topics and the issues and the discussions, but ultimately the show was going to be entirely from my imagination and completely from my flights of fancy. When I'm doing a show, I may be wrestling with a scene, but it's still entirely fictional. Then I'm much more likely to go right into devising and because it was a question of is my character human machine or both, there were a lot of things that I wanted to play with as far as that sense of inhumanity, or being non-human. I can project a giant keyboard on the floor of the stage, and type things out with my feet by dancing on it or things like that.

I did an autobiographical solo show a couple of years ago that was an hour long show, like the classic actor, this is my life, these are my challenges, to try to book things. And for that show I did both sorts of processes, where there were some things that I knew I wanted to do in sort of a storytelling style so I would write the text. And then there were other chapters of my life that I wanted to devise, I wanted to work with the performance or even work with a physical object. One of the things I ended up not using in the show. (Alan is now holding a baton with empty alcohol bottles attached to the ends.)

KYLA KAZUSCHYK: That was within reach?

ALAN WHITE: I brought it with me to Louisiana in the hopes that I would use it in something, because I didn't use it. It was part of the devising process of my solo show and, ultimately, I scrapped it from using it, but the way that I developed it was.

I have swords in reach, juggling balls in reach, puppets. I have all these things in reach. I love performing. I live for it. I was using it like a pair of double sticks. It's got two vodka bottles at either end and originally I was playing, I had the regular sticks with the tassels, when I was playing with it. And I wanted to find a physical way to illustrate alcoholism, because my father was an alcoholic and for a lot of my life and my family's life, we just judged him really harshly about, you know, why doesn't he just put down the bottle, why doesn't he quit drinking, why didn't he just make himself better. It wasn't until I was an adult and after my father had passed on that I really got some idea, which I got from theatre, by the way, of what that kind of addiction is like. And how a person struggling with that addiction can feel like they're in control, even when they're not. I think it helped me to feel a lot more compassion for him. I made this as like a physical representation of that, because when you twirl between the two sticks you're controlling it, but at the same time, one of these bottles of alcohol is always near you. When you push one away it rotates and the other one returns, so you push it away and it rotates, and so you can never get rid of it. And that was a representation of me trying to express the illusion of controlling your addiction. So that was a show where I used both writing text at times, and other times starting from performance to try to create something and devise. And I would take, I'd be like, Okay, I want to talk about this topic right now. I wonder if there's a way, how can I explore that, how can I express that, what can I do to build something? Do I play with something? I might even have gotten those bottles and tried juggling them for a while, or just moving them around, putting them on a table and picking them up and trying to and, ultimately, I built that particular prop.

KYLA KAZUSCHYK: It's such a potent metaphor—it's so clear that you're pushing something away and something's coming towards you and there's no way out of it unless you lose your balance, like that's how you're maintaining the entropy, the inertia.

ALAN WHITE: And then, when you lose your balance and that's kind of like that wake-up call, and not everyone gets that wake-up call. Some people don't hit that rock bottom that inspires them to make a change. My father was very high functioning with his addiction, he never hit that rock bottom that was so bad that he would seek the professional help that would have enabled him to change his life.

KYLA KAZUSCHYK: How did you develop costumes for that piece?

ALAN WHITE: The title of that piece is *Royally Unseen*, because again, geek. When I think about my childhood and my past and where my family's place was sort of in the history of the United States, I kind of see it through the metaphor of a kingdom. My dad was one of the first ten African American men to own a General Motors Buick dealership, when the company tried to integrate their ownership. My mother was one of the first African Americans to work with digital equipment corp in the early stages of the computer industry. There was a lot of being the perfect family and owning the house and having the kids and having the dogs. I always kind of saw it as this metaphor of a self-made royal family. And so, because of that I took this theme of royalty and Camelot and this fantasy kingdom. And particularly I chose Camelot because the Arthurian legend has this huge fall from grace and this huge tragedy collapse. My parents got divorced when I was about nine years old. So, for me that was that climactic fall and the crash of the kingdom. But the Arthurian legend stops at before, whereas my life went on in excruciating traumatic childhood detail that fortunately there are these people called therapists to help me with. So going on that theme, I wanted to have costumes. I really just wore one costume through it, which I wanted to have that sense of royalty so it's wearing all black, but I have a collared shirt. On this show, I had a lot of budgetary constraints, because I was producing this show myself out of pocket. I applied for grants and didn't get any. It was my first time applying for grants. So I went for things that would have a hint of royalty. I got this black button up with gold embroidery. This was sort of the perfect thing that I could wear. I had that and just some black slacks and I had a vest on over it and a pair of black sneakers with white soles that I wore and did not wear out in public anywhere until the show opened.

If I had had more resources—because through the course of that show I played myself, I played family members, kids in the neighborhood—I would have probably gone further in the way of costumes. But that show I was doing entirely on—all the money that I had to invest in the show really other than buying that shirt really went into renting the space, hiring a director and hiring a publicist, that was basically where my budget went. My props were all either objects I already owned, like I used a folding chair and I used well, a sword, because I have swords I bought when I had money. Of course I have swords. I had a folding chair, a music stand. The only props I had were a sword, a kitchen knife, and a baseball bat. I used my old laptop for projections, and the light and sound cues. So that was a lot, where the budgetary constraints came in for that one.

And also, with costume design with devising a piece, it would have a lot to do with the tone or the world of the piece that you're devising. If I was devising something that was even more sort of high fantasy or magical reality, then I would look for that in the costume pieces that I used, versus if I'm devising something that's trying to be much more grounded in our world, like if I'm devising a piece that's about sort of an issue of social justice or an issue of equity or something like that, but it is grounded more in the real world, I really want people to

FIGURE 3.20 *Alan White in their solo devised work, Royally Unseen (photo courtesy of Alan White)*

get that I'm talking about the environment and Louisiana, or to get that I'm talking about unequal access to medical and I don't want to go metaphorically into something, then I'm probably going to look for costumes that feel more grounded and more set in America 2021.

KYLA KAZUSCHYK: Thank you so much, Alan. Thank you so much for sharing your ideas. All your work sounds so cool. I want to see the transhuman show. If you ever do that, let me know where it's going. I'll buy tickets.

ALAN WHITE: We will see what happens next. My immediate next thing is I want to expand my solo show into an ensemble piece. I realized, when I was doing that show, when I was creating a solo show, one of the big discoveries that I made was that I had not looked at the issue of the treatment of women in fantasy and science fiction at all. The reason it came up was because one of the historical people that I had considered originally having in the show was someone who had fled from Britain because he lived in the mid 1700s and he had fled from Britain to India, because he was accused of raping a woman and to avoid facing trial he fled to the colony to hide from a law. And none of the historic sources that I could find, none of my research could find out—I couldn't find a source that definitively said yes, he did it or no he didn't, no one could confirm or deny his innocence or guilt.

And I was like, Okay, well, and I went round and round and round with that character, like I could just not talk about that, and then I read an essay from that someone had written a play where she was directing a show and hadn't dealt with the darkness, hadn't dealt with depression that an escaped slave that she was doing a show about had done and how she had basically cut off this character at the knees, by not. And I was like, Okay, well I can't talk about this character and not deal with this issue, right? That's just dishonest, I can't do that. And I was like, but I can't talk about this issue without talking about how objectification, exploitation, sexual assault have been treated and how women have been depicted in fantasy and historically, which is still very relevant.

As you know, anyone who's actually read the books of the *Game of Thrones* series. It reminded me of conversations that I had had with other people watching the show years ago where people use that same argument of, well, this is the cannon, this is how it is in the world, to justify that explicit, like fans talking about it, male fans talking to women fans justifying that explicit sexual violence being like, well, that's part of that world.

Which is the same thing as saying you can't be that character because you're Black and it's not canon. It's like, it's an imaginary world. And I realized you have the power to say I don't want this in my world. I don't have to read that book; I have to write that book. And that's where I decided, I wanted that character to go to a place of saying I don't want this in my world, but I only had 20 minutes of just me. And I was like this needs to be done by a cast because I want the characters that are being summoned to be a part of this conversation, to be a part of that dialogue and ultimately the main character to be the one to say, wait a minute, this is my world, I'm making this now, or this is how I want to interact with this fiction, I don't want this as part of my world, you have to go.

KYLA KAZUSCHYK: You could expand it so far; there's so much you can do with that. I'm so interested in the element of this gatekeeping in cosplay, how people say well that's not cannon so you can't do it. But it's fiction, it's fantasy—it can be whatever, let anyone do whatever! Why put those gates up? Why stop anyone from doing the things that bring them joy? And it is so connected to costume and identity and dress and the way that we want to express ourselves and the heroes that we want to identify with and for anyone else to tell us that we can't, why is that, why does anyone feel like they have to do that?

ALAN WHITE: But it's literally, at least what I've read is, it's literally where cosplay comes from, it's a shortened costume play, right? And it's like well why right, why not, but it starts when we're kids. It starts at the same time that children become aware of racial differences. It starts around age five or six. Some children, I think some people never learn it. Some people learn it but choose to reject it, and some people hold on to it all their lives.

KYLA KAZUSCHYK: Do you think that people that hold on to it feel like they're protecting something, like they have to protect themselves from something?

ALAN WHITE: Yes and no. Because it's different, it's all different people. Because it's not just people who have any one sort of racial identity, who gatekeep. A white cosplayer who is gatekeeping, who says well you can't be this person, because you're too dark or it's not cannon, is coming from a different place than a BIPOC cosplayer who says the same thing. I think the BIPOC cosplayer has grown up believing they can't be that person, so you can't do it either. Like, we can't be Batman, or we can't be Captain America, we have to be the Black Panther or Luke Cage or the Black superhero or the Black anime character, or we can't be the Japanese anime character because the Japanese anime character has lighter skin. And I think both of those people learned that around age five or six. I don't think they become an adult and suddenly start thinking like that. But I think it's something that's taught to them that they don't question because it's not necessarily directly taught to them.

I remember when I first learned about cosplay. I was dating someone at the time, who was a cosplayer and we were talking about going to a con together, and I was like, well I guess I would play this character, you know? It was a character, whose name literally is Jet Black from Cowboy Bebop. And my girlfriend who was white was like, well why do you want to play Jet? And I was like, well because Jet's Black, so, you know, I don't know a lot of Black anime characters, so I guess I gotta be Jet. I mean I don't know how I would make a cybernetic arm. He had a robot which was kind of cool too, I mean there are a lot of reasons to play Jet other than the fact that I thought he was Black but that was what was in my head—I have to play a character who looks like me. I hadn't actually challenged that programming, which I got, you know I can remember it as early as going back to when I was five and Star Wars came out, the first one, you know, *A New Hope*, before the introduction of Lando Kalrissian, and my friends telling me I couldn't be Luke or Han Solo or Gran Moff Targen because I didn't look like them. I could play Chewbacca because he had brown fur. And this was when we were playing pretend in the school yard; this wasn't like performance for casting. The world of acting was far far into my future.

KYLA KAZUSCHYK: Do you think that it'll change, do you think that that culture will shift?

ALAN WHITE: Yes, I do. I think it is changing, but I think it'll become a minority, I don't think it'll ever be gone completely. Because ideals get passed down from person to person and passed down through generation to generation so as long as there are adults now who still think it, they will pass that down to their children. There are children who rebel against their parents if they know what to rebel against. To choose that particular battle to rebel against, children always rebel against their parents, but there are so many different delicious beautiful things that children can choose as the topic for that rebellion, this may not be the important one for them.

FIGURE 3.21 Alan White in Around the World in Folk and Fairytales. Photographer: Tom Gosselin (photo courtesy of Alan White)

ARTIST SPOTLIGHT: MIKAELA HERRERA

Here, Mikaela Herrera shares ideas about collaborating, devising, and developing costumes from a dramaturg's perspective.

KYLA KAZUSCHYK: How do you define devised theatre? What is it to you?

MIKAELA HERRERA: I look at it as a collective, as a creative collective, but we are working together. It kind of depends, because I approached devised theatre like we came together and talked about ideas and then I composed the script and then I went back to my team and we just revised that. But I've also worked on pieces where it was an improv kind of deal and we just made notes as we went along.

KYLA KAZUSCHYK: I think that that's part of what I'm learning is that it can be a lot of different things. There are different ways to approach it. What would you identify as advantages to creating devised work? Why work in this way?

MIKAELA HERRERA: Well, the reason that I fell in love with theatre was that it was a collaborative art form, and I feel like the best way to show your team that this piece belongs to them just as much as it belongs to you is by working on a devised piece. Because each person is going to be handling a certain section or a particular area and then when you come together, like look, this also belongs to you. Though I sat in the space of like the director I'm like no I'm just as passionate as you are, and that just made it so much more exciting, knowing that people are just doing it to do it, but I had passion behind it.

KYLA KAZUSCHYK: Like that sense of ownership, you feel like you can really own the work, it's not someone else's work.

MIKAELA HERRERA: Right and that's also exciting because it's like, working on other plays and stuff, you feel like a sense of pride and depending on like the subject matter you kind of, you're like, Okay, this is something I can relate to I understand what the characters are going through, but you'll never fully understand exactly what the playwright, or what the characters are thinking in that material. Whereas if you create a devised piece, you're like Oh well, I remember sitting here when we put together this scene, I know exactly what it's supposed to feel like.

KYLA KAZUSCHYK: That's a good description. We can never get inside of a playwright's head; we're always just interpreting what we think their ideas were. But in devising it's our own heads.

Can you tell me about how you've approached creating costumes for pieces you've worked on and maybe talk me through examples of stuff that you've done or plans? How would you approach creating costumes?

MIKAELA HERRERA: I think, out of all the devised pieces that I've worked on, my favorite was—it makes me seem biased, but of course I am—my favorite was definitely mine. And my approach to costumes, since I was kind of doing an anthology, they all had the same theme or same idea, but they could all stand alone. So I was like all right, what if you dress the actors in slip dresses, like little nightgown-looking things. I thought of like really thin silk with a little lace on it, and the idea was to have them changing on stage. If they were going to be portraying a new character you'd be like, Okay I'm going to put this lab coat on now. Or I'm going to put some glasses on, but you would still see the dress that they were wearing so it kind of gave it some ambiguity and helped to add the idea of a liminal space.

KYLA KAZUSCHYK: What was the reasoning, I guess you touched on with the liminal, why does the audience see them change, why was that important to you to see them transform?

MIKAELA HERRERA: I wanted to play around with the idea of just being in existence. It's like not necessarily this show is taking place in one set location. But it was kind of like putting the audience in my head as I recall the things that I'm writing about so they were stories that I have experienced in terms of like, Okay well, this is how I see them when I close my eyes and remember what I went through. It was this weird thought bubble, and I was like how do I portray a thought bubble on stage? I had started writing and my big piece that I was doing was about skin color band aids. And then, in the midst of the Black Lives Matter movement, band aid came out with the skin color band aids and so I was like oh I gotta rewrite this whole piece and change what I was talking about. And then we met and it kind of fell to the back burner, but I never really went through and finished it, it was just kind of done.

KYLA KAZUSCHYK: That approaches the bigger question of when is a work of art finished? How do you decide? Is it ever finished?

MIKAELA HERRERA: That's true because I could just keep revising forever if I wanted to.

KYLA KAZUSCHYK: And the band aid piece—such a cool example too of how devised theatre can be so nimble. You can speak to a moment in time, and then as time, as society and culture changes, you can change the work you're creating to reflect that, and you can do it so quickly.

MIKAELA HERRERA: Yes, and I thought it was interesting because, one of the main topics that I was talking about is, I think I was like six or seven years old and a friend of mine was in an American girl doll fashion show, and they needed an extra person and so she invited me, and when I got there, I was the only girl whose skin was a little bit dark and so I had to play, like the Pocahontas American girl doll I don't know what her name is, Kya maybe. But I had to play her, and so I had these pictures of me just looking really sad because all of the other girls got books or cameras or a little puppy dog and I had a basket filled with corn husk dolls. And it just felt wrong, and it wasn't until later on that I realized, I was a senior in high school and I was like, wait a minute that was really messed up. And so I kind of sat down and started looking at it and then I started thinking about other experiences that I had lived through growing up in a small town in the middle of Texas, and I was like, oh my gosh. There was this one point where our band director would put band aids like over our fingers if we have nail polish for marching band, and the same for earrings to cover earrings. And one kid couldn't take his earrings out and so my band director was like let's just put the band aid on. But his skin was too dark for the band aid and so he took electrical tape and put it on his ears and I kind of thought about it, I wasn't close with the kid but I was like, can you imagine how dehumanizing that would feel? I was like why doesn't band aid come out with these actual things? It seems so normal, so second nature. But it took a movement to be like nude isn't the color nude it's the color of whoever it is. What defines nude? I got off on a tangent.

KYLA KAZUSCHYK: I am happy to go on that tangent with you, because I think it's interesting and it manifests in so many other arenas as well. Bandages are one example, but we can also talk about nude undergarments, nude crayons, why was flesh color always like a peach tone? We know, like you're saying, it's obvious that flesh is a bajillion different shades. Why was there a flesh tone that was associated with whiteness?

MIKAELA HERRERA: Exactly, and so I was like, Okay I've got to talk about this, and then they came out, and I was like, Oh well, I'm really happy that this is happening, but at the same time, it was like, man, now I have to talk about why do I think it took so long, you know?

KYLA KAZUSCHYK: And that's worth reflecting on too. Why didn't it happen before? And why isn't it still more widespread? Thinking about undergarments, like there's a few undergarment lines that have a whole range of shades. But not everything.

MIKAELA HERRERA: Yeah or even makeup, watching people apply makeup, looking at lipstick names it's like, Oh well, we're gonna put this nude shade on and then it's like a very, very light brown. That's definitely not what my body looks like. And also like with just the state of the world right now, and theatre kind of being pushed on the backburner as we figure out everything. It didn't feel like the right time anymore, because with all the entertainment that I turned into it's been a form of escapism. And I want people to really sit and listen to what I have to say. And right now, I just felt like maybe this isn't the time for it. I'll set it aside, keep working on it, I can always come back to it when I'm ready.

KYLA KAZUSCHYK: It's hard to gauge that because I look at entertainment as that too. I don't want to think about reality, I want to go to another planet. But I think that there will be a time and place and an audience for reflections on humanity as it stands. Have you worked on other devised pieces, have you worked with other people on their devised work?

MIKAELA HERRERA: Yes. I was the dramaturg for *Dream Logos* with Nick Ericskon. And then Covid happened. I also worked on *Upgrade* with Anthony. That was where I was really inspired, I really loved his process. We would meet weekly, and he would be like, this is the topic of today's meeting and then he would have fun theatre games that we would play that related to the topic, and then we would sit down and be like, Okay well, what did we learn from this game, and how can we apply it to the world that we're creating? And I was like I'm having a great time, I want to do this, too. And it was drastically different from working with Nick. With Anthony's I felt more hands on because he was my friend, and he would ask me questions and I kind of felt more open and in a position in which I can give my input. Whereas with *Dream Logos*, Nick was like this is what we did last year, this is what I need from you, what do you think of this and I was like, Okay. And I was just excited to go to Edinburgh, so I was like, I'm not complaining.

KYLA KAZUSCHYK: Can you tell me more about *Upgrade*? Can you tell me about what it was and how it became that way, and what was your role on it, were you dramaturg on that too?

MIKAELA HERRERA: Yes and no. I was more like a creative advisor. It was me, Kain, Mary, Kayla, and Zoey, and Angelle. So it's just like a bunch of power houses all in one room, and all of the people in there kind of had like a focus that they did. It was interesting because I came in with the perspective I had worked with Anthony before as a dramaturg. And so that was where my mindset was. I was kind of looking at the things that he brought in, I was like, Okay, I don't know if this would completely work, this kind of contradicts this part of the script like that sort of thing. But it was really fun because we came in and he was like all right, this is my idea and I had these topics that I had to choose from, and I think one of them was like looking into how 24-hour establishments work and he was like I want to go visit them, I want to know what it's like working at one of those at a place that never sleeps. And then he was like I want to talk about robots, and we were like, Okay, and then he was like robots, 24-hour establishments and queer people, and we were like, Okay, this is a very interesting grouping here. And then we kind of combined some of those ideas from where we'd branched out. And we ended up with *Upgrade* and we were like, dude, what if there was like an apple store or like a Sears where you could go and buy body parts. And then he was like, well with that you know if that becomes the norm there's got to be some sort of weird black market like deep web thing that's happening because I mean that's us now. I don't see why that would go away and I was like, you have a very good point, and then we were like well, what about if some like giant Disney-esque monopoly comes in and takes it over and then from there it became *Upgrade* and he made it an interactive process. When you came into the actual space, you got a sticky note and then whatever color your sticky note was that was your group, and so you saw certain parts of the show in a different order than the other group, and then you came together in the final spot, where it was a big battle.

KYLA KAZUSCHYK: That's so cool!

MIKAELA HERRERA: It was so much fun.

KYLA KAZUSCHYK: You all worked together to create it? Were you performers as well, or were you just on the writing team?

MIKAELA HERRERA: I was just on the writing team, because at the time that it was taking place, I was working on *Private Wars*. A lot of the people who were on the devising team did end up working on it. Mary stage managed, Kain did costumes. Everyone had their specific area, but we all did come together, once we picked the topic and we started, we came in, again those once-weekly meetings and we started to develop the world of *Upgrade* and who these characters were and what their relationships with other people would be. And then Anthony was like, Okay, I think I have like a solid amount of information, I'm going to write the script come back we're going to read it, do some rough blocking just so I can see it and then he just made edits and then kept bringing it back to us until finally were like, No, this is the one.

KYLA KAZUSCHYK: That's such a good example of a collaborative process and it sounds like it was so positive too, that y'all were able to really work together and value each other's contributions.

MIKAELA HERRERA: It was so much fun. Definitely. It was the show that got me excited to do mine and it was a way more positive experience than doing a quote unquote devised piece that had already been devised.

KYLA KAZUSCHYK: I can see how there will be challenges with that. I'm interested in that too. A lot of people I've talked to are so passionate about devising but I know that it's not always sunshine and rainbows. I have talked to people that are like, when it doesn't work it really doesn't work.

MIKAELA HERRERA: I think a lot of it is, I mean this goes for anything, but it's got to be the people that you're working with. When I was working on *Dream Logos*, it really felt that the backing behind that was that we were getting to go to Scotland. So we were kind of just doing whatever we needed to do to get it done and we were like this is the goal, this is why we're doing it. Whereas I felt like with *Upgrade* we were all passionate about creating something fun, something that we wanted to do. And I just love

Anthony so it was like the fact that you trust me to work on your baby, thank you.

KYLA KAZUSCHYK: That's a lot of good points, thinking about goals and vision and then collaboration and trust too. It makes sense that if the goal for *Dream Logos*, our goal is to go to Edinburgh, all right that's it—let's figure out how to get to that goal. But it sounds like with Anthony on the *Upgrade* project, the goal is to create something together and tell a story which is really a different goal. And both goals are valid.

MIKAELA HERRERA: It was definitely an instance where I was feeding off of the energy of the people that I was working with, so it was just kind of weird. I kind of was also like I want to do this, everyone else wants to do this, this is a collective mentality, I just went with it.

KYLA KAZUSCHYK: This idea of collective energy, that's so real and thinking about what the vision is and if you are creating something new or just revising something old because there's examples of devised work that starts with an existing idea and reinterprets it.

And I think that from what I understand of what Nick was trying to do with *Dream Logos*, like a group of people created this, I want to make a continuation of it, but with a different group of people, but it's not really their ideas. It is someone else's idea, so this is about ownership, it seems like it'd be hard to find ownership if it wasn't your idea to begin with.

MIKAELA HERRERA: Right, because he approached it with like, Okay I'm creating this devised piece with them, but he would just show us the footage from the last time that was performed. And then we just kind of stayed there and so he would send me the script and I would try and make updates and then when I got the script again, I was like well, why did you ask me if you didn't use any of it.

KYLA KAZUSCHYK: That's a good lesson about taking notes too, don't ask someone for a note if you're not going to take it.

MIKAELA HERRERA: I was like I don't want to waste your time and I don't want to waste my time either. It's a collective process, you have to be mindful of the others, the other people that are working with you. And I've definitely learned that during quarantine because this piece was the one thing keeping me together, and I was bombarding my team with stuff and I was like, oh my God guys, I'm so sorry I'm sure you have so many other things going on right now, it's not just about me and this piece.

KYLA KAZUSCHYK: That's such a valuable lesson, if you ever want to work as a director. I think directors often have that singularity of vision, but they didn't think about the fact that everyone else involved is working on a bunch of other things, not just that one thing. It can be hard to keep in mind.

MIKAELA HERRERA: Yes, and that was definitely something that I've learned from not only my devising experience, but just working in theatre in general, because I was like hey I'm so sorry but I'm going to have to take a step back from this and it's not that I don't care, but I just can't, you're coming to me with so many things and I can get them to you, I just need a moment.

KYLA KAZUSCHYK: That's an important lesson too, to figure out where you want to draw your boundaries and how to set them. I'm curious about your work as a dramaturg, and how you would compare the experiences you've had with dramaturgy in devising and dramaturgy for scripted work, how is it different?

MIKAELA HERRERA: Oh, my goodness, it is so different, and I think that was the biggest thing for me, that I had gotten so used to working with already scripted pieces that trying to approach it by creating my own, it was like being hit by a bus. Like from all angles, I was, Oh, my goodness, and I remember when I proposed the idea, they were like, Okay, well to do this you're going to have to have a very strong dramaturg. And I was like, well I do that, I was like that's like what I'm studying, and they were like, Oh okay great. But it was one of those moments where I was like, man, if I could go back and start that process again, I would want another person on it with me, because it was just information overload all the time. I had to look from all angles. Because working with scripted pieces or with a separate director, they've already had their moment with the script—they know what they want. And so they're like, Okay, I want you to break down this section, and then we will regroup in a few days and then I'll have you break down this one. And then I would just compile my research and give it to them, or lay it out for the actors, whatever was needed. But with mine, not only did I have to find it, but then I also had to retain it. And then, when it came to writing there were certain things that I wanted to reference, and I had to make sure that I was fact checking myself for certain things. It was coming from my head, so it was like trying to remember things and then also be like, Okay this actually happened, right now, I have to like, back this up. I would be flipping through my folders or going through my computer like, I know I had this somewhere I don't know. And it was definitely a challenge. And I don't know if it was just an instance of where I was so passionate about something that I let myself front more emotion than I did logic. So that could have been the issue, but if I were to do it again, I would want another person with me to bounce ideas off of and kind of be like, hey, this is what I'm looking for, can you help me find it.

KYLA KAZUSCHYK: That's like the whole importance of a dramaturg for any project. To have someone to hold some of that research and to bounce ideas off of, that can be so helpful on any project.

MIKAELA HERRERA: And I think a lot of it too, for mine specifically was that I mean, being a dramaturg is such a loose thing like there isn't a firm definition, so I like to look at it as being an information designer, that's what I'm doing. And everyone does it differently, and so I think I had a hard time letting someone into my space. Because I had gotten, I was like, this is how I do my work, this is how I present it and I can be really flexible when it comes to my director, but it was a matter of not being territorial with something that I was very passionate about.

KYLA KAZUSCHYK: It's hard to do, really hard to do. And it's hard to think about too because being passionate is also what makes it sustainable, because you care about it so much, that is why you want to keep working on it. But then that also can be to the detriment of the project.

MIKAELA HERRERA: Yes, and I mean I could go back to the very beginning of this conversation and be like what's the overall importance of devised pieces? Balance.

I mean that goes for everything, but as we've been talking about it, I really just, you know it was again the logic versus emotion, especially for a piece that is me, that I was putting me into.

KYLA KAZUSCHYK: You're not alone in struggling with that. So many of the MFA acting students when they do their devised thesis project, they often make it an autobiographical story and they deal with that same thing, like, I'm so close to this story, how do I tell this story, and I want to tell it in a way that resonates with the audience, but the process of doing it is important to me, too, and they don't often work with dramaturgs. It might be helpful to have someone to bounce ideas back and forth with, so it's not just their own ideas. And I think that that's interesting about the idea of devised theatre as a collective. There's so much solo devising but this is really a different thing, to be creating a one person show and doing all the devising yourself, without reflection from anyone else. It's a totally different thing.

MIKAELA HERRERA: Right. You asked me to define what I thought devised theatre was, and I was like, Oh, I think it's like a creative collective, but I didn't really think about just writing a piece by yourself. Because it's the same sort of process. I like to look at creating art as more like a scientific process than it is like literary, or humanities based. You have the process; you have to do the research and then you have to put it together and then you actually have to go through with the project. It's kind of like moving through like a scientific method, here's my hypothesis, this is me testing it out, that sort of thing.

KYLA KAZUSCHYK: I'll pick up the thread of the idea of science versus art. That's such a huge idea and it's interesting to think of them as being separate but maybe they're not. Maybe any process of creating art is a scientific process.

MIKAELA HERRERA: It's just so crazy to think about because growing up, I was taught that these are two very different things. They're like oh people in STEM think this way and people in the liberal arts think this way and I'm like, No, I do both. I don't see why we have to separate them, especially for a process like devising. Because if you're creating a piece by yourself, you are, in a way, creating this like, experiment. Because if you're doing it with other people, then it goes back to that collective and you are all kind of tackling different things together, but it's really like, I can't get over the scientific process idea, to do it by yourself that's crazy and that seems really hard.

KYLA KAZUSCHYK: All the actors I've talked to said it's really hard. And that ties back to all the ideas of what has made the pandemic so hard is that we're all on our own, each person is so isolated, that's what makes everything harder. We are meant to be interacting with other humans.

MIKAELA HERRERA: Right it's crazy to like start coming back to it and being like, wow my thought process has changed so much because I want to interact with people, but I am so used to just being by myself or staring at my screen and talking to another person and like, I don't know if I know how to interact with people.

KYLA KAZUSCHYK: Right? It's like everyone's going to have to relearn it.

MIKAELA HERRERA: I get weirded out like, if someone's really close to me in the grocery store and I think about the times when I would be at a concert just surrounded by so many people and I'm like, that wasn't overwhelming?

KYLA KAZUSCHYK: That it feels like so long ago, and to think about in terms of theatre too, like I'm struggling with this right now, like I miss theatre so much but also, I feel nervous to do theatre with other people.

MIKAELA HERRERA: It feels weird. I was just thinking about what next semester is going to look like and thinking am I ready to like be in this space again? I don't know if my bandwidth ever really recovered. It definitely took a hit and I don't know if I can handle certain things I just don't have the stamina anymore and I'm afraid to bite off more than I can chew.

KYLA KAZUSCHYK: It is going to be an experiment, like you said. And what isn't an experiment?

What advice do you have for artists approaching devised work, whether it relates to costumes or anything—what should you take with you into devising work?

MIKAELA HERRERA: We briefly touched on this earlier, but it would definitely be being mindful of the people that you're working with. Again, it is so easy to get wrapped up into it and forget that other people are also trying to figure out balance. And then also be open to other people's ideas because it's very easy to put yourself into a piece and start creating it in your head and you're like, Okay, well I want other people to work on this, but I'm going to try and help guide them to the idea that I had in mind. But I love when I think one thing and then I sit down, I talk to someone they're like, Okay, this is my idea and I'm like wait wait wait wait, I don't know how you got there and I don't know how I got here but let's put them together, because I think it's going to be amazing. It's just a matter of listening to each other and it's a lot easier said than done. I mean theatre people love to talk and they have so many ideas. But that was the biggest thing for me was being open to these ideas, because I was coming from what I know a director does. And from taking directing as a class. You don't want to give the people you're working with like, I want you to do this, this, and this, and I want you to get here or say it like this. We want to help guide them. But that's not how I feel devised theatre should be because, again, it's supposed to be all of y'all coming into one. In order to do that, you have to be all ears, no judgment, there is no such thing as a bad idea. And letting a barrier go. Like how I was telling you I had a hard time letting another dramaturg into my space even though now looking back at it, I really wish that I did. Because I was just very protective over my spot and, of course my own experiences, but I have to be willing to be vulnerable with another person, especially if I'm going to be staging these things—I'm going to be giving them to the entire world.

KYLA KAZUSCHYK: This is such a great point, the idea of being open and being vulnerable, I think that relates to everything. That relates to all the aspects of developing a devised piece, and also a scripted piece, and directing as well as creating costumes. In costumes, when we're designing, we are so often like, I designed this for you to wear it, but the actor is the one who's going to be wearing it, the audience is going to be the ones who are going to be seeing it. It could be so much greater if it's not just one person's idea, and if everyone else can contribute to it, it could be something even more wider reaching than just one person's idea.

MIKAELA HERRERA: Oh for sure, and the costume thing happens even with scripted pieces, because you go in with this idea and then you could be like actors on stage dress rehearsal right and then you're like, oh man, you know this isn't going to work so you got to go again.

KYLA KAZUSCHYK: You have got to be flexible; you have got to be willing to go again and to let go of things and to open yourself to other ideas.

MIKAELA HERRERA: Another reason why I fell in love with theatre in general but, more specifically, devised theatre is that it's fleeting. It's always changing and it's never going to be the same. And that's so exciting because it's like, if I don't put myself into this piece now did I miss out? Because it's never going to be the same piece that it would have been if I worked on it.

KYLA KAZUSCHYK: Oh that's so inspiring I love how you put that—that resonates with me so hard! That's what I love about theatre too, that it's fleeting. And that it's this moment and then it's gone and the energy in this room at this time is not going to be the same, even if it's the same show the next night it's going to be a different energy.

MIKAELA HERRERA: All of these different people with different experiences coming back into a room and the way I feel today probably isn't going to be the way I feel tomorrow, so why would I expect that of anyone else?

KYLA KAZUSCHYK: And we do! This is such a useful lesson too. That we do expect people to be static, but people aren't static, we're all always changing. So why wouldn't ideas change too? And the point that you made that I've never actually put the two and two together is that, if I don't contribute what I have to contribute to this piece it's not going to be the same as if I didn't! I'm so impressed that you have found that value in your own voice. That's awesome.

MIKAELA HERRERA: Thank you because people are always like, Oh, you know, like fear of missing out sort of deal, and I was like, Okay well how do I make that not that.

KYLA KAZUSCHYK: And I'm so glad that you had that positive experience on *Upgrade* where you saw how it could be when everyone brings their ideas and the person facilitating the ideas listens to all their ideas and incorporates them.

MIKAELA HERRERA: Yes, me too, because I kind of feel like I, though I didn't hate working on *Dream Logos*, not in the slightest, I thought it was a really cool piece, and I was really excited to do something I'd never done before. I don't think that I would have been willing to put on a devised piece myself or take on the project at all if that were my only example because like I loved being in all of these different productions at LSU and then kind of watching how one production meeting or rehearsal ran and moving on to the other ones, and how they influence each other. I was able to see that in *Upgrade* and I was like, Okay, I love the way that you are running this rehearsal or you were talking to us in these production meetings, this is what I want to do as a director, because I feel like it's a very healthy work environment, I feel like it's a safe space. I'm not afraid to say anything.

I love that I can see bits of how Anthony was running things in other projects that I've worked on. I worked on *448 Psychosis* with Angelle who also worked on *Upgrade* and I could see the similarities in there, too, and Angelle brought things from her internship that she did over the summer and I was like, Oh, this is so exciting. And it was weird because, not only was I devising an actual piece, with people, but I was devising the creative environment, too. Because it was changing as I went. I was like, Okay, well we're going to open it this way, and what didn't work last time, how can we kind of make things more concise and how I'm listening to what people are saying, and it was just always changing. It was fun.

KYLA KAZUSCHYK: And I love what you mentioned that you're evaluating what didn't work, constantly evaluating our practices as we're creating stuff. And in these ways, I think that our experiences with theatre can shape all our experiences. How am I interacting with students in the classroom and in the costume shop and how can I make that better and how can I make that more collaborative? There are ways to do it, all these can feed each other if we listen to our experiences.

MIKAELA HERRERA: Yeah because it'll start from the ground up. If I went in just kind of feeling blah it wouldn't grow any stronger. And so I was like, Okay, I had a really positive experience here, I feel like that is a good place to start, and if the people that I'm working with want to change something about it, let me know and we can talk about it. I always like to open up with like name, pronouns, something good, year, whatever and so I'm like well maybe someone feels like not comfortable in sharing all of this information and I'm a very open person, and so, Okay, well if you don't want to share with us, you don't have to share that next time we meet or anytime we do another introduction—I have that in mind, you know.

KYLA KAZUSCHYK: That's something I work on, trying to remind myself that my personality is not everyone's personality. Because I'm also a very open person and I'm like, let's do this let's all say this but not everyone feels that way, and figuring out how to help people to feel comfortable not just aligning to my obnoxious personality.

MIKAELA HERRERA: Oh, I feel that, and that was another really exciting part about my devised piece is that I was working with people that I had never worked with before. So I was super excited to get everyone into a room and I was like, wow I have all of these great minds that think so differently than I do. And to just have a sit down and then be like, Okay, this is what I was thinking, this is what I was thinking, do you see where we aligned here—okay now let's go from there. And it was just so exciting and it's like a puzzle, like I was putting together a puzzle. And it wasn't like any of the pieces were missing, they just kind of appeared as I was doing it, and then by the end it was collected.

KYLA KAZUSCHYK: How did you assemble the team?

MIKAELA HERRERA: Oh my gosh it was a lot. So I remember Suellen and I sat down and we were like, Okay, these are the people that we know. And so, these are people I've worked with before, and she was like these are the people I've worked with before and I was like, okay cool so we push those two together, and then we also had spaces that we couldn't get. And so I would reach out to other people in the program—be like hey, I need a stage manager, do you know someone? And then I just was bombarded with like different numbers and I would text them and be like hey are you interested in doing this and they're like I can't but I know this person. And then, it just kind of moved around like that, until I had my team, and I said, oh wow this is such an interesting group of people like I'm super excited to have y'all working on this because, like the idea was to tell a story or tell a set of stories from like me growing up, and like Suellen growing up, and the idea was like, Okay, I wish, these are things I could have heard growing up. A little bit more taboo stories that are very applicable to growing up as a female identifying or passing person. But I had a lot of people who were minorities in other ways than the way that I see myself as a minority, and I was like, Okay that's a very interesting perspective to work with because we both have the same goal—we want to be seen, but we want to be seen in different ways, so I'm like, Okay, well, this is how I feel and they'd be like I think that's really great But what if you approach it from this angle. Because like my goal was to reach more people and I couldn't do that if I stayed closed off.

ARTIST SPOTLIGHT: CARRIGAN O'BRIAN

As the Lead Program Representative and Teaching Artist at the National Theatre Center and the Eugene O'Neill Theatre Center, Carrigan O'Brian has developed lots of devising skills, as the following interview reveals.

How do you define "devised theatre"?

Devised theatre is a collaborative or ensemble-driven theatre technique that requires starting from "scratch," as opposed to starting with a script.

What are the advantages to creating devised work?

There are so many benefits to creating devised theatre and making this type of work! In a devised theatre process, everyone in the ensemble is relying on each other and held equally accountable. Everyone gets a voice in the process and during rehearsals, collaborators are usually forced to be very present with each other and fully in tune with their instincts since there is no road map/text to follow. All roles are equally important, and there are no "lead roles'" and "secondary roles," which allows for a non-hierarchical structure. In devised theatre, there is a clear objective for everyone the whole time, and there is liberation in the fact that you can change the piece at any point. Devising is also accessible to all theatre artists regardless of economic status, age, experience, background, language, disability, etc. Oftentimes, a devised theatre piece can be done on a low budget, so that's another plus.

How do you approach creating costumes for devised work? Any tips or strategies that have been successful?

Sometimes I've worked with a costume designer throughout the whole devised theatre process, who observes some rehearsals here and there, but mostly collaborates with the director about what costumes there should be/what the world of the play should feel like. This process evolves over time. Other times, the costume designer is actually a part of the ensemble, also working as an actor in the process.

I would say at the first rehearsal if you're the director/devised theatre facilitator, ask everyone there who has costume experience or purposefully find/pick an ensemble member who has costume experience so that they can be thinking about costumes throughout the whole process and also be a part of creating it.

I've also been involved in a lot of devised theatre pieces in which the ensemble wears black or neutral colors and puts on different costume "accent" pieces since each actor is playing more than one character.

What advice do you have for artists approaching devised work?

Be open to not having a "road map" and not knowing what the timeline/storyline looks like. Have patience with yourself and your peers—the story will come organically if you don't push it.

Always remember the audience will be taking in this story you're creating for the first time, so don't forget to think of them and come back to the reason you're making this piece/the question you want your audience to ask at the end of it.

If you're talking/generating ideas more than everyone else, take a back seat and ask one of the quieter collaborators if they need help or have any ideas.

Have a good sense of humor throughout. It may feel like you're doing the impossible at first—keep pushing through and know your authentic truth is enough and will get you to the next phase of the piece you're creating. When you're feeling "lost at sea," or when you're frustrated, look to the "ultimate decision-maker" or director for guidance or address your needs and concerns to the group. Oftentimes if you're feeling it, then someone else is, and talking it out will help you navigate the next step.

Always record your rehearsals—either via video or by taking notes. You never know when you will want to reference a prior rehearsal.

CHAPTER 4
KNOW YOUR RESOURCES

PULL CAREFULLY

Devised work can be a prime example of the "hurry up and wait" principle. While you are waiting for decisions to be made, you can be pulling multiple options, or at least familiarizing yourself with the options that are available, so that you are prepared to pounce on them when the time is right, i.e. when the show is cast or the characters are set.

Don't pull too much or too little. Pulling racks and racks of clothes is just making more work for someone (possibly you) down the line, in selecting what items to fit and in restocking eventually. Pulling too little is a problem too. You don't want to get into a fitting and run out of options before you find something that works. Pull with the characters in mind, or ideas and themes before the characters are developed.

For example, I designed and created costumes for a dance piece that was based on the history of Congo Square in New Orleans. I met with the choreographer to discuss her vision for the piece before she cast it. Her idea was that the dancers would embody the spirit of the musicians who were enslaved there and they should look like ghosts. I pulled a rack full of skirts, petticoats, and billowy blouses in a range of shades of cream, beige, and off white. Once the piece was cast, I called each dancer in for a fitting and styled looks for them from the rack of pulled garments. I never even measured the dancers. I just had them try on a bunch of things and then altered everything to fit as needed. Having the rack of items in a range of sizes, all appropriate for the world of the piece, saved a lot of time.

A useful tool for visual communication is to dress up dress forms with pulled costumes. Showing collaborators clothes on forms is better than showing them clothes on hangers or flat. It takes away the extra step of having to imagine what the pieces might look like on human bodies. Collaborators don't have to spend energy on that extra cognitive step. And as a costume designer, it can help you to start to envision what the different looks will look like all together on stage. As you develop the looks, make sure that the photographs you show to the director are styled very closely to the intended final looks so that they get clear impressions of your ideas.

Pull a range of options for each performer, like a closet of clothes that might belong to that character. This can be a way to give performers agency or ownership of their character, working with them to select clothes from their character's "closet" to wear on stage.

Often the most effective costumes are the ones that do not stand out at all. I have worked on a number of contemporary shows, both devised and scripted, where I hear comments from audience members following the show, akin to "Well, you didn't have to do any work, right? It looked like the actors were just wearing their own clothes." In the moment, this can strike a costume designer or technician as an insulting dismissal of their time, talent, and effort. However, critiques of this sentiment can actually be viewed as high compliments. If the performers made the donning of costume garments appear so effortless and natural, the work of the costume crew has resulted in the creation of apparently authentic characters. This is true in both traditional and devised theatre, yet in devised theatre it sometimes takes much more energy to arrive at a set of realistic looking costumes.

DOI: 10.4324/9781003181170-4

FIGURE 4.1 *Dancers on stage in Journey to Congo Square (photo courtesy of Vastine Stabler)*

FIGURE 4.2 *Costumes for dancers representing ghostly apparitions in Journey to Congo Square were created by calling dancers in all at once, without having any measurements of them, and styling them in looks from a rack of pulled costume pieces (photo courtesy of Vastine Stabler)*

KNOW YOUR STOCK

This is another place where doubling of roles is a double-edged sword. It takes so much labor to maintain stock, but if you are the one doing it, a benefit to that is that you know it well. Knowing what is available will make pulling so much easier. If possible, put in the time to familiarize yourself with stock. My perspective is from university theatre and professional theatres affiliated with university theatres. If you have stock available to you—use it! It is like shopping for free.

If you are the one responsible for keeping stock well organized, you know how much work that is and also how helpful it is. Many stock managers agree that if you cannot locate something within five minutes, you might as well not have it. It is worth it to take the time to keep stock organized. Utilize whatever space you have in the best way possible. At many universities, costume storage is in a building repurposed from another department, often consisting of many separate rooms. When restocking, even if you are in a hurry, you can at least put items back into the room with like items, making them easier to find later.

If you have access to a costume stock, maintain a working knowledge of what is contained in that stock and where things are kept. If you are also the one responsible for keeping this stock organized, devote the time and labor necessary to keeping it organized, so that it can be possible to pull from it quickly and efficiently. Pulling from stock can save money and time, though it can end up costing more time in the long run if you over pull, as you will have to spend time restocking and reorganizing.

Know your sources, and know the particular challenges associated with each source. Useful sources for costume pieces may include secondhand stores, the mall, fabric stores, the internet, or rental partners. It is also essential to know your skill set and your labor pool and budget your time accordingly. You must know your own speed, including exactly what you are capable of delivering and in what amount of time, so that you do not promise things to yourself or others that you cannot deliver. It helps to be as fast as possible.

To sharpen your ability to estimate how much time projects will take, keep track of hours in a written log. Write down what time you start work, and then when you wrap up, take note of the time and what you accomplished during that period. If you are supervising students or workers, have them practice this logging of time and accomplishments as well. It feels satisfying to look back and see concrete evidence of improvement, as in, "wow, a month ago it took me four hours to lay out and cut out all the pieces of a garment, and now I can do that in just one hour!"

While working on *Love and Information*, many characters were added to the show very close to opening night. With a few days to go, seven out of the ten actors in the show ended up playing Flight Attendants, in addition to the dozens of other characters they were already playing. Because I knew exactly where our navy blue suits and separates were in stock, I was able to pull them quickly. After brief fittings, I made the necessary alterations quickly as well. To complete the look, I ordered some plastic wing pins and red, white and blue scarves online, which arrived in two days. Without being familiar with these resources, I would not have been able to accommodate the last minute additions of characters. In traditional theatre, there are still sometimes last minute additions, but they happen on a much smaller scale than in devised theatre, and there is usually more time at the beginning of the process to make decisions and plans.

Love and Information became ten performers portraying over a hundred specific characters, some added as late in the game as final dress rehearsal. The day after the second dress rehearsal, the director approached me with concerns about the population of the airport that we had created. These concerns were not apparent when we had begun the process, in November of 2016, but in late January of 2017, airports were suddenly prominent in the news, as the president of the United States at the time began proposing travel policies discriminating against people representing certain religions, ethnicities, and nationalities. Two days before opening is too late in the process to make significant changes to the set of any show, yet it is not too late to make adjustments to the costumes. After discussing possibilities with the director, I pulled a yarmulke, a kufi hat, and a scarf that could be worn as a hijab. I reviewed the script and what characters had been established, and determined what characters could be adjusted with the addition of these accessories. Costumes for devised work possess the power to change the piece as necessary, in a way that can quickly update the story being told, drawing it into an immediately wider and up-to-the-moment cultural context.

KNOW WHAT IS OUT THERE

Know what sources are available to you. Maintain an honest awareness of exactly how long it will take you and your shop to construct or alter something, in what stores you can shop that are within driving distance, what these stores have in them, what is available online, and how long it takes online orders to get from vendors to you.

Frequent trips to the mall and to secondhand shops keep me familiar with what color palettes and styles are trending and what is available where. I often go out for a browse before characters and themes are set, so that I have an idea of what is out there and then I am ready to pounce on it when necessary.

FIGURE 4.3 Love and Information *at Louisiana State University (photo courtesy of Vastine Stabler)*

FIGURE 4.4 *Performers on stage in a scene from* Love and Information. *Adding and subtracting layers can allow performers to transform quickly from character to character (photo courtesy of Vastine Stabler)*

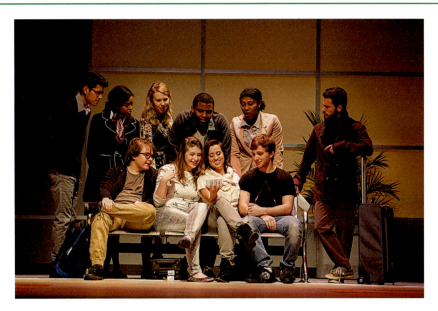

FIGURE 4.5 Love and Information *on stage, featuring flight attendants and a pallette of dusty neutral colors inspired by diseased chicken entrails (photo courtesy of Vastine Stabler)*

One challenge to designing costumes for university theatre or professional theatres affiliated with universities is that every purchase made has to be exempt from sales tax. In theory, every retailer should be able to do this, but in practice, not all stores comply with this requirement. This can be very frustrating, but it is not worth arguing with an underpaid cashier over. Through trial and error, discover which stores in your area will do tax exempt purchases and frequent those stores when shopping for a show. Often ordering online will allow for purchases to be tax exempt. Ordering online saves the legwork of going to stores, yet comes with its own set of pitfalls. Sometimes orders take longer than expected to arrive, and sometimes things look different in person than they did online, or they are actually different measurements than described. Another idea to consider is sustainability and ethical consumption. This goes back to the principle of knowing your stock. Pulling is the easiest way to limit your carbon footprint. From there, the second best way is to shop secondhand.

There are so many advantages to buying things from thrift shops or secondhand stores. Not only are they generally less expensive, but also items naturally look lived in instead of brand new. This can help to form authentic characters.

ARTIST SPOTLIGHT: MAGGIE MCGURN

Performer, writer, costume technician, and educator, Maggie McGurn discusses creating her solo devised thesis performance, working on new works, and the potential that devising holds.

KYLA KAZUSCHYK: How do you define devised theatre? What is devised theatre to you?

MAGGIE MCGURN: That's a tricky question because I think it can be so many things to each individual and each project is going to be a little bit different. I think in my Statera presentation, I defined it as theatre that gives you a voice. Because I was defining it as devised theatre being something that you as the artist or you as the ensemble are creating and therefore your voices as artists are going to be interlocked with that. And I still feel very much like that is the case. I've worked on projects that I didn't personally write, but you also get the sense when you're working on something that's being created throughout the process, that you have an agency in it, or that you are paving the way for that project in a way that a performance that has had many performances in many different venues isn't doing. With a show that has been well established, you can always have your own take on it. With devised theatre, you don't have anything to see what other previous productions of this thing look like, and so you really have to decide as an ensemble or as a group, or as a creator, what it is for you. I think that there is something really exciting about that and also it can be very intimidating at the same time.

KYLA KAZUSCHYK: I agree, and that's kind of rolled into the next question which is, why do it? What are the advantages to it and, in your experience, what have been the positive effects of doing it?

FIGURE 4.6 Corner of 26 and Lost, *written, directed, and performed by Maggie McGurn (photo courtesy of Maggie McGurn)*

MAGGIE MCGURN: I think it's a great challenge, that it pushes you as an artist in new ways, in new and exciting ways and also terrifying ways that are exciting as well. Because you're kind of pushing yourself into new territory constantly with devised work, and so you can't really lean back on old habits as much. You have to keep pushing forward and push through those challenging moments to kind of get out on the other side of it. And I think, at least with my experience with my thesis project, I don't think I have ever been as nervous as I was before going out on stage for that piece, because it's so personal to me. It's personal because it's a personal story to me but it's personal because I created it and I decided all the blocking and everything. I feel like I'm going out there and I'm like baring my soul in a way that I haven't done before, but it was also so exhilarating in a way that I had not experienced either. When I stepped off stage I was like, Oh my God I just did that, I created something and I performed it and it was amazing. The feeling of it was like the surge of adrenaline. I think for artists, you always do kind of get that but I hadn't experienced it at that height, because I felt like so much ownership over this thing that I had created and brought to life.

KYLA KAZUSCHYK: That's so exciting! have you evolved your thesis project since then? Have you gone back to it, have you performed it ever again?

MAGGIE MCGURN: I haven't. I've thought about it a lot and I've watched it and I thought, how would I do things differently now? And it's interesting because it's so personal that in some ways it was a very cathartic experience, because it was kind of dealing with how I was viewing where I was at in my life at that time. In some ways it feels like that piece has also kind of allowed me to move on from that. In some ways it would feel weird to go back to it because I'm in a different place in life and so it's almost like well if I was going to do a piece now what would I have to say now? But that's I think what's exciting about thinking about my thesis. I felt really great about what I created then. There are things looking back on it that I would want to improve or change but it's also about what would I do next, what would be the next project, knowing that I have that experience behind me and I haven't figured out what that next project is, but I have started feeling like it's time to start writing something again.

KYLA KAZUSCHYK: I remember you talking about working with a group devising in Richmond, right? Whatever came out of that?

MAGGIE MCGURN: It kind of splintered apart, which was okay. I think it's really hard to create something from the ground up with an entire group of people, unless you all know each other really well and know how each other works and kind of know each person's strengths.

Obviously other people would have a different perspective on that, but I know I'm very personal with my writing. I like to kind of hoard it to myself until I feel like it's ready to share, which is not always a good thing. I realized that is at times something that holds my writing back from being better because I am so cautious about sharing it sometimes because it's personal. And so I think that that makes it difficult for me to write with a group and that's something that I definitely want to work on and get more comfortable with but I don't know that that project was the right time to do that.

KYLA KAZUSCHYK: Do you have visions of another project that you would do with a group?

MAGGIE MCGURN: Not as of right now. But I am in a show that is not really devised, but it is a new script. I think working on a new script is very much in that devised world because we're creating these people and what this is going to look like, for the first time.

It was actually supposed to open a week before we went into lockdown last year. But we are slated to open it in spring of 2022. So we've met a few more times to do readings on zoom and that's been a really fun process. And the director brought in a movement coach and so bringing in that concept of movement with developing this character and who this person is, I always enjoy that.

KYLA KAZUSCHYK: Everyone's approached lockdown in different ways but that's interesting that y'all just kind of put a pin in it and will come back to it, and that you still had zooms to stay fresh on it, and that there is a plan to go back to it.

MAGGIE MCGURN: Yeah which I was very excited about because we were like literally a week away from opening the show and when Covid started and everybody was like, Oh well, this will happen for two weeks and we'll be back and it'll be fine we're going to move the show to May. We quickly realized that was not going to be the case.

I think that goes into the idea that devised work is so many different things and it's in so many different projects. Either it's like you are creating it alone by yourself, or you're creating it with a group or you are bringing somebody else's kind of devised or written script to life for the first time.

KYLA KAZUSCHYK: Even if it was devised and then it's getting on its feet for the first time, that's still creating something new. How do you approach creating costumes for devised work, how did you create the costumes for your thesis.?

MAGGIE MCGURN: Well, I don't know because I just wore jeans and a T-shirt.

KYLA KAZUSCHYK: But why? Why did you make that choice?

MAGGIE MCGURN: I chose an outfit that I wore frequently that was fairly generic and that could exist within all of the different time frames of my show. Because I was dealing with moving in between the past and the future, and it just seemed like an outfit that would fit me as a kid and me as a recent college grad and me as sitting in my apartment in Chicago and trying to figure out what I was doing with my life. Because it felt weird to be dressed up to tell these stories because in most of these stories I wouldn't have been dressed up in them. So I was thinking something casual and something comfortable and I needed to be able to climb around on the piano and move around, so I didn't want to wear anything that would be restrictive to my movement. And that seemed like the best choice, I guess, and it was a T-shirt so I wouldn't get too hot.

KYLA KAZUSCHYK: It's so interesting to me how much of what we do as costume designers is really intuitive. A lot of what we do comes from development and training, and there are specific means to design characters, but if you are just tapping into what is important to tell the story, that's what you just described. What are the requirements? I have to have motion, I'm thinking about what the character would wear in these situations and what would work for all of those, that's costume design.

I'm curious about the costumes for the piece that was about to open. Did y'all have costumes, what was the plan? Did you work with the costume designer?

MAGGIE MCGURN: Yes. So the play is, it's like a family kind of, it's a hard play to actually describe. It's like a family drama but it's not super realistic. It has elements of realism, but it flows in a way that, there seems to be some kind of like I don't want to say supernatural element to it, but this kind of like a surreal, I don't know how to describe it. But it centers around this girl who is a teenager and she's talking about her family and her parents are divorced, and how that is affecting her at that moment, and her relationship with her step mom and her stepfather and her parents and

FIGURE 4.7 Trying out costume and set pieces in rehearsal for Corner of 26 and Lost, written, directed, and performed by Maggie McGurn (photo courtesy of Maggie McGurn)

I am playing the step mom and all of the characters are onstage for pretty much the entire show.

We each had our own station and kind of like our worlds that we exist within, and so there weren't really any costume changes there were things that we would add on. I had an apron and at the very end, I had long black gloves that I would put on. But it was mostly, in a similar way to my thesis, one costume but that's traveling with you, through these different times and different interactions. It kind of embodies who that character is or says something about. My character was a nail model and very prissy but she loves to cook and so she had this bright pink cardigan and these high waisted kind of I want to say they were floral fitted pants. I could be wrong about that they might be black, for some reason I'm picturing them as being floral, with stiletto heels and there was a black tank top underneath because at the end, I had just a black tank top and long sheer black gloves with nails connected to them. Yeah she's a very dramatic woman, this character.

But when we go back into a more steady rehearsal process, I think we have a new costume designer so it'll be interesting to see what the take is, maybe it will go in a different direction. I think it will definitely change. The script has changed, not a lot but there's been some changes. So even though we were like a week from opening, we thought we were very ready and now we're kind of shifting the world of this show a little bit.

KYLA KAZUSCHYK: That's so exciting to be working on something that's brand new.

MAGGIE MCGURN: Obviously we didn't plan to do it over the course of this long a period of time, but when you have that time that you can kind of figure out what would we want to change, we have a whole other year.

KYLA KAZUSCHYK: Timelines are something else I wanted to ask you about. In terms of your thesis project, how did you approach developing the timeline for that, did you give yourself deadlines? How did you work out what you're going to do when?

MAGGIE MCGURN: That's a great question. I've never been really good at giving myself deadlines, but I knew going into the program that that was going to be the end product, that we are going to have to write our thesis show.

I think that I had the idea from the beginning, knowing that we were going to write this thesis, that I wanted it to be a personal story, and so throughout the time I was writing little short stories to figure out what exactly did I want to say and what stories did I want to include. So I had all these stories. I didn't end up using them all, but it was like oh this story flows nicely into this story and I had that song that I wanted to incorporate but I wasn't sure how I wanted to do it. I had a conversation with Nick at one point, I don't remember what he said, but we were just talking about it, and something he said made it snap into focus, and I was like, oh my God that's the thing that weaves all these stories together. Because I hadn't had that. I was like what connects all these stories if they're not linear, if they're not being told in a you know A to B. And I was like, Oh, this is it, this is the thing that connects them all, it's the thing that flows them all together, and so that then once that clicked into focus, I was like, Oh well then, it's all centered around the piano because it's all centered around the song and suddenly the blocking clicked into place and the whole set clicked into place.

So it wasn't so much a deadline, as it was figuring, writing things that I wanted to say, and then having certain moments that made those pieces fit together. And some of those decisions were made very late in the process. I just remember sitting in the black box, and I was just laying on the floor because I had the studio theatre. That was like a space that was coveted because that's where we were going to perform, but we had to schedule out who was going to be in and at what time and I was like, I had the studio tonight, which is great, but like I don't really know what to do right now. Like laying on the floor and that was the moment that I was like, it's just the piano, all I need is a piano. Because I had had this elaborate set planned out that's like here's a couch here's a chair and I was like, what am I gonna, how is this even remotely going to flow in any kind of coherent manner?

KYLA KAZUSCHYK: That it's so interesting that you started big and then distilled it, you really thought about the story. And you had a vision. I think people do this a lot, they start small and it gets too big, but you had a big set in your mind, a lot of pieces, but that wasn't working to tell the story.

MAGGIE MCGURN: Yeah absolutely, which is interesting, because I think when I go to write creative pieces, oftentimes it is like a piece of dialogue and then it's like, Okay, I have this one little piece, how do I expand this into an entire story? But when I'm working on academic writing or anything like that I always start with like, Okay, what are all the ideas that I want to get out and then, how do I distill them and I'm just realizing this as you're saying that, maybe I should do what I do with those academic pieces and bring them into devised work or into my creative writing.

KYLA KAZUSCHYK: You could! I'm also interested in what you said that you knew you had stories to tell, and it was going to be non linear it wasn't going to follow a regular linear progression.

To me this connects to theories of feminism and theories of alternative storytelling, whether devised or not. We're taught the story has to be A to B to C and that's it, but it really doesn't. There's so many other structures that it could be.

MAGGIE MCGURN: It also opens up a lot of possibilities for what you want to say. I can play with time. If I'm telling a story that's linear then I'm just like, Okay, well then I'm just telling a bunch of stories about my life in succession, which didn't seem super powerful or really what I was trying to do. I wish I could remember when I wrote each section in relation to one another. But because my thesis started with me, at least what was the present moment for the show, which was like the future, it wasn't obviously the present moment as in like, I am standing in front of you as an actor. It was starting at me in my car trying to figure out if I was going to go to LSU. And then all of the story is happening and then coming back to that moment, and I remember being asked well, who are you talking to in the show like, who is the audience, if you're talking to them, and I was like I think the audience is me. Because I think so often, when I was in that place which is the present moment of the show, I was driving around Traverse City all the time trying to figure out what I wanted. And when I was sitting there, looking at the bay trying to figure this out, I would always be running through these things from the past instead of thinking about the future. And so it was that idea of like I'm telling, I'm talking to myself about all this stuff which isn't helpful because it's just this cycle that is hard to break, but the end of the show is breaking out of that and moving away from it.

KYLA KAZUSCHYK: Taking a step. I am so interested in the idea of "who is it for?" Sometimes it's so clear, as in, Okay we're going to put on *The Music Man*, it is for all the retired ladies that are going to come see it, we need to sell them tickets that's who it's for. Or, well we're creating this new work and it's for young audiences, but we still gotta sell tickets. I think that there's so much room, particularly in devising, to be like maybe it was for you. Maybe it was for you to have that experience, for you to articulate that story to yourself and learn from it and grow from it and it doesn't have to be connected to selling tickets or resonating with other people even. It's for your own personal growth and that has just as much value as anything else.

MAGGIE MCGURN: I really wanted it to resonate with people, and I was really worried that it wouldn't. Because I was like I'm telling all these personal stories like why would anybody care? Why does anybody care to go listen? Why write my personal story, what does that matter, you know? Not in a self-deprecating way, but there's so many stories to tell, why now tell this? I don't think I thought of my audience, who I'm creating it for, as being me. I think, in some ways, yes, it was because I think it was cathartic, it was a way of processing it, but I think I was just looking at, when I was speaking to the audience, I thought of it as an actor if you're like alone on stage as a character you're like who am I talking to? Am I talking to the audience because I want them to help me figure it out, or am I talking to a scene partner, and who is that scene partner, who are they supposed to be, is it your best friend, is it your mom, is it your significant other? And the person that I was putting the audience into was myself. But I really wanted, and I was hoping that the more specific that I was about my experience, the more it would resonate with other people. Because I think when you get specific about things it's easier to relate to somebody than just having like a broad generic story, which is what I was hoping would happen. But it is interesting now thinking about who I was hoping to affect. I don't think I thought about that at the time.

KYLA KAZUSCHYK: Did you ever talk to the audiences? Did you get feedback from people that saw it?

MAGGIE MCGURN: I did and I had people come up and tell me particular stories, I remember one, there was an undergrad student who was like the devil in the basement story is like, just like, I feel that. I had somebody stop me in the hall and be like I remember when I was in my early twenties and didn't know what I wanted to do and felt so lost and I felt that in your show, I sympathized with that. I think in one moment of the show I was going off about like what is my generation, what do we even care about, like what are we, what do we stand for? Are we just entitled is that what it is, like we just think we should get things we want? And I had an undergrad come up to me and mentioned that part.

The more specific you get, certain things are going to resonate with certain people, it's not all going to resonate with everybody. But you start seeing yourself when people go into detail about their own life, you know? And that's what I was hoping would happen and so I'm glad that I got some responses that it was happening.

KYLA KAZUSCHYK: This is humanity! We are who we are because we overlap with each other, yes the whole thing together is your experience but there are parts of it that overlap with other people's experiences and exactly what you said that the specificity of it is what can make it universal, you're trying to say something general, you're trying to make something authentic and true to your experience and different parts of it happened to resonate with other people.

MAGGIE MCGURN: I'm not going to say that my life has existed in a bubble and nobody has experienced what I have experienced, and I was hoping that that wouldn't be the case and I knew that that obviously wasn't the case. But I think it does open up those lines of communication, talking to people about things that you wouldn't necessarily bring up, like, Oh I didn't know that you also felt really lost for five years of your life, you know? Or like, Oh, I had a relationship like that, or whatever it may be. You start feeling connected to people through what you've created.

KYLA KAZUSCHYK: That is the best part of theatre. Those things wouldn't come in just regular conversation but theatre is a place where they can come up and then there is space created to talk about them.

MAGGIE MCGURN: Yeah exactly, which is why I think that aspect of devised theatre, something that you create resonating with other people that connects you with other people, is such a powerful feeling. You feel it when you're in any theatre production, because that's what we hope to do is connect with the audience and connect with each other as artists, but when it comes from something that you've created from the ground up and people connect with it, there is a deeper level of that and feeling of connection.

KYLA KAZUSCHYK: It's even more meaningful. I met with Camilla and I talked with her about how she created costumes for her thesis project, *Nightmares Are Dreams, Too* (more on this in Chapter 8) and she talked a lot about working with the performers and you were one of the performers. What was that experience like for you? What was it like working with Camilla on her thesis project and collaborating to create that costume and create that character?

MAGGIE MCGURN: It was really, really cool. I loved it. It was amazing because the costumes informed so much about how you move and how you act and behave. And to be a part of that and have this amazing costume created with me in mind, and then be able to actually bring it to life and just the costume that there was no dialogue or speech or anything you're just moving around in this costume, so how does it affect your interactions with the other costumes and that was so interesting. It was really fun, it was a great experience.

KYLA KAZUSCHYK: How did you come up with it? Did Camilla come to you and say you're going to be an eggshell human creature or how did that idea develop?

MAGGIE MCGURN: If I'm remembering it correctly, she told me what she had in mind for me, and I was like yeah I'm all about it, which was exciting, because it was this thing that she had envisioned and she had envisioned it with me in mind, and then I got to see it in the drawing and then I got to try it on, and then I got to move in it. And because it was so flowing and it was so long and the sleeves covered my hands, and so, you don't suddenly have your hands and you can't really move fast because you're moving with all this fabric, so it was very flowy and so that affected the way the flow of my movements. It felt very stately and very elegant and it was interesting to watch and interact with all of the other costumes and see how those costumes were affecting how those women moved.

KYLA KAZUSCHYK: Did you all plan out how you were going to interact before you did it or did you come up with it as you went?

MAGGIE MCGURN: No it just happened organically. We did it twice, we did it once in the studio theatre, and then we did it once at the art museum. It was very much like just moving in a space and reacting to things that are happening around you and creating interesting pictures as you're moving. You're like oh it'd be so interesting if I interacted over here, or if I was just standing next to, or, there's something really interesting happening over here and I either need to balance it out by going over here, or I want to be like a part of it. So it was very organic and it was very improvisational in a movement based way.

KYLA KAZUSCHYK: That's so cool! It is so creative.

MAGGIE MCGURN: I know I was so honored that she asked me to be a part of it, and I was so glad that I got to be a part of it.

KYLA KAZUSCHYK: I haven't heard of any other improv like that. I've heard of improv with objects or with a costume piece, but that was so driven by, like each character had a certain costume that really affected their movements and probably they all affected them the way you said you felt stately, I think other ones felt grimy. Because what you're wearing brings up those feelings for you and then that influences how you move in the space, driven by the costume.

MAGGIE MCGURN: Well I think that's always a thing, right? When you get your costume for your character and it's always this exciting thing of like oh I'm going to feel like I'm finally in like, something has clicked into place. Because your clothing is so important, it really affects you. But this was all wrapped up in this costume, it wasn't just that there was a piece of it, it was the whole thing. It was how does this particular, to be hyper focused on how does this piece of clothing make me feel, and how does it affect the way that I move was also really interesting just thinking about the things that do affect us so strongly. Things that we put on ourselves and the things that we carry either physically or emotionally.

KYLA KAZUSCHYK: And in such a stark contrast to your thesis project like, I know I have to be comfortable, jeans and a T-shirt. But for Camilla's project, it was like this is not going to be comfortable, it's not going to allow you to use your hands, figure out how you're going to move with that.

MAGGIE MCGURN: Though I do think that I might have had one of the more comfortable costumes.

KYLA KAZUSCHYK: Relatively.

MAGGIE MCGURN: I didn't feel like at any moment that I should slouch or that I should, there were certain things I was like I will not do that in this costume and if I do, if I get down, if I sit on the floor and lay down it's going to be very purposeful and elegant. They're just like certain movements that didn't make sense in that costume. And I wanted to honor that costume because that was really the thing. I don't want to go against what this thing is telling me to do because my job is to highlight this thing and to bring it to life.

KYLA KAZUSCHYK: And ultimately it's the same thing as telling a story. If you have a script your job is to honor the story of the script but without a script, it is like the costumes are the script, your job is to honor that. That's so interesting. And it's so interesting to think that it existed in that time and place. There was one at the studio theatre, there was one at the museum and that's it. It existed for that and the people that saw it and interacted with it and it's not going to be created again. It is what it was.

MAGGIE MCGURN: I think there's something really exciting about that because it just had its moment, had its place. It did feel like performance art.

KYLA KAZUSCHYK: What advice do you have for artists approaching devised work?

MAGGIE MCGURN: I think it's the same advice that I try to give myself, which is really difficult to follow, but it's just don't be afraid to fail. Because I think that that is the biggest hindrance when you're creating something. If you're afraid that you're going to do it wrong or if you're afraid that it's going to be terrible you won't create it. And so you just have to dive in. And just ride the waves in some ways. There are going to be days where you are like I don't know what I want to do with this and I don't know if it's any good. But coming back to it. And coming back to it again and again, and not just walking away from it.

KYLA KAZUSCHYK: Yeah, working through it and riding the wave! That's a great way to put it.

ARTIST SPOTLIGHT: ANDREA MORALES

Performer, director, writer, and educator Andrea Morales discusses her take on solo devised theatre and her perspective as an actor collaborating with designers and technicians to develop costumes and tell stories.

ANDREA MORALES: I think everyone should do devising. Because so often as artists, and I'm speaking about myself right now, we're perfectionists and we're really structured and we want to get it right the first time, and when you're devising that simply does not happen. And even if you hit on something that's amazing you still have to kind of flesh it out, you might hit on something that could be amazing at some point in the show that you're devising but you don't know where it quite fits yet. And so just the idea of having to really embrace the unknown, not knowing exactly how it's going to turn out and not knowing exactly what's going to happen. Once you embrace that rather than fighting that it's really freeing because you're in a space to just create.

KYLA KAZUSCHYK: Absolutely and so much can come out of that. How do you see the range of devised theatre and how we define it?

ANDREA MORALES: It's hard to define devised theatre. Generally I would define it as just theatre that is created without a script or theatre that is created from an idea and not knowing where the beginning middle end are going to fall and those kind of evolve and emerge for you.

So I think for the devised MFA work that we do at LSU, for me personally, anyway, it was devised. I had some ideas and I really didn't know how they were going to go and my end result was not at all what I thought it was going to be.

I was really happy with it, but it was not what I thought it was going to be at all. I thought it was going to be about working in a restaurant. I thought my piece was going to be all about what it's like to work in a restaurant. What came out of some of the work that I was doing by myself when I was devising is the idea of what if we're comparing the idea of waiting on tables, to the idea of how you have to wait on getting roles and auditions in the theatre world. That was not what I went in with, but it just kind of came out of that and it was interesting because I think there was a lot of humor that came out of my piece from playing with different things and seeing what would happen, but there was also a lot of vulnerability that came out of the devising process. Because even though there are things in my life that I can look back on now and laugh about and find joy in and realize, wow I've really grown since then, going back to those times where I was struggling as an artist as a human, there's a lot to be explored there. Having the freedom to explore that was really difficult and yet also really freeing because you know theatre is the art of empathy and often we're not empathetic with ourselves. We are really hard on ourselves as humans, we're really hard on ourselves as artists. Since my piece was pretty autobiographical, it was nice to step back and be like okay what if. And how do I show this theatrically instead of exactly what happened to me? How can I show the bigger picture of humanity, of how tough it is to grow up, to not have to live paycheck to paycheck, to have to look really deep into yourself and say is this what I want to be doing, how long am I going to keep doing this? Digging into some of those topics was difficult but also incredibly rewarding because it made me discover things about myself as a human and as an actor. And isn't that why we do what we do?

KYLA KAZUSCHYK: These are big questions, too. I love the idea of autobiographical work as thinking of yourself as a character and being able to distance from yourself as knowing who you are and thinking about how you could connect with other people. That's such a cool idea.

ANDREA MORALES: Yeah it's tricky and I didn't really think to do that at first. That was something else that came out of the devising process, what would your character be named? The character of you doesn't have to be Andrea. Who would this other person be? It also kind of became this thing, where like future Drea was looking back at a younger person, not necessarily even myself, but just a younger person. What is the advice I would give to someone who was an actor who'd made the move to a big city like Chicago and was pounding the pavement trying to get acting jobs, waiting tables to make ends meet, feeling lonely because this is not where you are from. And how can I kind of talk to my younger self and give myself that advice? That was something in the devising process I also came to. Because even though there's a lot of autobiographical stuff in my piece, there's a lot that is also there for theatricality so that I could try and make the audience feel what this character was feeling, feel the isolation, feel the loneliness, feel the judgment of an industry who thinks that you're not Latina enough or too Latina or not brown enough but not white enough either, and just trying to theatricalize some of those things so that the audience could really feel what Isabel's journey was, being stuck in an apartment in a blizzard in Chicago and suddenly being forced to think about her life.

KYLA KAZUSCHYK: It's that thin line between specificity and universal ideas. Things that are specific to us are universal to the human experience.

ANDREA MORALES: Absolutely. One of the loveliest things that someone said to me after this piece was, she's like, I totally can see even though I'm not like you she's like, I'm Black you're Mexican she's like but I totally understood exactly what you were going through and every second of that even though my experience has been very different than yours, she's like, there was never a moment through your struggles that I didn't identify with. And I actually was like, tell me more about that, because for my own growth and rewrites I wanted to know. And she's just like, I think that so much of our struggle as artists as humans can be relative to other people, but for her and specifically we're talking about what is it also like to be a person of color and, more specifically, a woman of color in an industry that has underrepresented us, marginalized us and often put up barriers that make it very difficult to do what we love to do and how do we work towards opening those doors for others, you know? And so I was like well let's start by writing what we know, start by taking something like an idea of our experience, our personal experience and making it accessible to others. I don't know if it was Gloria Steinem that said it, but some wonderful feminist said the "personal is political." When I started thinking about that, I think my show broke open in certain ways, because it wasn't just about like, Oh, this is my MFA project I'm going to try and play all these characters and look really good in front of the people, it became more.

And a lot of people do that, and I mean, that's something that I think is very different and unique to LSU's thesis project, because if we were doing the more traditional thing, where you went and did your little program in front of the agents that came. All you're really doing, and that is trying to be like well, this is the monologue that makes me look the best, this is the song I sing the best, this is where I look the best and I shine and there's nothing wrong with that, if that is what you are wanting to take into the world with you. What I appreciated about LSU's program is that having this devised piece, I still was able to showcase some things that I did well. I did play different characters, which is one of my things that I think is in my wheelhouse. But it also allowed me to dig a little bit deeper. I had to work a little bit harder, I had to do the work as an artist and I think that's much more fulfilling, as an artist, as a playwright, as an actor. That's one of the gifts of devised theatre is I had some flexibility. I didn't know exactly how it was going to go. I was constantly having to work and challenge myself, and there were a lot of days that I was just like, well that didn't work at all, pitch it and try and figure out something else.

KYLA KAZUSCHYK: You build resilience, the more things that don't work, the more you get closer to things that do work.

ANDREA MORALES: Absolutely, and that I think is so important because, as artists, we have to build that resilience, the ability to bounce back. Whether it's just from you had a bad audition kid and you gotta just go to your next one, or when you have a situation like a global pandemic that shuts down your workplace, how you keep artistically active, how do you keep moving forward, how do you devise solutions to teach acting, stage design, set design, costuming, how do you do that, in a box this big? I think devised theatre lends itself to such an interesting thing, because it makes you have to improvise. It makes you have to think about what might work and what might not. I think we all as teachers have had this, the day that the zoom doesn't work or that a student's sound is cutting out, we just have to keep going and work with what we're given. As I was devising I was given a couch, a table, any costuming or anything is really going to be whatever you want to bring to it. You've got these just very few things, how can you create something out of that? By starting with just something that is very basic you're able to be really creative and think like, what can I do with this Bears jersey that I'm wearing? What can I do with a notepad and an apron to communicate how I'm trying to fill all these orders for all these different agents? Things like that, just very simple things that also give you the flexibility if you do want to continue working on this piece and take it places that everything can fit neatly into a box in your car if you needed to so that you can go to fringe festivals, you can go to different theatre spaces and make it accessible. Because I think right now, and probably for the next few years, the theatre is going to have to be on a budget in a way that it hasn't been before. And that goes from Broadway to academia to regional theatres to community theatres. I think there's going to be a lot of one-person shows, two-handers, things like that that don't require the big sets and lights and band, and all of that, because right now theatres are hurting financially, so the idea of just keeping it very basic. I want to be in the room with and watch other artists on stage. Right now I'm much less interested in the bright and shiny backdrops. I just want to have that human connection again.

KYLA KAZUSCHYK: Connection, exactly. So many of us are craving that. You mentioned accessibility and I think that this ties into it, too, that theatre kind of went too far. Broadway shows are so expensive, not everyone can afford to go to that, but they have to be that expensive to pay all the artists that worked on it. But if we scale down and keep things smaller and more intimate then the tickets can be cheaper, more people can come to it, it can be open to a wider range of audiences.

ANDREA MORALES: Yeah absolutely. Even before the pandemic I discussed with students and had lots of chats about the idea that theatre isn't for everybody, which made me really sad when my students would say like, it's not for me. And I would say, why is it not for you? Well that's what rich people do or that's what rich white people do. And you know that broke my heart to hear that, but at the same time I've been faced with many times in my life, a situation where one of my best friends is in a show, and I want to go see them and I cannot afford a ticket. It's expensive. And theatre needs to be accessible because theatre is for everyone. We saw how *Hamilton* blew up on Disney plus and I was so on one hand overjoyed that people were getting to see *Hamilton* and getting to see how amazing it was. But on the other hand, feeling very sad because some people can't even afford Internet to have their children going to school right now. So again, even though *Hamilton* you didn't have to pay, like the $250 theatre ticket you're still having to pay the 9.99 a month, so again it's kind of accessible, but not really there yet. So how do we work towards making theatre accessible and also just encouraging the artists who are making theatre? I think we are going to go through a trend where casts are smaller, everything is scaled down, and so, how do we let our audiences know that that's okay? It's okay, we don't need the big show-stopping musicals, we don't need to go see *Wicked*, it's perfectly okay to go into a room and have two actors on stage in minimal costuming with a very minimal set tell a story because we're still there, having that community together and connecting with each other in a way that we haven't been able to. The idea of being able to be in a room with an audience, where we can laugh together or sigh or groan or snicker or whatever it is. I'm craving that so badly as an artist, because even though so many theatre companies have been super innovative and done these streaming productions or zoom productions I miss hearing the audience laugh and react and being in that space together. We've just really been missing it. I'm really hoping that theatre companies as they're restructuring right now trying to figure out, how are we even going to stay open. But that they're really prioritizing the accessibility factor, that the idea of getting people being able to come to the theatre and see the show is more important than the $20,000 set behind you, and going back to the idea of very basic theatre. We were talking about devised theatre because it allows us flexibility. I'm perfectly fine in a theatre with just the house work lights up if somebody comes out and tells a story.

KYLA KAZUSCHYK: And draws you in.

ANDREA MORALES: I'll just listen, because that is important to me and I'm hoping that that is important to other people, so that, as we start reopening the theatres we're keeping those things in mind and not at the risk of not being able to pay our artists. I think that's the other thing I'm concerned about other than safety, right now, in going back into that space and acting and everything. Covid, of course, makes me a little nervous, but with vaccines and masks and protocols in place I'm not as worried about that. What I am worried about is that we're going to go back to this sort of thing where it's like we can pay everyone except the actors. And what am I willing to accept, how hungry am I to work? And likewise, are we going to stop paying people what they're normally paid? The designers should be getting paid what they're supposed to get paid, you know? So I'm really hoping that as new infrastructure, well, first of all I'm hoping new infrastructures are being put in place, but I'm hoping that the ones that are being put in place we're taking those things into consideration, the safety of our actors, our designers, of our audience and then the accessibility to our audience, the accessibility to the community. Maybe we do have to do a show outside in a park. But if we can invite people to come and just spread the word—Hey this theatre is open and they're doing this thing—I think that's amazing, and I would go and I would hope that people if I was in a show out in the park that they would come.

KYLA KAZUSCHYK: It's the question of accessibility and also like you said, sustainability. We can't ask anyone, actors or designers or technicians, to work without getting paid. That has got to go and that's one of the things that I'm worried about, that once things start to come back that people will be so hungry for these experiences that people who have privilege will take the experience, just for the experience. And people in producing roles will take those people that just want the experience that will work for nothing, and then people that can't afford to work for nothing, are going to be excluded, again, how do we avoid that?

ANDREA MORALES: I don't know the answer to that. I think for me personally, I just have to remember how hard I've worked in my life, and what I won't do. It doesn't serve me as an artist to go back and work for free, no matter how hungry I am. If a theatre company, especially if it's a professional theatre company and they come to me and they're like we're gonna do we're gonna do the show and you're going to be the lead and it's going to be great but we're not going to pay you, I have to say no. Let that opportunity go to someone who is of privilege that can do it, or what would be the best was if everybody was just like no we're not going to do that. And even though I'm not a huge fan of social media, it has allowed us to stay connected during the pandemic. I also think that, right now, we can really help each other out in the theatre global community by saying, hey this theatre company just said that they would have me in this role but they're not going to pay me. Being able to call someone out on something like that—that's not the best theatre practices right now. And I know there's a Facebook group for New Orleans actors that has done that a couple of times during the pandemic where they posted things for technicians and actors and there's been words in the description like "really great opportunity," nothing about pay, nothing about safety protocols or anything like that. That's something that we have to think about too is, not only do you need to be paid, but you need to be safe. And what money has the theatre invested in the idea of keeping you safe? We're so close. We're so close and we've all got that pandemic fatigue, where we want things to go back to the way they were in the before. But we're not there yet. So even if a theatre company wants to throw a bunch of money at me right now and say you're going to do this, and then I walk into the space and everyone's unmasked and everyone's just chilling out I can't do that either. So what I've encouraged myself to do as well as other actor friends is just to really think long and hard about what do I need right now. What do I feel are best practices that I need before I'm going to go back into the theatre. And the thing that's going to be really difficult is it's … it's gonna be a pain in the ass for a while.

KYLA KAZUSCHYK: And you talk about empathy, this is the crux of it, we have to think beyond our own safety, we have to think about the communities that we're in.

ANDREA MORALES: There's so many unknowns right now so you're right empathy is challenged right now. Because I think part of being empathetic right now is making sure that everybody is safe. That is difficult because we all have very different definitions of what is safe right now.

The idea of loving others and having empathy is very tough right now, because there's so much unrest. And I don't know when that will go away. And so I think for myself right now, I just have to be really patient, which I'm not good at. And most of my friends who are artists are really struggling with that. But I would rather wait, and do this right and safely. I'd rather be patient.

KYLA KAZUSCHYK: Even though it's hard. This point of patience, I want to tie that back into devised theatre. How do you approach a timeline for a devised project? How are you patient with yourself, how do you put parameters on yourself and how do you create a timeline?

ANDREA MORALES: That was probably the most difficult part about doing the devised piece. Ultimately, you have the timeline, you're like April 9 you're performing it, it's like, well, I better be done. But you know once I accepted to go to LSU I was already kind of thinking about a couple of things that I might do, from the beginning. Because one of the things I liked about LSU's program was this idea, so I was just like, what if I just kind of started thinking about this a little bit, and then allowing myself the time to sort of just daydream, like what if I did this, or what if I did this.

And then I think what got really tough is when we were really needing to kind of buckle down the semester before, and then the semester of the project. It was trying to find time to be creative to allow yourself time to really explore and play, while you had all your other things from being a grad student going on, your assistantship and your other classes and just other life stuff.

The biggest thing I learned to do and it sounds silly, but I would set timers on my phone. I would set the timer for 20 minutes and for 20 minutes I would just take an idea and walk around and talk it out and sometimes I'd record it and sometimes it was horrible! I would listen back to it and like, well there's nothing there, and I just chuck it.

Sometimes I did just 20 minutes of like I'm going to watch somebody else do this, so for 20 minutes. I would watch John Leguizamo, who is one of my inspirations. I would just watch what he did, or I watched a Lily Tomlin video or just seeing what other people were kind of doing.

There were a couple of books we were given to read that had some writing exercises in them. So, I set a timer for 20 minutes, I'm just going to write blindly with this prompt. Then, when I started kind of getting more comfortable with things, I would set up my video camera for 20 minutes. And try out some dialogue I'd written or tried improvising through an idea and again, sometimes I would go back and watch those and just be like, Oh God, this is terrible this is never happening. But other times there was something like, maybe just even like a minute of content there that I'm like, Oh, but I like that, then I can pull.

I also realized that, I can't remember who introduced this term to me, but it was called exquisite pressure, which is kind of like the pressure that you get when you're at a deadline and you're like I have to finish this, this has to happen right now. I wouldn't go quite that extreme with it, but what I would do is maybe wait until ten minutes before I was supposed to leave my house for the day to go to school. And I give myself that ten minutes to just write down whatever. And again a lot of the time it was nothing but sometimes there was one sentence and kind of a stream of consciousness thing that I might be able to use because, with just that pressure of ,you have to leave in ten minutes, you have to get to school, if you're not at school on time you'll get marked late, you'll disrupt the class—you don't want to do that. Or I would do it right before I went to bed, like I'm so tired, I feel like I'm going to die, but for five minutes I'm just gonna write this down. I still have pages and journals of like just my stream of consciousness writing because sometimes there was something in there that I was able to pull or even like later down the line I'm like, that's really interesting, that's not for this show, but maybe I can put that somewhere else. So for me just the idea of kind of setting those time limits for me was important. And then, once we were getting down to the nitty gritty, like now you're two months out, now you're one month out, having meetings with either an advisor or making a meeting with another cohort member to say, hey you want to look at this and I'll look at yours and we'll give each other notes.

For me anyway it gets to a point where I have to collaborate. I'm such a collaborator and creating on my own just doesn't work. I might have annoyed people at points, but I really was that person in the cohort who was like hey, you got five minutes you want to listen to this thing I'm doing. There were many great moments where suddenly just having someone else take a look at it were so helpful.

It's so helpful, I think, to kind of find your group of people that are going to help you along this journey, people that you really trust. People who are going to give you constructive criticism, because you need it, you know? If somebody is just like, it's great you're so good, that doesn't serve you at all—you need the person that's going to be like, this doesn't work try something different, or that sounds too much like this.

So just really being open and being willing to collaborate is really important, and it's hard because this is something coming from you, coming from your heart and your soul and there were a lot of days that I'm like this just sucks I'm never going to be able to do this, and then there were other days that I'm just like I totally got this. It's just remembering that each day is going to be different. Because it is live theatre and it's different every time. But if you can really just let yourself be vulnerable and commit to telling the story that's really, that's it.

KYLA KAZUSCHYK: That's the crux of it. I'm so excited for all of this, everything that you've said. I know you're speaking from an acting creating directing perspective. It applies to everything, everything you just said, I could tell my costume students to think about their costume designs, it truly applies to everything. Finding your group and finding feedback and collaborating. That ties into devised theatre and theatre as a whole that like, we're not creating studio art, we're not existing in a vacuum or not by ourselves in our studio. And if we are, then we need to get out and find more people, because the whole point of it is how it connects with other people and how other people are going to take away from what we're putting out there.

ANDREA MORALES: Absolutely, and I think that that's one thing that has been so challenging during this time of pandemic because we haven't had that connection to each other. It hasn't quite felt the same. And I know for a lot of people, even though I'm an extrovert there's something that's kind of become oddly comforting about being in your little space, and so the idea of kind of putting yourself back out there is challenging. But we still need this connection and it might feel uncomfortable at first to be having a zoom conversation with someone but really it's good to just connect and maybe step outside our comfort zone a little bit, and realizing that it is possible to create theatre over zoom, to share moments. My parents twenty-fifth anniversary was over zoom, my mom retired over zoom, my best friend just had a baby, we had a beautiful shower over zoom. So yeah, it's weird yeah it's a little awkward the internet sucks sometimes and you can't connect and you can't hear, there's the person that loves to leave their mic on when you're trying to talk, or they're like laying in bed while you're trying to teach. But all of that, much like theatre, much like devised theatre, you figure out solutions, you figure out ways to make your existence in this little box successful. You figure out the ways that this box does not confine you and that you can reach through and connect with someone else during these weird times. And I think as artists that's one of the reasons that we have excelled in this virtual world because, even though it is not necessarily comfortable or not necessarily familiar, we're still able to imagine what it might be. We have these great imaginations as artists. I mean just the idea that we can change our world from, yes technically we're staring at a screen, but what else could it be? And I think for me that's the biggest thing with devising, is remembering how much fun it is to just imagine what else could this be.

KYLA KAZUSCHYK: Can you talk a little bit more about how you approached costumes for devising? You talked about using pieces as inspiration and being flexible.

ANDREA MORALES: I think that one of the things I love about devising most is the idea that something that I'm not necessarily savvy in like costume design or set design I suddenly have a lot of freedom to play and to get advice from designers out there who can help blow things open. As far as costumes and some of the work that I've done there, what I tried working with at the very beginning of my piece was just the idea that I was just going to be in a T-shirt and yoga pants. And the idea that what would happen if I added a costume piece that was simple like just a scarf that could become a wrap, a tie, a headscarf, that kind of thing. And even though that was eventually something that I ended up cutting from my piece, because I think I was getting a little too clumsy with it, the idea of creating my characters, using different costume pieces to kind of train me was very helpful. I had a character who wore glasses and so I tried rehearsing it like putting the glasses on taking the glasses off to be the different character. And that wasn't really working, but the idea of having the costume piece there to help me explore what is it like physically when the glasses come down on the nose and then they go back up if you're when you're using the glasses versus not. I think, having the piece of fabric to kind of create different things helped me find physically different levels to characters that I wasn't sure how that was going to work. With costumes it was such an incredible thing because, even though I ended up, I wore a Bears jersey, because I was in Chicago, but I did wear yoga pants, the idea that I could kind of put on my little server apron in certain scenarios and then I'm a server and then take it off. That really was my only costume piece that I had. But having the flexibility to play with the pieces and having them morph from costume pieces into props into set decoration, that was something I did use a lot in the devising process of what if there's clothes everywhere, what if what if Izzy's just a messy character and there are clothes everywhere, so there were a couple times I went into the devising room and just threw clothes everywhere and tried, what if I'm putting this on as this person and again, even though I didn't necessarily end up doing that for my final project, I might someday go back and actually utilize that because I love the idea of being able to add a piece take it off and become someone else quickly.

I have always been an actor that feels like my character isn't complete until I know exactly what they would be wearing, whether I'm literally wearing it or if I've kind of tried it on in pieces, and so I know what it represents to me. Character like that is something that is so important. And I think one of the things I would like to do as a next step for my piece, which has been, I've been looking at it here and there during quarantine, but I would love to have a costumer come in and like tell me how does it work better, does it work better with the costume pieces, does it work better without, what can you use to make this character more clear when you're playing this character, do you need a costume piece, do you not need a costume piece? So being able to have that collaboration with someone I think would be really helpful because, since we were kind of on our own, and we didn't really have a design team that's something that I didn't really, everybody who was looking at me for this piece was more looking at it from the acting perspective, and I would have loved to have a little bit of feedback on what else I could do.

But one of the best experiences I had at LSU, and this was not my devised piece, but this was when we did *Airline Highway*. Because I was playing, originally, an ensemble member, and it was so refreshing to walk into the room and to have, you asked me, well tell me about your character, tell me who this person is. And it's almost like the clothes found us. You were like, I have this, and this, and this. And then, when we found it, I was like, there she is, there's my character, that's exactly who I've been wanting to be. And so I think if we were to jump back to devised theatre is there a way to collaborate with someone who maybe just has five or six things on a rack, maybe some of them aren't even clothes, maybe there is just a big long piece of China silk or something, and how can we take that and how does it evolve the story and the character?

My husband hated what I wore for my thesis project. He's like why did you wear a jersey, that was so literal, that was so, I don't understand why you did that. I'm like I didn't have a costume designer! And he's like well clearly it was like hey but.

KYLA KAZUSCHYK: It sets the scene: it's the Bears, you're in Chicago.

ANDREA MORALES: Exactly! I thought it worked for what it was. But I think that, so much of the time, particularly working in smaller companies and things like that, the idea of really taking the time with the costume designer to really figure out who you are and what your clothing says about you sometimes gets skipped over. Not always, but sometimes it does and it's weird but I will always remember my *Airline Highway* experience because of that, and because when I got put into a different character Emma did the same thing, it was like let's take a look, let's find what feels good for you here.

And only one other show that I've done in the last couple of years, do I remember that was the same thing, and that was when I did *Native Gardens* at Southern Rep. I was playing a character who was pregnant and the costume designer was just like, Okay you're out gardening and you're eight months pregnant, of these things here what is calling to you? And I'm like those stretchy pants, yeah. So let's put those on and let's see. So the idea that in a devised piece, you have the freedom to go so many different ways and if you incorporate into your process having just pieces, even if it's just different pieces of fabric. How does that change you as your character? How does that shift your transitions? Because often in devised pieces you're playing different characters. Several of us in my MFA cohort were playing different characters in their pieces and some of them are really clear and some of them are a little muddied. And so I'm wondering what it could have been if we'd had some more time to really put in that extra layer of the costuming into that, because having that freedom to design is also such an amazing thing, and it can really shape the piece in a completely different and beautiful way. And I think that my piece would have benefited from that and I think several other people could have really benefited from the idea of what happens if I try this just to see, same as you would with a line of dialogue, what if I tried this, well that didn't work, what if I try this fabric, oh suddenly I realized, Oh, I feel very different with this it changes my posture changes my characterization. What happens if I go even further and try another piece? Having the ability to have pieces of costuming that you don't exactly know where it's going to go, it doesn't have to be the finished piece, it doesn't have to be beautifully tailored but where is it going to lead you as far as your character's journey? And I think that that is so cool because again with devised theatre you don't always know where you're going to end up and that allows us freedom as artists, freedom as designers to be like, I don't know what's going to happen, but let's find out.

KYLA KAZUSCHYK: I agree, I think there's so much more room for collaboration with the MFA thesis project. There's room for more experiences for everybody. I'm so glad that you had a good experience on *Airline Highway*. I had so much fun creating those characters with y'all and creating those costumes. Though none of us intended for it to be a such an exercise in flexibility, this is what theatre is, like you say like improv, devising, that's what it prepares us for. No one could have known at the beginning of that process where your role was going to go. And then it did, and we had to be ready for that and I'm so proud of Emma that she was ready for that, to handle that and to work on that with you and that y'all arrived at something that wasn't where any of us planned, but we got there together.

ANDREA MORALES: It was incredible and I've got to point out your research that you did with that, and I mean it was such a gift that we were so close to New Orleans. Your photos that you had even before we started the process at the very first read through where we had the designer presentations looking at all those different people because New Orleans is just such an amazing plethora of characters and color and design and mixed patterns and all and all of it, so I mean even just looking at those pictures there, I was like, Oh that's interesting, all that's really cool, oh that makes me think of this character. And having the flexibility to kind of play within that is such a gift. Because there are also the processes where you go in and they're like, this is what you're wearing and you're like, Oh, but it feels like this and they're like, great, bye and that's the end of that. I feel that it is so much more rewarding when you have that collaboration. I walked out of our fitting the first time with you and I'm like, I love my costume. I love it. I love my costume, I'm so excited. And that's a great place to be as an actor. It's like that was the missing piece, now that I have the shoes and the dress I know it's gonna blow things open and it did, it totally did. And it really didn't take that much, it took you and me having a ten-minute conversation and then maybe a 20-minute fitting that completely changed everything. So it's the idea of if we just take the time to collaborate, we can create some of the most beautiful things out of that, and really realize that we're working together, that the costumer and the actor and the director and everybody, we are a team. It's not just like, Oh hey stupid actor put on this this costume or hey look what the costume designer, but rather having the freedom to have those conversations, having the freedom to say these shoes are super cute I'm never going to be able to wear these for two hours without feeling uncomfortable. Feeling comfortable to say that, not feeling like a diva, or not feeling like, Oh I just broke the costume designer's heart by saying that. I'm always like I don't want to hurt anybody's feelings, if they've done all this work, and then two hours later, my feet are bleeding and I'm like ,you should have said something. So just having the freedom in the collaborative space to feel safe to say what about this.

The thing they teach us in improv is, of course, "yes and." "Yes and" I will do this. But I think as we're moving forward in this world where, because consent is becoming so much more important on so many levels, it's also okay to say "no, but." So the idea of "no I don't think I can wear those shoes, but that other pair you have is super cute and I would love to try these on." Or "no, I can't wear these

FIGURE 4.8 *To start research for* Airline Highway, *a show about people living in New Orleans, I walked around the streets of New Orleans and took pictures of people. I printed the photos and brought them to design meetings, rehearsals, and fittings to communicate about what sorts of costume pieces we could use to represent characters*

shoes right now, but maybe we can stretch them if you really love the look of them." Having that willingness and flexibility with each other. Because I think that consent is something now that we're really focused on in the theatre world in a way that we haven't. Finally. It's about time. But that's not just about the consent to work the stage kiss a certain way, it's also what do I feel comfortable doing in rehearsal, what do I feel comfortable saying to my collaborators.

And finding that balance of wanting to do everything and be open and also saying I really truly don't feel comfortable doing this, but I'd be willing to try this. Creating that compromise, I think, is so important, and I think that compromise is the nature of collaboration anyway, or it should be. And when you're working on a devised piece, being able to compromise is huge, because you might not be able to have the stage lights that you were hoping to have in the situation or you might have a hard 25-minute limit on the 40-minute show that you wrote. So how do you scale it back? Being able to make sure that everyone in the room, not just you, but everyone in the room feels comfortable, feels safe, and beyond feeling safe feels confident in what they're doing. That was something that I think I heard at Statera, which is the idea that you're not just feeling comfortable with doing something, because I can say, to feel comfortable doing that I feel comfortable, but do you feel confident in doing that is different. Do you feel confident wearing this dress on stage for two hours, do you feel confident in letting him massage your arm? And having the flexibility for you to say you know what I feel comfortable with it, but maybe we could try something else, because I don't feel really confident right now with this, like I can try it, but if there's something else we can try, what would that look like.

KYLA KAZUSCHYK: It's like you said about imagination, having the imagination to visualize something beyond the given circumstances. Does it have to be this or can you imagine something different than this.

FIGURE 4.9 Characters in costume on stage in *Airline Highway*, inspired by the people of New Orleans and developed in close collaboration with the performers

ANDREA MORALES: We've had to do that. I had to do that this fall. Because with Covid, there could be no touching and yet we were doing a little showcase and there had to be a moment of intimacy where my actors had to be six feet apart and masked. I was like well how do we do this, and we did it with sort of just like we kind of created this weird interpretive dance, and there was like a reaching moment, and it was like everybody else on stage kind of like softly froze so you just saw the two of them do a reach. So it was kind of a weird moment, but I think the audience was able to understand they have a connection.

KYLA KAZUSCHYK: I appreciate your ideas and your perspective so much. You have been able to articulate a lot of the stuff that I've been thinking but haven't been able to articulate. Thank you.

ARTIST SPOTLIGHT: NATHAN YNACAY

Nathan Ynacay has designed and built costumes and scenery for a range of scripted and devised works. Here, he identifies some challenges with collaborative art.

NATHAN YNACAY: I think that devised theatre is, on paper, putting together a show from a singular concept and then using collaboration to further the concept into a fully realized piece. And then I started thinking about what exactly is devised theatre in and of itself and it's like there are 15,000 categories of what devised theatre is.

New works being created through rehearsing is certainly devised theatre. Nathan also points to musicals that start with an idea, like *Company*, or Sondheim's exercise in writing an entire musical in three quarter time and coming up with *A Little Night Music* as including devised aspects. Nathan and I worked together on costumes for a show called *LMNOP: A New Muzical*, where we employed many lessons of flexibility learned from devising and improvising.

NATHAN YNACAY: Improv exercises that become theatrical things are also devised theatre pieces, even improv itself is like literally devised theatre pieces that are happening. So I think that all of these things kind of use the same set of skills to come up with a theatre piece. It's just when you are actually doing a full devised theatre, we have like a sentence or an idea that we are striving for, and we are going to come up with this while we are actually in the rehearsal process, that uses 100 percent all of the skills that you would need for these other types of devised pieces. It's just whether you're using it like 100 percent or if you have a script to begin with. Even *LMNOP* because we didn't have the music until halfway into the process, and it's a musical. That's definitely like, we don't know what this thing is going

Know Your Resources **87**

FIGURE 4.10 *Costumes are key to telling stories, especially in unscripted work, as seen in Nathan Ynacay's The Three Fates (photo courtesy of Nathan Ynacay)*

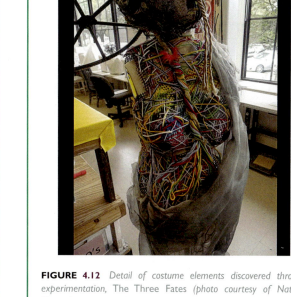

FIGURE 4.12 *Detail of costume elements discovered through experimentation, The Three Fates (photo courtesy of Nathan Ynacay)*

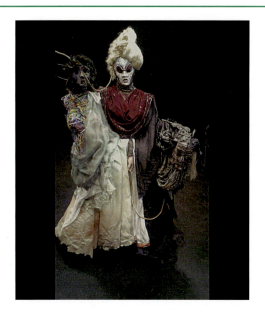

FIGURE 4.11 *Inspired by the story of the Three Fates, Nathan devised and created this combination costume/mask/wig/puppet using a variety of materials and techniques. Without a script, the movement of the artist in the costume is what drives the performance (photo courtesy of Nathan Ynacay)*

to sound like so we don't know if the images are going to clash. So when we did finally get those images, it answered a ton of questions about the opening number and how that scene actually would move around in the story.

Maybe the question of what is devised is how much do we know and how much are we filling in, and then how flexible does it need to be.

Nathan worked on a version of Dracula that involved many flexible elements. The timeline for the project was extended multiple times, often pushed back because of the global pandemic and eventually taking several months from inception to production. The third draft of the finished script included 90 pages of dialogue, a cast of 15, and a budget of $2000 for the whole show. To save money, Nathan sourced pieces from thrift stores and built costumes out of his own supply of fabrics. As ideas evolved and characters changed, Nathan drew stacks of renderings to communicate ideas to the team. "I've done 50 drawings of costumes and it's like the drawings are the goal to strive for, but it's going to be super flexible."

Members of the company working on Dracula take on multiple roles of acting, designing, choreographing, producing, and writing. When doubling up on positions like that, it can be a challenge to step back and see the big picture of what is working and what is not possible. And, when responsibilities of each position are unclear, the process can get frustrating. A big opportunity for excellence in Dracula is the use of blood, especially for a piece that will be performed outdoors, in a space without laundry facilities. There are many possible solutions to how

FIGURE 4.13 *An early draft rendering of Mina, created as the script and the character developed (photo courtesy of Nathan Ynacay)*

FIGURE 4.14 *A sketch used to communicate ideas for a costume Nathan would build for Mina to wear in the promotional photo shoot for Dracula, which took place before the script for the show was written (photo courtesy of Nathan Ynacay)*

to depict blood onstage, but a decision as to how the team is going to do it must be made early on so that costumes can know how to move forward.

NATHAN YNACAY: Part of it is that they're wearing too many hats, the other part of it is that they don't understand what it takes to maintain that. And they also have said before, like, Oh it's our aesthetic for things to get dirty and grimy and we like that. But that's not how that works. Every show should have the same visual impact, so if someone is covered in blood at the very beginning of the show then blood is no longer significant in the show. And it's just them not understanding that yes, costumes and scenery also is artistry, it isn't just we're giving you a playset to play on, we are also telling a story and making carefully chosen choices.

If members of the production team are involved in conversations earlier on in the process, it would be easier for everyone to be on the same page of what are the parameters of what is achievable.

The question of how performers will move in their costumes, and how important is it that costumes represent accurate period silhouettes is another question that needs to be answered as early on as possible. Should they wear corsets, or do they need to be able to crawl around on the ground?

NATHAN YNACAY: Well, either you want total movement or you want some movement, but you cannot ask me, as someone being paid a very small amount, to be able to give you the world without justifying it. Like, unless you can point to the script and say at this scene I'm going to do a backbend, at this scene I'm going to do this. I've asked the choreographer things like that, and finally she was like oh yeah at the end of Act Two Lucy is going to be held up by her legs like a stuck pig by Dracula. And I was like, Okay you're wearing a nightgown, your who-ha is going to be hanging out. So after that conversation I was like, Okay, so I guess we need like a combination under there. She gave me a very specific moment, I can plan for that. That is a great example of you telling me what you need and me being able to provide for it. But it is unfair, unless we have the facility and the people. You can't ask us to give you gymnastic level ability to move or you're just going to get T-shirts, at which point I don't want that on my resume.

I think that there's a theory of collaboration and devised theatre. But there's still a problem in that the directors and the people that are devising the piece don't understand what the technicians or the designers, what our job entails. So there's not any consideration for any of that. So because they don't know what our job is, they make choices that affect us in negative ways without considering that we are going to have to work on this as well. We understand the devised nature of theatre, we understand that it's a strain. But you're making very difficult choices that because it's devised theatre it could be thought of in another way. And then, sometimes in my experience they've never felt the need to explain it when

Know Your Resources 89

FIGURE 4.15 *Promotional photo for a devised and immersive interpretation of Dracula, set in a vineyard in rural Oregon. Costume designed and constructed by Nathan Ynacay (photo courtesy of Nathan Ynacay)*

FIGURE 4.16 *One of many renderings Nathan drafted based on the source material for the Dracula project. He used sketches to express ideas about the characters as they evolved (photo courtesy of Nathan Ynacay)*

FIGURE 4.17 *A fitting for a bride of Dracula, trying out ideas in the performance space (photo courtesy of Nathan Ynacay)*

FIGURE 4.18 *Costumes for the brides of Dracula eventually evolved into a mix of distressed layers (photo courtesy of Nathan Ynacay)*

I ask them or when I challenge them on it. Like, why is the dripping necessary in this blood? Why the dripping element? You want the splash, so if I'm telling you that it won't show up, do you want the splash or do you want the visual impact of gore? And then them choosing the splash because it feels good as the performer, it gets them in the mood for the scene. And they're the ones with the power in this situation because they're also the producer and the directors and I don't think they understand how much work goes into things.

The scenery has gone through like, five different looks and because it's a wandering theatre production in a vineyard, the space is 1000 feet by 500 feet, and so they're like, the world is our oyster so they wrote in seven locations. And then they go, this is a lot why did you design so much, and I'm like, because that's what you wrote. Maybe don't write in a carriage. They have Dracula in the castle at one point and then Jonathan Harker runs to one door, it's locked, then runs to the next, it's locked. He runs through a third, he turns around and says, all the doors are locked I can't get out. And it's like, you want three doors. If we are devising and writing things ourselves, why not write things that are achievable?

I think a lot of healthy collaboration comes down to humility and how we teach humility and empathy and it's baffling that the whole point of us being theatre artists is empathy—that is like our main thing. As designers or performers or directors, how is it possible to compartmentalize enough and put that aside and not actually practice empathy for each other, where does that get lost?

NATHAN YNACAY: I think it gets lost because the emphasis has always been on what they see, so the performer and the direction. Like even like the size of names of people on playbills—like they'll put the producer at the very top. Why not just do alphabetical with a blurb of what their job is or even like I feel weird about separating producers, technicians, whatever, actors, why not put everyone's name at the bottom of the thing like a high school production.

Especially thinking about it in terms of devised theatre, if the whole point is that we're collaborating and we're wearing lots of hats, why are we still bringing our egos from all of our silos into it? How is it possible to let go of that and to emphasize with each other and understand that we're all doing a lot and trying a lot and dealing with a pandemic and dealing with the stress of the limitations of the budget on top of everything.

And it comes down to storytelling too, what does it take to tell the story, and what do we need to tell this story? Do we need to wear corsets, or do we need to bend at the waist?

Devising is not perfect. I can see the idea in theory of what's cool about it, but then in practice we need to answer the question of how people are treated, how we can treat each other fairly, and how we can create productions. And it expands to all kinds of theatre. We need to be treating everyone with equity, no matter what, whether it's scripted or devised, and we can't overlook that.

Sometimes people are short-sighted. People have a hard time seeing beyond their own ego and beyond what's in front of them and seeing things from other people's points of view, which also, shouldn't be what theatre is doing for us. When I watch a work of theatre, I can see other people's point of view. So why can't we as we're going into creating a work of theatre really think about how much time and effort and labor and legwork other people are putting in to create the dreamy dreams that we're dreaming up?

Before Dracula, this company created a production called *Neverland*, which was a version of the story of Peter Pan. Audiences got up and walked seven times to different locations throughout a vineyard as the story unfolded around them.

NATHAN YNACAY: It was interesting, but it was long. It was very, very long and there were so many locations and there could have been so many cuts that happened to it. And I think the cuts didn't happen because the people that were writing it weren't the ones watching it because they were in it.

So they said at the beginning of Dracula that they were going to reduce it, and they did, to their credit. But we never had feedback from *Neverland* from the producer and the technicians of like here's our post mortem and here are things that happened with this and how you can improve. So they didn't correct some of the issues that they could have corrected if they had the information. So we still have seven locations and talking to them about like, even requesting things of like, hey format wise, the script has 50 scenes—can you go ahead and separate them by day? Like, these clusters of scenes are all in one day or one evening, page break. And the writer was like, well we don't want to think about that, while writing. And I was like, Okay, well, you need to understand if the story centers around a creature that only comes out at night, you need to know when day and night is. And then also like you don't have to think about this, but the next script you write, if it's this important to distinguish between day and night you're going to need time for people to change. So you need to build in lines that are like, "oh, I'll go change" or like, "I'm off to bed, I will go change," or something like that to justify them walking off the stage and coming back on. Or don't acknowledge it but be aware that this logistical thing has to happen because physics.

It can be frustrating when all the power in the room is given to the director. If everyone on the team is just in service to the director, this is not actual collaboration. There is room for actual collaboration, though. And there is room for other forms, stories told in new ways, stories told by puppets, led by costumes. We have just scratched the surface of what is possible with online theatre.

NATHAN YNACAY: I did costumes for one zoom show which was a conversation between God and two angels, a Jewish angel and a Christian angel, talking about Covid safety or something. It was basically a PSA for like wash your hands. It was early zoom theatre. We now have eras within zoom theatre, what a wild time to be alive. It was a PSA propaganda-type feel of like stay six feet apart, wash your hands, very topical. I underestimated the creativity of blocking. They told me that they were just going to do from the bosom up and I was like but I can give you more and they were like but we're just doing from the bosom up, and I was like Okay, and then I did design a fully realized top for the angel, the Christian angel was like a nun. And then for the Jewish angel, it was more antiquity, or whatever. And they didn't do any interesting blocking and it was like, Oh okay, that's boring, to sit and stare at the camera. That one was okay, but it was also just people sitting and talking at each other.

It comes down to all these questions like who holds the power and how are they going to use that power. And how much power does each of us hold? How can we set boundaries that protect our art and our own safety?

NATHAN YNACAY: I'm trying to be more honest with theatre companies. Just, I don't know, just calling out wildness sometimes is hard. I understand power structures and stuff but I'm trying to find a better way of just constantly reminding people of like, no, if you don't know how it gets put together and you just expect me to do it, that's not how that happens. And that's not how that's going to happen.

And I also told them, considering the pay, and I'm not saying this because I'm embittered about the lack of payment, what I'm doing is making sure that you understand that you have had the power to write this show. If you gave us time to actually collaborate on it, we could have put together a really cool show, with only ten people. But you didn't include us in that process, so no, this wasn't a collaborative effort. And also you all aren't paying us enough to do this and you don't have the infrastructure to do this. We will try to attempt something, but you need to start looking at designers and technicians as the experts and asking us if something is possible, and when we say no, respecting that.

It's going to take a lot for the whole culture to shift, but I think that the more that we can do to speak up for ourselves, and to speak up for each other and to point out inequities and to point out when things are unfair and to point out when things are impossible. And on the flip side to that, also listening to and accepting other people's suggestions, then maybe that's going to create a culture of everyone listening to everyone's suggestions eventually.

NATHAN YNACAY: Early conversations, even if they're hard conversations. Sit down and think through it. During Dracula they've been telling me like, Oh, the book is available, we're doing devised work, you should read the book. That's 400 pages from a dead white guy. I'm no longer interested in putting my time and effort into reading classical pieces of literature. I'm willing to read the greatest illustrated classics version that will take me a day to get through. You're asking us to read this novel instead of the script because you haven't finished adapting the script and we're also doing a ton more research for the visual elements, like that's on top of other stuff. They have a dramaturg so that should be a portion of their job. They don't understand what a dramaturg is actually supposed to do.

Realize that people's time is important so let's front load some of the work into the heavy thought process. It cannot just be in the room, or if it is in the room process, for the sake of design and for a limited budget, you need to give them just these 15 elements and say like, hey we don't have the time and effort to be able to do this amount of work, we can give you two custom pieces from your devised thing, depending on how big it is. And we can give you access to anything in our house. And it's like it gives you freedom but it still involves rules. The rule of gravity still applies during theatre, everyone. Physics still applies during theatre. Financial constraints still apply for theatre. And time constraints. We live in a physical world, we need to plan in a physical world. We cannot plan in an ethereal plane. And that's the advice I would give to people and that's also for producing heads of like, yes, we know that it's difficult to sit through long meetings, but like, let's sit through long meetings. I heard of a process where the designers read the script together and talked about the process. That is an example of collaborative theatre where it's like, yes, I know that not everyone wants to sit through a meeting, but I would love to sit through a meeting like that.

The realities of racism and sexism are at play in the dynamics between us as collaborators. What is safe or easy for one person may not be comfortable or even safe for someone else. Nathan describes working with a director who was especially patient with all collaborators:

NATHAN YNACAY: During the conversation with the director, I definitely asked her about things, and she was saying, like part of the way she talks with designers and stuff is because of being a female-bodied person in theatrical spaces and being the one with power, her being questioned by actors of like, why are you in this room. Like just dealing with sexism in general, so she has learned how to taper responses and like how bad it feels to be treated poorly so it's I'm not going to treat people poorly now. And I think I try to implement that but it doesn't happen all the time.

There are so many variables. Dealing with a pandemic is real, this is real trauma that we're all going through and everyone is processing and we're not equipped to process it, this is unprecedented times and it's making everyone's patience lessen and making it harder to deal with each other. And I would also add to that that part of what's missing is the best parts of theatre, like being in a room and seeing something happen on stage and having that exchange of energy between the audience and the performers—we haven't had that in over a year now.

NATHAN YNACAY: Yeah I'm not a fan of devised theatre anymore. I would much rather have carefully planned theatre with themes."

ARTIST SPOTLIGHT: EMMA ARENDS MONTES

Emma Arends Montes has used principles of devising in her work designing and building costumes for dance, for scripted theatre performed in person, scripted theatre on zoom, and in teaching classes and supervising wardrobe teams and costume shops. Here, she discusses ways to use the resources you have to truly communicate and collaborate with people.

KYLA KAZUSCHYK: The more research I do, the more I realize, everything is devised. Many of the projects that we worked on might not have been labeled as devised theatre but we kind of were devising. And the first one that comes to mind that you've worked on is your designs for dance. Can you talk to me about your process designing for dance and how you do research, how you approach creating the costumes, how you work with choreographers, all that stuff.

EMMA ARENDS: What an interesting project that was. The main challenge, well it wasn't even a challenge, because everyone was so great, but there were 11 different choreographers and they all had their own specific image of what that dance would look like and what they wanted their dancers to look like, which is great. I think that's probably the best thing to have is a clear vision of what you want. Because if you don't have that, it's chaos, it's absolutely bonkers. But everyone I worked with had a pretty clear image about what they wanted and what they didn't want. I joined them in rehearsal to see how the dances were going and it just so happened to be the only time that anyone could meet whatever that's fine, I will join you there. And really I just went in with an open mind. There was nothing set, there was nothing that said it has to be this way because of xyz reason. Everything was open. So just going in with an open mind and listening to what people want and thinking about things that were feasible. There were some things that I was like I don't know exactly how we're going to achieve that but that's okay, we don't need to figure it out right in that second. Just being open and being like, Oh okay like maybe we could do this, maybe we can't I don't know.

And then, after those initial meetings with all the other choreographers, I created collages. Actually before then, I asked them if they had a specific image in mind so if a certain leotard comes to mind, or a certain image, I asked them to email me that image and after I took that image, I did a ton of more research for similar images or whatever the emotions that they were telling me.

One of the ones that I distinctly remember is from "Black and White" by Todrick Hall, which is a fantastic song. The main thing that the choreographer really wanted was a transformation. He wanted something that was black and white and seemed very structured at that time, and he wanted to change it into something colorful and something flamboyant and luscious. So I took that and I made a collage of black leotards with white fishnets and white other things, but then also took those same white fishnet skirts and found them in color and came up with this idea that we can mix these so there's color within the white.

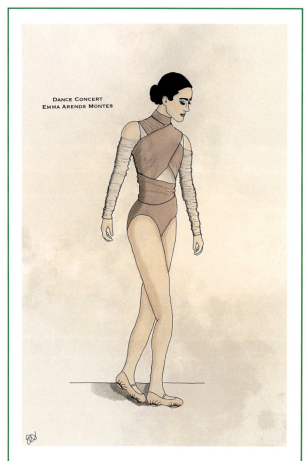

FIGURE 4.19 *Rendering by Emma Arends Montes, freelance costume designer and technician (photo courtesy of Emma Arends Montes)*

And then we can create a quick change for the dancers. It started up, as straps, and then the straps would be white up above and they had epaulettes and when they released them, they would come down into a skirt and they would be all colorful.

So with these collages and this idea in mind, I brought it back to the choreographer. He loved it, he was like that's so great like I think the one thing he didn't want was like I think one of the leos had pants and he was like I don't want that, and I was like, Okay that's fine no pants.

I did that with pretty much all the choreographers. I did in-depth research into every dance and went to the rehearsal and it helped with the collages and the ideas of what we could do, and then having that second meeting with the choreographers and trying to set that up.

And then moved on to the next project, which was to create renderings for these costumes that would be the final product and seeing what worked best for everybody. And that's kind of where it ended with Covid.

FIGURE 4.20 *Rendering by Emma Arends Montes, freelance costume designer and technician (photo courtesy of Emma Arends Montes)*

FIGURE 4.21 *Rendering by Emma Arends Montes, freelance costume designer and technician (photo courtesy of Emma Arends Montes)*

I made these collages and then I made the renderings and then I ended up bringing it back to the choreographers with the renderings and saying this is kind of my final thoughts about what this could look like and also still not married to any idea, nothing was precious at this point, anything could be changed at any point in time. One of the big things was one of the choreographers totally changed her mind about what she wanted midway. And I was like, that's fine, we can make something else. I was going to go back and make another rendering and then Covid happened so that didn't matter anyway.

I think the other big change was that I did a rendering for "Elephant Wars," the big group number, which I don't think we ever decided if I was going to make anything, or if I was just giving them this collage and then they would have to go find stuff. Which is also part of devised theatre, being able to say okay when do I take control and where do I let people have their own creativity and claim it for themselves.

And then, in that rendering I put boots on the girl, and they were like nobody's wearing shoes and I'm like, Okay, no one wears shoes, I guess. I guess let's just make sure the floor is super swept and nothing's on the floor.

KYLA KAZUSCHYK: I really admire how you're able to make choices and come up with ideas and let go of them so easily. I think that that's something that stops a lot of designers in their tracks, that they're like, this is my only idea, it has to be this! And then when they're thrown for a curveball as if, like well we're not wearing shoes well this doesn't work, then they're not able to quickly think of something instead. And that's one of the things that I really am impressed by with your work that you're like, Okay that doesn't work well let's move on to the next thing. You're able to take changes in stride and just come up with something else.

EMMA ARENDS: I think my time at LSU taught me that. I was definitely not that way in the beginning. I don't think I was at all, I think there were some things that I was like, No, this is the way it has to be, this is the way that things must go. But, over time, I was just like, no it doesn't, no. It doesn't have to be that way in order for it to be good.

I think, particularly with *Diary of Anne Frank*, I remember being like it needs to be historical, it needs to look a certain way, or we're not doing it justice or blah blah blah and then yeah that was all over the place, not on just my end. I learned to just let it go and realize that every production is going to be different.

KYLA KAZUSCHYK: It truly is and I'm glad you brought up Anne Frank. I was your advisor on that project, and I remember guiding you towards like, this is *The Diary of Anne Frank*, it's a play about history, do your research about who Anne Frank was, who Nazi soldiers were, what they wore, what women wore at that time in history, what men wore at that time in history. Do your specific costume research. We were going into that not as if it's a dance about elephants or it's a dance about black and white, it's not a devised piece about the actors' ideas, it's about a girl who lived.

And you did that research and you brought it in to the director and the director said no. We never could have anticipated that. I remember that being such a challenge because I also was coming to that with the idea that this is a period piece, this is about specific people who lived in history. We want to do them justice by depicting them accurately and I thought it would be a good experience for you as a graduate student to really look at 1940s silhouettes but the director really threw us for a curve.

EMMA ARENDS: She did. I mean, I think we still achieved the goal of having 1940s silhouettes, kind of. Not 100 percent.

KYLA KAZUSCHYK: Do you remember how the director explained her concept? Because you came with that initial research, and then how did she explain what she wanted to do with the show?

EMMA ARENDS: We had one meeting and we were like, Okay, this is the game plan we're going to say, do you want dance wear, do you want street wear, because those are going to be two different things, and we need to accommodate for actors, we need to figure that out now. And she did not have a clear image at all. She was like, I kind of want it to look like street wear, but I want it to be movable like dancewear. And I also want it to have the silhouette of the 1940s, but not clothes from the 1940s. And we all were like, what does that mean?

Thank God for Modcloth I guess, because that's kind of what we ended up doing and then also I remember the colors were kind of all over the place. I remember her talking about how she likes a distinct color palette but not boring, so it couldn't be just like four colors, I think I ended up choosing six. And then also she did not want Nazis, but there were Nazis. And then, for a split second there was a cat. And we were all trying to figure out who the cat was and what the cat is. Do we need to dress somebody like a cat?

KYLA KAZUSCHYK: I could have never anticipated that would be our experience on *The Diary of Anne Frank*. I think this speaks to challenges. It's the challenge of working with a director. I have regrets about honoring the story in looking at what we did. But we did what we could with the collaborators that we had. And in that situation, the way it's set up is that the director has all the power and the director is at the top of the hierarchy and everyone else is just following the director wherever they go and the director is a little bit open to following other ideas. But it also comes to this idea of vision, which I think is such an interesting contrast. You talk about the dance choreographers you worked with. They had such specific vision that they could communicate to you. And in contrast, the director on Anne Frank, I think didn't know what her vision was.

EMMA ARENDS: I don't think she had a clear vision, the entire time.

KYLA KAZUSCHYK: I think that getting to Modcloth like you said was so helpful too, because that was visual images that the director could just say yes to, like, yes, I like those, the collage of images that you showed her from the Modcloth catalog. And that's what we provided and that's what we put on stage and it wasn't historically accurate, but it had that feel of the 1940s.

EMMA ARENDS: I can't believe we did that. Honestly, what a whirlwind.

KYLA KAZUSCHYK: I think looking at it in hindsight and thinking about what lessons you pulled away from it, if one of the things you're able to learn is how to let go of stuff I think that's really valuable. And I learned that too, because I had the idea that, no she has to look like the pictures we've seen of Anne Frank, she has to look like that. Well, if that's not what the director wants and the director is making the decisions, then we have to all let go of that even if it's not exactly what we agree with.

EMMA ARENDS: Correct. I mean I feel like there's like a level where you have to stop, like maybe if some things were really offensive. One image that comes back in my mind is the Nazi symbols which are important to the story, but she didn't want to put them in there and I don't think we ever ended up doing, but then we did decide that we were going to do the stars of David, which I'm glad we did that, because that actually is a representation of what happened.

KYLA KAZUSCHYK: It is interesting to think about who the audience is and what the audience is bringing with them, and like, why are we telling stories? Are we telling stories to educate students about history? Are we telling these stories to articulate things about history? Are we telling stories to resonate with students? I have a lot of unanswered questions there.

EMMA ARENDS: I do too. There are so many things that I don't think I will ever get a clear answer on and I guess that's okay. I learned that I need to let things go and how valuable a person is that has a clear vision. People that have clear visions and clear ideas of what they want, excellent. It is so much easier to collaborate.

When I worked at Stagedoor, I worked on a production of *Eurydice*. And the director who worked on that show had been wanting to do this show for years. And he had such a clear image of everything he wanted to look like. He wanted Eurydice to wear a red dress, he wanted a blue swimsuit on her, he wanted a clear water scene and like we had probably we had three different hour-long meetings solely about the water that's going to be hitting the costumes and the actors. It was a lot of talk about water but I'm very thankful for it because everybody knew what they were supposed to be doing, which is great. And then he had a really clear image of how he wanted the stones to look and he wanted them to look creepy but he wanted to look like they were having some sort of fun with it. And then, of course, like the three stones turned into six stones. With those images and that clear vision it was super easy, just to be like, Oh yeah we will put cheesecloth on these things, we got a bunch of black outfits and then they'll have creepy makeup and creepy hair and that was a great show.

KYLA KAZUSCHYK: Another project you designed was *Gloria*. How did you approach *Gloria* as far as devising ideas with the director and coming up with stuff and designing the costumes?

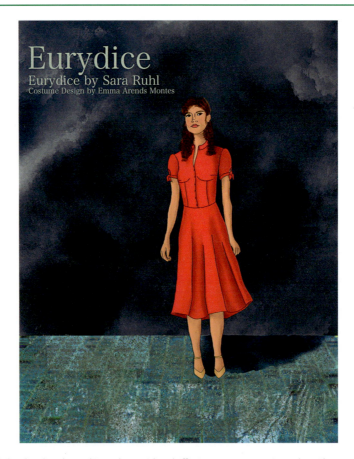

FIGURE 4.22 *If you are skilled at digital rendering, this can be a quick and effective way to communicate about ideas as they evolve. Rendering by Emma Arends Montes, freelance costume designer and technician (photo courtesy of Emma Arends Montes)*

EMMA ARENDS: The sacrificing on the show happened throughout the process. I remember one actor saying, "I want to change my costume entirely." And instead of just going in attacking and being like no absolutely not, we're not changing anything—it's way too late for that now, which it was, it was way too late for anything to change—I went into that situation with an open mind. It was the week of tech, it was very late in the game. And I'm glad I did come in with an open mind, because it turned out that this guy just wanted to tuck in his shirt and get glasses. And I was like, Sure okay here's your glasses and your tucked-in shirt. Because it went from a surfer dude to a nerdy dude I was like alright cool this is your character development and what you decided your character needs to be, I'm here to support you for it. Just maybe use different wording next time.

KYLA KAZUSCHYK: I think that this is a useful lesson too, that if the actors aren't happy, nobody's happy. If actors aren't comfortable in their bodies and in their clothes and in their makeup then it's going to be a problem for everybody, so you might as well work with the actors, rather than against them.

EMMA ARENDS: Oh, one thousand percent because if they're not comfortable in their things, or in their character, if you could help them, why not? Just do it, just help them.

KYLA KAZUSCHYK: Especially because most things are possible like you said, even if it's the last minute, like Okay what changes do you think you need, how can we accommodate those changes—let's figure it out.

EMMA ARENDS: It'd be different if I went in and he was like I don't like any of my clothes and they all need to change and then I'd probably be like no. It can't all change because we don't have time for them to change. I think that's also part of devised theatre, finding that balance of like, what do you stick to and like what do you throw away. It's always a dance, and I feel like the dance is also determined by time.

KYLA KAZUSCHYK: Thank you for putting that so clearly. I've been trying to put my finger on that, but it's definitely a balance, and it is always determined by time. Is this project open-ended or is opening night set and patrons have tickets and they're coming to see people wearing clothes? They have to be wearing something.

EMMA ARENDS: I think that's probably where devised theatre can get hairy because you don't always know when it's going to open. When you put that definite date on it it's kind of like this is when it's supposed to end. I mean granted with *Gloria* even into performances it changed, but there's only so much you can do after it's open.

KYLA KAZUSCHYK: Well, that leads me to another show that I want to ask you about your experience with that changed a ton after opening, which is *Airline Highway*.

EMMA ARENDS: I remember it being tech week and it being chaos.

KYLA KAZUSCHYK: Here's my perspective on *Airline Highway*. I designed the costumes for that show, and you were the wardrobe head. I finished the designs, worked with the actors, went to USITT (United States Institute of Theatre Technology) conference, left you in charge of it, got a call from you, so many things have changed, there have been cast changes, there's been actor changes, there's been character changes, what do I do? And I was so grateful to have you in that position because I had worked with you a bit and I trusted you to make decisions and I trusted you to look at the design of the show and be able to figure out, okay, this is the world, these are what the characters were, this is who the new character is, and let me work with this actor to figure out something for this character to wear. I am so impressed that you were able to do that. I'm so grateful that you were in charge of that.

EMMA ARENDS: It was such a tumultuous time too. Not only was it just these cast changes, but the reason behind it was just so gnarly. So it was an emotional time. It was an emotional time for everybody in the cast and crew. I really felt the need to step up and be like, Okay y'all if you want to be part of the show, and you want it to open you don't want these people to bring us down, we can do it, we can do this. We've done it before, we can do it again, it's going to be okay. And I just kind of reminded myself to have that kind of attitude, especially with the actors who have gone through this horrible thing. And just being very supportive, especially to Andrea who really killed it, she really killed the game on *Airline Highway*. I remember her distinctly because, like for the redesign of this, I guess, but not really. I just followed your advice.

KYLA KAZUSCHYK: It was an evolution. You evolved the design.

EMMA ARENDS: I just followed your advice of just finding outfits that I knew would fit Andrea and not putting any pressure on her necessarily but having her be able to be comfortable in her new role which was way bigger than what it was before and honestly, I think, better than what it was before.

And being like look I have these clothes and I have them in these kind of outfits so why don't you look through these things and see what your character would wear during this scene. You know what's happening in the scene, you know what your character is doing. I think it helped not only myself but it helped her build her

FIGURE 4.23 Airline Highway *on stage at Louisiana's Swine Palace, after multiple cast and character changes. As head of wardrobe crew, Emma collaborated with performers to style new outfits from racks of pieces pulled by the costume designer*

character more within a very short period of time, so I think that was super helpful. And I believe that helped with everybody who had to change roles. There were two or three other people that had to change too, to figure everything out. I remember that and watching that transformative experience of these actors and how cool it was just to be a part of that, I think that was probably one of the best experiences I had at LSU, was just like being able to be a part of it, and help people achieve a goal during a really tough time.

KYLA KAZUSCHYK: I'm so proud that you were able to take that away from that experience, because it was really tough, it was challenging and I'm so impressed that you were able to look at this as like, how can I help, how can I be sensitive to these actors and everyone who's working on this and what can I contribute to this that can help people to feel comfortable. That's awesome.

You also were sensitive to the integrity of the design, to the extent with which that is important. For me, as a designer I would have been fine with honestly whatever y'all figure out that works is okay, but you did think about what was my vision for the whole show and how to continue that and so I'm impressed with your sensitivity to everyone and your desire to help and that you are proud of helping. I'm also impressed with how quick thinking you were. It happened fast, the events went down, one cast member had to leave the show, and one cast member had to move into a different role, and then the ensemble had to shuffle around. But for Andrea, the cast member moving from ensemble into a main role, you had to find that stuff within a few hours in between your classes and the show laundry and all the other obligations you had of the day. You had to find time to pull stuff and put it together and then fit it on her and then put her on stage that night. You worked so quickly, you were able to pull so quickly, you were able to communicate with the actor so quickly and so efficiently and she was able to go on stage and tell the story. What a success!

EMMA ARENDS: Honestly, what a time. Well, and then also not only just helping the actors, but then with the crew and everything, that was bonkers, not only doing the supervising of this evolution of the design, but also the supervision of crew members who have to deal with this, things that they probably would never deal with, you know?

KYLA KAZUSCHYK: Was everyone else on the crew undergraduate students? Were you the only graduate?

EMMA ARENDS: I think so.

KYLA KAZUSCHYK: Yeah that was quite an experience but it's a good example too. I've talked to a lot of people so far about devised theatre and a lot of them are coming from the acting and performing and even directing mindset. And to a certain extent, yeah costumes can be just okay—pull something out of your closet and put it on, figure out. We can do that, but not always. And they're not necessarily attuned to figuring out designers and wardrobe crew and run crew and stage managers—all the other aspects of what's happening backstage to put a show on. I really value your perspective on this because you've had experience collaborating with all those different members and listening to their perspectives and being sensitive to them and really working together with all of them and helping them to work together.

EMMA ARENDS: With costumes, we're one of the main gateways between the technical realm and the performative realm. Because I just feel like, Okay, think about scenic wise, like how often do you have to collaborate with an actor about the way the stairs look or the way the stairs work? Never, you never have to do that. Same with lighting and sound and props even though perhaps I'll give it to them a little bit. But with costuming we interact with them way more than anybody else.

KYLA KAZUSCHYK: We work really closely with actors.

EMMA ARENDS: We work very closely with them, we know what they're thinking generally because for some strange reason we also give off this effect that, like we want to hear all your problems, right now, right here. We hear the problems, we hear the challenges, we hear the praises, we hear the development of the show as it's happening. So I feel like we have a very interesting perspective when it comes to doing designs and technical designs. And the performative acting director side, if that makes sense.

KYLA KAZUSCHYK: Totally and it's so true and I wondered about this myself too, why do actors feel so comfortable telling us so much? You work on a show, and maybe you're meeting these actors for the first time, and then you have a fitting with them and they often want to tell you their whole life story, everything that's going on with them. I wonder if it's connected to the vulnerability of changing clothes and taking their clothes off and putting different clothes on like they feel like we're instantly closer than we actually are.

EMMA ARENDS: I think that it has a lot to do with it, the intimacy of changing clothes and changing who you are and then also I feel like it has to do a lot, because we also do a lot of character analysis as designers so we both have this connection to the show, and to these characters and maybe they see that too, they're like, Oh, you get it, you understand me, I will tell you everything about my life.

KYLA KAZUSCHYK: I'm hoping to make the connection between collaborative processes in theatre and collaborative processes in the classroom and I've had the opportunity to work with you in both arenas. We've talked about the shows that we've worked on together and I'm interested in your perspective on the process of collaborative decision making in the classroom, the stuff that we practiced with maskmaking and with advanced stage makeup, what's your take on that? Do you think that you would take practices that we practiced and try them in your own classrooms? Do you think that they were effective? What do you think?

EMMA ARENDS: I personally enjoy it. I think it gives an opportunity to students to claim the class as their own being like, Oh, I really want to learn about this, this is what I want to do, and this is what I think we should do. I enjoy that part and I also like hearing other people's perspectives because while I'm like, yeah we should learn this, we should all write papers, because we're all going to write papers and everyone else is like, I don't want to write a paper and this is why, because I don't want to do research and I'm like, Well okay, but we still need to do research, so how about like a presentation, do you want to do a presentation? No, I just don't want to do research. Okay, well, I guess, I will do research, but you don't have to. It's things that you just really never think about until those challenges are there. Because we all have different perspectives and we all have different learning styles that I think are important to meet with our students and that's something I do take with me when I teach people—meeting people where they're at, rather than set these expectations that maybe that person can excel at.

So, I think that's important—however, I do also want to say, I think you did it well, in a sense that there were certain skills and goals that we needed to achieve, but there were different activities in order to achieve those goals. And I think that's where it could get dicey. It's similar in collaborative theatre, it's like if this person does not have a clear idea about what these goals need to be then it's going to be dicey. So I think that that could be a thing too, and maybe that's why we would end up with classes where people were like, well I don't care what we do and not have an opinion about anything because maybe they just weren't clear about what the goals or the skills that they're learning were.

KYLA KAZUSCHYK: Clarity of goals, that's important.

EMMA ARENDS: Because I bet if somebody was like, Okay well the goal of this project is to learn how to write a 25-page paper I bet people would be like huh that goal does not sound like what I want. Not that that would be one of the goals that's just like an example, but it's good to start somewhere, rather than starting at zero.

KYLA KAZUSCHYK: And figuring out what the shared goals of the community are. What are the goals of the group? What goals do you have that overlap with goals? Like if it's one person's goal to write a 25-page paper, but nobody else's, then maybe that's not going to work as a goal for the whole group.

EMMA ARENDS: Yeah exactly. And then also it's similar to like what is your learning style? Because everybody learns things differently. I'm a visual learner, I have to see you do it in order for me to understand how to do it. People like reading—maybe they're like I want to buy this book because this is the only way I'm going to learn how to do it.

KYLA KAZUSCHYK: Diversity of tactics with learning styles, that's key to education. And being sensitive to that too, being sensitive with everybody's different needs. Everyone's educational needs are going to be different.

EMMA ARENDS: Yes, one thousand percent and I think that's what I really pulled away in my teaching style is meeting people where they're at and then also understanding goals that we're all trying to achieve in this class or even production. The question is always like, what is the goal?

KYLA KAZUSCHYK: And if everyone's not on the same page for the goal, then how is it going to turn out? If it's one person's goal to make money off the production, but one person's goal is to do something weird and experimental that might not make money then it might not end well.

Another point that I'm interested in your perspective on is this idea of reciprocal mentorship. I think it is connected to meeting people where they're at. And it's something that I am trying to do. I think it's something I've been doing, but I'm trying to articulate what have I been doing and why is it important, and is there value to it.

I know a lot, but I just know different things than students know and if I am to approach our mentorship relationship with just being like, I'm just here to tell you everything I know and I don't care about what you know, I think that that is putting us both at a disadvantage. Because I think, even though you're coming in as a graduate student and I'm the graduate professor, you have had experiences that I haven't had before. And I can learn from your experiences in the same way that you can learn from my experiences. So as a professor, I want to be open to your experiences, and I think that there's room to do that with undergraduates too, even though they're usually younger and have had fewer experiences, but they've still had different experiences. We found that with makeup class too. Some of the students came into that makeup class with so many experiences that we could learn from—they were just different from the makeup experiences that we had had.

What are your thoughts on this about the idea of reciprocal mentorship? Do you think that it's something that could work, do you think that it's something that you've seen in practice, what do you think about it?

EMMA ARENDS: I think it definitely can work, and I think it's probably the best thing that has worked for me and my students, understanding and balance. I can learn things from my students and I can learn from their experiences, but there are some times that what they're saying is just not correct and that's okay, but they need to be able to be in a similar respectful relationship between me and my students being like, Okay, well I'm not always going to be right, you're not always going to be right, and I think we both need to be able to be humble and be able to be like, Okay, you're right that I was not correct here. And own up to that and be like, Okay well what would you do differently or something like that. Particularly I think about my intro to the theatrical design class versus like costume practicum or costume construction. In that class I kind of had more of a leadership role and being able to be like, Okay, that is not exactly what we're talking about, but I can see where you made that connection, like, I get the connection of why you would think that, but this is actually what we're talking about. Versus in costume construction and costume practicum, like we could also be doing that being like, Okay that's not exactly correct, but this is how you do it, but then also having their talents come in being like, Okay, well, this is how I've been making a straight line, and then they show me and I'm like ok seems to work, keep doing what you're doing I guess. And being open to those ideas of, Okay well, maybe it's not exactly how I would do it, but like it seems to be working so and I guess if it doesn't work, then I guess we'll find out.

And I also just think it has to do with the idea of making mistakes. I think this world takes mistakes way too seriously. Mistakes happen, but it's not the end of the world. Like just because I got a stitch wrong doesn't mean that somebody in the world is having a heart attack right now and dying or something. I've noticed that people are afraid to make mistakes. Like they just are terrified of it. I don't know, maybe I just grew up differently, but I'm not afraid to make mistakes. And if it happens, it happens and I always did the best I could do. And I'm willing to learn from them, but they still happen. Which is also I feel like a really long rant of like, how mentorship I think should be is being like, Okay we're both people and you obviously have more knowledge than I do in this situation, but you're willing to learn from me as well about things.

When I worked at Stagedoor, we had a student, he was 14 and he was not interested in performing in any shows, he was like, I do not want to do that, I want to be in the costume shop and learn how to do that and I was like, okay. And I remember it's like the first week, and they were like, so you're going to have the student follow you around for the next three hours. I was like, right, cool did not expect that, especially since I have two shows and like 90 kids to dress but yeah sure why not let's have this kid follow me around. I would tell him stuff and we would do stuff together. He taught me how to tie a knot on my string super fast. And now that's how I tie all my strings because it's literally the fastest way I've ever learned how to do it. And if I didn't listen to this 14-year-old kid I would never know how to do it.

KYLA KAZUSCHYK: I love this idea of humility. You articulated that so well, and that is exactly what I've been trying to put my finger on. That if we are not approaching any situation, whether it be collaborating in the costume shop or in the classroom or designing a show or working on a show, if we're not coming to it with humility, then how are we going to form an idea together? How are we going to grow and listen to each other? It's impossible.

EMMA ARENDS: It is impossible, and then I feel like, especially in collaborative production settings and what I've seen, always one person that feels like they have to fight for their voice. They always have to fight for their position in the production. And I'm like, well why even fight, you're in the show you're doing the stuff, you don't need to fight, you're here. If you obviously couldn't do it, then why are you here, you know?

KYLA KAZUSCHYK: I think this is directly connected to people being afraid to make mistakes. I think that people haven't been in enough situations where it's safe for them to make mistakes, and I think this is something that we can provide to the extent with which we have agency over the costume shop. In your future as you go on, if you work as a shop manager, and I'm going to do more of this as I work as a shop manager, like doing everything I can to help people to feel comfortable that it's okay to make mistakes. Because if they're just afraid, if they come in on edge to make mistakes, I think that leads to that attitude that you're saying about, like, I have to fight for my spot, I have to fight for what I have, I have to fight to defend my ideas when it's like, if we just create something from the get-go and it's like, well, I can have an idea, and it could be wrong, I can explain something and I could be incorrect, but then it's okay. It's okay, then we can just move on from there.

EMMA ARENDS: I think you're one hundred percent correct and it's not just in theatre, but I think in the world in general, people are afraid to make mistakes, because they're in environments that won't allow them to, which I think is bullshit. Because there are so many people that I'm like, yeah maybe you shouldn't make a mistake if you're a pharmacist or a surgeon, that's totally understandable, don't make mistakes. But we're putting on plays for crying out loud. And God knows, there have been a million mistakes in theatre, and in film.

KYLA KAZUSCHYK: So it's humility and it's also resilience, I think that that's what you're touching on, the ability to admit when you've made a mistake and then just move forward. You talked about that, with your collage communication too, like, Okay we're not going in that direction, fine, let it go, let's go in another direction. Being able to hear, Okay, no that's wrong that's not what you want—okay let's find something different, and not just immediately feel like you have to be defensive like, well, this is my idea and the reason why this idea is like this is because it has to be—well it doesn't.

EMMA ARENDS: No apparently it doesn't and I also feel like that's a weird balance too, of like where do you find the balance of like, it has to be this way or it's disrespectful or it's just awful.

KYLA KAZUSCHYK: Well, this is the danger of collaboration. And that's the same danger of corporations is that it's so many people just doing their one part, and not seeing the big picture, so that in the end, when we look at the big picture, we can be like, that was the whole picture? And it comes back to a director's vision too. If it's the director's responsibility to have the vision of seeing everything come together, or if it's a truly collaborative process where everyone can see everything that's happening. I think that that's what has not happened on these projects that we've collaborated on. We've contributed something, but without knowing everything else that was happening until the end, we don't know what we could have done. And it has to do with power and agency too. That's what I think about when I reflect on Anne Frank, is that there was no room for us to say no to the director. And that's how everything is set up, like it's the director's way or the highway, there's no back and forth communication unless the director chooses to be open to that, but if the director doesn't choose to be open to that, then it's a disaster.

What advice do you have for people collaborating, for people creating costumes for devised theatre, for people designing for dance, what are the salient pieces of advice that you would like to give?

EMMA ARENDS: For the designers, I think my best advice for you is just be open minded and to realize that, even though it wasn't exactly maybe what you wanted, or what you envisioned it to be it doesn't necessarily mean it's bad. It could be its own beautiful thing, especially with

FIGURE 4.24 *To fit* Small Mouth Sounds, *a show produced on zoom during the global pandemic, Emma pulled costumes during the day and placed them on racks in the offices used as dressing rooms and filming locations by the performers. In the evening when performers came in, they tried on various combinations and discussed with Emma and the shop manager/cutter/draper through zoom (photo courtesy of Emma Arends Montes)*

FIGURE 4.25 *With multiple costume options available to them just off camera, performers were able to add and adjust costumes as moments were devised and added up until opening of the show (photo courtesy of Emma Arends Montes)*

Airline Highway, that was a beautiful process out of a horrific situation. That would be my advice to the designers: if something is precious to you, I guess hold on to it, but really save it. If it's not for this show it's for another one.

And then people that are creating devised pieces of art and want to create something beautiful, have a clear image of what that beautiful thing is. Know all the details, know the colors, know the size of it, know exact details of what you want. It makes the process so much easier and much more successful if you have a clear image. Yes, it can be fun to explore and do all that stuff but do the exploring before.

KYLA KAZUSCHYK: It goes back to the question of time—time is always going to be a limit.

EMMA ARENDS: Time is going to be a limit and I think you would be way better off if you come into that first production meeting with an exact image of what you want. And what it should look like.

KYLA KAZUSCHYK: That's awesome advice. Thank you so much.

CHAPTER 5

"SHARE YOUR BABY OFTEN"

NOTHING IS PRECIOUS

Nothing is precious. This is true in devising … and in *everything*! We are passionate about our work and it is important to us, but the more we are able to accept that anything can disappear at any time, the more we will have the capacity for resilience and creativity.

A story that illustrates this point is a graduate school folk tale I heard secondhand. I am not sure if it is a true story or not, but it goes like this: students were assigned to complete full color renderings for a show. They did all the research, created rough sketches, developed their ideas into finalized designs, painstakingly rendered them in detail, and brought them to class. The professor asked each student to choose their favorite rendering, the one they had worked the hardest on, spent the most time on, the one they were most proud of. The professor then collected all these renderings, tossed them into a metal trash can, and set them on fire. This is a harsh way to learn a lesson, of course. I think hearing the story and imagining it happening to you serves enough of the purpose with less trauma. Renderings can look like beautiful works of art, but ultimately the production on stage is the art. Renderings are a communication tool. All renderings are working renderings. Cultivate your own resilience. Be able to let go of anything, even ideas you have invested large amounts of time and energy into.

Be ready to let go. Figure out *how* to let go. Build stamina. Learn how to release yourself from the hold of your ego. This is not easy! Yet it is possible. It takes practice. We can be so devoted to our work, things can *feel* precious. Indeed, it is a positive thing to care about our work, but the more we are able to open our minds, the more space we create for bigger and better ideas. The whole is greater than the sum of its parts. This is what makes theatre different from studio art or fashion design—we are not here to express any one singular vision, rather a collective vision, reflecting multiple perspectives.

Costume designer Camilla Morrison often says, "Share your baby often. In fact, don't even call it your baby!" When we keep our ideas to ourselves, the fear surrounding those ideas grows. If we share our work often, the anxiety is lessened and the ideas have the ability to grow and improve from the contributions of others.

A brave costumer must enter into the process being unafraid to try new things, ready to accept ideas from new sources, experiment with techniques never tried before, and maintain calm as chaos creeps into the equation. We can become so attached to our ideas that we lose sight of the bigger picture and slight the potential for collaborative art. If we share our ideas with a variety of people, we can generate new ideas from expected or unexpected sources, and the resulting work becomes even more cohesive and multifaceted.

Part of embracing the chaos of devised work is being ready to let anything go. My initial color scheme idea for *Love and Information* was based on microscopic views of diseased heart and brain cells. As the piece developed, the director felt that a palette of "dusty neutrals" would be more appropriate for the world they were creating in rehearsals, so I shifted my key inspiration pictures to photographs of diseased chicken bodies (an image also referenced in the text). The beige, peach, and mauve tones combined with the tones of grey, black, white, and dusty green from other research images. Maintaining the somewhat scary view that nothing is precious leaves you open to new and bigger ideas. An initial idea a costume designer had

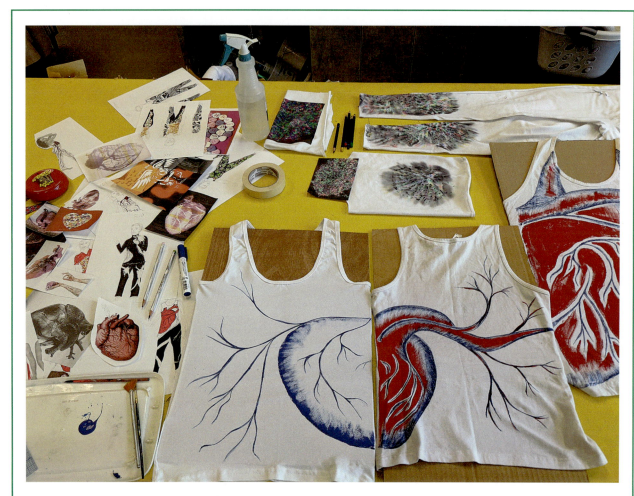

FIGURE 5.1 *While experimenting with dye and paint treatments on Savage/Love, I was grateful for both the physical space of the costume shop, and also for the opportunity to bounce ideas off other people in a shared space*

independently may seem like the best possible solution to a problem, yet when thrown into the collaborative think tank of an ever-changing work of devised theatre, other collaborators might offer fragments of new ideas that coalesce together to form something greater than any one of them imagined individually. Costumes are one piece of a larger puzzle which becomes the presented work.

First dress rehearsal of one of the scenes from *Savage/Love* went exactly according to plan. The scene is about two people who pass each other every day at their mailboxes, each one hoping the other is noticing and sharing their longing. In the end, they do see each other and make a passionate connection. My research images included photographs of large-scale coordinating tattoos. The idea of tattoos ties in to the theme of reckless passion that leads to lifelong scars. The piece was staged with the two people standing still on opposite sides of the stage, facing the audience, as dozens of other people ran around them in every direction. At the point where they began to connect, they faced each other and walked toward each other, eventually embracing. This staging was partially built around my idea for costumes that, on their own, looked like a random assortment of incomplete lines and partial shapes, yet when the two performers embraced, created an image in which the lines formed larger connected lines and recognizable shapes including geometric hearts. In other scenes, the performers appeared again, still covered in bold and incomplete lines, yet when surrounded by other people, the connections remained incomplete. When the piece traveled to France for its next stage of devising, one of the performer's custom hand-painted garments got lost. From the States, I advised my assistant to find him a plain white tank top and black yoga pants to wear. I was disappointed that some of the magic of my idea had been lost, but I had to make the most achievable choice with the given circumstances. The show was able to be presented and the story was still told,

FIGURE 5.2 *Savage/Love* on stage in the first iteration at Louisiana State University

minus one of the costume details but plus the contribution of international performers.

Costume designer Emma Arends Montes describes the practice of letting go: "I think that's also part of devised theatre, like finding that balance of what do you stick to and what do you throw away. It's always a dance, and I feel like the dance is also determined by time."

ARTIST SPOTLIGHT: SARA OSI SCOTT

Sara Osi Scott is an artist, performer, creator, and educator. Here, she discusses devising as growing, dreaming, and being able to let things go.

SARA OSI SCOTT: You asked, how do you define devised theatre? And things that came to mind were inspiration, themes, and growth, rather than the traditional art of a theatre piece.

By growth, I mean just the expansion of an initial idea, and of course the story arc even expands as well, but there's a different type of expansion that for me feels like growth, development. When I think about devised theatre, those are key things. The reason I mentioned inspiration is because usually it starts with an idea. Of course everything starts with an idea, but it may be a song, theory, a painting, it could be anything, the shape of the cloud that you saw on your way home from cycling, and it starts you on this journey of discovery and questioning and it's just an exciting place to be.

KYLA KAZUSCHYK: I love that idea of growth. A scripted piece is stagnant, it is one thing, but a devised piece is always growing, in its nature it's growing.

SARA OSI SCOTT: Right, ever evolving. So what are the advantages of creating devised work? The fact that it's ever expanding, there's this organic discovery process that happens, either internally as you're writing if it's a solo piece, but devised theatre usually is more collaborative. So via collaboration, there's this bouncing around of ideas which is a beautiful thing and really to me, it's community. It's community storytelling at its sometimes strangest or rawest. It's a chance for a community of people to get together and discover new things about that inspired

FIGURE 5.3 *Savage/Love* costumes, inspired by large-scale tattoos that fit together like a puzzle

idea. It's again not restricted by traditional expectations of a static theatre piece. So those are some advantages to creating devised work.

And the next question was how do you approach creating costumes for devised work. I've only done it once, with my own one-person show which I don't know if that's really devised—actually you know I would consider it a form of devised theatre. I used my experience, because that's all I really know. Consider the setting, the stage and your space where you are going to be performing this piece. For us it was a studio theatre, so we used that minimalistic backdrop and played off of that with kind of minimalistic costumes, paying attention to blocks of color and letting that tell the story, going down from bright colors to more subdued and then black at the very end, so that everything was more monotone at the end.

And also costume changes—considering what you do. If you have costume changes during your piece, what do you do with the costumes? Do they become other costume pieces?

Does a shirt transform into a headscarf or whatever? Those are things that I think are really great, especially for devised theatre that is traveling or moving because you can use less and do more, do more with less. So those are some things that I thought about with creating costumes and any tips or strategies that were successful for that.

Look at the script with blurred eyes. I know that sounds strange but to look at it and see Okay, what are the general shapes that I see in this piece and what are they saying. How can that be communicated via costume color, costume style? Costume changes also, are there any underlying plots or things that you want to emphasize in your devised theatre piece? And when I say underlying, you know things that are maybe not as overt in the text or the action. How can that be communicated in costume? How much do you want to reveal through costume from the beginning to the end? So those are some things to consider that may be successful, maybe.

KYLA KAZUSCHYK: I love that idea of blurred eyes. You could approach sets and lighting that way too, like what

FIGURE 5.4 *Sara Osi Scott onstage in the first scene of her devised piece. Photo by Mackenzie Andrews (photo courtesy of Sara Osi Scott)*

FIGURE 5.5 *To show a shift in mood, she changes her costume from bright yellow to black. Photo by Mackenzie Andrews (photo courtesy of Sara Osi Scott)*

really needs to come across, what is the core of the story that really needs to come through, the silhouette, the overall color, what do you really want the audience to take away? That's great.

SARA OSI SCOTT: Right, exactly, and the last question that you said was what advice do you have for artists approaching devised work? Start early. If you have a deadline, then start early. If you don't have a deadline, if you are just devising, then dream frequently. Lots of daydreaming, lots of listening to yourself, listening to what comes to you as you're daydreaming and sitting with it, giving yourself ample time to decide to do that. Allowing yourself that joyous space to just be in a place of creativity is just so beautiful and being in a time crunch is like the antithesis of that.

It can be really tough sometimes, and I know some people do well under time pressure, but I think with devised theatre it's important to allow yourself that time to explore all areas. It's ever evolving. There may be a performance that you do and then it may change based on your response, the audience's response, the response to the audience's response, who knows, you know? But you learned. Your lived experience is how you grow.

Allow the ideas to flow. Don't force. Try not to force. I don't like to say don't do this don't do that, but you know try not to force things. There may be something that you think may work at the beginning, but if it doesn't seem to fit then it's okay to release it, it may come back in a different form.

It's okay to go with what is working at present.

TRY NEW THINGS!

Mental roadblocks can impede the creative process in all aspects of theatrical production. Designers, directors, technicians, and performers all feel stuck from time to time. One way to get unstuck is to look to alternative sources of inspiration and challenge yourself to simply begin.

An activity that can help strengthen this muscle is Music Inspired Design. Assemble some art supplies. This can be anything at all. If you have access to watercolors, colored pencils,

FIGURE 5.6 *A square of blue fabric becomes a versatile costume piece, here worn tied around her waist as a skirt. Photo by Mackenzie Andrews (photo courtesy of Sara Osi Scott)*

FIGURE 5.7 *Supplies assembled for music inspired design activity*

markers, specialty paper, that's great. If you can grab scraps of notebook paper, pencils, pens, crayons, that will work fine too. If the most accessible medium to you at the time is a paint program on your computer, that will work well for this activity also.

Play a song and draw/paint/create what you see in your head when you hear that song. It can be abstract or literal or a combination of both. Having only the length of the song to finish the work will challenge you to make choices and commit to depicting them, understanding that anything can be thrown out or changed later. This doesn't have to be the final form, but you might unlock a kernel of an idea that you can build upon.

At the end of the song, stop working and reflect on what you created. Does it clearly express what was in your mind's eye? Did you discover something unexpected? What would you adjust if you had more time?

You could also do this activity in a group, and then ask even more reflection questions when you look back on the work you devised. Are there through lines throughout the work? What themes begin to emerge? Did someone else articulate something you saw in your imagination, too? How could we combine and blend these ideas?

In general, when you are feeling stuck, look to nature, look to all forms of art—inspiration is everywhere. Set a boundary, give yourself a limit, start to create, and see what comes up!

The line between costumes and props is one we know to be blurry. When we look even harder, the lines between sets, sound, lights, and costumes become less like hard lines and more like grey areas as well.

After sharing my research images for *Savage/Love* with the lighting and projections designer, he incorporated some of the ideas and images into the projections. After listening to the music selections made by the sound designer for *Love and Information*, I had a clearer idea of what particular style of contemporary clothing some of the characters would wear. For example, a character that listens to Bjork or the Postal Service might wear a Joy Division hoodie. In educational theatre, a transparent process can be mutually beneficial to teachers as well as students. I found that by sharing my work with my students at every stage, they gained a clearer picture of the process, and I gained insight about style and aesthetic from a younger generation.

FIGURE 5.8 *Mixed media collages created quickly, inspired by music*

An idea or method that worked for one piece may not be right for the next piece. This could pertain to the style of renderings, research, or collage.

Another helpful practice is keeping a bank of ideas. Many artists talk about how it can be easier to let things go if they do not go away entirely. Perhaps an idea you felt was a great idea still is a great idea, just not for the piece at hand.

MORE TIPS FOR COLLABORATION

Invite ideas from as many people as possible. In the costume shop community, this could be students, workers, or passers-by. The more perspectives, the stronger the ideas can be. Talk about your ideas with anyone who has time and space to listen. Ask questions, be curious, listen to perspectives different from your own. Seek out as wide a range of voices as you can. Listen to perspectives of members of the production team, from performers, from students in classes, from friends and family. Often people outside of theatre can point out things we thought were obvious. Be open to letting your ideas evolve and expand as you learn and grow. The conversations in this book are arranged into chapters aligning with the themes of the discussions, yet you will notice that many ideas overlap. Everyone I talked to spoke about the importance of healthy collaboration, of being open, honest, and flexible.

ARTIST SPOTLIGHT: RACHEL BARANSKI

Rachel Baranski is an incredible collaborator. Here, she discusses how she has developed ways to work together with artists of all ages to devise and create.

In her work with Applause Youth Theatre in Cary, North Carolina, children and adults have been creating devised work together without even calling it devising.

> *I would have just called it like "student driven." That's part of the beauty of it is that we have so many different personalities and we want to always place a priority on everyone has a story to tell, we need to hear what people have to tell.*

FIGURE 5.9 *A larger-scale version of the music inspired design activity. Don't be afraid to make messes. You can always clean them up*

Working as an ensemble can help people learn how to listen and how to express ideas. The sense of ownership and investment in the work increases when it is work they are creating themselves. And stories can be about anything! If it is important to the youth to tell a story about a superhero, a nurse, two cats, and a mermaid, then let's figure out how to tell that story. What costume pieces do we need to indicate these characters? Applause has experimented with a number of different formats throughout summer camps, after-school programs, and track-out programs for year-round schools.

One example is a camp that is focused on creating a story that will be performed for the parents at the end of the camp. Youth work with grown-up instructors to develop the story they want to tell, and they also devise their costumes.

> *So we might give them a white tee shirt and a white cap, and then they might paint it or cut it or glue stuff on it, or tie it or whatever they do and create their look. And the same with their scenery or props. They're determining what's important for what they are working on, and it's very informal.*

Rachel describes her work as a puzzle, and I think the same metaphor can extend to describe the collaborative process of devised theatre.

> *I think that just having like our project, it's just another piece of the family puzzle. Our metaphor that I always use is a puzzle and it's like sometimes the puzzles are small, the pieces are little, sometimes they're big and sometimes they have a sharp corner and sometimes they're round and sometimes they've got a bunch of holes and sometimes they've got a bunch of bumps and we need all of this, all of those pieces. Sometimes the puzzle piece gets a little piece of the picture peeled off, but it still fits. We just want them to feel like, I feel like kids need to be heard, like everybody just wants to be heard.*

And by inviting everyone's voices into all aspects of the process of creating theatre, we can help people to feel seen.

Another devising project at Applause was for their kindergarten, a 5–10-year-old age group program. It started as an experiment with delegating roles and responsibilities.

FIGURE 5.10 *Music inspired collage created by artist Lindsey Muscatello*

We started with like, take a story and then we're going to act it out, and then we moved into take a story and then we're going to make up our own version of it, and then we moved into take a story and then like, just think, learn about beginning, middle and end and use that as an example, then throw it out and make up our own thing and then we sometimes ditch the story altogether.

The group would alternate art classes with acting classes with the idea that they would all learn and practice all the art techniques. In this case what the instructors learned was that what they initially thought was important turned out to be not important at all.

It was just that everyone wanted to be creative and there were kids who were like oh I don't know anything about acting and I just really love to make things. Their little souls were fed and the kids that were like, oh my gosh I just have to act all the time, their little souls were fed and then you know you see them and their little heads are all bent over the same project and whatever they're doing.

Students would get very serious about all of it, and very proud of their work, even coming up with their own publicity and marketing, making signs advertising their show and hanging them up around the building.

This illustrates the key principle of *flexibility* within devising and creating. Sometimes it makes sense for roles and responsibilities to overlap, and other times it makes sense to encourage participants to focus on the parts of the process that bring them joy. Why not?

This "yes and" concept applies to everything like for us. We might not be able to dump actual sand onto the classroom floor and make your beach, but what else could we do?

And for facilitators and instructors working to make sure that each person's voice is heard and each soul is nourished, it is about developing a level of tolerance and patience,

FIGURE 5.11 *Students devising work as part of the town of Cary, NC STEAM camp. Costume items like an apron and a crown create distinctions between characters (photo courtesy of Rachel Baranski)*

assessing what the group needs at any particular moment and accepting it.

Like okay, well guess what, we were going to play five drama games and we were going to try to act out Jack and the Beanstalk but we're on the first drama game because they love it, and we'll just stay here, it's fine.

When brainstorming ideas, hold on to the attitude that, whatever happens, it's fine. Whatever idea comes up, we will either find a way to incorporate it and it is okay if that means the show is super weird, or we will save the idea in a "parking lot" or a "later list." This is helpful when a lot of ideas are bubbling up and time is running out. Even if you don't end up going back to the idea, whoever shared the idea knows that somebody heard their idea and wrote it down, so they still feel validated.

When the town of Cary made Juneteenth a holiday, Rachel had the idea for devising a project based on a children's book. The book is told from the perspective of a little girl, about what she sees and experiences on June 19, 1865, and ends when she goes to sleep that night. The devising idea is that families could work together to imagine and tell the stories of what happened when the girl and her family woke up the next day. What might be different?

There's so much freedom in devising. I love how open ended it is and how there isn't any one person's perspective necessarily, there's no playwright's perspective telling it.

It can be difficult to find children's plays that meet all the needs of a group, which can include very young actors, teenage designers, and audiences that range from toddlers to older siblings and parents. To find a published work that is interesting and challenging to that entire range of individuals, while also having some sort of moral integrity and positive messaging is a challenge.

There's a lot of freedom in building it from scratch. It's helpful to be able to kind of shift in the moment depending on who you've got in the room.

Another example of an Applause devising project is a summer camp where teens select songs that they like and work with a musical director to figure out how to incorporate them into a musical. For research and inspiration, instructors and students try all kinds of different tactics. Sometimes they walk around

FIGURE 5.12 *Student-created marketing materials for their devised work (photo courtesy of Rachel Baranski)*

Costumes for this camp are minimal. Because they write it from their perspective, in most cases they come to the camp wearing what their character would wear, styled out of their own clothes. In the event that they devise something more elaborate, like the story of Clip Clop, the famous tap dancing horse, students figure out how to represent characters using what they have at home and can bring in to use. (Clip Clop was made out of a blanket off someone's bed.) The stage where they perform is actually a movie theatre, shallow and with no wing space, so they have to be creative based on the limitations of the space, which is such a useful skill to sharpen for a career in theatre.

> For the rest of it is basically just inviting suspension of disbelief to enter this crazy world where they just break into a song that you heard on the radio on the way there and the story is cuckoo and amazing. There's like a rawness to it that really appeals to me, this idea of like, we can MacGyver a show together with our like, q tips and dryer lint and like, poof we made a play. There's something really appealing about that.

It is like you are distilling down to the most vital. What do we really need to tell the story? How much do we really need to get the idea across? We can show just what is most essential and trust that the audience will accept it and fill in everything that needs to be filled in. Theatre often attempts to be so hyper realistic, but does it really need to be? Elaborate costumes are beautiful, but they are also so expensive and time consuming. Costumes can be more abstract—they can suggest a character and leave room for audiences to imagine.

From the perspective of a producer or a production manager looking at the big picture and considering the budget for the whole show, you might have to say no to a scenic designer wanting to purchase a fancy door handle. Do we really need that door handle to tell the story? And if we get that door handle, it means we cannot get the crinolines that we need.

For a production of *The Little Prince*, performers used hoop skirts in a creative way. When they knelt down, the skirts collapsed around them, and when they stood up, they were volcanoes!

Using a base costume, like leggings, camisoles or tee shirts, and shorts, and then adding pieces on top of that to identify characters works for many reasons. It is a way to be sensitive to students' individual boundaries. It saves the time of waiting to change clothes entirely. It saves the budget of buying entire costumes.

> That was definitely a conscious decision. It's like we're not going to be able to do this otherwise. And especially because I didn't want the kids to feel like they failed. I didn't want the kids to be like we can't do it, we can't succeed. So we let them

outside and take pictures of anything that catches their eye, sometimes they look at works of art, sometimes they play improv games and develop a list of words and non sequiturs to use as a jumping-off point. Because they are creating the shows themselves, it is possible to welcome and include a really wide range of people. Shows have incorporated a student's service dog. When a student who uses a wheelchair participated in the camp, the students modified choreography and staging so that she could be comfortable participating.

> I have to believe that it's because of honoring the voices, honoring their voices, I think. I think it creates a different vibe. It reinforces the intimacy and the team sport-ness of theatre. I mean you're always working towards a common goal together, that's what an ensemble is: diverse people working towards the same thing. But I think there's a difference. There's a difference when what you're implementing is you, your thoughts, versus when you're implementing someone else's thoughts.

do what they can where they can succeed. And that has been working pretty well, I think. I think it's good for everybody's creativity to not get too literal.

What makes you more creative is working within parameters and boundaries and figuring out how to create something within those limitations, so that, when your limitations expand, you can easily create something more elaborate and realistic and expensive, if it is possible to do it on a smaller scale. Limitations build that creative muscle.

Timelines vary, but generally the production team (grown-ups) meets a month before auditions. The grown-up team creates the framework for the students to work within. From there they have five weeks of rehearsal and one week of tech. Rehearsal and tech sessions are short, two hours or less, and done by 9pm. It makes sense to be cognizant of people's lives and ask parents what they need. How can we make everything more accessible? It is worth it to work on finding ways to ease the length of rehearsals. The escalation of relaxed to super tense wears on everybody. How can we massage that timeline better, to give everybody the time they need for rest and for life outside the theatre? There must be a way to adjust from casual to super stressed. The scale always seems to tip drastically from casual to super stressed.

A part of it that hurts me the most is that we have been emphasizing the kids and their families, this whole time, like we've got you, this is about you, is about our journey and that's the truth, and we have a show to produce. So it's like at some point, it becomes, like, the scale tips, and it goes from student-driven student-driven student-driven play you know, try whatever, rehearse, like play around and try new things and brainstorm to like cut, you're cut off, you know no more ideas we've got to implement and it's like that is so upsetting to me on so many levels.

One of the most difficult and also most vital responsibilities of a producer is saying no. Looking at the scope of the entire big picture and figuring out what can stay and what should go is a challenge. When working with students, the challenge is increased by the dimension of simultaneously producing shows and providing learning opportunities.

Applause approaches the tech rehearsal phase of production understanding that it will be a slow process, making time for collaboration between everyone. Rachel is interested in continuing to evolve systems as they grow, to give more opportunities and responsibilities to students and to really think about the services they are providing to the community. Devising many short shows instead of producing one longer scripted show allows rehearsals to be shorter and more students to practice directing and more students to be cast.

So many places just keep doing things the way they have always been done, but they are not aware of what's working and what's not working and they're not even aware that things can shift. We can always be improving, we can always be making things better, we can always be making it so it is a better experience for everyone involved.

Applause Youth Theatre started out as something affordable for parents to take their kids to. Now that there are more options for families, delivery of services has changed.

Theatre people will find theatre where they need it and that's great, but non theatre people need us too and so we are evolving our community value into a more service-driven focus and like not being shy about really, kind of, like we are going to do theatre—we're called "Applause Cary Youth Theater," it's rooted in theatre and that's what we do, but really what we're building, it's really not your monologue skills. Its like you are more confident to speak in front of someone else, you understand how to breathe and relax your shoulders and you have worked with a team of people that you didn't know, and everybody's different and growing social and emotional skills in people. I'm focusing on things like community partnerships that we can do. How can we reach the people out there that don't know what ice cream is instead of just being like the sprinkles on someone's ice cream? We can be both. And so, this pandemic shut down has given us, we have virtual classes going on, and we have some community partnerships going on, we have after school workshops going on with elementary schools because the PTA was concerned that the kids are socially isolated. It hasn't been hard, it has felt really natural actually, dropping the theatre agenda and pushing the people agenda, through theatre, has been awesome.

So we have a partnership with an organization in town that provides services for people who have food insecurity or job insecurity, and they have this job training program and we're going to partner with them. They wanted to work on public speaking skills, so we're going to do some improv classes with them.

There's an organization that supports folks who are experiencing homelessness and we have partnered with them for years, and while the parents are in their training classes and workshops, they have a big family dinner once a week when they have a cohort of people that comes through and when there are a lot of kids and the parents are in workshops we send in a drama teacher to just do drama class.

I want it to feel like anybody can come and imagine and be creative and work together and play. Like you can do that, even if you're not an actor. I want to focus on that more.

Honestly, why not. Why not focus on the things that can bring us together and help everyone rather than the things that keep us apart. It doesn't really matter if you identify as an actor or not, you can still get together and make something up. Someone might have more training and experience as a designer, but someone with less experience can still put something together, figure something out. We may have different experience levels, but we all have ideas to share.

> What I always felt like, with adults, it is like, here I am, look at me, it's about me, and the kids are always like, what can we do? It became a we, instead of a me.

It takes practice to learn how to release that ego. It's not about who has the most lines in a printed script, it is about taking all this junk and creating something together. It takes all of us. Everyone is important to the process.

> We don't want you here because you're the best actor, or because you're the best stage manager. Like, you might be, but we don't care. We want you here because you're you. You're the best you, and that is why we need you.

There is space for theatres of all kinds. There is space for polished, scripted commercial theatre and space for more raw and maybe more rough around the edges unscripted theatre.

It is hard to get comfortable with a final product being a little rough.

> And we're still all working on that because, at the end of the day, there's going to be little botches, because they're kids, like somebody was too quick on the fly rail and the thing crashed into the deck, like, it happens, you know? Somebody will miss their entrance because they couldn't find their shoe in the green room, it happens. That kind of thing happens, but my goal for myself is to be more comfortable with like, you know what, actually, so and so is barefoot in this scene because we didn't get to the shoes, and that's fine. Or, we didn't even make that flat, because we ran out of time. And that's on us as grown-ups, to not see that as a deficit.

And to figure out how to accept it. This question of process versus product, this is what capitalism teaches us too, that the product is everything and the process doesn't matter, but in reality it is the opposite of that. The process is everything and the product could be fantastic or not, but, why does it matter?

> And frankly, when you nurture the process, the product is going to be amazing because all the little gears are turning and they're all together because everybody has their place, and like, whatever their place is, whatever their thing that they add is part of the big picture.
>
> We used to have to do our mainstage plays outside. It was just a horrible setup. Particularly the spring play, it was always like, is it going to rain, isn't it going to rain? And I had to tell the parents like, unless you're a meteorologist, don't talk to me about the weather. Don't ask about it, don't tell me about it, unless you study it. I had the number of the national weather service, which was a terrible idea to have it, I'd be like creeping around the woods calling them like, Okay, if you had a child on stage. And we developed this motto: Something will happen, and then we'll all go home. At the end of the day, it's like, so what? We had one show, it rained, we lost all of our tech. We opened in the drizzle, and the next night it stormed, and we went to our rain date and it rained. And we waited to call it, because it was like, Oh, this is going to move through, this is a thunderstorm, like is this going to pass, like what are we doing. So we waited and waited and waited and waited. And all the kids were so bummed. And we made the call to cancel it. And literally, like ten minutes after that call, like everything had, like all the channels, like you can imagine, the government springing into action and canceling the thing, the sun came out. I had to order pizza because I was like, Okay, we have to at least feed them. The kids are all sitting there and they're bummed and the sun is out and the pizza is on the way, and we look out, and this huge rainbow is in the sky. It was beautiful. And we all came out of the shelter and stared at it, and then we had a pizza party. And it was like, well, we didn't do our play but, like, so? I sure love you guys. I mean was it the thing that everyone wanted? No. And it was still a good thing. That's how it goes. Sometimes you just have to eat pizza.

Eat pizza and experience nature! You can't control nature. There are so many things beyond our control.

> I really think, to bring everything full circle, if you can make everyone feel heard and seen, you can do anything. There was one project we did, where we interviewed some older members of the community about their holiday memories. We ended up taking a lot of their narrative and then kind of creating scripts around it, and then we performed it. I had no idea that that was devising. We just kind of made it up. This is so funny to think about it as like a thing. This is just kind of what we do.
>
> I won't say working for the government is easy all the time. I won't even say it is easy some of the time. But the work that I get to do is a great platform, and so I want to make sure I'm using it. While I have this, I want to make sure that I am using it.

CHAPTER 6

GET INVOLVED!

THE IMPORTANCE OF REHEARSALS

When you have a script, you can read it and visualize the characters. When there is no script, how can you visualize where the characters will come from? One way is to watch it happen in rehearsal.

We are subject to time constraints, and we must consider healthy boundaries and the value of labor. For performers, directors, and choreographers, rehearsal time is likely the bulk of the time requirement, especially if they are only working on one show at a time. For designers, we are often working on multiple shows at a time, and for designers/shop managers, we are also orchestrating the production of multiple shows at a time. Add in teaching and service requirements to the frame of educational theatre, and it can be untenable to attend rehearsals every night on top of everything.

In my experience, I have found the benefits of attending rehearsals to sometimes be enough to outweigh the exhaustion. I recognize that this comes from a place of privilege as well, which is important to think of, especially in terms of the time we ask from students in educational theatre. It might not be possible to attend many rehearsals. Maybe rehearsal times can be adjusted. Many students have jobs on top of classes and rehearsals. Many artists, students and non-students are also parents. It is possible to create art in a way that is accessible for everyone, so why not create an environment where everyone can participate?

If you are present in the rehearsal room, you can see the characters start to take shape and you can start coming up with ideas of how to dress them, instead of waiting until the characters are fully formed.

Attending rehearsals sends the message that you are a part of the team, helps to alleviate an us versus them mentality that might emerge. Communication does not need to be a debate between directors and performers versus designers. It is possible for all participants to come up with ideas together. If you show up at rehearsals from the beginning, performers/directors/choreographers will feel more comfortable with you. When trust is established over time, communication becomes easier.

Also, you can use time in rehearsal to sketch. For me, drawing is quite difficult and takes a lot of time anyway. I can spend that time at my desk or in a chair in the audience at rehearsal. Another advantage is seeing the performers' bodies as you draw, as well as seeing the movements that they do and starting to think about garments to suit these movements.

The more drawings you do, the better. For one thing, because practice helps your rendering skills to improve, and for another, this is a corollary to the "nothing is precious" principle. If you have only a few costume renderings that you have spent a lot of time and energy on, it will be harder to let go of these ideas than if you have a lot of quickly drawn rough sketches of ideas. It can be easier to adjust ideas before they are fully formed, and easier to include more perspectives. Collaborators might feel more comfortable saying no to a rough sketch.

In a typical design process, a costume designer might attend one or two rehearsals, usually included in the rehearsal schedule as a "designer run." This can help the designer to see the movement and blocking, entrances and exits, and the formation of characters. A character that may have seemed shy in the first reading of the script might appear sarcastic and outgoing on stage, as individual actors bring their own points of

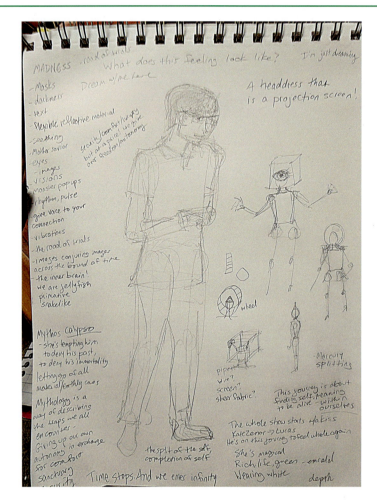

FIGURE 6.1 *Notes and rough sketches I drew during rehearsal for a show that eventually became* Dream Logos. *The lighting and projection designer would often attend rehearsals and experiment with different looks, which inspired me to start thinking about costumes as possible projection surfaces*

view to the formation of the character. In a devised process, it is imperative that a designer attend as many rehearsals as possible. Not only does this send the message that you are a team player who is invested in the whole project, it also begins to provide the answers to such questions as: Exactly how many people are in this scene? And are they playing specific characters? Do they need to be able to do cartwheels, back flips, or high kicks in this costume? Does the costume need to be specially fitted so that the performer may safely do tricks on aerial silks?

On *Love and Information*, the number of people on stage in each scene continued to change up until opening night. At some points, the actors on stage had an integral part in the scene, while at other points the actors had the purpose of moving furniture to set up for the next scene, or comprising the background of a busy airport. In rehearsals, I was able to see their individual characters forming. Some characters ended up being very specific, like flight attendants, security guards, custodians, and children, though those distinctions were not all finalized until a few days before the show opened. In *Savage/Love*, some of the pieces involved performers standing or walking on stage, while others involved the aforementioned backflips, lifts, and incredible tricks on aerial silks. By attending rehearsals and watching the shows develop, I was able to fill in the blanks of the scene and character breakdown paperwork that I was initially unable to do. Seeing the actors' movements informed how stretchy or how loose fitting garments could be.

While working on *Love and Information*, I observed the director leading the performers through a number of warm-up exercises at the start of every rehearsal. I could see relationships and trust beginning to form between members of the ensemble as they gained awareness of the connections between them. This awareness shapes the characters and the ensemble. Individuals discover who they are in relation to each other.

FIGURE 6.2 *To explore the idea of using costumes as projection surfaces, I brought to rehearsal items that could augment the shape of the body while still allowing performers to see and move. Here, the performer is wearing part of a collapsible laundry hamper as a hat/mask, and knit fabric I stretched over a rigiline frame as a circular glove*

Because no single character exists on their own, it is helpful for a costume designer to see them all together, instead of only seeing them one by one as they come in for costume fittings. Being present at rehearsal shows the director and the actors that the costume designer is an active participant in the company. This makes it easier for them to trust the costume designer, to listen to ideas about costume and to feel comfortable offering their own ideas.

CREATING CHARACTERS

Sometimes characters shape the costumes, other times costumes shape the characters! Costume pieces can inspire ideas and propel the development of characters, scenes, even settings. This ties in to another vital principal—be prepared!

When I brought my first collection of research images for *Love and Information* to director Tara Ahmadinejad, she was particularly interested in the pictures of celebrity couples in various stages of connection and heartbreak. Specifically, the photographs of famous people in airports seemed to invoke this complex desire that so many of us have, to simultaneously revere celebrities while asserting that they are, as tabloid magazines put it "just like us!" After our first meeting, I refined my research further in this direction, amassing copious photographs of celebrities in airports. This research not only influenced the look of the costumes: it actually shaped the setting of the whole show. The director saw that the duality of an airport as being a relatable site for both connections and missed connections helped to tell the story. So, while often it is the given environment that offers clues to the potential expression of the characters through costumes, on occasion it is the costumes that give clues as to who the characters can become and where the play can be set. And because I came to early meetings prepared with lots of research images, it was the costume perspective that shaped the course of the entire show.

Bringing costume pieces or even objects that might become costume pieces to rehearsals can inspire performers to tell stories or invent characters in different ways. You can

FIGURE 6.3 Love and Information *set in an airport*

collaborate with projections and lights as well. Anything can be a hat, or a projection surface.

After *Savage/Love*, choreographer Nick Erickson invited me to collaborate on another devising project, again originating with students in Louisiana, and then traveling to France and Scotland. This piece, which eventually became a show entitled *Dream Logos*, began with no written script at all. Nick was inspired by the philosophy of Carl Jung and the logic of dreams. He encouraged students to bring their own ideas and to work together to develop dances and scenes. The cast and crew were fluid, as students decided to what extent they wanted to contribute and participate. As much as I wanted details set in stone, I really found that I had an easier time the more I could let go of wanting that. Maybe it only feels easier to design and build costumes for projects that have a script, characters, and a cast because that is what we are used to. If we let those things go, we can be more open to experimenting and we can learn new ways. And, it can be more possible for more people to participate.

For example, one student had an idea he wanted to express about the mind's descent into madness. He shared poetry that he had written and other students improvised physicality and movement. They worked together on this piece over weeks in evening rehearsals. I knew that the plan for the show was that it would be performed on stage by a group of students at the end of the semester in Louisiana, and then some of those students along with other students would travel to Europe and perform the show there. So costumes had to be comfortable and flexible to support movement, had to fit on multiple performers, and had to visually support the theme. While watching and listening to the performers come up with the scene, I thought of the image of a straitjacket. I talked the idea over with the performers, they agreed that it could evoke the theme of madness and would work as long as it didn't actually restrict movement. Considering budget and always working to save money where possible, I bought inexpensive loose-fit long-sleeve white T-shirts and stitched strips of white knit across the front and around the sleeves with the edges hanging off like straps. I made a few small, a few medium, and a few large, and handed the stack over to the performers. The loose fit allowed them to wear the shirts over whatever else they wore, which helped to accommodate quick changes as well as the need for the costumes to fit unknown performers.

Stretch fabric is your friend, especially when facing unknown variables. Another scene in *Dream Logos* started out with aerial silk performers exploring the dichotomy between darkness and light. Sometimes in rehearsal they worked it as

FIGURE 6.4 Dream Logos *at the Edinburgh International Fringe Festival B (photo courtesy of Andy Phillipson—Livewireimage.com)*

FIGURE 6.5 *Performers on stage in* Dream Logos *(photo courtesy of Andy Phillipson—Livewireimage.com)*

FIGURE 6.6 *Stretch knits can be durable and versatile (photo courtesy of Andy Phillipson—Livewireimage.com)*

a duet, sometimes as solo aerial performance, and sometimes as aerial silk performance over dancers on stage. The two performers working on the duet were students with very busy schedules, pretty sure that they would perform in the Louisiana segment of the run, but not sure if they would be in it for the Scotland run. When creating costumes, it is always ideal to have the performers' measurements first … but that is not always possible, for any number of reasons. We can waste energy being frustrated about this, or we can find ways around it. For this duet, I made an estimate, leaning toward too big instead of too small. Another ideal situation when creating costumes is having time to build and fit mockups made out of inexpensive fabric before going into final costume fabric, but this is also not always possible, especially in devised work. If scheduling only allows for one fitting, you've got to start with final fabric and leave room in it for changes. So I built a "darkness" costume and a "light" costume, each out of stretch fabric. When the performers were able to come in for a fitting, I pinned out the excess, essentially quickly draping the costumes on the performers' bodies. These costumes worked for the performance in Louisiana, and then different performers wore them in Edinburgh.

If I could have gone to Europe with the show to fit costumes on new performers, I would have. A big part of creating costumes for devised work is learning to let things go. Create what you can with the time and resources you have, offer it as something that can help the performers tell the story, then relinquish control and trust your collaborators. The show and the people in it will be stronger when they are comfortable and confident in what they are wearing.

Another aspect of the *Dream Logos* story that performers wanted to tell was about seductive snake goddesses. As this developed into a scene, I talked to the performers about shiny reflective snakeskin print stretch fabric that could reflect light and enhance their serpentine arm movements. Like the darkness and light piece, I couldn't get measurements for all the performers, we weren't sure who was going to be in that scene, and it was likely that different performers would be in it when it traveled. So I approached it in a similar way, building boxy long-sleeve tops and shorts to start, and taking them in to fit each performer as it became settled who would perform in that scene. Another ideal is having time to prepare for scheduled fittings, and fitting performers one at a time. It is nice when that

FIGURE 6.7 *Without measurements or multiple fittings, I built these stretch garments to be larger than necessary and then fitted them on performers in one fitting, talking to them about what they like*

can happen, yet it is possible to work within whatever time and space is available, maybe fitting multiple performers at once, maybe in between scenes during rehearsal. This can feel stressful and hectic at first, but like everything, it gets easier the more you practice it, and it is easier the more you prepare and organize as much as you can. The corollary to "know your speed" is "be as fast as possible."

INVITE PERFORMERS IN

A concrete strategy for success in creating costumes for devised work is to invite the performers in and really listen to them. Talk to them about what they do on stage and who their characters are becoming. Meet with them in advance of fittings if possible. Listen to them about what makes them feel confident and comfortable. Include at least some of their suggestions into the final looks. Prepare more options than you think you need. I have found it quite helpful to meet with the performers in the costume shop and take a few minutes to listen to their perspectives on the piece. For *Love and Information*, I prepared for fittings by making a list for each performer of what scenes I thought they were in and who I thought they were in those scenes. Before we even started trying on clothes, I went over the list with them and made changes as necessary. For example, "Are you the one who is keeping the secret? Who is the other person to you, a friend? A lover?" I scheduled 45-minute long fittings so that we would have time to try on lots of different clothes and talk about what felt right, who they wanted to be, and who they believed they could be. It was a delight to see them visibly grow in confidence as they looked at themselves in the mirror, often crediting some detail as solidifying a certain character, as in: "Oh, he wears basketball shorts? I get it. I see who this guy is now." It was helpful to hear their input, i.e., "I think this character is the type to wear sunglasses and a scarf in the airport." Because I had pulled a variety of options and because I knew exactly where in storage sunglasses were kept, I was able to provide the pieces to complete that character almost immediately. This flexibility and efficiency allows the

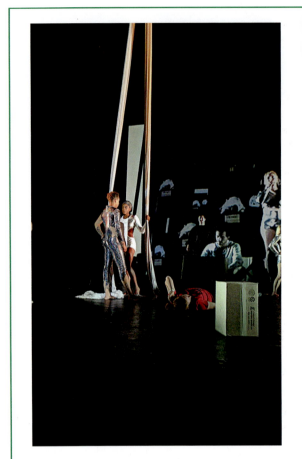

FIGURE 6.8 Dream Logos on stage at Louisiana State University. One performer wanted full length leggings, the other felt more comfortable on the aerial silks with no fabric behind her knees, so I cut her leggings into shorts.

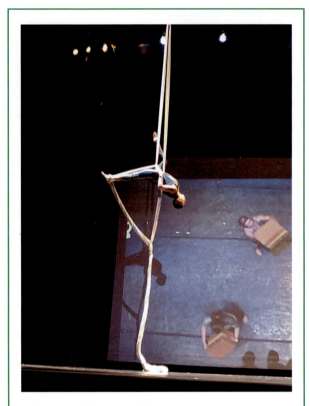

FIGURE 6.9 A scene in Dream Logos as performed in Louisiana, costume designed and built with no measurements in one fitting. Anything is possible

costume designer to truly be a part of the process of adding meaning to characters through costumes.

Some suggestions for successful fittings:

- Be prepared! Pull a range of options for each person, including garments in multiple sizes. Make a plan of what you would like to see on each person, and be ready to change it up as you go. Prepare in advance of the fitting, as soon as the show is cast, by communicating with the team about what to expect in fittings. Compose a document (or edit the one included in the appendix) describing intimacy policies and distribute it to everyone.
- Communicate clearly—express your thoughts in words and listen carefully to others. Err on the side of *over* communicating instead of under-communicating—reintroduce yourself, don't assume that the performer knows or remembers exactly how fittings work. Explain to them and point out on the rack or hand them what you would like them to try on, then say something like "OK, I will step out and let you change in to that. Please open the door when you are dressed and I will come back in." At the end of the fitting, thank them for their time and let them know that you will step out so they may change back into their own clothes.
- Always start with undergarments and shoes. These are the foundations of any costume and must be established so that the rest of the costume fits comfortably and appropriately. If a performer will wear their own undergarments for a show, make sure they bring those undergarments and wear them in fittings.
- When possible, make light conversation with the performer while you are adjusting the fit of their costumes. Do what you can to help them feel at ease. Never make any personal comments about their size.
- Encourage performers to ask questions and share ideas. Ask them how they feel, if they feel closer to their character, if they were expecting anything else or might need anything else.
- Don't forget to take photographs of each look. Make sure you have a space with bright lighting and neutral

FIGURE 6.10 *On the silks, a performer in a white stretch velvet costume that helps tell the story and facilitate her movement. On the ground, a dancer wearing her variation of the snake goddess costume*

FIGURE 6.11 Dream Logos in Edinburgh, Scotland. A performer I never met wearing a costume I built for a different performer. Stretch is your friend! (photo courtesy of Andy Phillipson—Livewireimage.com)

FIGURE 6.12 Elements of the show, including the cast, continued to change throughout rehearsals and throughout the run of the show. If costumes are able to be used on new performers, they are. If not, that is okay too (photo courtesy of Andy Phillipson—Livewireimage.com)

FIGURE 6.13 *One of the snake goddess costumes I designed and built for* Dream Logos

backgrounds. Maybe tape marks on the floor to make it clear where the performer and photographer should stand.
- Keep your fitting room stocked with supplies you might need, including safety pins, pencils, washable markers, measuring tape, scissors, elastic, twill tape, scrap fabric, and a notebook or clipboard or laptop/tablet/phone to take notes.

I recommend printing out your fitting photos if possible, especially when working on a show where the scenes are fluid. You can cut them apart and spread them out over a table to visualize the progression of each performer's looks as well as what they look like together with the other performers in costume. If a performer gets added to a scene in rehearsal, you can look through the stack of photos of outfits you styled for that person and add one in. As the timing for the show settles in to what it will be, you can make adjustments based on what quick changes will be possible. Will that person be able to change their entire outfit, or should they add a jacket or subtract a scarf to become a different character? Another way to organize

FIGURE 6.14 *Snake goddess costumes on stage in the Louisiana version of* Dream Logos

FIGURE 6.15 *After the performance in Louisiana, Dream Logos went to Scotland. Performers made changes to their costumes yet the original spirit of the piece remains (photo courtesy of Andy Phillipson—Livewireimage.com)*

FIGURE 6.16 *Fitting photos for Love and Information. I anticipated the need for lots of quick changes, so I tried to think of as many ways to identify different characters by adding or subtracting layers as possible*

photos, reference them, and move ideas around is by storing them online in a place everyone on the team has access to, like a google drive.

FIGURE 6.17 *I styled a variety of looks for each person in* Love and Information, *so that we would have options to add as the scenes they devised grew*

The pandemic affected communication in so many ways. In socially distanced in-person fittings, we had to figure out how to describe with words all the things we would have done physically. Zoom theatre caused us to ask a lot of performers—suddenly they are their own dresser, electrician, engineer, and more.

In the *Savage/Love* fittings, I talked to the performers about what sort of movement they would do in the piece and had them try it out in the fitting room to make sure the costumes could accommodate it. Some of the aerialists had very specific preferences about how tight or loose their garments should be, and what parts of the body needed to be exposed or covered up. In these instances, it is important to defer to the performer's preference, to ensure their safety. A costume designer is intimately connected to actors and can help them find the best possible wearable tools to use to tell the story.

Sometimes, when devising, there is no way to know whether an idea will work unless you try it. During the first few rehearsals for *Dream Logos*, performers and the projection designer were interested in grey morph suits, full body stretch unitards that cover the whole body—feet, hands, and head

FIGURE 6.18 *It can be fun to talk with actors about the characters they are creating and work to devise costumes together*

FIGURE 6.19 *Fitting photos printed out, cut apart, and spread over a cutting table in the costume shop*

included. Their vision was that everyone in the cast could wear one. I bought one and brought it in to rehearsal. It was stretchy enough for a few different performers to take turns working in it, zipping it up right over their rehearsal dancewear. With the digital projection mapping effects created by the projection designer, they did create some stunning stage pictures. What we learned, however, that we probably would not have learned if we had just tried the suit on in the fitting room, was that it actually impeded the performers too much. They were able to see through the fabric when all the lights were on, but in lower lighting situations, they couldn't see clearly. The fabric covering their feet made it quite slippery, and the gloves covering their hands made it difficult for them to climb the aerial silks. So instead of buying more morph suits, I bought and built tank tops, shorts, and leggings of white and grey stretch fabrics, and we accepted that the projections would just look a bit different when they hit performers' skin.

Sometimes specific characters emerge out of devising processes, and sometimes they do not.

ARTIST SPOTLIGHT: SIOUXSIE EASTER

Siouxsie Easter describes how she has worked with performers to create characters and devise costumes to express those characters.

SIOUXSIE EASTER: I got started in devising quite a while ago. I had my own theatre company. It was a group of us who were actors who got together every weekend. I was more of the director, but I did act and stuff too. We worked on a show one time for almost two years. We actually created the characters from scratch and I was the director, I was that sort of eye giving the actors the prompts and exercises and improv to do. And then we had a playwright in the room. I would go "write that down!" or he'd write some things down, or he would start to take the language and the dialogue that we made up during improvs and he would add to it. So we came up with this play called *Gargoyles*. David Dannenfelser is the playwright with the

FIGURE 6.20 *Experimenting with a morph suit and projections in rehearsal for* Dream Logos

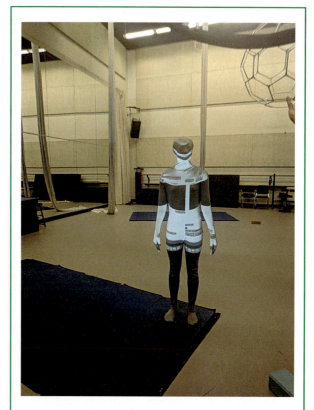

FIGURE 6.21 *Projection technology allows the performer's costume to be the projection surface*

company. It was about these people who ended up on a self-help weekend on an island and all the different reasons why they were there. That was really fun.

We approached costumes for that the way that we approached the creation of character. It was actor driven. For that one in particular we didn't have an independent designer. So they would start to write things about their personality and then we started digging into color, like what's this person's color scheme? Well, if they're on the island and they're going to go to the beach, are they going to wear a bathing suit? Are they going to be all covered up? How are they going to do that? Are they the big floppy hat kind of person? So we really did it through a series of questions. I would have loved to have a costume designer because we were pulling from our wardrobes. We really approached it according to the personality of the actors. It mostly stems from the actors.

I did a devised piece with a group of students. We were in England at the time, and so we did it about the history of Bath, England, which is where we were. We found this really interesting woman painter that a lot of people didn't talk about. So we devised a piece based on her. The costumes for that really came from looking at research photos of this woman and trying to cobble something together. We went to a rental costume place and sort of pulled some things together that seemed to be like her.

I did another piece here at Wells about famous women who graduated from Wells. We took a look at, again, research. What do these costumes look like? We had a little stint with Hillary Clinton, because she did come to Wells one time to speak. So I pulled a suit out of my closet because the students didn't own any dress suits. So I go, "here you go, here's a suit, looks very Hill like." So that's the type of projects that I've done, a lot of projects based on real people, interesting random real people that you find places that their stories don't get told very often. I've also helped birth a few more devised projects where people are taking aspects of their life and melding it with other people's lives and sort of creating a character based on different autobiographies and going that way.

KYLA KAZUSCHYK: When you work on those group projects, how do you delegate responsibilities? How do you decide who's going to pull from the costume storage, who's going to pull from their closet?

FIGURE 6.22 Dream Logos on stage at the Edinburgh International Fringe Festival, wearing costumes that do not impede movement (photo courtesy of Andy Phillipson—Livewireimage.com)

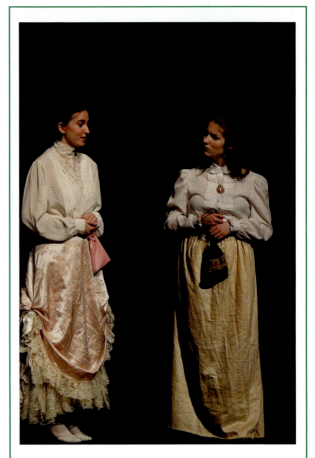

FIGURE 6.23 LeAnne Weber, left, and Katelyn Costello, right, in As the Ivy Grows, devised by Wells college students Ally Collins, 2020, Luke Lauchle, 2020, Abby Hauf, 2021, Michele Pradella, 2018, Kaetlyn Stinson, 2020, and LeAnne Weber, 2019 (photo courtesy of Siouxsie Easter)

SIOUXSIE EASTER: It really just ends up being a volunteer basis. It's sort of, one student goes, "well I have a black shirt, do you have a black shirt? What size are you? Here you go!" The only devising I've done with designers is really a lighting designer. I've not had the privilege of working with a costume designer in a devised situation.

And I know that costume design is so wonderful and so much beyond that. It would be great to have a designer in on the process to listen to the actors and really sit and watch and scribble down stuff about their personality. And do some mockups and talk. The beauty of being able to talk to the actors as well about their costumes, instead of the traditional practice where the actors are, a week before opening, they're given their costumes after several fittings and they're like "Oh well, here's what I'm wearing." And then they have to adapt in the moment, rather than sort of the costume adapting to them along the way.

KYLA KAZUSCHYK: Or them developing together! What I'm really excited about is if the costume designer is a part of the company from the beginning, they can be present in those rehearsals, in those conversations as things develop, and the costume can develop along with the character.

How do you determine timelines for your devising works? Do you just let it go as long as it takes, or do you set deadlines?

SIOUXSIE EASTER: This one I've let go as long as it's going to take because it just is. I love setting a deadline. I love saying "And we're going to put this up in November" and then we're like "oh it's done." With the project I did at Wells, we did that in one semester. And then we put it up at the start of the second semester, and so that was bound by time because of semesters. So we met once a week for 15 weeks and created that piece.

FIGURE 6.24 *Ally Collins seated on top of Luke Lauchle in* As the Ivy Grows, *devised at Wells college (photo courtesy of Siouxsie Easter)*

FIGURE 6.25 *Wells College student Michele Pradella in* As the Ivy Grows *(photo courtesy of Siouxsie Easter)*

KYLA KAZUSCHYK: Do you create a timeline other than the end or do you just say, well, it has to go up at this time, so everything has to be done by then?

SIOUXSIE EASTER: We do some, like tech has to be the week before and then this is the opening. And then I sort of sit back and watch the process as we go along and then I'm like, hang on, we're going to want to set some things in stone along the way. Let's do our final script five days before tech so that you all can memorize any of the changes or anything like that, but then the rest of it, I leave pretty loose. I know, in my mind, we should probably be at this point, but some of those really cool things are found midway through the process when we just want to be done and you're like—ughhh. And then we have to reengage at that point in time. So you don't want to cut it off too early, because the middle, the very middle of the process, all the way up to like two weeks before tech is such a … it's not fun.

It feels like we don't know where we're going, and this is hopeless, and then we get a big push and I think having a costume designer say today we're going to play with parts of these costumes I've been thinking about, could really be that push because, especially if you're working with students, until they get their costume they don't feel complete.

And I'm sure you've noticed for character, they just don't feel it until they've got their stuff.

It would be really great to have a costume designer in the room that could bring in little bits and pieces along the way, not just your rehearsal shoes the first week, but here's something else I'm thinking about and see if that changes character too. I wonder, have you had that experience, if that would change a character, based on what you bring in?

KYLA KAZUSCHYK: Yeah, absolutely and sometimes it goes the other way too, like if they're rehearsing something and the character changes, then the costume has to adjust to meet that too. And sometimes if you give them a piece like a hat or an apron or a corset, a corset totally changes it!

SIOUXSIE EASTER: Oh yeah, guess what, you can't breathe now—enjoy!

KYLA KAZUSCHYK: Or you have to figure out how to deal with this like how is it going to affect your posture and all your characterization?

SIOUXSIE EASTER: Yeah that's really neat how it goes both ways.

KYLA KAZUSCHYK: Do you practice non-hierarchical decision making in your classes?

SIOUXSIE EASTER: Yes, I do, and it's so funny because it's so hard for the students to accept that type of work when they first get there. Because they're so used to doing, they've arrived and all they've done are their high school junior musicals for four years, and we get into my classroom and I'm like, Okay so we're going to just explore the scene and who do you guys want to be and, Okay, so when you feel like moving, move when you feel like being still, be still and they're like, what why. Should I sit down now and I'm like, don't ever ask me that question. If you feel like in your head, should I sit down now, sit down and then we'll look at it and go with what works, what doesn't work, and I do that with my blocking too. I know the play very well, I do my research, I know my interests. And I shape it, but that decision making is so empowering for students, even though they don't think it's empowering in the beginning they're freaked out, but I do love that.

KYLA KAZUSCHYK: How do you work with them to cross that bridge of being scared of it to taking choices and making risks?

SIOUXSIE EASTER: I really piss them off for a while, I think. I frustrate them for a while because they are like, just tell me what to do, why can't you be more specific, why can't you tell me and I'm like, because it's time for you to start exercising your own choices. And it's time for you to really have opinions. Uta Hagen always says we should have an opinion about the world around us, you need to have an opinion and I want to know what it is, and this is a gift to you, to be able to give your opinion. What do you think, you know?

I worked at Shakespeare and company, when I was in my late teens early twenties, and I just happened to land a job in the box office there, and you know it's all these wonderful wonderful people that worked there that Kristen Linklater and Tina Packer and Dennis Crowley all these great people and I'm a little box office girl, and so I'd get off my shift, and I would go down to the main outdoor theatre and I would sit on the hill and watch Tina direct the actors and I would just sit there and watch and one day she leans over to me she's like you, you and she always called me Cindy Siouxsie because my best friend was Cindy and she couldn't tell us apart, she didn't, she didn't know me from anybody, she said, what do you think about this, this moment I'm like what. She's like it's not working, what do you think?

And I said um, maybe if that person came in, just like in the third line, and then they moved over there and she's like all right we'll try it and she tried it and I was like, completely empowered you know, and I think I'm the greatest director in the entire world, because surely I directed this whole play and you know she'll always remember that moment and me.

But, to think about that, that sense of wow, maybe I can do this, maybe I'm worth something more than this box office role then. And so I guess just really talking to the students and helping them understand that it's a gift and not a punishment, that it's something for them to take.

And now, if I ask a student, what do you want me to call you, do you go by Kathleen or do you go by Kathy and they say I don't care, they also get a little lecture from me because I'm like surely you do care. You wouldn't want me to just call you, I don't know—some derogatory name— you really do care. Tell me what you care about, tell me your name, which is the core of who you are. I have a very specific name and that's who I am. I'm not Sue and I'm not Susan and so I think that the thing that I do with the students is to get them to start to care and be invested in that.

KYLA KAZUSCHYK: Do you think it's starting to care or just starting to feel comfortable expressing that they care?

SIOUXSIE EASTER: I would say yeah, more feeling comfortable to express that they care and also they've sort of developed this I don't care attitude, a lot of times in junior and senior year because teachers are always saying no, not that way, no not that way, here's your lines, here's your everything you have to fit into is right here, you know, and so they give up on caring maybe.

KYLA KAZUSCHYK: I just recently started incorporating non-hierarchical decision making into my costume classes, into mask making and stage makeup and costume construction. Like starting the beginning of the semester asking the students, what do you want to get out of this? I have a million things I could just tell you, but you could look them up on YouTube. I think that, now that we have YouTube, now that we have the internet, universities started before we had all of this, so universities need to adjust to fill in something that students can't get otherwise.

You have access to information, you're not just coming to me as a fountain of information, you're coming to this community, because we can be in community with each other and bounce ideas off each other and grow from each other, like that's the whole advantage, that's the reason that we're here in a class together.

SIOUXSIE EASTER: That's an interesting thought because professors used to be like holders of information, we knew more than anybody else, we studied harder and longer than anybody else, but now it's like yeah my carburetor is out so I'm going to YouTube for how to fix that. We're doing things you've never thought you would fix or do because you can.

So I teach devising also. I'm going to be teaching it this summer in England and I think I'm going to have the actors also take on designer roles. By default, sometimes when I teach that I'm like, Oh and I'll take care of that for you guys and I'll take care of this for you, that's not really designing that's actually being hierarchical where I'm like, Yeah I will do the costumes I will do this and I will do that yeah so I need to let them into that a little bit more.

KYLA KAZUSCHYK: Devising can be so many different things.

SIOUXSIE EASTER: It's wonderful when you just get this idea and there's a group of people. The tough part is killing the darlings. One student has this juicy monologue that they've written for themselves and they just can't let it go and you're like it doesn't work, it's not working in this piece, we can keep two lines from it, you know?

KYLA KAZUSCHYK: I think that's a valuable lesson too, to know that nothing is precious. It feels so important, but you can—it's okay to let it go.

SIOUXSIE EASTER: We killed pages on our piece about the women of Wells like, Okay well that's gone, you know. We just kept putting up those big sticky pads on the wall and just kept writing on them and kept writing on them, and we just had tons of them, and that was fun to look at.

KYLA KAZUSCHYK: When you throw stuff out, do you totally throw it out, or do you save it for other projects?

SIOUXSIE EASTER: I roll it up and I stick it in the corner and I stick a label on it, and if we need to bring it out for something else we bring it out for something else. Everything's kind of got a box or a space. Like, Okay we're gonna look at this again, it didn't work for this show, but it might work for that show. They did that in musicals. It's called a trunk tune, and it was a song written for a show that doesn't work for the show, and so they put it in a trunk, like put it away, and then they get it out for a different show, and they adapt it to that show and it's called a trunk show.

KYLA KAZUSCHYK: You work in analog like that, on physical sticky note posters, you find that helpful?

SIOUXSIE EASTER: I do find that very helpful because the students will get up and work with them too. You'll throw them a marker and they'll get up and I actually learned this at an ATHE workshop—that to buy the markers that smell, like the different flavors and not flavor, you're not eating them, they smell like, well you want to but they smell like different things—the students were so into those markers. They'd be like I want the raspberry one, I'm going to write something down, and then they get the raspberry one to write it down and they were totally into the markers. It was the silliest thing, but I loved it, it worked.

KYLA KAZUSCHYK: There's probably research behind that, the sensory connection. Maybe people are motivated by the different smells and they make them want to generate ideas.

SIOUXSIE EASTER: They were really into it and they started to figure out their favorite color. Sometimes I'd come in the morning, and I would just slap three of them up, and I would write a word at the top of each one or I'd write a question and I would say the first ten minutes are silent and here's your markers and it was really cool to watch just stuff come up on there and then be like, Okay, this is our first improv today we're going to take this first sheet—let's go, let's do a silent sculpture, based on that, okay now I want you to create a three-word scene, based on this panel and then we're going to do a character based on this panel, who's going to tell me a one-minute monologue, write a one-minute monologue about this panel.

And it's all time based. You have one minute to do this, you have five minutes to do this, because then there's no time to think you just have to go.

KYLA KAZUSCHYK: Time limitations I'm sure are very helpful.

SIOUXSIE EASTER: Do you ever just put a bunch of clothes in the middle of the floor and tell people to have at it and see what happens?

KYLA KAZUSCHYK: I haven't yet. I have brought in pieces to rehearsal, and sometimes not clothes. I've brought in, you know the fine line between what's a costume and what's a prop, and what could become a costume, like anything can be a hat, right? Or a piece of wire, a hanger. I've given those to performers in rehearsal and see what they come up with and see what becomes a costume or what becomes a character.

SIOUXSIE EASTER: That's fun. I would love to do a piece just with pipe cleaners. That would be fun, that would be really cool to costume based on that.

KYLA KAZUSCHYK: It would be cool to have like a vast amount of pipe cleaners.

SIOUXSIE EASTER: You could twist them up together, that would be fun.

KYLA KAZUSCHYK: I just put that in the trunk. That's a trunk idea.

SIOUXSIE EASTER: I'll be waiting for it, the pipe cleaners. Let me know, send me a link.

KYLA KAZUSCHYK: Or maybe it's one of those things that starts as pipe cleaners, but then it becomes something else, like give the pipe cleaners to the actors and they can make the shapes and then give the pictures of the shapes to the costume designers and they can make them.

SIOUXSIE EASTER: That's a cool idea. You can make the silhouettes and then you can make a set from them too, or props from them.

KYLA KAZUSCHYK: Sure, yeah build the whole set out of pipe cleaners! It's a medium that is accessible, we all know how to bend a pipe cleaner. Give that to people that understand wood and metal and have them make it out of wood and metal. I'm so excited that we're generating ideas!

SIOUXSIE EASTER: That would be really fun. We're doing it. We'll collaborate.

KYLA KAZUSCHYK: Yeah, why not! Do you have advice for artists approaching devised work? Based on your experience, what advice would you give to people?

SIOUXSIE EASTER: I really would say you can't really be prepared for this type of work, but you can be in the sense that you need to, especially if you're using the inspiration piece, you have to know that inspiration piece backwards and forwards. Unless you're planning on all the research coming from there, but if you're saying I'm going to do a piece on Moby Dick and you've never read Moby Dick, like, just because you think it's cool is not a great reason for a piece to devise from. You also should be in love with the inspiration piece. Otherwise, in two weeks you're going to burn out completely and you're not going to enjoy it at all. Joan of Arc, I've been working on this piece for two years. I do love her. There are days I hate her and I argue with her, but for the most part, I think it's really fascinating. I want to keep researching and going. So make sure you pick the right inspiration. Make sure it's something that you can buy into and that you and the group of people that you're working with, everybody buys into. It should be an inspiration that inspires everybody.

And then you also really have to take days where you're the leader and days when you're the follower and you have to make those equal. To look at that, like, Oh I've really driven the conversation for the past couple of days, I'm going to be quiet and listen for a couple of days and see what new thing comes with because if you're in a devising group and one person's driving their idea, then it's not devised piece, it's a directed piece, right? Whether that person is an actor, designer or a director they're directing the piece that they keep saying, and they railroad everybody else. I'm a facilitator a lot in devised theatre, where I'll sit and listen listen listen and then I'll say hang on one second what did you think about that, you look like you want to say something and then I'll pull something forward from the people who don't talk. So, be prepared to talk, be prepared to listen.

KYLA KAZUSCHYK: I love that because that's advice for everything. That's true for any kind of collaboration. That's true for any kind of relationship. Be prepared to talk, be prepared to listen. It's going to be more fun and more fruitful if it's give and take.

SIOUXSIE EASTER: Absolutely. You've worked in classrooms for a while and when the conversation is just pushed by one person over and over again, even if they are so smart and they did all the homework and all the rest of the slackers in the room didn't do their homework it is still annoying. It doesn't open it up, you know.

And I'll say, Hey what did you think about this and they'll say, Well I didn't read the chapter, like, Okay, but I'm not talking about the chapter I'm thinking about this subject, what do you think about this subject. You don't have to regurgitate to me what the chapter said, although you should go back and read the chapter because that's how we learn, too. But what do you think about this?

I have a couple of students who have never really seen theatre that are in my classes this year. And it's mind blowing. There is a student in my directing class this year who has this really interesting perspective because he's a visual artist and he tends to come at that approach, and like, Okay, great see you didn't have to speak theatre talk to tell me what you thought about this, you know?

KYLA KAZUSCHYK: There has to be some kind of balance between a base of knowledge and then alternate perspectives.

ARTIST SPOTLIGHT: RACHEL ENGSTROM

Rachel Engstrom shares her unique perspective as a costume designer who has collaborated with students and professionals on forms of scripted and unscripted performance in different regions of the United States.

RACHEL ENGSTROM: I think that devised theatre is something that's created by a particular group of people for, usually it's a singular project but for a particular purpose. There can be overlap with theatre, there can be overlap with circus, there could be overlap with puppetry, there can be overlap with music. So it's just kind of whatever that style that that group of people wants to do. There's definitely some companies that have a particular style. There's one

FIGURE 6.26 HamlEt at the OC Centric New Play Festival, directed by Tamiko Washington, costumes by Rachel Engstrom (photo courtesy of Rachel Engstrom)

company I worked with in LA that had a lot of dancers and gymnasts in their company, in addition to actors, so they did basically like physical theatre, so lots of like circus elements and things. They called it choreographed movement. So sometimes there were dances like, where there were dances in a script. Because they would usually start with a classic script like Shakespeare or the one thing we did was Hercules, so like myths and things, things that are in the public domain, and then they kind of mess with them and set them, sometimes in a different world, like different time period or more fantasy. And so they had their particular style that they did, and I think other groups have a kind of thing where they make the entire scripts like with that group, so it kind of depends. I think the biggest or the first like, distinction between different groups is, are you starting with an existing story whether it's a rewrite of a classic or even just a basic storyline or are you starting completely from scratch and you're going to build a script out of an idea or a piece of music even but that's more common with dance-focused things.

KYLA KAZUSCHYK: It's interesting how that is kind of devised, too, like whether you're starting with a theory or an idea or a myth or music and then devising the work around that—pretty much what choreographers do is they're devising.

RACHEL ENGSTROM: It's interesting because I work with a lot of different choreographers in my job because I primarily design for the dance department and they all have different approaches and so now that I've worked with some of them multiple times it's just like, Oh I kind of know what they're doing. And so, like the ballet professor she will sometimes do classic ballets that have choreography that was done by a famous choreographer and she's recreating a thing. Other times, she will, like she did this amazing piece about Frida Kahlo and she devised the whole thing, working very closely with the lighting designer and a projection designer. At the time it was a student costume designer, and we remounted that piece so I handled the costumes because the student wasn't there anymore, it was years ago that they designed it, but it was like their design, we still had the costumes and remounted it. But that was something that she devised completely from scratch and I can't remember if the music was original. We do a lot of stuff with original scores of music, which is always cool because sometimes they get the music and then they choreograph to the music, other times they choreograph a dance and then music is made for it.

KYLA KAZUSCHYK: That's so cool!

RACHEL ENGSTROM: Yeah so it's just kind of like different things, and sometimes there's live music and sometimes it's recorded and it's really kind of neat.

KYLA KAZUSCHYK: The musicians create based on what they see the performers do?

RACHEL ENGSTROM: Actually there's this really cool piece, we're opening our dance concert next week and there's two pieces that are outdoor pieces that are going to have small audiences and one of them is a piece where the audience and the dancers are all wearing headphones. And there's three different pieces of music, so you get to choose which piece of music you listen to when you watch it so everybody has a slightly different experience and even the dancers are all choosing one of the three pieces. But all three pieces were created by a DJ composer so it's a very synth-like mix—it's all like mixed samples of music like a DJ does but done for this specific dance piece, so that they came to watch it and they videotaped it. And then the choreographer was telling me that the DJ is actually using that music then because he owns that music, he created it and he's using it in shows that he's doing at like small venues and bars and stuff, and he's using some of the video like it's very highly edited or like filtered so you can't see who the actual people are in it, so it looks like outlines of people, but it's like the video of the dancers doing that dance that he's projecting for people to just enjoy at the bar to dance to themselves. It's really cool. So I think it's neat when people create just things out of nothing or out of an idea.

KYLA KAZUSCHYK: Yeah, totally, that example sounds so interesting. It's like post postmodernism, to take something and turn it into something else, and then turn it into something else you can't even see what it was at the beginning. That's so cool and the idea of there being three separate pieces of music. I don't know a lot about dance, but it would have to just be the same timing right? And then it can be totally different as long as the counts are the same, right?

RACHEL ENGSTROM: Yeah, pretty much you can use any of anything as long as the counts are the same, and so you get very different emotional qualities from it. They set up a thing like basically you scan a QR code and it brings you to the website and you have three options, and it has a countdown for when you're supposed to press play so everybody presses play at the same time and has just like short little descriptors of the different pieces of music so like, one says, I think, like playful energetic upbeat and like another one says, traditional melodic or something like that, so you just kind of choose and it's interesting because in dress rehearsals I saw it multiple times, so of course I listened to each of the pieces and it gives you such a different feeling. It's weird. I liked one and three the best. But the ending with two was so different feeling and like the ending of a show when you see it, that feeling that you have when you leave the theatre when there's something like that completely like a twist at the end or something. And it was just so interesting. It was really cool. I had doubts along the way, as to how it was gonna work for sure. I was like this is an ambitious project for pandemic times but the composer that she chose was really up for the task and was able to meet all the deadlines that were needed from our sound engineer, so it actually turned out really well.

KYLA KAZUSCHYK: I bet that made dress rehearsals less tedious too, like you're watching a different show three times.

RACHEL ENGSTROM: Oh yeah, and with dance shows the one nice thing is that they're very short. Like this was an eight and a half minute piece. That's an advantage.

KYLA KAZUSCHYK: And you designed the costumes for that?

RACHEL ENGSTROM: Yeah and this choreographer, generally she does very pedestrian style so like stuff you can buy off the rack. And so it was canvas joggers and T-shirts or tank tops but the color scheme was inspired by the brick they were dancing on and the building they were dancing in front of, with like a little bit of navy blue thrown in for contrast, and so it was kind of funny because each individual dancer had a different combo but, as a group, they looked so good together and I realized that it was literally the colors from my wardrobe, my personal wardrobe. I was like, Man, now I understand why I'm like I can't figure out which one's my favorite because there's usually a favorite costume or like, Oh that's the one I would wear personally, but this one, I was like I would wear every single one of these that's so weird and then I was like, Oh that's why.

KYLA KAZUSCHYK: Was it a challenge to think about, like when I have designed for dance I really think about the tone of the music and like if it's happy upbeat joyful that's one kind of design, but if it's traditional, that's a totally different look.

RACHEL ENGSTROM: Well, that's the thing about working with different choreographers is I've been able to see how differently they work, and so, like the ballet professor I was talking about, she's very about the music. And so it's very important to design to the music for her. Others, it's about their concept, what they want the audience to feel, or what they're trying to say. Or sometimes, like there was one where it was like, make them look like sea creatures, but not cheesy like fake fish and stuff so they had kind of like a seaweedy feel and color scheme to them. But this one, it was about perspective and how multiple people can be seeing or hearing the same thing and have a different experience in a different perspective. And so she wanted every single person to be different, but all within like the same thing, so they literally each had the same pants. I found a pair of pants that was available in like six different colors. Apparently it just happens to be the color scheme, I think it was just what the fashion industry decided was in right now. So, and then just bought T-shirts and tank tops to match based on what would look good on the dancers. And since it was kind of one that was not about the costumes because there were so many other elements, like it was in a different place other than a theatre and they had this like sound element that was so unique. That one was just kind of like make it so that they can dance and have an interesting color scheme. And then it ties to the concept with every single person being different, that every single person has a different perspective. So it's kind of like a simple one, but then others like this other, the other piece that is outside, is kind of more akin to like a happening. It's about 23 to 30 minutes long and the music is live, all computer digital music and it goes around this lake that we have near our building and she basically just wanted to invoke the spring equinox. So every single one of them was in metallic and pastels to try to hopefully catch the light and they had leggings and then different asymmetrical outfits. Some had kind of like tunic dresses and skirts and tops, some had these really flowing pants in a bunch of chiffon and stuff and so once I saw them as a group, doing the dance I was like, Oh, they look like they're summoning a spring goddess or like doing some sort of like ritual like almost like religious or even or some kind of cultural ritual or something. And it's a public space that they're doing it in and so people were just going to be walking through. A lot of people would just avoid it or some people just walk through and the dancers just kind of went around them. And this one guy was coming on a path and we saw them across the lake and he sees them and he just turns and goes up an extremely steep hill because he was walking and then all of a sudden just saw like these women all walking in a perfect line doing like long sweeping motions with their arms and legs in pastel floaty costumes so it was it was just hilarious to see how people reacted.

KYLA KAZUSCHYK: You weren't trying to get an audience, it's just whoever encounters it is the audience?

RACHEL ENGSTROM: Right. And so like their intention, there's four performances next week for these two pieces, so the intention is that they're inviting classes so students can go see them and inviting their family or whatever, and then just whoever happens to be walking by can watch it. That said, I mean the nice thing about it is that they're not selling tickets to it. It is all just like free invitation-only kind of thing so it's going to be interesting to see. I hope they have enough people show up and everything. It's a different form. I like how they're playing with form, but it is a challenge, because we're doing things where we haven't done them before when we have students who are constantly ending up in quarantine because they live in dorms. All right, we've learned a lot from this and if we need to do this again we know what we will do differently. So, because you know when they say, Oh I don't think I'm going to need that much technical support and then you find out what the actual thing develops to be it's like, Oh you actually need way more technical support than you thought. Because you developed it through rehearsals and with truncated time and everything.

I think the biggest challenge with devised theatre is having to set parameters or being comfortable with saying and being told no. Because sometimes—as much as you can think an idea is cool and as much as you want to do it—sometimes with time and resources just the answer has to be no and then you have to not get hurt about that or not get distracted by that and be like, Okay, so what is really the root idea of what I wanted that I couldn't get and is there an alternative to doing that?

This outdoor piece she originally wanted LED lights. And originally it was supposed to be less dancers, and same with another piece was supposed to be less dancers, and I'm given the same amount of money, regardless of how many dancers they cast. And because they're outside I had twice as many shoes I had to buy as I normally do because on marley floors they dance barefoot a lot. And shoes are expensive, so there was a certain point where I was like, Listen, LEDs are probably not going to happen, and she was like, okay. She's like, Well, maybe we'll save that idea for another semester. Do you think there's a way we can still get the idea? The idea was like sunlight streaming through the trees, and like spring and the equinox. So I was like, What if we did some metallics and tried to get the reflection from the sun? It may or may not work, depending on how the weather is and in North Carolina you can never count on the weather. So that's what we did, and it didn't fully get the reflection and look and the light that we wanted, but even with LEDs during daylight from that far away you're not going to see them. So it's, you know, it's like, that's a great idea choreographer, but here's how I think it's not going to work and here's some alternatives, and fortunately she's someone who's very much about the educational process and we can't do everything and is very open to ideas, so she was happy with the final product, I was happy with the final product. I'm sure in the future there's gonna be some LEDs on some costumes when we're on stage and can control the light conditions and make those actually visible.

KYLA KAZUSCHYK: Was there a lighting designer or you're just doing it daytime with natural light?

RACHEL ENGSTROM: We have a lighting designer for the project and because one of the pieces, there was a pointe piece that was one of those ones that was choreography from a famous choreographer that was just replicated. And that one was on the stage with a lighting designer and because there's gonna be a film release with the two outdoor pieces and then two pieces that were done inside those four are going to be released on a film for people to see. And so that piece had a lighting designer but the other three pieces of the two outside were like, Yeah we don't need lighting, we're just going to use the sunlight. And the other one, theirs was in the lobby and our lobby is basically like a wall of windows. And so they were just using the daylight because they liked the quality at a certain time of day when the light streams and you get really beautiful patterns on the floor and everything, and so they were using the quality of that light, particularly. So that's why we didn't have a lighting designer for that, but it was interesting. It's very difficult, too, because it resulted in us having three tech weeks in a row. The choreographers only have to be there for their piece. I had to be there for all of them.

KYLA KAZUSCHYK: Yeah division of labor is always going to be a big question. Sometimes directors really only see the one thing that they're directing. But the costume people are doing costumes for every show, the lighting people are doing lighting for every show. And in that example you described, yeah, like you can just use the light that's around you if it's site specific you don't need to build the set, the set is what's around you but they have to wear something, unless they're nude.

RACHEL ENGSTROM: Yeah, and I mean it is a smaller concert than normal, less dancers, less costumes and we didn't have crazy builds. We built the one that was outdoors around the lake but we were able to over hire that, some of that labor, but that's the other thing too with the last three semesters. Our practicum class enrollment, because we're hybrid classes now for distancing we only have students like half the number of students that we normally have so that's half the number of hours. And we just didn't get that many student workers and then people constantly being absent, for you know, usually related to, Oh, I have to wait to get tested because I got a call from housing, that I got an exposure and it's just like Okay. From the beginning, we underestimated how much labor and tried to count in for those anticipated absences and we still, just the timing of them, it was like there was one cluster in the dorms and it just seems like it knocked out half of our students, literally 50 percent attendance for almost two weeks.

KYLA KAZUSCHYK: Did you adjust your production timeline because of that or did the opening days stay the same?

RACHEL ENGSTROM: Well our schedules constantly changed. That's probably the biggest mess with Covid that we've all collectively complained about.

KYLA KAZUSCHYK: This principle of flexibility is something where I think devised theatre makes us all stronger and more well equipped to handle things like that too. Even when working on a scripted piece, you've still got to be so nimble. Everything can change because of a global pandemic, or because of anything—there's a million reasons why stuff could change and you've got to be ready to throw stuff out and start over. And it's so hard to do that because we're taught that things have to be so regimented and analyze the script and have the cast and that's that but the cast might change, maybe it's going to be a small cast, maybe it's a big cast, maybe it's these students, but then they graduate. Everything can change, no matter what.

RACHEL ENGSTROM: Oh yeah its flexibility and thinking outside the box, finding nontraditional solutions to things. A lot of the devised pieces that I worked on out, I moved here from like L.A., Orange county, and I worked with a lot of small theatre groups that either didn't even have spaces, or would rent spaces and some of those things were the most innovative pieces because they more often than not wanted to create an entire world—like we're not setting it in the '50s, we're not setting it in America, it's not set anywhere, it's set in the world of the play.

I did a 30-minute version of *Hamlet*. And it was basically like the highlights of *Hamlet*. The whole thing was steampunk and an extremely diverse cast, and it was just so phenomenal. The interesting thing is *Hamlet* I have done

FIGURE 6.27 HamlEt at the OC Centric New Play Festival, directed by Tamiko Washington, costumes by Rachel Engstrom (photo courtesy of Rachel Engstrom)

FIGURE 6.28 Using Shakespeare's Hamlet as source material, collaborators devised this 30-minute show (photo courtesy of Rachel Engstrom)

at least four times. I did *Rosencrantz and Guildenstern Are Dead* and it's just like it's crazy like what people can do with different things.

KYLA KAZUSCHYK: And that comes back to what you were talking about before, starting with a story like, Okay, everyone knows the story of *Hamlet*, but this is something totally different. Like we are going to that and turn it on its head and put it somewhere else, compress it.

RACHEL ENGSTROM: My thesis project in grad school actually was with a director who I then later on worked with on a bunch of devised pieces. He had a company that had gymnasts and dancers, and it was *Two Gentlemen of Verona* but done with YouTube music. So, like a play with music, I mean kind of like a musical but like not exactly and then it also had physical theatre, so it was choreographed movement and circus acts and stuff. And it was the craziest thing, and it was set, the people in the city were all in like very '50s kind of like Norman Rockwell style clothing to try to evoke that perfect like American dream kind of feeling. And then the outlaws in the forest were all a biker gang like, think like '80s, '90s biker gang and then there's a military aspect, and so the military we chose was Air Force, and the reason was because the director's dad was in the Air Force so I mean you just had to choose a military and so we were just like American Air Force. And because we wanted to give the idea of America and everything. And my professors, when I was presenting my project, they could not grasp the concept that it was not set in the '50s. Because they had a huge issue that I used relatively modern looking military uniforms and then biker outfits that were very a la '80s and then '50s clothing and I'm like but all this stuff exists right now, people wear '50s clothing now. They just could not grasp it and they were like, What, when is it set, like where does this take place, why? And I'm like, these are chosen for the almost like archetypal qualities of these specific things like the '50s clothing evokes a very specific feeling to Americans. It's not about the time, it's the feeling, it invokes this wholesomeness that nothing is wrong, everybody is in their place and the purpose of that being chosen is to show that she breaks out of that because she doesn't want that, and then she ends up with a biker gang because, like that's the last

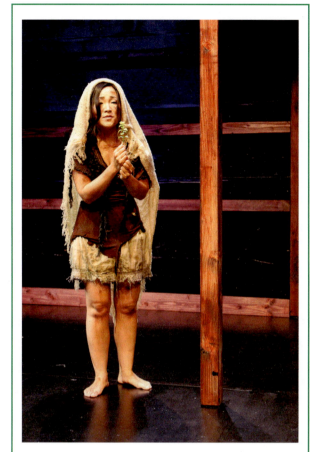

FIGURE 6.29 HamlEt on stage in a small black box space on Chapman University campus, Orange County, California (photo courtesy of Rachel Engstrom)

place that you would want your daughter to end up is with a bunch of bikers in a forest. So it was interesting to try to convince them that that's what happened. And the interesting thing too was, the cast, who were all undergrad actors, got it instantly. They understood it, they got it, they were like, this is cool.

KYLA KAZUSCHYK: I'm excited to see how that will change too as young people get older and as young people have more leadership roles in theatres. I think there's going to be more openness to throwing whatever we've expected out the window and doing something new. My students are so interested in doing something new. They're not interested in, no one wants to do a traditional *Two Gentlemen of Verona* for sure.

RACHEL ENGSTROM: It's amazing just to see this generation, they're just like blowing everything apart in a good way, like they're just like, Yeah no, this is not okay, this is who I am, this is where I am and we're going to form this world the way we want to. It's fascinating to me to see because art always kind of leads culture. People think that art is a reflection of culture, which it is, but it's always at the forefront of the culture. And I guess you can see it most when you look back at art history, you know, like people think about it and they're like, Oh yeah Picasso. Well, think about when Picasso was and what life looked like, are you kidding me women were still wearing corsets and he's like putting up art like this. People don't always necessarily see the art that is happening and, like the Shakespeare thing. We assign production critiques for our practicum class, it's one of the few homework assignments they have to do, and because of the pandemic they're watching streaming things. So I assigned *Romeo and Juliet* that was streamed by the Globe and it was great. It was like this interesting kind of modern take and everything and it was pretty fast paced and I was like, Yeah they can pay attention to this. I have two students this semester and they're both psychology and dance so they're not theatre majors at all. They have not taken any theatre classes like, this is the only one, this practicum. And neither one of them had ever seen Shakespeare done. In their minds, they thought Shakespeare was in Shakespearean clothing like it's going to be this all the time and that's all—they were like, This is so interesting and I'm like I've never seen Shakespeare done in Shakespeare's time, ever. And I have seen dozens of Shakespeare plays performed. Never once was it actually set in that time period, and I was like, Oh you guys aren't even seeing art. It's always interesting to see how students make me reflect on my own life and, like their experiences, and the older I've gotten, I'm like man, I really had an awesome childhood and like I had so many opportunities that were like given to me and encouraged for me to take. My parents encouraged me to take opportunities and be bold and do things, and it's interesting to talk to some of these students and it's like you're a theatre student and you're scared to move away from your hometown, you're scared to talk to people, you're scared to ask a question in a class that you are paying lots of money for. It's almost just like what did people do to you that made you afraid of asking questions like, who yelled at you for asking questions.

KYLA KAZUSCHYK: A lot of people probably did. Like with standardized testing.

RACHEL ENGSTROM: It's shocking because it's just like, Oh, I was just raised in such a wholesome environment with support. I encounter a lot of kids who are very like I was, but I encounter other kids who clearly were just raised with fear. And it seems to be more common. I don't know if it's more common, or if it's just a difference in geographical area, because when I taught in California I taught at Huntington Beach high school, which is in Orange county which is like, it's a super rich school. Some of my students' parents were like millionaires, it was crazy, it was a culture shock. The students here are very, it's a state school, they're your average college student, half of them are working three jobs and going to school full time. And it's rare to have the student who's, like my parents wouldn't let me work because they said school is my full time job. We occasionally get one of those and it's because their parents were smart enough to put away money, able to put away money or they had a grandparent who left them a bunch of money. People have very very different circumstances here. Whereas in California, like all of these kids just came from obscene privilege. They were amazing students, though, very, very different than what you think on the surface, like they were very polite. It was interesting to see them talk about their parents, too, because some of them came, I mean they were all theatre students and some of them came from very capitalistic republican parents and they were kind of like, Well, my parents are paying for my college so I'm going to major in theatre because they're paying for it.

KYLA KAZUSCHYK: It is so interesting how culture is regional. I think the point you make about fear is really interesting because I encounter that with my students too, and I think that one of the antidotes to that is devised work. And if students are so hung up on what's the right answer, like I need to know the right answer tell me the right or wrong answer, what do I need to do to get an A—that's the problem with education—they're not learning to think for themselves. And you can do the same thing in a scripted show, like what's the right line reading of this line, but if you're devising something together with students, the line isn't even written, there's no right reading of it, there's no right answer, y'all have to figure it out, you have to come up with whatever the answers are for yourself.

RACHEL ENGSTROM: Yeah and it also gives them a great sense of ownership over the work too, and sometimes it allows for almost like a personal catharsis or I see this a lot, especially either with the director, or if there's a playwright involved or somebody who's in the production team, where it can be extremely personal or a way to kind of like work through trauma or a way to solve a problem. That's always interesting to me too because then it can be like for the people involved, it can be such like, an emotional journey and some of those things can be just like, I mean you work on a show for a few months, and it can be something that you remember for the rest of your life. There's a handful of shows that I've seen that it's been over a decade since I've seen them and I still have vivid memories because these shows were so amazing. And I can guarantee you, not a single one of those was a production of *The Music Man*. Every single one of them was either original, something completely off the wall, or something that, for some reason, the time in my life I was going through something and it just struck a nerve. And I think that's the beauty of theatre and that's what I miss most about live theatre right now is, I mean, I've watched the streaming things and stuff but like I don't feel anything.

KYLA KAZUSCHYK: It is so true that doing stuff on zoom is not the same as doing it in person. I know we talked about collaboration like we can only express so much through a computer screen, even if we're working together to create something. We're working on a production right now that's all going to be streamed through zoom and you can listen to someone and respond to what you hear but it's so different from having the energy of being present with someone in a room. There's nothing that replaces that.

RACHEL ENGSTROM: Yeah and that's so weird too, because it's energy and there is no other way to describe it, but there's also no tangible way to like measure that or measure the transference of emotions.

There's also a difference in vision and hearing, like the ability of seeing something in person, as opposed to on the screen. There's something that happens to it that flattens it on the screen or something or your connection. And then hearing too, like that's the one thing with masks. I'm all for these places that did masked production—like all of our dance shows they're all masked and they're dancing so you know we just make sure that it goes with the costume and it's fine—but to do a show where people are talking, and if you have the masks and they're not clear masks you're making that less accessible to people.

And so that brings up another question which is, we were going in a good direction with making theatre more accessible to people. Children's theatre does sensory shows and everything, and so I think there's a lot of good things going, but I hope that all of the stuff with Covid doesn't impede the progress we're making in other areas.

I hope people remain innovative without just being like, Oh, we innovated with zoom productions, so now let's ride that wave for a while. It's like no, let's keep innovating at this pace. We know we can do it now, let's keep doing it.

I really think American theatre, a lot of places, especially when you get outside of big cities and you look at what some community theatre models are, they're doing the same things over and over and over again and it's like, I don't want to have to go to a big city or go to like very few choices for actual artistic theatre. I don't know if that many people can see the level of art that we can raise theatre to, because I feel like culturally, art is seen as inaccessible to people, to the average person. Some art museums are doing things like making free days and some places have student rush tickets or pay what you can nights and everything—but even still. People don't see theatre, people don't even try to seek it out or look up or find out about pay what you can nights unless somebody tells them because they automatically discount it by saying, it's not for me. I'm not going to understand it. But then sometimes that's always one of the things I love doing is taking a friend who has never been to see live theatre and take them to see something so weird or just like something they wouldn't expect. One of the theatres in town did *Silence the Musical* so it's *Silence of the Lambs* and it's basically making fun of some of these really misogynistic things that are in the original movie and it's a very stylized, very satirical version of the original movie. And my friend was like, you're taking me to a musical—Okay, I guess sure, and it was like, well I'll buy your ticket and he was like okay well I've got nothing to lose then, and so we went and he was like that was the funniest thing I've ever seen. See, it can be funny.

And so now, since then he's gone with me to like two more things and it's just interesting. One time he came with me to the ballet and people kind of dress fancy for the ballet and he was like, Well, I'm gonna wear jeans and I was like, Okay, he wore jeans and a Metallica T-shirt. Like dude, okay we just have orchestra seats, but that's okay that's fine and you know, like some people looked but it's also I mean there's people in like full three-piece suits with bow ties and then there's other people in jeans and a T-shirt.

KYLA KAZUSCHYK: I think there's room for all of it. We created those cultural norms that you have to dress a certain way to experience something, but you don't really have to.

RACHEL ENGSTROM: Right, we're all just sitting in the dark anyway.

KYLA KAZUSCHYK: Exactly.

RACHEL ENGSTROM: It's so interesting and like that's the thing is, I always like dressing up for shows because it gives me an excuse to, and I think a lot of people do and that's another thing that I think is fun with theatre, is you can play with the audience, you can be like, Hey when you come see the show you should dress like a cowboy if you want to. It's fun, because then it brings people together in the audience when you're standing in the lobby beforehand, you can be like, Oh, I like your outfit you know.

So I think, with devised theatre and site-specific theatre and stuff it's playing with the audience, it's engaging them in different ways it's making them experience something that they haven't experienced.

And hopefully with the pandemic, I think a lot of people have realized that life isn't about the stuff, that it's more about the experience and the people. And connection. Hopefully theatre can kind of grab onto that and be like hey, people want connection. And do more innovative things because the ideas are out there, people just need to take a chance, and there's so many complications to trying to get funding, space, all of those things and somebody to give you a chance. Thankfully, like academia, you can do a lot of stuff that I don't think you'd be able to do in the real world, unless you had a very supportive producer.

KYLA KAZUSCHYK: That's why we should do everything with academia, while we can.

RACHEL ENGSTROM: Yeah the weirder the better, like some of my colleagues always say they're like I don't know why we do some of this weird stuff all the time, the students need to learn the classics and it's like why? Why? I mean like they can study them in their academic classes, because yeah, theatre history is important, but study what history was so that you know what it can be.

I mean occasionally throw in a classic because, why not, and you can usually save some money on royalties if they're old enough, but I mean also throw in a classic and mess with it, do something different. It's so common for companies to do that with Shakespeare. I think we need to start doing that with more stuff. But it also gets a little dicey with copyright and all that legal stuff. I want somebody who has like a good handle on that stuff before going on a venture, because you know it's like the Beckett estate with *Waiting for Godot*, that's such a brilliant piece, you could use such cool things with it, but I don't know how closely you could get to doing inspired by Godot. There was one thing I saw, I guess it's like performance art, this guy was standing in an airport with a sign that said Godot. He was just waiting. Like, he stood there for like an entire day or something. I love that stuff from like the happenings from the '70s and, like all the flash mobs that were super popular in the '90s, and I don't know I guess they're still popular but that kind of stuff like pop-up art. You know pop-up galleries are a thing now pop-up boutiques or things, pop-up restaurants, like let's do pop-up theatre, you know? We need to stop saying we are theatre and we do things in this box and that's the only way we do it. I think it's the direction we're going. It's just a matter of time, and when I get excited about things, I just want to hit the ground running and you know but it's hard because then there's life.

KYLA KAZUSCHYK: Tell me about your trap music project.

RACHEL ENGSTROM: Oh well, I don't know a ton about it, yet. They're workshopping in the fall to create the script. They have an idea of the script. The playwright is an alum and her son is a DJ and trap artist and so he's going to be in the piece, he's like the musician in it and then there's going to be ten actors in it as well and it's going to be filmed sort of with the idea of a music video. From what I've gathered so far it's going to be about young people starting out in trap music and starting a music career. There's a lot of questions still at this point. Which in academia, is a lot harder because they want you to nail things down like so much earlier. The actual production will be next spring. So it's just kind of weird because it's going to be devised, but our final design presentation is in October. So okay to me that says we're not starting the design process till the fall because even if we started it in the spring, everything could change. And it's now become a pattern that we have costume designs, but we don't have a cast. And like, yeah I can present conceptual designs, but as soon as I get a cast, it might entirely change so you're really creating twice as much work for me because of arbitrary deadlines, because this is the model we're using, and this is how it has to go for the shops. And yes, I get it our schedule is extremely complicated, extremely tight to the day, but also it's almost an act of futility to present a design that I know is going to change. So what's the purpose? What's the purpose of designing it and so like, my answer when I talk about that, like to my supervisors, is basically like, well just present what you have like, then present research or present whatever if you don't have like renderings and it's like, yes, but.

In everybody's minds as much as people want to say that they don't like that it's like, Okay yeah I understand it's going to change, and you can say that, but it still gets stuck in their minds what you present at the presentation. And so then, from that point on, anytime you make changes you feel the need to have to justify those changes as opposed to during a normal design process, you would just be still designing and not have to justify it to anybody, except for maybe your team. It's interesting and then also like personally it kind of gets stuck in my brain and it's not necessarily how my design process works. And so it's like, I know I can design on the fly. I can design very quickly. I can design based on what actors say in a first fitting and change things, but then I get push back because I'm doing things later than planned, or all this and it's like, well, but that's not always how it works so then you're constantly asking for exceptions and it's like, well if you're constantly asking for exceptions this isn't actually the model that we're using, so why do we keep saying this is the model we're using? I don't understand why we couldn't have, hey, the scene shop needs the set designs much earlier than the costume shop does so let's have the scenic design present on this day and then two or three weeks later we'll have the costume design presented like, why can't we have two different deadlines? Oh, because there's not enough time for meetings and everybody's schedule. So it's so many moving parts and so many people involved.

I think sometimes devised theatre works better when it's small groups of people.

People who have longstanding relationships, you know how each other works, you know that when that person is short with you that they're not actually mad at you, that they're just tired, you know they're just getting straight to the point, because there's not time for certain things. But other times, like every time I work with a new choreographer there's a certain amount of tiptoeing around and like trying to figure out how they are, and do I have to be the utmost professional at all times, keeping them updated every little step of the progress, or are they the type who's going to say you're the professional I trust you.

It's nice because now I have some choreographers where I know I can make color decisions without asking them. I know I can just buy the fabric, because we talked about it enough that I know the direction it's going in. I don't need their approval before every single purchase. Whereas others, I might say, oh hey I ordered swatches, let's look at them together, even though I already know which one I'm going to order, and have the conversation, so that they can then see why that's the best choice. I think things are expedited when you have a longstanding relationship with people, especially when it's with the director or the choreographer. I think that's also why a lot of design teams will stick together. Like you'll have the same group of people and it's a comfort thing or, especially if you've had successful shows you know it's like well we've done this before let's do it again. And that's always nice.

KYLA KAZUSCHYK: I'm curious, how do you see hierarchy playing into these collaboration conversations? Is there always the hierarchy of the director and the choreographer saying what's what, is there room for everyone's voice?

RACHEL ENGSTROM: Well, I think it really depends a lot on personality. And sometimes you need somebody who's going to be the leader and especially when you have those larger groups of people, I think having one person who is ultimately in charge is good when you have a large group of people, because somebody needs to just make a decision, otherwise you go back and forth, back and forth forever.

But I think in small groups or in groups where the chemistry works, it can be really easy and natural to just collaborate together and I guess, I sometimes find myself like after design meetings going, Oh, I might have just stepped on that lighting designer's toes because I suggested a color or something, and you never know until you get like kind of that feedback from somebody when you suggest something and so it's always I think finding the polite way to suggest an idea, or I always like it when a director says, you know, like let's just throw all the ideas on the table, like it doesn't matter, everybody can throw out anything. And that's always kind of nice because you can build off of each other, and you can give each other good ideas and suggest things that are outside of your field. Personally like I've kind of done a little bit of everything up until I was in undergrad, and so I have interest in scenic design, I'm interested in lighting design, I'm interested in directing and writing I have interests far outside of theatre and it's kind of one of those things where it's like I have a little bit of knowledge about a lot of things. And so I might make some connection that somebody else doesn't. I also have a different perspective. I feel like our faculty especially comes from all over the United States, and so I don't think people necessarily always think about just how vastly different our country is.

I lived in like three very, very different places in this country. I grew up in a small town in the Midwest. I lived out in southern California and now I'm in the south, but a city in the south, not the deep South, but it is still the south. I think people don't necessarily understand how vastly different people's experiences are and at the same time how similar. In theatre it's important if you want to make your art relevant to the most people, you need to find the universal kernels of truth that are in it and highlight those and have everybody be able to fill in the details themselves.

Sometimes people just worry too much about a particular story and they don't dig into why are we doing the story, what is this story really saying to people. What are people, why should they experience this, what do they want, what do we want them to walk away feeling? Sometimes there's too much of a focus on the script and the actors and not enough focus on the audience experience, especially in academia, because it is focused on the students or their experience is the most important because, even if we don't have an audience we're still going to do this show but in the grand scheme of theatre, why are we doing it if we're just doing it for the same group of people over and over again?

I see this particularly with community theatres that cater to what I lovingly call the blue hairs, you know and it's like, yes, those are the people with the money, those people that support you and, yes, we love those people, but … We also have entire generations of people who feel like this isn't for them. And you know it's the age old argument of the theatres dying. The theatre has been dying for a thousand years. And it's because people just don't even know about it, people just don't even know because you're doing it in this space that is dedicated to this one thing. That, even if it has a beautiful prominent front as a lot of theatres do, they still don't realize how vastly expansive theatre itself can be. All they know is *Hamilton*, which *Hamilton* is great, I love *Hamilton*. But I mean if that's the most innovative thing that you've seen performed. The innovation is the fact that it became so popular. That's what made it amazing was because he did something innovative and then it became super popular. There are things that are done that are vastly more innovative, more off the wall, more creative but they're not being seen. And so it's a problem when it's a form that clearly does not translate as well on film and so it's, how do we bring it to that, and I mean film sometimes is a little bit of the answer—there's movies that are more similar to the theatre that are getting there, people sometimes engage with streamed theatre. But I don't know. I just hope we don't stick in the streamed theatre thing too long.

KYLA KAZUSCHYK: I hope we don't stick in anything too long. And like what you're saying about this community theatre I've heard that argument too that like well we've got to do *Music Man* because that's what the blue hairs are going to buy tickets for. I can see so clearly now that that's the same argument as "well we're doing it because it's the way it's always been done." That's how white supremacy is upheld! If that is the answer to it, it's got to go. There needs to be more of a reason or a different reason, besides "that's the way it's always been done."

RACHEL ENGSTROM: If you look at some of these shows that have always been done, a lot of them are extremely problematic. And there's no good reason to do them anymore. There's things that have cultural significance that are problematic that when you experience them or when you teach them in schools, you have to teach them with a caveat of "this is why this is problematic now and back then it wasn't" and use it as a teaching tool, but then there's other things where it's just like we don't need to be doing this anymore, why are we still doing this there's plenty of other good musicals out there. There's new musicals I mean for goodness sakes, look at the stuff people create on TikTok in 60 seconds. The creativity in the world blows me away all the time.

KYLA KAZUSCHYK: And now there's so many more avenues for us to create and share stuff with each other, I wonder about that, when I think about the idea of universities as a whole, like, I mean I've built my life on university, but now that there's TikTok, really, what is the point of university?

RACHEL ENGSTROM: I want theatre to be politically active. I want theatre to be in your face. I want theatre to challenge people's assumptions and challenge their beliefs. Get arrested, well, sometimes you have to do things that challenge things that are not like dangerous or are gonna get you hurt, but like, dangerous like you're gonna have people yelling at you, you know? And because I think it can make a difference, and I think devised theatre is the perfect thing to do that. When you take raw emotion and put it into a blender with all of these other things, and then create something, the potential is so great.

KYLA KAZUSCHYK: Yeah absolutely! I love the blender metaphor and it's so true that theatre has the power to shift consciousness, like storytelling in general. Stories are what shape our consciousness and our outlook. The stories people hold shape how they view things.

RACHEL ENGSTROM: Right and people don't always think about someone's backstory. And I feel like with theatre, since we have to study that, especially costume designers, we delve into a character's backstory and like why they would choose that coat over that coat and that you can apply that to people. Because everybody has a different backstory. You don't know what that person went through today. You know why this is and it's interesting because I noticed that people make assumptions about me because of the way I look and the way I sound. I can blend in different groups. I am perceived as a different person depending on where I am when I am and who I'm with. And it's amazing because the majority of my life I've been surrounded with academia and so I'm used to people who

FIGURE 6.30 Untitled Communion. *Costumes by Lena Sands, directed by Nancy Keystone in collaboration with Critical Mass Performance Group, REDCAT NOW Festival 2017 (photo courtesy of Steve Guther)*

assume like, okay you're relatively intelligent and tend to treat me with a good amount of respect, at least, like the average amount of respect you'd give your fellow human being. But I've been in other situations where people look at me and especially if I'm dressed really casually because I tend to just dress casual what's comfortable and or if I'm not wearing makeup or something. People will assume I'm one thing or assume I'm way younger and treat me so differently.

KYLA KAZUSCHYK: This is so interesting that people definitely make judgments based on appearances and based on dress.

RACHEL ENGSTROM: Oh yeah it's so strange.

ARTIST SPOTLIGHT: LENA SANDS

Lena Sands is a costume designer who has created incredible work on a wide range of devised and scripted pieces.

FIGURE 6.31 Frankenstein, After Mary Shelly, *A Four Larks Production, directed by Mat Sweeney and devised in collaboration with the company, The Wallis, 2020. Costumes by Lena Sands (photo courtesy of Kevin Parry and Joel Hile)*

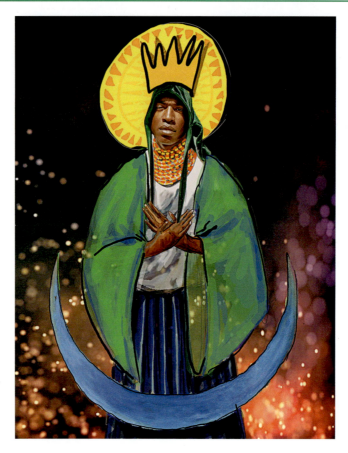

FIGURE 6.32 *Rendering created by Lena Sands in collaboration with performers for Mariology (photo courtesy of Lena Sands)*

FIGURE 6.33 *"These renderings are the start of the process for Mariology—a dynamic performance spectacle, exploring the Virgin Mary as a beacon of faith, source of comfort, and a weapon of colonization," Lena Sands (photo courtesy of Lena Sands)*

When working on scripted pieces, you have words on a page that lead you where you go, whereas on devised pieces, you start with an idea. As Lena Sands explains:

> An idea can be several pages of words that are just not together yet. With devised work, it is a very collaborative process. What is the story it is going to tell? What are the images we are interested in? Sometimes in devised work, you are still figuring out what the question is. Some companies approach scripted work looking for a question. When I did Baccae with the CITI company, we came to it with this framing of, well what are we doing here and how does this resonate with us? What are the questions that we have about why this is meaningful to us?

Instead of spending time making renderings, Lena went to almost every rehearsal. She brought images, music, clothes in for the performers to see what would stick. Every aspect was created in tandem with the performers in the rehearsal room.

FIGURE 6.34 *"These are 'personal Marys,' that is, Marys created in collaboration with the performers to bring some idea of what she means to them to life," Lena Sands (photo courtesy of Lena Sands)*

Lena traces her ease with working things out in rehearsal to a time she designed costumes for *Tales from Ovid*. She started by thinking about ways to depict humans turning into animals in very representative ways, like if a human turns into an owl, have them wear an owl mask. The director suggested she bring some fabric to rehearsal. Together with the performers they discovered creative, non-literal transformations.

> *I like asking the question together, I like the collaboration, the interaction of movement and performance with garments, and the devised medium is ideal for discovering those intersections of meaning. It exists to move to its fullest potential, or to restrict movement in a way that tells us something about a character. I love a good play. I love plays that ask questions that they don't know the answer to. Designers know a lot of different ways to solve things. Working in the rehearsal room as opposed to the page gives us more options. If you're writing, you are drawn to words, whereas in the rehearsal room, there is more space for images.*

When working on a devised piece that stems from a certain place, the first step can be looking at the source material and framing the question. Lena describes her process through the example of working on a "junkyard opera" version of the Frankenstein story. She started by reading the source material, Mary Shelly's novel, and asking questions like, what is the structure and who are the characters?

> *Then, look at a lot of images, pull images, share them with the team, start to make word association trees, to expand my thinking, bring it to a more subconscious level, to make connections, and then start drawing, sketching, always conversing, thinking about color, movement of color.*

She spent time sitting in rehearsals, watching them and sketching, being conscious of when they might be ready to incorporate a costume piece. It can be helpful to have a rack of costumes to work with ready for performers to play with as early as possible. This can give performers a starting point to talk

FIGURE 6.35 *Rendering created by Lena Sands in collaboration with performers for* Mariology *(photo courtesy of Lena Sands)*

FIGURE 6.36 *Rendering by Lena Sands for the "Baba Yaga" character in* How to Catch a Karen *(photo courtesy of Lena Sands)*

about what works and what could be different. Sometimes the shape of a dress is right but the color or the fit is not. The more we as costumers work with performers, the better. "I try to instill in the actors that I value their comfort, this is where this costume operates in the piece of the puzzle. Everyone is going to feel taken care of." Everyone is a piece of the puzzle.

Lena worked on an online workshop production during the pandemic where they decided as a group not to build costumes, instead to just see how ideas function, maybe as paper dolls or puppets. *Mariology* is a show about different images of the virgin Mary. Because the show is about the performers and their personal relationships to this idea of this person, Lena spent time talking to each actor about their own ideas and perceptions. She then took the textures and ideas from their research and brought it together. Actors brought a wide variety of images including Filipina Marys and Mary as a punk radical. Lena spent a lot of time with the performers, in rehearsal and beyond. They watched movies together, looked at images together, and over time created a shared vocabulary. This practice of collaboration mirrors themes in the show, asking questions like, "How can we make society more equal? How can we tear down the structure of an unequal world and create a more equal world?" When creating designs, Lena also stayed open to experimentation, trying out new mediums: "The media of these helped me solve them, ink drawing, I don't usually work in ink but I'll try and see where that brings me." Doing the workshop online allowed more people access to it, and opened up the possibilities of what they could create without the limitations of a physical theatre space. "We really honored the space of the online medium. There's no givens! Nothing is taken for granted!"

When approaching any project, devising or not, ask "What do we have, where are we doing it? And what are our questions? And what are our resources?" It is possible to work in an equitable way. It is possible to dream big while also acknowledging what is possible with the available resources.

Lena also worked closely with the performer in *How to Catch a Karen* on the development of costume.

Knowing from the start what the goal is and having everyone involved on the same page about that goal is essential.

FIGURE 6.37 How to Catch a Karen, *an online devised performance. Costumes by Lena Sands (photo courtesy of Lena Sands and the Naked Empire Buffon Company)*

Acknowledge the timeline and then set goals that are based on that timeline. Whatever you can do in the time allotted is going to be what it is. If possible, make the tech process longer from the beginning. With more time, tech can be a time to try things and figure things out. Devising can be a process of finding possibilities and can inspire you to find the potential in all things.

CHAPTER 7

PAPERWORK

STAY ORGANIZED!

Even if other aspects are in total chaos, keep in mind that you do not have to be. You do not have to let structured and clear paperwork go out the window because other aspects of the production are chaotic.

As a shop manager and teacher, I have a stock set of paperwork templates in addition to my stock set of slopers. This can help immensely when generating paperwork for a new show. There is no need to reinvent the wheel, but, with the wide range of forms of devised work … we may need to invent some new wheels.

Depending on the particular needs of the show, you may need to revise your standard issue costume paperwork. Your templates may need to take on different shapes. You may need to create more charts than usual.

INVENT NEW FORMS

Ultimately, figure out what will work for you. Existing devising resources may apply to your work. There are many publications on moment work. The guide from Complicite available online might apply to what you are doing, or it might not. Following are examples of paperwork I created to help processes go more smoothly. If these apply to your work, please take them and use them, or take the parts of them that work and adjust them to suit the particulars of what you are creating. I hope to inspire and empower you to create tools that will serve you.

Start with non-precious working documents that you, the wardrobe crew, and the performers can edit and update as chaos is organized. Try storing paperwork on Google Sheets or Google Docs or anywhere else online that is free and able to be accessed by multiple members of the team.

For *Love and Information*, one piece of paperwork that I used initially was a blank costume plot grid, which I printed out and wrote in the first draft of dressing lists while watching rehearsals. Because the lines were not ascribed to specific characters, I created an initial list of who says what lines, to which I also added notes on character details in rehearsal, such as "This person seems more arrogant," "This person seems more youthful," and so on. The page breakdown for *Love and Information* ended up being a 12-page-long grid, detailing what each performer wore in each of the 70 scenes, and where and when quick changes needed to take place. This kind of organization is essential to the practicality of creating art; it is the work that makes the final product on stage appear magical and effortless.

Look at the parameters of every project. If no boundaries exist, add your own. Check out the various examples included in the appendix.

ARTIST SPOTLIGHT: ADANMA BARTON

Adanma Barton sets a fantastic example of inventing new forms. In her work, she creates what she values, and she invents methods that work for her instead of adhering to any arbitrary rules.

ADANMA BARTON: Devised theatre is when you have nothing, and you collaborate with a group of people to create something. And that's why it's better than scripted work, because

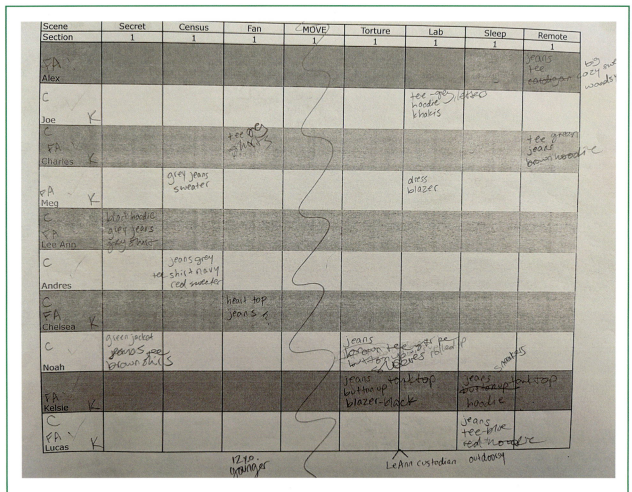

FIGURE 7.1 *I created this spreadsheet, filled in the information I knew, and left space to make notes in rehearsal as I observed each scene. Across the top are the names of the scenes. Down the left side are the names of the performers. My handwritten notes are ideas of outfits that might make sense for them to wear.*

the actors and ensemble have ownership of what they are putting out. It's a really amazing thing to watch, honestly.

KYLA KAZUSCHYK: That's a really clear and concise way of putting that: taking nothing and then creating something.

ADANMA BARTON: And something to be proud of, too. My kids were like, oh my God we did that, and I was like yeah y'all did that! You're trying to pretend like you're not an artist.

KYLA KAZUSCHYK: It's something tangible that you can look at and show them that they created. How would you approach creating costumes for devised work?

ADANMA BARTON: We did *Say Her Name*, and we decided to make the Black fist, but they were all female names, and everybody wore a T-shirt of that. Unless you have a very specific theme that you're devising under, the more neutral the clothes, the better, because then a prop or a pop of color or something adds more to the imaginative experience of the audience. You can always put on a doctor's coat and be a doctor. And then you can take it off and then you're still right back. Something neutral—that's why I always tell people—and comfortable because you should be able to move.

KYLA KAZUSCHYK: Because the movement can help tell the story.

ADANMA BARTON: Exactly. When I devise shows, in order to get what I want, I give them little mini assignments underneath the theme. Because a lot of times kids are like, I can't do this, I can't act, I can't write. And it's like, Okay I'm going to give you this assignment, you're going to go work with so and so and in 30 minutes you're going to come back and bring something back to the table.

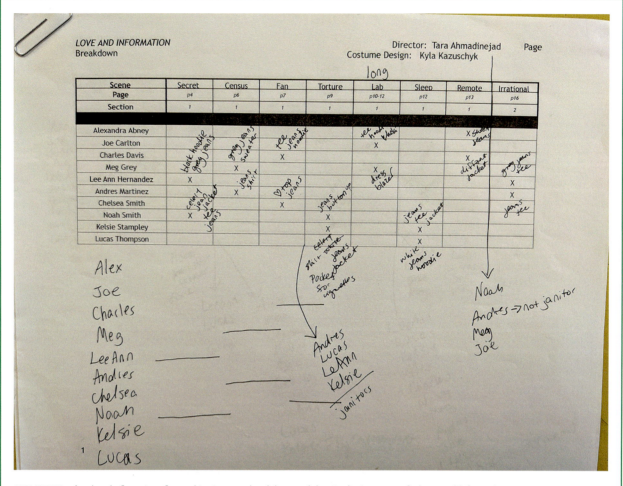

FIGURE 7.2 *Another draft version of a combination page breakdown and dressing list in progress for* Love and Information

I tell everybody when we start rehearsal, what've you got to throw on the table? Throw it right now, this is your one and only chance, you can throw it, whatever, you got a parking ticket whatever, you got an F on this quiz whatever. You, you think your life is over because your girlfriend broke up with you, but she was never really straight in the first place, and everybody knew that but you and so many things, right? So once all that's thrown on the table, then I'm like, great, all that's in a box, boom on fire, let's get to work.

You know if you guide them, if you have, maybe it's just me, I'm speaking for myself. I don't have some sort of form, it's not necessary. It's a skeleton, it's the spine, right? And then it's there, they're putting all the meat on it to make it a meat sickle. But I have to be the one to be like, Look we're going to do this play about *Say Her Name*— we're going to use the colors red white and blue but we're going to flip it, white being the color of honoring Breonna Taylor, blue being the color of interrogating the Louisville metro police department, and then red being the color of protesting in a pandemic.

Once that spine was built, then I'm like, Okay, I need you, what do you have? Did you write a poem? That's going over here. What did you do? What you got? You got that? Okay great.

And we bring in guest artists in order to inspire them too. Every Saturday I brought in guest artists. And some of them were from campus. I'm like, Hey guess what you can take this chick's class she just happens to be my friend too you know cause I had to have a White guilt conversation that I can't have. I know I can't have that so I called my friend who I know is well versed in all of these healing circles. She's doing all these racial healing circles, I love it.

And she spoke with the cast. And then I have a friend of mine who's working with the local Berea police department so she gave them like reverse idea of how

Love and Information Casting (as of 4 December 2016):
Section 1

Secret		A: Noah — asking, eager, then shocked, feels distant, standing
		B: LeeAnn — bartender, drinking not sorry
Census		A: Meg — attitude, sitting
		B: Andrés — remorseful
Fan		A: Chelsea — sassy, competing, actual parent, find it when they can't find / looking in magazines — preteens, juvenile jungle gym? hangout, climbing or sitting
		B: Charles — gay
Torture	— are they cops? — maybe in uniform? No detectives	A: Noah — shady
		B: Kelsie — not necessarily compliant — professional
Lab	Vacuum Leanne — 2nd date, cognitive dissonance — long ish	A: Meg — giddy, scientist, smart — at the bar, sitting on stools after work on a date?
		B: Joe — curious — 8 second inhale
Sleep		A: Kelsie — can't sleep — lying down in bed? facing audience
		B: Lucas — sleeping
Remote	there's no easy answer to this — urban / rural	A: Charles — uncomfortable, needs connection, fresh from the city — sitting at table
		B: Alex — lives in remote place, calm, can feel if its raining, a water

Section 2

Irrational		A: Andrés
		B: Lee Ann
Affair		A: Chelsea
		B: Kelsie

FIGURE 7.3 On this show, each scene had a title (the words in the left column), but the sequence of the scenes fluctuated until the show opened. I used this document to note which performer was in each scene, and then as I watched rehearsal I took notes on aspects of each character as they emerged

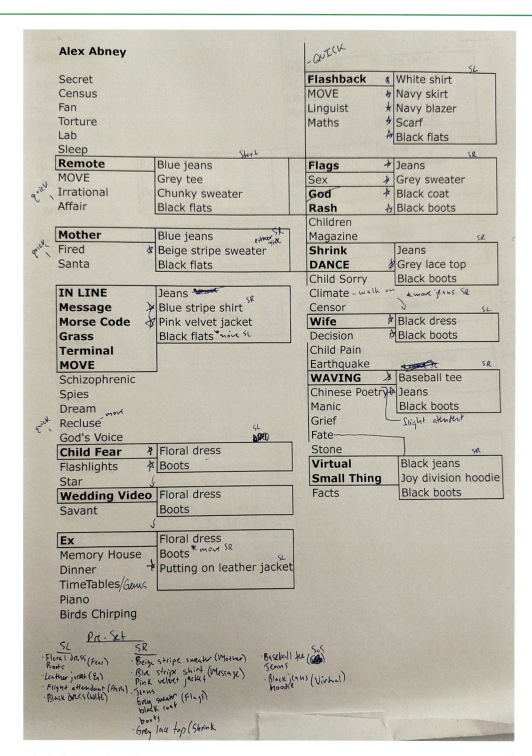

FIGURE 7.4 Draft of a dressing list used to communicate to an actor what they wear in each scene. I took the printed list to rehearsal and noted where actors exit and enter, considering whether they would have time to change entirely or just add and subtract pieces. Similar to a standard dressing list or tracking sheet, with the added challenge that on this show the characters never had names

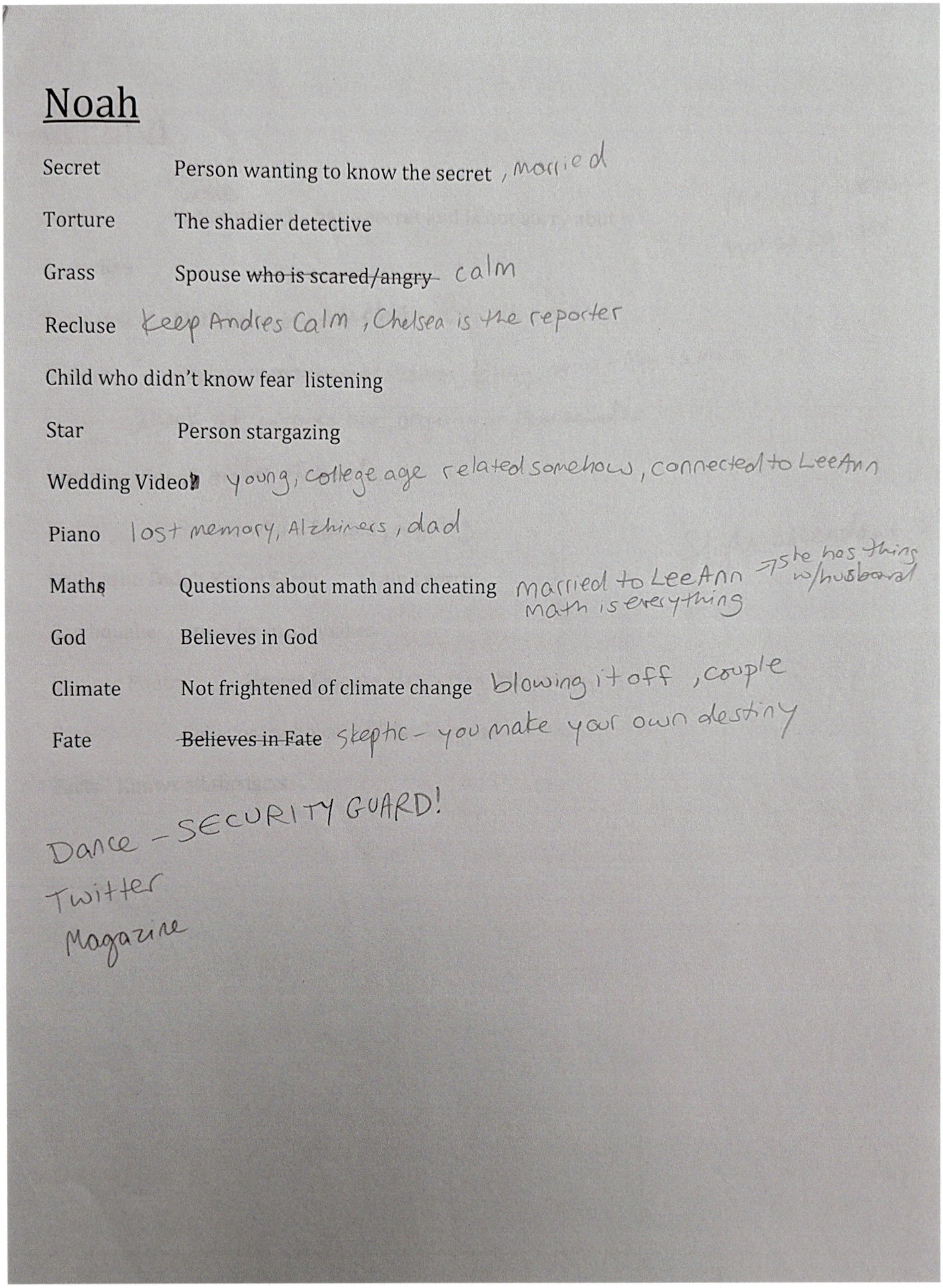

Noah

Secret	Person wanting to know the secret	, married
Torture	The shadier detective	
Grass	~~Spouse who is scared/angry~~ calm	
Recluse	keep Andres Calm, Chelsea is the reporter	
Child who didn't know fear	listening	
Star	Person stargazing	
Wedding Video	young, college age related somehow, connected to LeeAnn	
Piano	lost memory, Alzhimers, dad	
Maths	Questions about math and cheating married to LeeAnn ⇒ she has thing w/husband — math is everything	
God	Believes in God	
Climate	Not frightened of climate change blowing it off, couple	
Fate	~~Believes in Fate~~ skeptic — you make your own destiny	

Dance — SECURITY GUARD!
Twitter
Magazine

FIGURE 7.5 *I printed out this list of scenes and my impressions of the characters an actor is playing in those scenes based on my observations in rehearsals. I had this list ready to talk through with each actor when they came in for fittings, verifying or updating my ideas with information from the actors*

FIGURE 7.6 *Obinna Ilochonwu (Nigeria) and Raquel d. Garbanzo Nunez (Costa Rica) in* Say Her Name: Breonna Taylor, *a devised theatre performance created and directed by Adanma Onydike Barton. Costume design: Ami Shupe; video design: Daniel Chapman; film editor: James Monroe; sound editor: Jon Flikkie (photo courtesy of Adanma O. Barton)*

FIGURE 7.7 *In* Say Her Name: Breonna Taylor, *performers wear long-sleeved black T-shirts printed with a raised fist made out of names of Black women who have been killed by police (photo courtesy of Adanma O. Barton)*

FIGURE 7.8 *Costumes can be neutral and comfortable, allowing performers to move and to easily add and subtract pieces to become different characters (photo courtesy of Adanma O. Barton)*

good cops feel when stuff like that happens. Honey, when I said we went deep, Oh, the well was deep. See, but I didn't do it, that's the thing I did it, but I didn't, you know what I mean? I told them what to do, and then they did it, and then they brought it back and then I just organized the order and then had to watch a zillion million clips. I cannot wait until we can do theatre on a stage, are you kidding. I'm gonna have to find some way to add that to my CV. I'm a film producer. I produced a play film.

KYLA KAZUSCHYK: I love it! It is so true that the pandemic forced us to create all these new skill sets that we didn't have before. And producing film is very different from producing theatre.

And I think that what you're talking about is interesting, too, that being a facilitator is almost a different skill set than being a director. You're facilitating the creation, but like you said, the students are the ones creating it, you're just organizing it, you're not necessarily creating the direction of it.

ADANMA BARTON: There's no direction until there's an actual piece that's completed and I kept telling them that. I was like, You all can write all this stuff, I'm glad you're sharing all this stuff. You need to start thinking about where's this stuff going to go in the show. Because I have some ideas, but if you don't like these ideas, and there was a couple actresses that were like, No, we need to do this first and this and I was like, that's fine. And then, once we had a full-blown script we did a read-through of the script and I assigned people. Some of the stuff that people wrote they didn't do. Because like, Okay you're going to do this because I know you can do this better you're going to do that—that's when the directing starts. You can't direct until you have a script. So you have to facilitate in order to direct. That's what makes it actually harder, especially for designers. I know, I'm sorry, I know, I'm sorry, I know.

KYLA KAZUSCHYK: Do you work with a timeline? Did you create a timeline with specific deadlines?

ADANMA BARTON: Oh absolutely. We wrote for a week or so, created the script, created the skeleton of the script, practicing, having our guest artists come in, reshaping the script. A script was completely done by week two, so they learned it and filmed it week three, we edited week four and it went up. It was amazing because the cast being in all different areas when I'm telling you girl, we, the technical director is in Montana, he's lucky I'm an insomniac because yes I'll answer your email at two o'clock in the morning I'm up you know what I mean—I will look at this clip whatever. I got him over there. I got an actress in Chicago, I got an actress in Pennsylvania and boy, I got an actress two feet away from me, I can't even go say hi, in the dorms. It was too much.

KYLA KAZUSCHYK: It is a lot to coordinate.

ADANMA BARTON: But it was worth it, for sure.

KYLA KAZUSCHYK: Do you think that aspects of that will stay with us as we move past the pandemic? I'm like you, I can't wait to be back in person, but it's kind of an advantage to be able to coordinate with people all over, too.

ADANMA BARTON: It is, it is, I think, you know, we're theatre people, we are the tellers of the stories. If we don't tell the tale, how can we move on to tell others? This is like a once in 100 something year you know pandemic or whatever. And it's still the thing, it's still not gone. I live by the quote of Nina Simone: it's the artist's duty to reflect the times we live in.

Whether you think you can do it or not, whether you want to do it or not, you have got to do something of the moment, whatever that means to wherever you are.

For us it was Breonna Taylor because that's like right up the road, and there was national attention and kids needed to express, but for other people it's other things.

KYLA KAZUSCHYK: Do you think that is where devised theatre and new work comes in? It's more able to speak to the moment, rather than finding something that is scripted that speaks to the moment.

ADANMA BARTON: Totally, unless you've got I mean some people do have a playwriting or screenwriting or whatever connected to their programs. If you've got playwrights that are good at your disposal then yeah of course I can like procure you and say, Hey dude, I want you to write a play about NWA. And they'd be like "something like what?" I'm like, Yeah exactly that's why you're not doing it. That's why we're devising the show. Because the kids need to feel like they own it.

That's the thing about it, when they create the script themselves, there is an ownership to the work. They work harder at doing it right or making it right. All the time, I have to be like "stop stop you're doing too much you're doing the most." I had a sign, I was like you're doing the most, and my cross. I've still got my cross. There'd be times, where I'm just like (holds up cross).

KYLA KAZUSCHYK: Is that a reminder to come back to Jesus?

ADANMA BARTON: Yes. I would wait to see who would see it. And then, one of them would be like "Oh, we got

FIGURE 7.9 *Amoni Adair in Say Her Name: Breonna Taylor, a devised theatre performance created and directed by Adanma Onydike Barton. Costume design: Ami Shupe; video design: Daniel Chapman; film editor: James Monroe; sound editor: Jon Flikkie (photo courtesy of Adanma O. Barton)*

FIGURE 7.10 *In zoom theatre, like in film, small accessory details can help performers to make a big impact (photo courtesy of Adanma O. Barton)*

Jesus! Yo she put her cross up!" How are you supposed to control ten people in ten different places, you know?

Well yeah that's the cool thing about it, they were having so much fun, that it was hard to rein them in and say "girl your face is too hard, this is for film, this is not for stage, you do not need to be doing the most. That looks crazy, you look crazy" you know what I mean? So yeah, that type of stuff.

KYLA KAZUSCHYK: A lot of devising people I've talked to say devising is mostly editing, like it's starting with a lot of stuff and then distilling it.

ADANMA BARTON: Exactly, and that's what you gotta let people know upfront: don't get your feelings hurt. You need to have more material than you do time. Because that way, I mean if you really got your feelings hurt we can take two lines of your thing and put it in homegirl's poem, but you see how it makes her poem sound like trash, right? So we're not going to use your thing. If you want to do your thing as a movement piece, come back at me, let me see that story, beginning middle end as a movement piece—then we can talk. Because I do believe that there should be variety in devised performance. You have scenes, you have monologues, you have dance, you have original songs, there's so many things you can do.

KYLA KAZUSCHYK: And that can make it more accessible to a larger audience, too. Different things are going to speak to different members of the audience.

ADANMA BARTON: Exactly. The more variety that you can obtain in your group, the better. We had a student from Nigeria, we had a student from Costa Rica, so they got to do a piece talking about how America looks from the outside looking in. It was so successful. We wouldn't have that if we didn't have them. And everybody has their own talents and advantages and I just push that, like went on that, you know, not everybody were writers, but a lot of people are actors and that type of thing and usually the crew understands as you start to put it together, you'll hear the flow, you'll feel the flow, you'll be like, Okay, this needs to go, as you know, and everybody just bring something to the circle. Like today I need to read, this is a piece that I wrote, we'll be like all right.

And I always tell them to name the piece. "This piece doesn't have a name." I was like I'll give it a name by the end of the piece. Why? Because you have to organize. All right, if this piece is actually really good I need a name for it, so I can put it over here, this piece could be good for this section—that type of thing.

KYLA KAZUSCHYK: Did you invent your own system for organization or were you following other devised theatre models?

ADANMA BARTON: No, I invented my own. Because I mean I read them other books, don't get me wrong, like I read all the books, I got them all on the shelf but it's just—forgive me, but I'm really in my feminist decolonizing the curriculum bag, like, I'm in my bag. And all of these books that I've been made to read, to get this MFA were all like cis gender old white dudes. I even just had a fight in the department meeting the other day, because chick was trying to tell me I had to direct a play from the Restoration period, and I said, have you lost your mind? We're coming back from a pandemic, and you want me to do some crusty dusty ass *Tartuffe*? Have you lost your mind? I'm not doing that. I'm not doing that.

So I did, I created my own, but it's not because I didn't get stuff. You know, I read. Some people need walls and sticky notes, and that's cool. Some people are very visual with it. I'm actually visual with it, but I'd rather have it on a spreadsheet. Because spreadsheets then can get transferred to sound and to light and to whatever and then they already know the order of the pieces and stuff. That's just me. People that do the cards eventually get to that point anyways. I was just like maybe I should just go ahead and make the spreadsheet.

Because that's what I've come to learn in devised performance, the faster you can get stuff to tech, the happier they will be. If you get stuff to tech, they don't like changes unless it absolutely has to happen. The good thing about film is that you can do more changes than you would be able to do in a real show. So that's something else I've learned too.

KYLA KAZUSCHYK: I think there's room for that to shift. I was trained as a technician and we're taught that things have to be rigorous, things have to be standard, but just because we're taught that doesn't mean we have to perpetuate that. Things can be flexible, things can change.

ADANMA BARTON: I'm going to sit up in my house I'm gonna pop my IPA I'm gonna plop my Cardi B I'm gonna sit here and look at my thing and I'm going to be like yeah this goes here, this goes there just goes here, this goes there that's the flow yeah. Screw those white dudes.

Like what, I'm supposed to go and write a notebook first? I'm supposed to get a notebook of my thoughts, because you know in devised performance you bring your thoughts together. And then, after I have my notebook of my thoughts I'm supposed to get another notebook to go to my thoughts to look at some type of stage design. They wrote that back when people had time to do shit, we ain't got time to do, no. Create your own system, because then that way, it will work faster for everyone.

Because like I said you're the facilitator and you're the director, you are the end all be all you are the alpha and the omega, okay like Yes, they get to write the pieces, but you get to say no. I said no a lot. I said no a lot, I was like that goes too far, that doesn't go far enough, that sounds dumb like you know you have to be truthful. Like, what do you mean it sounds dumb, like read it again. Oh, I see like, yeah you repeated the same line four times for no reason, no, I'm not putting that in the show so go off and do something else you know.

KYLA KAZUSCHYK: Do you approach your classes the same way, do you create your own system for the way you teach your classes?

ADANMA BARTON: Yeah. I mean I got the syllabus whatever when I first got here, I was like okay so we're going to add this this this because, again Stanislavski right then we're going to take this away and it's very ritual for me. Before the Covid, before the rona, I insisted that my students clapped when I came in the room. Why? Because the sound of applause is such a great sound and we as theatre people, we do all of this work to seek that sound. So one, I love, I live for the applause, thank you Gaga, but two, I also clap back at them.

So we start with energy. We must. We start with energy, do the roster, do the warm up, what's the lesson, sit down and learn, ask the questions I know you gonna ask because I get older but y'all stay the same age and I know you gonna ask the same stupid questions but I'll answer them.

And then at the end, I have a meditation and yeah my little meditation bells, boom, end of every class and end of every rehearsal as well, so that way it's like the art is sacred. That time that we spent together, we're the only people who know what that feels like, you know what I mean? We get clapped in and we breathe out. And they get to go off about their day, knowing that there's a shift and they just did some awesome work. They might not be able to do math but they didn't ruin a show you know.

KYLA KAZUSCHYK: Have you been able to find ways to translate that to zoom?

ADANMA BARTON: This last show that I did was a film, it was I mean everything was on zoom but we had green screens. It just sucks. There ain't no other way about it because it's not a movie it's not a short film because I'm not there with the camera I got to only take what they've got. So that's kind of what we do, we kind of just created this like, it was beautiful, mirage collage of pieces and media I would definitely say was more of a theatrical media

FIGURE 7.11 *Ricara Moorman and Malcolm Andrew Link in* Say Her Name: Breonna Taylor, *a devised theatre performance created and directed by Adanma Onydike Barton. Costume design: Ami Shupe; video design: Daniel Chapman; film editor: James Monroe; sound editor: Jon Flikkie (photo courtesy of Adanma O. Barton)*

FIGURE 7.12 *Say Her Name: Breonna Taylor, Berea College Theatre (photo courtesy of Adanma O. Barton)*

devised performance, rather than a straight-up devised performance. Because there was so much media involved.

But it enhanced it, oh my gosh. When we juxtaposed the Black Lives Matter march on June 1 on 6/1, where doofus was like tear-bombing people, so you could take a picture, with the upside down Bible. And then on January 6, you like converse the numbers January 6 the day that the guy who shot Breonna and actually like his bullet killed her. The day this dude gets fired is the the capital riots.

So we got to, because we are in a film medium, we got to put those two together and challenge other departments to find their own Breonna. Yes, we know about George Floyd's actually got a trial. And Ahmed Arbury, his people are in jail. Not one person that shot all, what 32 bullets, 32 rounds in this girl's house, not one person's going to jail? The corruption oh. I could make another play, but I already spent myself on this first one so I said dang it I got to do a comedy so I'm not doing those sixteenth century are you kidding me. Ah, I was a slave what do you do, what do you want me to do? Oh gosh students need—the students do not need that.

I should have marched louder, I should have set more things on fire, I should have organized faster. I don't even know. Who knew the depths of greed, that people will sell out their own people. I mean I grew up in a military town so that's kind of beyond me like that's literally.

I didn't even know *Hidden Figures*, which was right down the street from my house, was going on until Pharell did the movie! And that's what I'm talking about. I'm here in Kentucky and I'm hollering. This is not just a play. The action goes deeper. We have to go back in the K through 12 curriculum, we got to start telling these kids the truth. Tell the truth. You'd be surprised how kids will actually absorb. I saw that on YouTube, some father wanting to pull his daughter out of school somewhere in Tennessee because they were learning about Black Lives Matter. And that doesn't align with his beliefs, because Black Lives Matter is "a terrorist organization"? Lord Jesus help us Lord I don't even know.

There's so many stories to tell. Which story do you want to tell and how do you want to tell it?

Do you want to include other people? Do you want to bring other people into the sauce because sometimes you can bring some dance people into the sauce. Sometimes you can bring like straight-up English people, like let 'em write poems and stuff into the sauce if you're having a hard time writing and then that way it makes it a multi-departmental or interdepartmental you know what the what the deans like to see.

KYLA KAZUSCHYK: Interdisciplinary, they love it.

ADANMA BARTON: Yes. Because I've done that. I've had women and gender studies, African American studies, like what's up communications let's do this thing.

Before the rona I was getting ready to do Pose the class with child and family studies. We were going to talk about how ballroom culture was like a whole entire theatrical thing and then we're also going to talk about chosen families and how in that time period, people would pick their family. It was gonna be battles, we were going to end with a ball, the final was going to be a ball and then here comes the rona—Oh, I wish, she would go away.

KYLA KAZUSCHYK: That class sounds amazing.

ADANMA BARTON: Yeah well it's there, it's proposed it's just it'll happen one day when I think about it. I tell my students all the time, like if you see something, if you don't see something, then it's your responsibility to put it there.

ARTIST SPOTLIGHT: PAMELA RODRIGUEZ-MONTERO

Scenographer, educator, and visual artist Pamela Rodriguez-Montero shares some of her ideas about the ways devising practices can enhance our work.

KYLA KAZUSCHYK: I'm interested in your perspective on how you define devised work and what do you see as the advantages to it.

PAMELA RODRIGUEZ-MONTERO: To me devised work has to do with any collective creation, any shape of art like performance or theatre or any storytelling that is created collectively, that is rooted in the group, in a group thought and in collaboration among different members and that we don't have any sort of idea when we're starting and they start to form as a collective.

KYLA KAZUSCHYK: And are there advantages to doing that versus scripted work?

PAMELA RODRIGUEZ-MONTERO: Of course they have, I'm going to say advantages but it's a different result. To me, devised work is creation that is starting from the narratives that the group brings and whatever every person in the group brings. I think it can be more creative as a process, you can allow people to explore different areas to interact in different roles, not only as an actor or performer. You can be a playwright, you can be a director, you can step in many different roles. And if we talk about educational theatre, allow students to cross different disciplines, at the same time.

KYLA KAZUSCHYK: That's a good way of looking at it, because we often try and do that in educational theatre with scripted work but it doesn't lend itself to crossing those roles as much as devising does.

FIGURE 7.13 Thumbelina *at Stillwell Theatre, Kennesaw State University, GA, 2020. Director: Rosemary Newcott; music director: Amanda Wansa Morgan; set, costume, lighting design: Pamela Rodriguez-Montero; sound design: Mikaela Fraser. Picture credit: Casey Gardner Ford (photo courtesy of Pamela Rodriguez-Montero)*

PAMELA RODRIGUEZ-MONTERO: I think devising does have a little bit more of that specific because the nature of it is so fluid that then you can add the fluidity into the work we are doing.

KYLA KAZUSCHYK: Throughout all of it. So, you have experienced creating costumes for devised work. How do you deal with that fluidity? We're taught the linear process of costume design. When you don't have that linear process, how do you do it?

PAMELA RODRIGUEZ-MONTERO: I have done scenography for devised work. And to me it's just more about listening, more about having that same structure of organic changes, going with the flow in ways that you are understanding where the group is going and you're shifting. You are offering options, you are having more conversations. And I think that's where the timeframe differs, like the process is a little bit different, because you have to have more conversations with your cast members and your performers and sometimes the people helping you design are the same ones performing, and sometimes you are performing. In my case I'm not a performer at all, but it could be that way. You are having those conversations. So it's more time, you are communicating and building a relationship and understanding what is the role of design at this moment. It's interesting to me it's just more, it makes the human process a little bit stronger in knowing, a little bit heavier and more involved in that relationship.

KYLA KAZUSCHYK: Absolutely. Do you have a template that you use for devising or do you just let it be whatever the specific project is?

PAMELA RODRIGUEZ-MONTERO: I think it's just more like a process like being prepared, soaking up everything that's happening, studying the materials, the reference materials in case we are like coming off of a tale or a poem or a song or something like that, whatever we are studying as like an anchor material inspiration, but I think we do follow a little bit of like the standard practice, gathering references, gathering our research. Doing all that will never go away. I don't think there's any moment in which we're not doing that specific part of reference, research and analysis.

But I think, in addition to the normal process, it is more like this conversations and this constant like free evaluation, which is something that is healthy and good in standard costume design, but I think for devising, is also very necessary to reassess constantly, pivot pretty much every day, every hour and rethink our choices.

KYLA KAZUSCHYK: It's so exciting and also very scary. I was very afraid of it at first.

PAMELA RODRIGUEZ-MONTERO: It feels a little bit scary, but I think since I'm Costa Rican and I have done theatre in different ways with limited resources or things in which maybe you are not fully in control. I think it does not daunt me because I know there's different structures. Coming to the States and finding the whole more structured technical theatre area and all that, it felt like yeah I can be a little more spoiled in this area but, like in Costa Rica I have seen performers doing their own costumes all the time, just naturally. And you're there as a designer maybe doing lighting, but like helping out with other choices or discussing like, Oh, I think this is the direction we should go with this other element. So I feel like that background of doing theatre in a more limited resource setting, I think it helps me be flexible and not be scared.

KYLA KAZUSCHYK: That's so cool to think that in other places in the world it's common practice for performers to create their own costumes. That's not common here.

PAMELA RODRIGUEZ-MONTERO: No it's not, it's not common at all. I wouldn't say in every production, but I think even low budget productions here, they will have that a lot when they go into their own closets and they bring stuff. It's just more like that low budget or like just a different process is a different thing but it helps out developing those conversations and allows the performers to have that awareness and the costumers to have the flexibility and that power to reach the performer, or not power, that ability to reach the performer.

KYLA KAZUSCHYK: The relationship with the performers is more accessible.

PAMELA RODRIGUEZ-MONTERO: It's more accessible and more just open dialogue, there's more trust, I feel like it when you're doing it this way. When you are devising, there has to be more trust, because you don't have the full control of everything. When you're doing research and breaking down your characters and having a lot more the process you're like just swimming in the same water, as we are all. And the performers also, so there's the relationship of trust. I think that is the most important, that you are flexible, you're trusting or being trusted. And you are all just doing honest work and trying to be present at the moment, which I think is the most important for devising theatre anyways, to be present, be there, you know? And it's hard. I think that's the hardest part, maybe this world in which we are like, constant emails, constant things coming in, but just trying to be part of the process, like an organic part of the process, you have to be there.

KYLA KAZUSCHYK: That's so inspiring because that applies to everything. The more that we can ask ourselves to be present in the moment, the more rewarding any process is going to be.

PAMELA RODRIGUEZ-MONTERO: I think that's true, and yet it's so hard to do. It's so hard to just be there, you know? Very hard.

KYLA KAZUSCHYK: I love your comparison of like we are all swimming in the same water. That's a beautiful way to look at it. So many production processes are set up in a hierarchical way where the director is the boss, and everyone else just serves the director. But in my experience in devising, I found that it's more like okay let's all jump into the pool and swim the same way. It's more fun and it's more rewarding than just having one person tell everyone else what to do.

PAMELA RODRIGUEZ-MONTERO: Yes, exactly. I feel like there's so many input channels. There's so many inputs, so many different thought processes and you can embrace a lot of voices. You can start processing different points of view. I think it makes it richer. It is like a dish, maybe. You can have plain foods, dishes with just one ingredient, and it might be okay, but if you add more things to it, it will get better, you know? If you're able to combine them to get them to mix well, to work, to do all that. I think that that's how I see it. You have more choices, more ideas and maybe your work here is to be able to catalyze them or be able to say okay I'm going to analyze what I got from this, and this, and this, and this input and I'm gonna try to make them all fit and all work cohesively.

KYLA KAZUSCHYK: I love this metaphor because everyone brings their specific spice, like someone that has more experience with costumes can bring their costume experience, someone that has more experience with performance can bring their performance experience, but that doesn't mean that each can't have input on each other's process.

PAMELA RODRIGUEZ-MONTERO: I love what you said, because it is not a hierarchical process. You're definitely questioning and challenging that definition that there has to be one leader or a boss, you know it's just not. We are all doing this and there are leaders in the sense of guidance and there are people who are in charge of certain things but it doesn't mean that they are bosses, or that's the only vision we're following through. It is challenging the standard practices and that's what I love about devising, because you can really get to understanding how to just question, to question authority, question the things that have been done before and why, and just understanding what leadership really is.

KYLA KAZUSCHYK: Absolutely. Do you find that there's crossover or similarities to devising and working in the classroom, in education?

PAMELA RODRIGUEZ-MONTERO: Oh, absolutely yes, I think devising to me tends to be one of the most fruitful methods of doing theatre or ways of doing theatre. Because of that, because we are in a classroom, there are so many voices and we are trying to give them as much as we can from all the topics while teaching them the skills to work in any setting and allow them to build their own critical thinking and build their own leadership skills and build our collaboration, so I feel like, yes we could do that as well, separately, but devising allows us to do all of it together.

KYLA KAZUSCHYK: Yeah, and build everything at the same time.

PAMELA RODRIGUEZ-MONTERO: That's how I feel. I love it. I think it's really effective and not even for only theatre majors. I think everybody should do a little bit of devising in college, to approach collaboration, to understand their own power as leaders.

KYLA KAZUSCHYK: That's so interesting. Do you have experience with that? Have you worked with people that don't have theatre experience in devising?

PAMELA RODRIGUEZ-MONTERO: Yes, I have, with Gina Sandi Diaz. She specializes in that specific kind of devising work with the people from all backgrounds and all levels of experience and yes it's interesting because it takes away a little bit of the daunting of like all this is, you know, this is the scripted, and this is a script, and this is what you're supposed to do, and allows people to put in a little bit more creativity. I'm not super expert on that. I have done more with people in theatrical settings like theatre students and all that, but I do think it's a great practice for everybody to develop many skills.

KYLA KAZUSCHYK: And especially to think about like liberal arts colleges, like if you're trying to get a well-rounded experience anyway, why not?

PAMELA RODRIGUEZ-MONTERO: Why not? I think it's essential. It's essential for many, even social sciences disciplines, just to be able to say, let's tell a story. Because sometimes we just say, oh Theatre, and we put like the capital letters on it, and then we put it up there, like this

FIGURE 7.14 Thumbelina *at Stillwell Theatre, Kennesaw State University, GA, 2020. Director: Rosemary Newcott; music director: Amanda Wansa Morgan; set, costume, lighting design: Pamela Rodriguez-Montero; sound design: Mikaela Fraser. Picture credit: Casey Gardner Ford (photo courtesy of Pamela Rodriguez-Montero)*

FIGURE 7.15 Thumbelina *at Stillwell Theatre, Kennesaw State University, GA, 2020. Director: Rosemary Newcott; music director: Amanda Wansa Morgan; set, costume, lighting design: Pamela Rodriguez-Montero; sound design: Mikaela Fraser. Picture Credit: Casey Gardner Ford (photo courtesy of Pamela Rodriguez-Montero)*

FIGURE 7.16 Thumbelina *at Stillwell Theatre, Kennesaw State University, GA, 2020. Director: Rosemary Newcott; music director: Amanda Wansa Morgan; set, costume, lighting design: Pamela Rodriguez-Montero; sound design: Mikaela Fraser. Picture credit: Casey Gardner Ford (photo courtesy of Pamela Rodriguez-Montero)*

FIGURE 7.17 Thumbelina *at Stillwell Theatre, Kennesaw State University, GA, 2020. Director: Rosemary Newcott; music director: Amanda Wansa Morgan; set, costume, lighting design: Pamela Rodriguez-Montero; sound design: Mikaela Fraser. Picture credit: Casey Gardner Ford (photo courtesy of Pamela Rodriguez-Montero)*

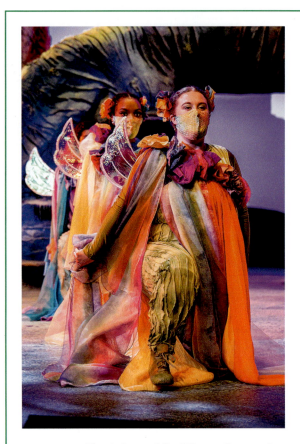

FIGURE 7.18 Thumbelina *at Stillwell Theatre, Kennesaw State University, GA, 2020. Director: Rosemary Newcott; music director: Amanda Wansa Morgan; set, costume, lighting design: Pamela Rodriguez-Montero; sound design: Mikaela Fraser. Picture credit: Casey Gardner Ford (photo courtesy of Pamela Rodriguez-Montero)*

shine bright stage, but this is storytelling, we are telling a story. That comes for everybody, we're just trying to tell a story, so it doesn't really have to be theatrical arts, it could be a story, it could be any discipline trying to express themselves through this medium. So I feel like that's important to just put out there, maybe your book can help people from other disciplines to take on storytelling.

KYLA KAZUSCHYK: Hopefully! Can you tell me about some examples of work that you've done?

PAMELA RODRIGUEZ-MONTERO: Yes, I did one, it was like I would say the most intense, that spanned for a long time as well, and that I had to do both not only devised work for concept and pieces and a lot of work through ensemble work as well, but also, I did work in traditional design as well, building and implementing in a traditional way. So it was a mixture and a hybrid of the process. It's a *Thumbelina*, we did as theatre for young audiences. We devised the script, the songs, we devised everything and it was very nice. Everything in the process got created by our students. And I designed along with them, so I designed as we were doing things. I would talk to them and show them the sketches and like this is where I am, what do you think. But it was something that they had their input and like they will tell me things but I finally also did my job as a costume designer and did all the process, all the sketches or like the implementation, I did it along with my shop manager and assistants in the shop, so it was like a mixture.

But just by devising it parallel allows the students or the performers much more empowerment, to come to me and tell me like I don't think this choice is working, I think this choice should be this way I'm not feeling comfortable with this, this headdress, maybe can we do this, and this and that or like this is how I'm planning to do my hair how, what do you think. So, I feel like just devising a bit and like doing it in parallel allows them to feel much more empowered to come to me and like, suggest, like just

FIGURE 7.19 *An interdisciplinary collaboration at the Zukerman Museum of Art. Mask design and construction by Pamela Rodriguez-Montero and choreography by Lisa Lock. Picture credit: Emily Knight (photo courtesy of Pamela Rodriguez-Montero)*

to say like, Oh, these are my thoughts, what do you think? And I will implement them, and they will be so happy to be like, I was thinking about this. That to me is like the future that I want to build. I want to build a costume design where the performers can come to me and say hey I feel like this is a better idea for this character and like what do you think, we can discuss it.

So it was a beautiful process, it was very interesting because it was hybrid. It wasn't finally a traditional play in the setting we presented it and everything but the process was 100 percent devising and to me my design process was very influenced by devising as well.

KYLA KAZUSCHYK: You said it was theatre for young audiences, was it working with young performers?

PAMELA RODRIGUEZ-MONTERO: No, it was just young adults but there wasn't like the youth. Young people but not like children.

KYLA KAZUSCHYK: So that's one thing that's really exciting to me about devising too is that it's accessible to all age levels. There are projects where people work with children devising shows.

PAMELA RODRIGUEZ-MONTERO: I want to try more out, I want to do more theatre for young audiences anyways because I have a son and all that, so I feel like it just lends itself very well to that. And if you think about it, we all have done a devising process with our cousins or our friends like anything when we're like oh let's dress up let's tell a story. So I feel like the structure is just right there, it is very connected to play, very connected to just play work as storytelling I would say.

KYLA KAZUSCHYK: I agree that it's absolutely natural and like you say that we put this capital T theatre on it, and now it has to be something else but it originated out of that play, that's where it started.

FIGURE 7.20 "The interdisciplinary collaboration was devised between myself and choreographer/performer Lisa Lock. We were invited by the Zuckerman Museum of Art to create a piece inspired by one of their exhibitions, A Peculiar Proximity to Spiritual Mysteries. The exhibition touched on issues of identity, race, immigration, and cultural origins. We both are immigrants so we decided to collaborate instead of working solo. We visited the museum and responded to the piece Map of Migrations by Michelle Murillo. It was a beautiful collaboration in which each one listened to each other and led each other in our respective areas." Pamela Rodriguez-Montero (photo courtesy of Pamela Rodriguez-Montero)

PAMELA RODRIGUEZ-MONTERO: Yeah it's just basically playing and doing things and having that ability to be creative, to have fun. I think what devising allows them sometimes is just not to be so serious. It allows us to find a seriousness in our work through play.

KYLA KAZUSCHYK: Yeah because, like you said, why not? Like, why not enjoy what we're doing?

PAMELA RODRIGUEZ-MONTERO: Yeah I mean, I think we all enjoy doing like capital T scripted theatre, but it has a lot more restrictions and a lot more expectations. I think devising removes a lot of that structure, removes a lot of that expectation and allows more organic process.

KYLA KAZUSCHYK: And more voices. I think that's important too, what you said about students feeling empowered to tell you their opinions. I love the idea that anyone would feel comfortable sharing their voices and how they're feeling about something.

PAMELA RODRIGUEZ-MONTERO: I think that's very important, how you're feeling and how it's working and if it's doing what it needs to do for you. I feel like maybe just that devising process gives that platform, builds confidence, builds trust, and like then you're like, Oh yeah, well come to me if you have anything and even for other shows that we have done before. After that they will be like, Oh yeah, they know because the trust has already been built so I think that's why it's so essential, especially for costume designers I feel because sometimes there's like this power dynamic and it's not like healthy. It's like all the costume and the directors have like this much saying about what a person is wearing and maybe they don't have as much of a chance to give the feedback and say like, Oh, this is just what I'm feeling, you know? So I feel like devising could be a good way to bridge that allows us to have more connection, to empower people to say what they are feeling about their stuff.

KYLA KAZUSCHYK: Absolutely. It's going to be a healthier process and it's going to create stronger performances. We know that when a performer feels uncomfortable in their costume they're not able to give their best performance. And if they don't feel comfortable saying that they don't feel comfortable then, how is that going to end? It is not going to end well.

PAMELA RODRIGUEZ-MONTERO: I think in general it also allows them to see how the process works, understand the design side a little bit more, because they have done it and understand why we make choices and how it is. I feel like it helps all in so—it's a beautiful way. It does generally take a little more time. I believe it is different, you have to plan for it differently and that's where production managers and artistic directors have to understand that that's different, but if it's done in a classroom setting I feel like it's perfect, it lends itself so well for everything.

KYLA KAZUSCHYK: Yes because we're setting up the time frame, so why not choose to spend more time on those conversations early on, than on anything else?

PAMELA RODRIGUEZ-MONTERO: Yeah, that's true. This was wonderful, thank you for inviting me to have this conversation.

KYLA KAZUSCHYK: Thank you so much for sharing your perspectives. I worked on a couple of devised pieces and then I had the idea to make this book, and then once I started working on it I realized like this book cannot be just my perspective, because it's the same thing—it's like what's the point if it's just the director as the boss, and the director's vision but not including everyone else's visions? Why have it be just one voice, when it could be lots of voices and it could include lots of perspectives?

PAMELA RODRIGUEZ-MONTERO: And there's so many people doing theatre and I love that you are a costume designer who is also working on this particular take on devising. Because it's so different, it's nice to see it from a different perspective from the designer's perspective or the director's perspective—maybe it's good to see it from all different perspectives.

KYLA KAZUSCHYK: I think you kind of covered this, but what advice do you have for costumers doing devised work?

PAMELA RODRIGUEZ-MONTERO: Well, for me, I would say just keep an open mindset, trying to enjoy the process and not be too serious in the sense of like you are being very serious and you're doing a lot of serious work, but your work comes alive through play. Your work becomes as you go, as you play, as you play with different possibilities and as you collaborate. So if you're super structured and you have expectations that are so rigid then just let loose of that, adjust your methods to enjoy and to allow a little bit of the creativity and the organic part of devising to take over in ways.

CHAPTER 8

BEYOND THEATRE

Skills developed in devising and creating can be applied beyond the work. It is possible to come together in groups and collaborate without oppressive hierarchy. You can use consensus-based decision making with casts, production teams, classes, and more, to ensure that everyone's voice is heard and the whole truly becomes greater than the sum of its parts. We can all learn from each other, and the process of creation of art can be praxis for a world that is accessible and equitable.

NON-HEIRARCHICAL COLLABORATION

We have been taught that hierarchy is essential to everything, but is it? Who says?

This idea of hierarchy is directly connected to white supremacy. It pits one person as the boss and everyone else involved in roles of service or servitude to the boss's vision. Devised theatre can dismantle this idea. In a devising process, everyone's voice matters. We can share more and compete less. It is possible to create community. When creating collaborative art, we are interdependent on each other. We can try new things and find other ways of working.

If the structures we have inherited are no longer serving us, we must recognize that and find and implement better ways. It is going to require a diversity of tactics to create something new. Maybe a model that could work for you could be one that is semi-hierarchical, with people sharing various leadership responsibilities. It will take an honest assessment of what is happening in order to change it. Do we need one person to be the boss and everyone else to serve them? Could we imagine and implement a sort of creative anarchy? Anarchy doesn't mean no rules, it means collective responsibility. Take responsibility. Accept that you will make mistakes. Acknowledge when you have made a mistake and work to change and to improve.

The idea of process versus product is a false binary. It is possible to engage in a process where participants learn and grow, and also through that process arrive at a product that can be shared with audiences, and audiences can learn and grow. You can have both, all! Theatre and art can be sustainable—there is room for variation on every model. Most binaries are false binaries—almost everything can be a mix. Costumes can be structured garments and costumes can facilitate movement. Costumes can indicate specific characters sometimes, and other times not. Costumes can be a mix of items specifically designed and items performers bring in and feel comfortable wearing. Costumes can be the primary means for telling a story, and you can tell a story without costumes.

What we know as "western" models often perpetuate oppression. If we are just drifting along with the models we were given without actively questioning why we are doing things, we may be passively continuing harmful and oppressive practices. It is possible to reimagine everything.

Even the widely accepted "Aristotelian" structure that we learn as the standard for script analysis, a linear story that takes the shape of a pyramid, reflects the worldview at the time of Aristotle. Alternative narrative structures can challenge the linear form. Maybe it served the people of ancient Greece, but does it still serve us in the world today? Could it be possible to adjust our whole worldview to one that is eco instead of ego, operating from a mindset of abundance instead of scarcity? The structure of the stories we tell and the way we organize to tell those stories, all this can shift to align with our values. Do we need to value power, competition, and control, or could we

FIGURE 8.1 *A structured costume to indicate an otherworldly pilot in* Dream Logos *(photo courtesy of Andy Phillipson—Livewireimage.com)*

create a culture that values collaboration and interdependence? Could the skills we develop through devising help us to get there? I think so. Another world is possible, and it is up to us to create it. We get to create it.

Don't lose sight of your imagination! Trust your intuition, and be open to the intuitive ideas of others.

CONSENSUS-BASED DECISION MAKING

Flexibility, creativity, and effective collaboration are key skills for all theatre artists.

Consensus-based decision making is not yet commonly practiced in theatre, perhaps because not many people have heard of it or tried it. In my experience as an educator, costume designer, and leader in costume shops, I have found it to be extremely beneficial. People feel more fulfilled when their ideas are welcomed and their concerns are listened to. Students in particular feel more empowered to speak up when a culture of true collaboration is established. With more people bringing their ideas to the table, the art we create can connect with even wider audiences.

When I look back on my life, on the achievements I am most proud of, the experiences I am most grateful for, what inspired me, what has shaped me into who I am today, I think of experiences with theatre, and I think of Positive Action (PosAct). PosAct was a student group, not specifically connected to theatre, though many of the projects we worked on were connected to performance and design. We once built a giant inflatable dinosaur in the center of campus, and stood next to it handing out fliers that read "How many dinosaurs does it take to stop a war?" We organized concerts featuring local and touring bands in an English classroom at night, pushing all the desks to one side at the beginning of the evening, and cleaning up and setting the desks back in rows before classes would be in there the next day. (This was definitely a form of theatre.) At club meetings, when having group discussions to plan actions, we always practiced consensus-based decision making.

It didn't occur to me to try consensus-based decision making in the classroom until listening to Dr. Nicole Hodges Persley speak at the Association for Theatre in Higher Education (ATHE) conference in 2019. She described her practice of developing a syllabus for a class with the class. She talked about

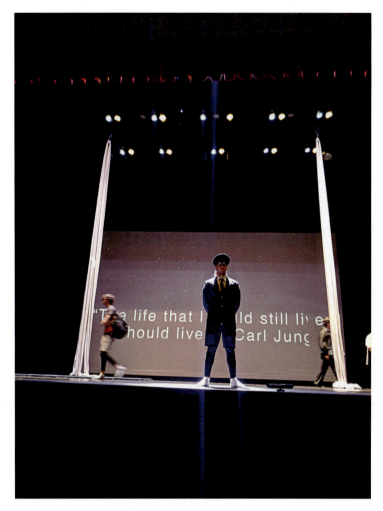

FIGURE 8.2 *The hat, jacket, shirt, and tie are enough to specify the pilot character; the shorts and leggings allow full range of movement*

coming in on the first day of the semester with a stack of books and posing the question to the class: "What ones do you want to read? What is important to *you*?"

This is one way to begin to dismantle the racism, classism, misogyny, ageism, and ableism inherent in the teaching of the commonly accepted "canon" of plays.

In costume technology classes, unlike dramatic literature or history, we do not have a list of books, but we do have a list of projects. So now, on the first day of class, instead of giving the students a syllabus, I come in with a list of possible projects and we devise the syllabus together. We talk through class policies as well, and collectively come up with agreed-upon policies that serve all of us.

A system that has been helpful in ensuring that everyone's voice is heard involves the use of hand symbols.

One person serves as the facilitator of the discussion. For groups new to this practice, the person bringing the practice to the group can be the facilitator, but once a group has experience with it, people can take turns serving as facilitator. The facilitator listens, encourages each person to share their thoughts, and shares their own thoughts. When it sounds like the group is on the precipice of a decision, the facilitator calls for everyone to weigh in using hand signals. For example, if the idea in question is a class policy regarding late work, and many people have voiced the opinion that any assignments turned in late should be worth 50 percent credit, the facilitator can call it to a vote. Everyone that agrees completely with this idea puts thumbs up. Everyone that disagrees puts thumbs down. Anyone who doesn't mind either way puts thumbs horizontal, halfway up. If anyone, even if it is just one person, has thumbs down, instead of the motion passing, it goes back to group discussion until the group collectively arrives at a decision that no one gives a thumbs down. Maybe late work should count for 75 percent credit. If you are trying to decide on something more

FIGURE 8.3 *Performers on stage in a later evolution of Dream Logos. One character wears a grey and white tank top and leggings that I designed and dyed. Other characters wear their own clothes (photo courtesy of Andy Phillipson—Livewireimage.com)*

sensitive, or if it seems like people are feeling pressure, you can have everyone but the facilitator put their heads down when they vote, so no one has to know who gives a thumbs down.

Additional hand signals that can help to enhance group communication include wiggly fingers, stay on point, and direct response. If someone is saying something that you wholeheartedly agree with and want to amplify, you raise your hand with your palm facing you and wiggle your fingers. If you really, really agree, you can use both hands. If someone is veering away on a tangent that is not crucial to the decision at hand, you can raise one palm with your thumb facing you, and with the pointer finger of your other hand, point at your palm, encouraging the speaker to stay on point. If someone is making a point that you have a direct response to, you can alternate both pointer fingers back and forth. This is to be reserved only for instances when you have something to bring up that might cancel out the speaker's point. For example, in the question of accepting late work, if someone is saying that late work should never be accepted, but you know that it is university-wide policy for late work to be accepted for partial credit, you could do a direct response so that the conversation moves toward an idea that will work within the parameters of both the immediate and the larger community.

I have found that this system is extremely helpful at both making decisions efficiently and ensuring that all voices are valued equally.

The problem with "majority rule" voting systems is that they give power to the majority, the most dominant voices, while voices that have been marginalized continue to be marginalized.

There are so many benefits to consensus-based decision making. Like devised theatre, it allows space for everyone to be heard. Everyone can be on equal footing. Everyone has ownership, or buy in. In educational settings, instead of teachers struggling to get students to do the things you, as a teacher, think are important, they are doing things they believe to be important. There is still a built-in power dynamic, but the struggle can be mitigated. Transparency with communication is vital, just like in collaborative art. We exist in community. We depend on each other.

FIGURE 8.4 *In* Nightmares Are Dreams, Too, *designed and built by Camilla Morrison, performers improvise movement based on their costumes and move through the space without speaking. Costumes are the driving force of storytelling (photo courtesy of Camilla Morrison)*

FIGURE 8.5 *From Carrie Bellew: Sam Quiones' book* Dreamland *was utilized as source material and students used Tectonic Theatre's book* Moment Work *and their exercises to develop and devise a script based on the opioid crisis in America. Students worked in conjunction with two other schools, Gulfport High School and Valley High School in Louisville, Kentucky to create three different plays that were presented together at the South Eastern Theatre Conference annual convention in 2020. Title for their show* Is the High Worth the Risk? *(photo courtesy of Carrie Bellew)*

FIGURE 8.6 *Young artist Lincoln Johnson manipulates fabric and objects to devise costumes and performances*

CIRCULAR MENTORSHIP

The model of a teacher being a font of knowledge and the system of education as students coming to that fountain is not only outdated but extremely toxic, oppressive, harmful, and unnecessary. Now that the internet exists and continues to become more and more accessible to more people, we as a culture need to seriously rethink the models of universities and theatres. When these institutions were invented, they were the only places people could go to learn or to be entertained. And they were exclusionary. For years, only white male landowners were allowed to attend universities and have access to the knowledge contained there. This created the culture that education was for them, and not for anyone else. Some forms of theatre perpetuate similarly exclusionary practices. Tickets can be expensive and invented norms of theatre etiquette can cause many people to believe that theatre is not for them.

If we acknowledge that existing systems are outdated and harmful, the next step is to take a step back and start to reimagine what could be. What is the point of higher education? What is the point of theatre? What can these offer in ways that YouTube/TikTok/Instagram/the internet in general cannot? What can we offer?

The first step toward dismantling oppression is to identify where we have power and privilege and identify how we can use that power in a positive way. Theatre at large, institutions of education, and especially costume shops contain lots of opportunities to reshape everything in a more equitable way.

We can create and sustain communities. We can encourage and support and challenge one another. We can nourish interpersonal interactions. We can offer space to practice and space to give and receive feedback. And this applies to everyone at all experience levels.

Mentorship can be reciprocal! Teaching is much more interesting and exciting when everyone involved, teachers and students, opens our minds to ideas outside of our own perspectives. This applies to collaborative design and creation processes as well. Some of us have more experience and training in particular disciplines, but that doesn't mean ideas can't be expanded by input from people with less experience. Actors can influence costumes, costumes can influence actors, there is room for all sorts of spaces to overlap.

Devised theatre can be a blueprint for healthy forms of education. Traditional schooling often suppresses autonomy and indoctrinates people into the habit of accepting hierarchical structures without question. In many Indigenous cultures around the world education eschews authoritarianism in favor of self-directed play. With time and space to play and explore and pursue ideas, individuals can develop in healthy ways. And we can learn how to cooperate with each other through creating with each other.

The practice of creating devised theatre mirrors practices of popular education. It can be praxis. When starting a devising project, participants bring their own experience and knowledge. Through sharing ideas, we identify patterns, and themes begin to emerge. Together, we come up with new ideas based on shared knowledge. As the process continues, people are practicing skills and planning actions, and then applying everything they have learned along the way together. At all stages of the process, unequal power relations are being challenged. And at the close of a project, there can be room for reflection and feedback.

The process of creating costumes can be praxis for equitable communities too. Connection to the world and to our humanity is inherent in all theatre, and especially powerful in devised theatre. Because the process for creating costumes for devised theatre goes hand in hand with the process of creating the work that will be presented, the costumes are deeply connected to the characters and to the stories they tell. Chaos is inescapable. Fear of chaos can prevent powerful stories from being told. Fear of the unknown can close the door to opportunity. As theatre practitioners, our job is to tell stories and to create magic. We are creating new worlds never before believed to be possible. Costumes are what create the fully fleshed-out characters that inhabit those worlds. It is possible to tell stories and to forge connections. We learn who we are through relationship to each other.

ARTIST SPOTLIGHT: SUELLEN DA COSTA COELHO

Suellen da Costa Coelho has designed and built costumes in her home country of Brazil as well as in venues across the United States. Here she discusses ways to practice truly equitable collaboration in theatre and in education.

SUELLEN DA COSTA COELHO: If I had to define some devised theatre it is like some show that starts without a script, like most of the idea and the gathering of the artists is a collaborative process.

I think the advantage to working with devised theatre is the idea that you don't need to decide everything, and I think the idea to have some people collaborating with you. Bring in their ideas, because, I feel that we are like a captain of the ship that we can just guide people towards to bring the idea and transform it into something that's usable in the stage, since we have the knowledge in how to build it and how to develop this but the advantage for me is to have a lot of minds together in

FIGURE 8.7 *Performers in an immersive devised dance and physical theatre piece, Spring 2021 (photo courtesy of Suellen da Costa Coelho)*

created a mood board and then the colors started to come up and then together, and then we could see what they wanted as a color for the show, and we really heard their voice about this.

Then we set up the day to go to the storage. And they chose their clothes and we talked about the colors that we had before, the colors that we talked about before in rehearsals and they were like, Okay, I like these, but we can change we can paint? I was doing the alterations for them like since I have the knowledge, they don't have this, but everything was decided together. They decided what they wanted to wear and then, of course, thinking about the process that we had before, for the first dance show, after we had these conversations I designed some renderings. I did some renderings to present to the director and then he liked it and I presented to the dancers, too.

And we built in the costume shop and brought to the dancers, to start to rehearse with. And it was funny because we had the process that, I developed something like a crown of flowers, and we got together after the rehearsal and they said, we can't dance with this, and I said Okay, it's okay, what do you want to do with this? And they changed it, they changed the crown of flowers, so they can dance, to be better for them and it was totally cool to be part of this, and they decided that. They were like, Okay, we are going to change that and it's going to be in this way and it is okay. I think this is my process, like let it go and really listen to the dancers.

a collaborative process, that it's going to be more rich than just one person thinking about this.

The two examples that I have were dance and it was funny because it was kind of the same process, I think maybe I'm creating a pattern for that.

I had a conversation with the director. He talked about his main idea in the first case was like about the environment, about the recycle work, like recycled materials. The second one was more about empowerment, empowering women's voices. My idea was to bring some theoretical work—like for the first one, I brought Dali and the second one I brought Anne Bogart as a text. And the first one was Dali as a painter and say hey, This is like what I'm envisioning for that is like this woman in the desert and for the second one we were talking about the violence to choose something and to choose the art and to define art.

And in the first one, I was bringing paintings, and they were talking about the ideas. In the second one, I told them to bring some images like, send to me, I can print, then we can talk about this, how it's going to be this process, what do you think about this imagery what do you see what's your idea? And it was nice because we put the images together on the wall and then

KYLA KAZUSCHYK: It's a great example that you had it fully designed, you had the designs realized, you gave them to them and then I'm so glad that the performers felt comfortable approaching you and saying, this doesn't really work for us. And you, instead of meeting that with combat and saying well, you have to wear it because it is a costume that I designed, you said, Okay well, what do you think? What could work? And together y'all developed the idea. I remember these flower crowns, we worked on them in the costume shop, it was like a crown of flowers and it went over the whole head right?

SUELLEN DA COSTA COELHO: Yeah and they had like some neck collar and they said, Okay, we can change and they put the neck the collar on top of their head and they had some flowers in this direction and it totally worked, the pictures look beautiful of the show, it's totally okay.

KYLA KAZUSCHYK: That's so cool that they discovered that in rehearsal too, that they took a piece, and just wore it in a different way, so it's still the same piece and it still communicates the story that you're trying to tell. And I love your story of the other piece that you worked on where you went with the performers to storage, had them pick out things that they wanted to wear. Did you feel

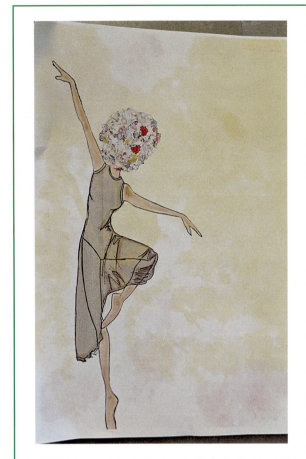

FIGURE 8.8 *Rendering by Suellen da Costa Coelho. The initial idea was a wire frame that rested on dancers' shoulders with wire-stemmed flowers wrapped around it encircling dancers' heads (photo courtesy of Suellen da Costa Coelho)*

like that helped them feel comfortable in their costumes? Did you feel that they were more excited about their costumes?

SUELLEN DA COSTA COELHO: Yes, totally, and it was really cool to watch too, because they went to the storage and I said, go have fun! and they started to pick like clothes and say, Okay, this is not like the color that we were talking about this is not like the way that we talked, can we cut here can you do this and it was really cool. There was a lot of energy in the room to find this to like be thinking about costumes and it's funny because most of the dancers told me that they said before, like, I have a lot of leotards but it's much fun to come here to do this. Most of them said, like I danced since I was a kid, like I have a lot of leotards, but coming here and like and also they asked like what did the other person choose what the color that she choose before me, and we talked about these and said, Okay I'm going to pick this color because I think it's better to match with the other dancers, and yeah it was a lot of energy in this moment.

KYLA KAZUSCHYK: But that's so cool to think that they're already thinking about their work as an ensemble and they're thinking about how their piece communicates with the other pieces in the show and I like what you mentioned too about like it's a collaborative process, everyone has a voice, but you know as a trained costume designer and technician you have more knowledge. You have more experience in how to alter clothes, what is possible. You know about dying and painting, so you know what is possible, so you can come bringing that knowledge and they can come bringing the ideas and you can go back and forth about what do you think is possible and what might be possible.

SUELLEN DA COSTA COELHO: Yes, that is a, I think it is a Greek sentence, that says that, like the man is the head, but the woman is the neck. I feel it is the same. It's so funny, I figured out that I think, for me the process was like that, like they're like the head of the piece and I was like okay, maybe I was the neck!

KYLA KAZUSCHYK: That's a great metaphor. Okay you've had these experiences designing costumes for dance. I'm curious as to how the way that you worked on these projects translates to other costumes you've designed. Do you think about these principles of collaboration when you're designing a scripted show?

SUELLEN DA COSTA COELHO: Yes, I think devising releases your ego. Devising theatre releases your ego. Like you don't, you can't be attached so much. That's something that I learned with you in the beginning, like if they don't want to wear the clothes that day it's okay and that's releasing a lot of your ego. And when you have a problem, like with a scripted show and, like the actors are so used to go to the dressing room and say yeah I'm going to dress this and it's like the costume design option choice. And then when the actor said I'm not going to wear this or I'm not going to wear this hairpiece or not gonna do this like it's normally a great like a big problem with directors and costume designers and at this point, after devised theatre I can say, Yeah, whatever like, is it gonna be a problem for the show? No, nobody's gonna die and it's gonna be okay, and I think the other thing is to release your ego with your director. If they say I'm going to take this off, I say it's ok. I think it helps a lot for the process of scripted theatre.

KYLA KAZUSCHYK: Yeah that makes sense, totally, that it allows you to move forward and to let go of your attachment to something which is really hard to do because we care so much about our work, we put so much effort into our designs. We do care about them, but

FIGURE 8.9 *After rehearsing with the flower crowns as seen here, dancers had the idea to flip them upside down so the flowers stretched over their shoulders instead. The original spirit of the design remains, and the piece is even stronger because the dancers feel safe and comfortable and know that their voices are valued*

it's hard to see the bigger picture that like if we put this aside, it can be something else.

SUELLEN DA COSTA COELHO: Yes, yes I think it's a really good learning experience to learn to let go. It is still hard sometimes.

KYLA KAZUSCHYK: It takes practice. You can cultivate it. The more you practice, the easier it gets.

SUELLEN DA COSTA COELHO: Yeah and I think again the sentence about the neck because it's something really good to learn about directors too. Like, okay you don't want this, but maybe you can have this. Like, give options what you want, for the director and the actors.

KYLA KAZUSCHYK: My next question is what advice do you have for artists approaching devised work, either choreographers or dancers or costume designers. What advice would you give?

SUELLEN DA COSTA COELHO: To listen. To really listen. Like, of course, we have, everybody has input, I have input when I start the show, I have an idea. But, as every time that we start some art project, it's really hard to create exactly what you have in your mind, to come out exactly in the same way that we imagined it before is like the ideal world. But to listen. I think it's better. You're going to get close to what the people want, if you listen really listen, not just putting your idea inside on top of everyone.

KYLA KAZUSCHYK: I think that goes to everyone, too. Like that could go to directors and performers too. For performers it's on them to listen to why the costume is like this, and what is important about this and for directors too, to hear the needs of everybody and organize all that together.

Regarding reciprocal mentorship, we've been talking about how the principles of collaboration can also apply to what we do in the classroom. You've been studying to be a teacher and you've been practicing being a teacher. And you've seen how I practice being a teacher, as your teacher. And thinking about ways that we can set up communities where everyone's voices can be heard, and everyone can listen to each other, what are the

FIGURE 8.10 *Dance costume direct application dyed by Suellen da Costa Coelho (photo courtesy of Suellen da Costa Coelho)*

connections that you see there? How does this work apply to the classroom?

SUELLEN DA COSTA COELHO: How the devising knowledge applies into the classroom?

It is going to sound repetitive, but I think it's like a great thing to release your ego. About, do you think it's important for you? Like it's not important for me for some students to learn how to draw a hand in a very perfect way, or to stitch the best collar like when starting, when learning how to stitch a shirt at the costume shop. But the most important thing is you're going to be able to leave the costume shop and do some other stuff and train more.

Because it's not going to be perfect the first time, but he's gonna understand the process, he's gonna understand how to set up a machine, how to cut the fabric and it's going to be much better the next time, is going to be faster the next time then I'm not gonna be so attached to all, like all the details like oh, this is not like this corner is not perfect, you need to do all the thing again like you need to do all the coat again. No. The knowledge that he had until here, until this process and to this corner and you saw that this corner didn't work very well it's gonna be part of your process is going to be part of your next clothes.

Like Legos, you build some stuff.

This is the process. And I think this is the same for devised theatre like maybe the first one is not going to be perfect or maybe like something that some dancer is going to decide at the last minute is not going to be what you decided what you wanted, but it's something that he decided or she decided and the next one he's going to be more empowered to understand that okay I need to make more like other choices or think more about my group. I think it is the same for the classroom.

KYLA KAZUSCHYK: Like in the short time we have with students, the best thing that we can offer them is an understanding of a process so they could take that process and apply it to something else. And the next time they try, they can practice more, rather than having one specialized area of knowledge, but not knowing how to seek that knowledge and how to incorporate that knowledge with the larger project.

FIGURE 8.11 Costumes devised by Suellen da Costa Coelho, in collaboration with the aerial artists (photo courtesy of Suellen da Costa Coelho)

FIGURE 8.12 Immersive dance and physical theatre costumes designed by Suellen da Costa Coelho in collaboration with performers (photo courtesy of Suellen da Costa Coelho)

SUELLEN DA COSTA COELHO: Yeah and I think they need to understand that, because they get so stressed about oh it needs to be perfect, I need to finish this now, I need to do it in this certain way, and no it's not about this, it's about enjoying the process.

KYLA KAZUSCHYK: So in mask making and advanced stage makeup we practiced collective decision making, which is a skill that I have connected from devised theatre and non hierarchical leadership that I'm trying to implement in the classroom. And you were in both of those classes. What is your perspective on that? Do you think that it is helping, do you think that it needs to be modified, do you think it's something that you would try, this process of everyone making decisions together?

SUELLEN DA COSTA COELHO: I think I am probably going to use that in my life as a professor, like to make decisions together. But I think you do that, and then you make them stick with the decisions. Like okay, we set up that we're going to show a portfolio at the end, we're going to show a portfolio at the end doesn't matter how you're going to do this, how long you're gonna take to do this if you're going to do this, like in your last day before you present your portfolio, but you're going to present your portfolio. And I think it really works, sometimes some students are not going to understand that, but at least they're going to have the practice to experiment.

Because, something that I can notice about other classes is that we don't have a chance to experiment with process, to experiment with a lot of materials. And this class, advanced makeup and mask making, we could experiment a lot. And this was like, I know how to do a face cast because I tried so many times. The first two times were terrible, but the last one that I did with Jolie was perfect.

But I could do this, I could have this process, I didn't feel guilty when the first time didn't come up like really good, because I knew that I had more chances to do that again, and again and again to be good at this. I think this makes a huge difference for the students to have this time to experiment with something.

KYLA KAZUSCHYK: I agree. I'm so glad you took that away. Kind of connected to this is something that I'd like to hear more about your perspective here, that a lot of the university system is built on this model that the professor holds the knowledge and the students come to the university and come to that professor to get the knowledge. And I can see a lot of problems with this structure and I'm interested in your perspective on it.

SUELLEN DA COSTA COELHO: No, I think it's an exchange. It's always an exchange. I don't have the whole knowledge, I have more experience, just that. I know that some stuff is not going to work, like just to look. It's funny, when I started at the costume shop, I remember that I was stitching something, and you came from another place, and said the machine is not sounding good. And another day I caught myself doing this with one of the students. Because it's just about the experience, but they can bring so much for us like they have other knowledge and to be open for that is the best part of being a teacher. To be open for the knowledge that the students bring and the way that they see other ways to do stuff other ways to build the process.

Sometimes it's hard to let it go like we have in the advanced makeup. Sometimes it's hard, because you see that the process is not going to work but, you can tell to the students, you say you should put more vaseline and the student is not going to put more vaseline and then she has to cut her own hair. You told them! But I think it's not like something hierarchical that is going to become from up to down, it's always like an exchange. I had just had more experience. And I really don't want to be part of the white supremacy to think that I'm the knowledge, I'm the truth.

KYLA KAZUSCHYK: The world is much wider than that. And we have knowledge and experience and students come with different knowledge and experience. There were examples of that in advanced stage makeup. Some of the students would come when they demonstrated techniques that I didn't know, that I had never seen before. And it's just because that's what those students had focused on and they learned it somewhere else, and they brought it to us, so the classroom can be a space to share all these ideas.

SUELLEN DA COSTA COELHO: Something that I learned in this process too I think was I don't need to have the best cut crease eye. My student can be better than me and that's totally okay. I'm just here to support the students. Because I remember that I started the class for advanced makeup I said hi I'm not the best at makeup. But I could be some asset for them in other stuff like in the way that they research, in the way that they present their work, the way that they think about the process, how they do the prosthetics because I like the prosthetics. But that's why I think it's totally an exchange and if more professors think about that it would be much better, much more enjoyable to be a student.

KYLA KAZUSCHYK: It's so hard to do, because as professors, when we are put in leadership positions, we feel this pressure, that we have to be perfect at a cut crease but a cut crease is really hard! And so you feel like because you're the one up there, teaching it, you have to be the best at it. But exactly as you explain, you don't have to be, you just have to create a space where students can practice it and you can bring other assets, you can bring your knowledge of prosthetics or something else. In the way that you encourage the space and the way that you help them think about research and then they can teach each other how to do the cut crease or what have you.

SUELLEN DA COSTA COELHO: Yes, I totally learned this here, I was like no I need to be the best one because I'm the grad student but no, I can be the best in other stuff. It's okay, I can be good at enough stuff.

KYLA KAZUSCHYK: It also sends the message to students that they don't have to put that pressure on themselves. If they see us being transparent and vulnerable, as people in leadership positions, like look, I'm not the best at this yet, but I'm going to keep practicing. I think it sets it up that it's okay for them to keep practicing.

SUELLEN DA COSTA COELHO: Yes, it's pretty good. I think this is the real exchange with the students is the real learning. Like when you think you know everything, that's the moment that you don't. If you think you know everything, that's not true.

ACCESSIBILITY AND EQUITY

The nature of devised work is innately more accessible than scripted work. It is organized so that anyone may participate, regardless of their experience level. The skills that we learn in devising can be applied to scripted work, like being flexible and open-minded, and listening to everyone's voices. It is possible to create and hold space for everyone to share their perspectives.

When we create costumes, we can choose to work towards making the world we want become the world we know. Everything is possible in some way, and everything gets easier with practice.

Devising can make more space for audiences to be active and involved participants instead of passive spectators, even if it is just inspiring people to question things they did not question before. We can listen to everyone's voices. We can create space and hold space and amplify each other's voices. The work we do in theatre can be connected to the work we do towards creating the world we want. When we create something, we can always think about access. Who is this for? How can they get to it? If we are not actively working to dismantle ableist and oppressive white supremacist structures, are we just perpetuating them? Right now it is easier than ever to make a video or get to something on the internet. Anyone can create. Everyone has a story to tell.

ARTIST SPOTLIGHT: EMILIO RODRIGUEZ

Emilio Rodriguez is creating theatre in a way that is both equitable and sustainable, proving that it is possible!

KYLA KAZUSCHYK: What do you think are the advantages to creating devised theatre?

EMILIO RODRIGUEZ: I really love that it's collaborative because I think that sometimes when theatre is in the hands of one person exclusively it can sometimes only represent one person's opinions or one person's values and so being in a more collaborative setting, hearing everyone's voices and creating something from scratch that really resonates with whatever the community we're working with interests are, I think those are the two reasons, that collaboration and that community response.

KYLA KAZUSCHYK: It's totally different than just taking a script and showing it to someone. There's room for much more back and forth and more communication.

EMILIO RODRIGUEZ: I think sometimes you know, taking this script and like, let's do *Mary Poppins* but we're going to respond to what's going on in the world now. It's like trying to fit a square into a rectangle or whatever the phrase is—circle in the square—but instead of like, okay what's going on right now and then let's write a piece about what's actually going on right now, or if we want to make it metaphorical, we can, but that it's a new piece that's responding to that, rather than trying to make something else be a different thing.

KYLA KAZUSCHYK: I wonder why we do that so often. I have worked on so many of those productions like "it's *Mary Poppins* but" like why?

EMILIO RODRIGUEZ: I'm so fascinated by that too. I feel like it's never been a strength of mine, or an interest of mine, to really do that, I think the only time I've maybe done that is like with *Romeo and Juliet* in college, because everyone has to do a Shakespeare show in college. That's when I just started directing. But other than that I haven't really felt that need. I think because I'm also a playwright, I've always had an interest in new work or creating something from scratch, so I think it just depends on the interest and I think if we have more playwrights maybe in leadership positions or more different theatre technicians, different areas of theatre, costume designers in leadership positions, sound designers in leadership positions, lighting designers in leadership positions, I think that is going to make our theatre so much more exciting and that's how we're going to get away from the rules of the past, of this is how we do a show and go into more exciting territories.

KYLA KAZUSCHYK: Do you think that that shift is really possible?

EMILIO RODRIGUEZ: I hope so. I mean part of me is an optimist and believes in the abstract things. I think the biggest thing is going to be funding and audience, because if you can get the funding for it and you can get people interested in it, then no one can argue that it's a valuable method, but I think if one of those two areas fails or doesn't succeed, then that's when people start questioning, is this really a viable source. So I think it really comes down to having someone on that team who can get the funding and someone on the team who knows how to take this theatre that is resonating with communities, but also make it marketable so that you actually get the people coming to see it.

KYLA KAZUSCHYK: And it's kind of disappointing that it always comes down to money talks, but that's what makes work sustainable.

EMILIO RODRIGUEZ: Yeah because I mean who wants to work for free? I mean maybe if you're like super super passionate about the project but we also tell people, artists need to get paid, so if we want that model then we do have to make money or we have to get revenue into the project as well.

KYLA KAZUSCHYK: Somehow, yes. How do you approach creating costumes for devised work? Do you have examples of the projects you've worked on and how you create costumes for them?

EMILIO RODRIGUEZ: So this student just sent me their rendering. I have an example of something that a student just drew. So we're doing this project with NALAAC, the National Association of Latino Arts and Culture and we are writing and working with students. So I'm the lead writer, but the students are essentially giving me the idea and the schools and the parents as well.

It is about restorative practices, but told through the lens of superheroes. So they're fifth grade students and so they're telling me, Okay, and then the heroes do this and then this will

FIGURE 8.13 *Jazmine Kuyayki Broe and Joshua Zambrano in* Mirror on the Wall, *a Black and Brown Theatre original adaptation of* Snow White. *Lead costume designer: Saawan Tiwari (photo courtesy of Emilio Rodriguez, Erin Elliot Photography)*

happen, it's gonna be a crystal ball, and then I'm putting that into actual dialogue form.

And they're also designing the costumes, they're working with a costume designer named Nicole "Broadway" Avery and she is teaching them about costume design and how to make renderings and so here is the costume design that one of our students came up with. This is for the villain character and she is a fifth-grade student, she was saying, you know, maybe a mask because villains always are hiding who they are, and also because it's Covid times like it may be fun to just have a mask as well built into the costume.

And then you can see, like his hat, it has a money sign on it, there's a cane that's also a bird that matches his bird aesthetic and then a fancy fur coat so that was something that you know really having that teacher specialist come so that people aren't just like doing it completely cold, but they feel confident and they're given the skills and the resources and she was teaching them about the questions, how do you think about shape, how do you think about colors on this, so this one's black and white, but she eventually did color it in, and it was, I think, like the whole costume is black and gold.

KYLA KAZUSCHYK: I think that having that teacher is a really important element, because we're all capable of learning something if we have the right teacher, and so I think that community involvement is like okay, how do we give the community power, but how do we also give them the resources and tools, so that they can be successful in it, too, and it's not just here you can do whatever you want, it's here you can do whatever you want and we're going to make you feel prepared and safe and confident in trying this new thing.

KYLA KAZUSCHYK: I love that! That connects with everything, that connects with teaching and like so many of the people I've been talking to can cite that the advantage to devised theatre is anyone can do anything. But exactly what you just said, like okay do it, but we don't have the training, we don't have the background, we don't have the experience, we don't have any support to just do it.

EMILIO RODRIGUEZ: Yeah I think and that's where, for me, so I love devised theatre, but actually, I like to do it my own way, I don't like to take a lot of practices from other people because of that exact same problem that you had

FIGURE 8.14 *A costume sketch designed by a student for a devised piece at Black and Brown Theatre Detroit (photo courtesy of Emilio Rodriguez)*

like there's no there's no organization or structure, when I see other people do it I'm not saying everyone I'm just saying from my personal experience when I've worked with other people. And so it just becomes like a hot mess and then the play is like a bunch of ideas and then as an audience member you're watching it like, What just happened? But as a creator you're like, Oh my gosh this is so fun I got to give my idea. And so it was, like, How do we get that, Oh my gosh this is so fun I got to give my idea, but then also get the structure so when the audience is watching it they're like, Oh cool I get it here's the story, I can follow along. And so we typically do more linear plays but they're created with the community's input and with the community having a say in what the costumes look like, what the set looks like. So everyone has a say in everything but they're having a teacher guide them through all of the steps.

So I typically focus on teaching writing and directing and then I have someone teach costume design, someone to teach lighting design, someone to teach set design. So that everyone in the community feels supported in what they're doing and how they're being involved in the creation, too, but that when they invite their family and friends to see it, or when, if it's filmed, when they show it to their family and friends on YouTube or whatever platform we put it on, that they're able to be like, Okay, I understand the story I'm not confused it wasn't just for you—it was a story that could reach a larger audience that you had a say in as well.

KYLA KAZUSCHYK: That's so cool and that really is so much so different from other devised theatre practices where like yeah it's great to focus on the process and yeah then it's a valid experience for the people involved in the process, but it's not an enriching experience for the audience. It can be both: it can be enriching for the performers and the audience.

EMILIO RODRIGUEZ: Absolutely, I always think, I think of theatre more in a business aspect, and I think some people misinterpret that as me being like, I'm greedy and how do I make all the money, but not in the sense of money, but

FIGURE 8.15 Mirror on the Wall, *a Black and Brown Theatre original adaptation of* Snow White. *Pictured are Joshua Zambrano, Kiana Douglas, and Jazmine Kuyayki Broe. Lead costume designer: Saawan Tiwari (photo courtesy of Emilio Rodriguez, Erin Elliot Photography)*

in the sense of being consumer centered. My brother was a business major, has an MBA and now works for Procter and Gamble and my dad was always like really big in leadership and both my parents were teachers, so I always think from the educational aspect, but then I also think of like, how can we be consumer centrist in our theatre so it's, how do we have like that Venn diagram of what we're passionate about as artists, but also what the community and the communities you want to work with are what they are passionate about too. Because sometimes we're like well, I really want to do this Shakespearean story, but everyone's going to speak it backwards and it's going to be translated into Russian. It's like, okay does your community speak Russian, do they like language backwards, do they even like this particular Shakespeare story? Maybe they like *Romeo and Juliet* but you really want to do *Measure for Measure* because it's exciting for you and it's like, how do you find that compromise of what's exciting for you, but then what is the audience going to get out of it because if we're really just doing it for ourselves, then maybe we don't need an audience for it, but if we're doing it for an audience, then we want to also think about what are they going to get out of it as well.

KYLA KAZUSCHYK: And it's really a balance because the scale can tip in the other direction too. I've worked at theatres that are like butts on seats, we just gotta sell tickets it doesn't matter what your experience is.

EMILIO RODRIGUEZ: Right *Mary Poppins*, no matter what.

KYLA KAZUSCHYK: Yes but there's room, it can be a spectrum, it doesn't have to be one or the other, there's room in between.

EMILIO RODRIGUEZ: Absolutely, and I think that's so important, and I think it teaches like not only compromise, but it teaches empathy as well, because I think it's so interesting that theatre artists are always like, theatre is all about empathy, theatre is all about empathy but then, if anyone says anything that they disagree with they're like I hate this person I'm deleting them off my Facebook—it's like, what happened to empathy?

And so I think what a devised process teaches is that understanding. Because sometimes we might have different opinions or different values of where we want this story to go but that's when we have to come to an agreement, come to an understanding, find that Venn diagram, find that commonality, which is a process. And it's not easy, but I think that, hopefully, that we get better at taking those theatre skills that we learn in the creation process and applying them to our real lives too.

KYLA KAZUSCHYK: How do you approach facilitating that, especially with children, how do you decide how to say no?

EMILIO RODRIGUEZ: I think, for me, it is important to have a team of people who are the designated leaders, a very small team where there's like two or three people that just are going to make a final call. Because sometimes you have to accept the fact that if you have three people saying this, and three people saying this, how do you make a final decision that blends both worlds? Because those three people are seeing it from their eyes and these three people are seeing it from their eyes, so having an outside person who's like looking at the larger picture. And I think, for me, setting that tone, from the beginning of, here's what the expectation is, setting the expectation in the beginning, that we're not always going to get everyone's way. It's impossible for everyone to get their way, because if you get your way, that means I don't get my way if we're conflicting with each other. So setting that up from the beginning, I think, is really important that that's a standard. So that way, no one is surprised. I think sometimes they set it up at the beginning like this is devised theatre and everyone's voice is going to be heard and everyone's voice is going to be equally mattered and then it gets to the end point and they're like, Well, you said that everyone's voice matters, but how come this person is 60 percent of the writing and I'm 20 percent? Because we didn't set that up from the beginning that it's not going to be able to be perfectly balanced like that. Because if it is perfectly balanced, then it also might feel like, that's where we start getting the plays that are all over the place and it's like, well we gave you 20 percent 20 percent 20 percent 30 percent so you got six pages and then you also get six pages, even though your scene is not actually done in those six pages it's like. It's fair, but fair is not always going to be creating the best show. So I always like to tell everyone involved that our ultimate goal is creating the best show, whether or not my ideas get incorporated at all or whether or not all your ideas get incorporated or some of your ideas, some of this person's ideas, some of this person's ideas. It might not be a perfect balance, but what we're all going to look at collectively is how we make the best show possible.

And sometimes making the best show means that my idea doesn't get included or maybe not all of your ideas. We have to find that balance. So I think that's really important, setting up that expectation from the very beginning, so it's not a surprise at the end. It's something that we review every single meeting that we have. I think that some of my students will say like, Okay, we get it, it's a collaboration, we're doing what's best for the show. But that way, we never run into a problem at the end of like my idea didn't get taken or you know I don't run into those problems. Yes, I annoy them every rehearsal though by saying, "Not everyone's idea is going to go, you know we have to do what's best for the show," and they get to the point where they're like we get it, we can regurgitate this now. But we never run into the problem at the end of like oh, my idea didn't get taken here because they know from the beginning that we're doing what's best from this for the show. And they're reminded at every rehearsal.

KYLA KAZUSCHYK: The more reminders the better, this is like the same principle of community agreements.

EMILIO RODRIGUEZ: Yeah I think that's probably because of my educator background slipping in. Both my parents are teachers. I always like to set that up when in the classroom too even when I'm teaching theatre that's not project based where it's just learning the skill sets of theatre. The same thing it's like what are the community agreements and I actually teach like all ages, preschool all the way to college and an adult class too. But with my college students, I was like, Okay, we have to come up with our agreements of like, how do we even have a discussion. Because so often we're taught that the point of a debate or discussion is to get the other side to believe, to be persuaded—you have to agree with my opinion. And so one of the first community guidelines we had is my opinion probably won't change, but your understanding of my opinion will.

So then it creates that impetus of like, you're not trying to change my opinion, I'm not trying to get you to change your opinion but by giving each other the space to speak, hopefully we both will have an understanding of why we feel that way. Which is the key to empathy. So I think those, like you said community guidelines, it's a perfect way to think about it, and really all settings should be having, schools, workplaces, relationships, I think that's just a great baseline to have.

KYLA KAZUSCHYK: Yeah it totally applies to everything and even the reiterating it at the top of every meeting, like you can never hear it enough, even if you feel like you know it, it's so easy to separate from it. This is probably connected, but how do you approach creating a timeline for a devised project? Are your projects all set? What determines when the deadlines are?

EMILIO RODRIGUEZ: Oh that's a great question. As of recently we've been doing it based off of grant deadlines, because typically these projects are grant funded and that's what allows us to pay the artists, pay the teachers, pay the educators all of that, you know have costumes, all that stuff that we love in our theatre world. So typically we work backwards from that so if they need a report by June 30 then we're going to probably want it done by May, so we have time to have reflection. And then we think back, is it a live performance, or is it filmed? And then deciding how many weeks we need to rehearse, how many unique weeks we need to write, how many weeks we need to brainstorm, how many weeks we need for production elements, and then venue rental because we don't have our own space—so planning backwards from that.

So a typical show right now, our shows range from about 30 minutes to an hour and we typically do about four weeks of rehearsal, and then writing process is anywhere from six to ten weeks and then before that production process, we want to give typically about a month to have just production meetings to go over what are all the things we want to accomplish, what are the things that have to align with the grant, where are the things that are meeting what the community asked us, and the other community partner, and all of that. So a process, including all of that can be what is that, like three, four months planning process, three or four months process that we outlined in the timeline.

KYLA KAZUSCHYK: You have the production meetings before you start rehearsing and getting on your feet together?

EMILIO RODRIGUEZ: Yes, it's something that I've just been trying recently, and then we also meet again as we're rehearsing during the rehearsal process, just so that everyone knows where they're committing to because with a devising process the script might change and we might take it in a completely different direction, and so oftentimes the designers or the production team want to book their schedule to know what's going to happen, but as we're creating the script it's like it might not be done by that time or it might change from what we originally pitched you, so having that time to be with everyone and prepare everyone to be on the same page.

What our process is too because our process for some of our shows is a little bit different than other people like the one we're doing now, where the students are really in control, so we want to make sure that everyone the design team understands that before they even go into the realm of the actual show and seeing the actual script so there's no surprises of like wait, what did I sign up for. We have that time to just meet and plan ahead and plan how we're going to build in our time to anticipate problems, how we're going to build in the rehearsal schedule time to make changes and to plan on making changes and to plan that a set will be built, and then a second draft of the set will have to happen when we're actually in the space trying it out. That a costume will be built and then as we're doing our blocking that costume might have to completely change because we thought we wanted this character in a dress, and then we realized that she's doing cartwheels and squats the whole entire show and a dress is just not going to work. And so maybe you can keep part of the dress but you have to like cut open the front, so that she has room to move her legs or whatnot.

So that I think that's been really important for me and I've learned from my mistakes, to have those production meetings earlier, so that they know to plan for everything to change throughout the process, so that if only a few things change and they're like, oh great only a few things changed, you told me everything was going to change, but if we don't prepare them for that, then if everything changes everyone's freaking out.

FIGURE 8.16 Superheroes in Disguise, *an original show by Black and Brown Theatre created with Ypsilanti Elementary students. Pictured is Bryce Foley. Lead costume designer: Dr. Nicole "Broadway" Avery (photo courtesy of Emilio Rodriguez, Erin Elliot Photography)*

KYLA KAZUSCHYK: It's hard to adjust to changes, especially because so much of theatre training is so rigid like it's going to be this and this is set in stone and that doesn't teach us to be flexible, that doesn't help us to roll with the punches when things have to change.

EMILIO RODRIGUEZ: Absolutely. I was talking to another one of my friends about this, she was doing a podcast about theatre and we're talking about directing and how, this is true for a lot of people, they think I'm brand new to directing because I often ask actors how they feel and how they want to be directed. And so their assumption of me is like, oh he's never directed before so he's asking like for ways to be, how to direct, but I'm actually asking them because I have learned from directing so many times that certain people shut down from certain things, certain people break from certain things, certain people excel with certain directions, certain people hate certain directions.

For example like line reading is like the classic thing is like don't ever give an actor line reading. Sometimes there are actors who are totally fine with the line reading and when we're filming especially, and we need to wrap and people are like we need to have dinner at 6pm or we can have dinner at 7 p.m. with me trying to figure out how to give you this note, or I can just give you the line reading and wrap it up but that depends on the actor, because some actors will tell you, No, please don't ever give me a line reading and some actors will say, Yes, give me a line reading then we can get over with, and some actors will say, Well, it depends, are we filming or doing live theatre and if we're filming, are we pushing our dinner break—you know all of those things.

So knowing all of those elements I think is so important for a director. Another weird thing that I've learned is weird is apologizing as a director. So many people have told me they've never been apologized to by a director.

And that was so weird to me because I think that's like part of my leadership process is being transparent and saying I messed up in this area and I'm sorry for that and how do we make this right. If we're making a play about restorative practices, how can I go through an entire rehearsal process without ever acknowledging my mistakes to anyone on the team and correcting those mistakes. But then when you do that, people are like, because like you said, people are so used to rigid

FIGURE 8.17 Superheroes in Disguise, *an original show created by Black and Brown Theatre with Ypsilanti Elementary students. Pictured are Leyla Beydoun, Daniel Alexander Rivera, and Bryce Foley (photo courtesy of Emilio Rodriguez, Erin Elliot Photography)*

theatre, and this is what a director does and they tell us where to stand, then they're like wait, have you ever directed before and I'm like, yes I've directed before and because things have gone wrong before that's why I do things the way I do things because I want to not make the same mistakes again.

KYLA KAZUSCHYK: And that applies to everything, not just directing, that's any kind of communication, if you open yourself up to see what someone else's communication style is, you can get there quicker, you can get there more efficiently, and you can get there with less harm, so why wouldn't you? I think that this culture of not apologizing and not admitting when you're wrong is connected directly to patriarchy and white supremacy too. That is stuff that is so ingrained in all of us. We were taught that this is the way it has to be but it doesn't have to be like that.

EMILIO RODRIGUEZ: Yeah it's so interesting and so we've often started incorporating restorative practices as part of our theme for a lot of our family shows. We call them family shows, instead of theatre for young audiences, which is a separate tangent about how you'll never see a show where there's no adults, a kids show where there's no adults in the room because somebody had to take them to the theatre or if they're in a school then there's teachers and principals and administrators there.

So yes, some adult is gonna have to suffer through this show if we don't make it accessible to adult audiences as well. I think of great Disney movies, like you can watch them even as an adult and they're still entertaining and there's still a story to follow and it might not be your first choice in a movie that you want to see, it might be more interesting to watch *The Godfather* as an adult but, like you can still be entertained by a Disney movie, and so we want to create more of that family aspect. And so I think when we ingrain these messages about restorative practices it's so interesting that sometimes the actors or the team will say something like can an apology really be a climax? And I'm like, well, yeah if the resolution after the climax is that they're going to change their behavior, they're gonna make up for the things that they've done or they're gonna go on a new journey, why not, and they're like, I just don't think an apology is that big a deal, but then, as we get into the process, nobody apologizes for anything they did! Someone just, you know, turns something in late and they're just like, well if we'd had a little bit more time and it's like, you could just apologize, and we can move forward and we can correct the situation so it's just so funny to me that, like from the theatre practitioner's side it's like how can an apology be a climax, but then not being able to see outside yourself and as everyone in the process makes a mistake they're like, the apology is the last thing that they want to say.

FIGURE 8.18 *Kennikki Jones-Jones in* Superheroes in Disguise, *an original show created by Black and Brown Theatre with Ypsilanti Elementary students (photo courtesy of Emilio Rodriguez, Erin Elliot Photography)*

KYLA KAZUSCHYK: It is so hard to see outside of yourself. But hopefully theatre can help us with that and theatre can get us there.

EMILIO RODRIGUEZ: I hope so too. I think it's a learning process—but yeah.

ARTIST SPOTLIGHT: CAMILLA MORRISON

In her work in theatre and beyond, artist and educator Camilla Morrison is expanding the realm of what can be imagined and created.

CAMILLA MORRISON: I believe that devised theatre is a performance-based art creation process. In my opinion, it focuses mostly on the process, and then the outcome is truly a result of the creation process as a whole. So if the process takes seven different directions then the outcome is ultimately the story the paths have taken to get to the performance. And I think it allows the piece to take on a deeper meaning and allows the artists to reflect on what is most important, and what is being told in the moment.

KYLA KAZUSCHYK: What are the advantages to this? Why do devised work instead of scripted work?

CAMILLA MORRISON: Well, I think that the biggest advantage that I found in devised work is a high level of collaboration with all artists involved. I think that when the artists know that their voice is important in creating the work and that everybody is being listened to and has a chance to really add to what's going on, then there's a high level of connection to the piece. And when everybody who's involved feels really connected to the piece, I think the audience can really see that happening too. There's such a feeling of possibility when the whole team is working towards a shared goal, while also knowing what their role is and what the individual goal of each person's role is as well. So if we are all working towards the same thing, then I probably have a different goal than the performers do, but we all are working towards creating something together, that's the ultimate goal.

So for *Nightmares Are Dreams Too* I started with taking my own experiences of what it means to be a woman in the world, and from there, I created poetry and started to create designs about what physically as a costume those experiences might look like. And then I asked people who were a combination of performers, scholars and more movement-based performers, I asked a combination of those individuals and then individuals who don't really perform, other designers, to participate as models in the piece. When I asked a person to be involved, I told them what the piece was about, and then we had a conversation about the topic and as we were talking about it, the piece sort of grew even more. So the process of creating that particular costume for that person who's going to wear it, they then were able to really take on and understand more of the story, because they identified with it as well, so that then really showed up in their performance and their characteristic of the piece.

KYLA KAZUSCHYK: That's so cool. Did you have models, examples of work that had been created, like this, or did you invent the form entirely.?

CAMILLA MORRISON: I did not look to see if anything like this had been done before. And it's something that just sort of developed. I originally thought about putting these pieces on dress forms, or maybe I thought these pieces would hang in a gallery, kind of like on the wall. One of the very original ideas that I had was a piece like that had been sewn into the wall and sewn into the floor, like a dress that was kind of like sewn into different places, but then, as it developed, you know I really thought about how the pieces would be much more meaningful on bodies, on people. And being able to see them move around, because I really designed the pieces to move, and I really thought about how the fabric would interact with the body and how that would add to the story being told, so it really developed from thinking about it more in like a gallery setting, well what if I put it on dress forms. And then it became very clear that it needed to be on people who could more inhabit the character and tell more of the story. So I didn't find anything, I didn't really go looking for anything like this ahead of time and luckily, the piece was able to really develop into what it needed to be.

KYLA KAZUSCHYK: And so the thing that finally developed into is performers moving around in a space, do you consider that theatre? How do you define that in the terms of like we're used to going to the theatre sit in the audience watch actors on stage, but what you created is different than that.

CAMILLA MORRISON: Yeah it was more of an interactive exhibit and I would still consider this theatre because there was still some sort of a stage and, when it was first shared, then it was in the studio—a black box theatre space—and there were platforms setup and the models wearing the costumes were in the middle of the space. And the audience just sort of naturally either sat in the seats or sat in the chairs surrounding the performance space and they were able to observe the performers moving. We talked in the fittings and as we were getting ready about how to interact with the audience. And one of the things that I told them that I was not expecting them to do is to try to explain the pieces to people. And nobody really tried to talk with the performers, because there was this invisible boundary and nobody tried to interact.

But then the piece grew even further, when we were asked to come to the LSU museum of art. In the museum, we were inside an art gallery and the boundaries really disappeared. Because the performers and the models really were interacting with the audience and at first, you know we sort of still had the sense of well, maybe there should be sort of an invisible boundary where you kind of ignore the people watching and maybe it should be still like they're observing you, but the performers really just kind of felt as they went on, they interacted a lot more with each other, they started to interact with the audience. They sat down next to the audience, the audience sat down next

FIGURE 8.19 *"Love and Expectations," designed and built by Camilla Morrison for Of the Earth, worn by Shelby Hazel (photo courtesy of Camilla Morrison)*

FIGURE 8.20 *Mercedes Wilson, Evleen Nasir, and Maggie McGurn in Nightmares Are Dreams, Too. Costumes designed and built by Camilla Morrison (photo courtesy of Camilla Morrison)*

FIGURE 8.21 *Rendering by Camilla Morrison for "Beautifully Emotional" in* Nightmares Are Dreams, Too *(photo courtesy of Camilla Morrison)*

to them and they had small interactions with the audience, or they would invite the audience to like sit on the floor with them and then they would drape the fabric of their costume over them, so it developed into something completely different when we changed our space. And it was amazing to see, and it was great to see, and it was much more lighthearted in the second space and the first one it was very serious feeling because of that automatic divide.

KYLA KAZUSCHYK: That's so interesting how the setting changes the tone of the piece. There's so many variables.

CAMILLA MORRISON: There really are so many variables with theatre like this.

KYLA KAZUSCHYK: Can you tell me more about how you developed the costumes? How did you develop a timeline? You designed them, and you built them and you fit them and you did special dying processes. How did you give yourself a timeline and parameters? How did you figure all that out?

CAMILLA MORRISON: Well, because this was for my MFA thesis I had sort of a deadline that I had to be working towards because I then had to write about the process, so I had to make sure to design and build and put the pieces on the stage somehow within a certain timeline. But I did find that I needed more time to brainstorm and design than I originally expected. I thought that the process would go pretty quickly, because I have a lot of ideas. But it ended up taking quite a while to design and then I did individually pattern and then specially dye paint every piece, so all of the fabric was modified in some way for each piece. And so, all of that process, it all took some time but I had that deadline of the performance when I had the black box reserved and I had the models who were coming to the space. I had to revise the calendar a few times to give myself a little bit more time to design. But I think that once the designs were created, and once I knew the direction that they were going in and I knew who the models were going to be, then it was much more fast to actually fabricate the pieces. But knowing that there was the ultimate deadline of needing to then write about things afterwards sort of motivated me to make sure to work towards that deadline.

FIGURE 8.22 *"Hungry Belly, Hungry Body" rendering by Camilla Morrison for* Nightmares Are Dreams, Too *(photo courtesy of Camilla Morrison)*

FIGURE 8.23 *"To Be a Woman" rendering by Camilla Morrison for* Nightmares Are Dreams, Too *(photo courtesy of Camilla Morrison)*

KYLA KAZUSCHYK: Like having an opening night! That applies to all theatre, the show's got to open when the show opens.

CAMILLA MORRISON: Absolutely yeah but because there was no original script to work from, the design process I think needed a little bit more time because the pieces needed time to start out as one thing and then grow into something else and grow into something else, as I dove deeply into those ideas. And because the ideas were all very personal also I needed time to process those things myself. They were all very personal and they all still feel pretty emotional to me. But at some point I needed to sort of say, Okay, this is the story that I'm telling and it is my story, but it's also my work and I'm putting it in front of people so, then you know, the process of building the costumes I didn't feel as extremely attached to them the whole time until they were created, and I saw them on stage.

KYLA KAZUSCHYK: And then you felt attached to them again?

CAMILLA MORRISON: I think so. I think I really felt very attached to them in the design process, because it was very much my story. But then when the model performers became involved and we talked about how they have had some shared experiences, then it became not only my story. So, then I felt still attached to them in that they're very personal, but at the same time, knowing that people who are coming to see it may also be identifying with it and I am not necessarily alone in these experiences, I think I was able to let them go a little bit more, and then sort of seeing them on stage in front of people was very meaningful to me.

KYLA KAZUSCHYK: What did you learn when you saw audiences interacting with them?

FIGURE 8.24 *"Carrying" rendering by Camilla Morrison for Nightmares Are Dreams, Too (photo courtesy of Camilla Morrison)*

devising process and decide for themselves what the story is. Those created two very different experiences.

So it's interesting. I really considered the audience at first more of an audience of onlookers, I want to give them all the information so that they have a full experience. But then moving to the museum taking some of that information away and having the renderings and the descriptions in a program that they could read either immediately or later or never, it was interesting to see, then, how willing they were to sort of approach the model performers. Or you know this immediate divide in the theatre.

KYLA KAZUSCHYK: It's interesting the way you talk about how it was personal to you and close to you, but also something that you know you're going to present for an audience. And the actors that I've talked to, Andrea was just talking about that, with her piece that she's creating something that's autobiographical, but it's not just me standing here telling my story like she theatricalized it in a way that she wanted it to resonate with audience members—that that's the whole point of it is not just to create something and leave it there, but to create something.

And yours had a tangible physical interaction with the audience members or even just like you're talking about the first stages, the audience reflects something, and maybe takes something away. That's so interesting and thinking about like when we have a vision for our work, how that vision includes what the audience is going to take from it.

CAMILLA MORRISON: I think that when I saw the audience interacting with the performers in the second and I don't really know what to call them—I call them models performers sort of they're both because they don't have lines, they are showing the costumes but they're also embodying the character, so they're both. So when I saw them, the first time with the audience more observing, I also had my renderings and the explanation of each of them fully available for the audience to come and see so they knew immediately what each of the pieces was supposed to be, and they had that knowledge sitting and watching. But in the museum space, there was a program that they could pick up and read if they wanted to, or they could just go look and observe and decide for themselves what the pieces meant, so I think that those two ways of interacting with the audience provided a different experience. Like whether you state in some way what the story is or if you let the audience then sort of become a part of the

CAMILLA MORRISON: So, for the first one, where it was in the black box space, I also had the audience take a survey. So, as they came in I handed them the survey that they would fill out that asked them things like what piece do you most connect with, and you know what stories do you see being told here and then some just identifying information. So I got to sort of interact with the audience in that way, where they didn't necessarily have to tell me, you know I identify as a woman, and also these pieces really spoke to me or I identify as another gender and these pieces spoke to me, so it was interesting to get those responses and then also some people were willing to talk with me, because I was also standing by the door, you know, encouraging people to come in and thanking people as they left, so I got to talk with the audience on different levels with that first piece. And so I think it was interesting being able to hear people's thoughts as well because part of my writing process was, I wanted to be able to reflect on understanding the audience's experience and what they

FIGURE 8.25 *Hannah Gudan wearing "Carrying" in* Nightmares Are Dreams, Too *in the Studio Theatre at Louisiana State University (photo courtesy of Camilla Morrison)*

FIGURE 8.26 Nightmares Are Dreams, Too *at the Louisiana State University Museum of Art. Hannah Gudan wearing "Carrying," designed and built by Camilla Morrison (photo courtesy of Camilla Morrison)*

would take away from something like this, so I'm glad that I was able to hear someone's thoughts on this aspect of performance.

KYLA KAZUSCHYK: I'm really curious as to how this influenced your work, moving forward. Did you take aspects of this towards the work you do in linear costume design?

CAMILLA MORRISON: I think that certainly the work with actors, I very much like to talk with actors in fittings and whenever possible about the characters and who they're inhabiting and the stories that they are telling and how I can support that and through costume design, so I think that I really value the collaboration with the performer. And that's something that certainly was enhanced through the process of doing a piece like this. And I think, also the willingness to let things develop as needed. I think that there are some instances when we create designs and they're final and they really have to be final in order to move into the costume shop and happen quickly, but there are small things that can continue to grow with the performer and when we are working with them. Like maybe they need some sort of insert in their shoes or something to feel more comfortable or to feel a different way, or if they need small accessories like rings, or something like those tiny things can also tell more of the story, so I think I feel more in tune to small details like that and wanting to not only know what my idea of the character is that I've been talking with the director before the actors get to rehearsal but then also what are their ideas for this person that they have been or this character that they have been researching and thinking about throughout the rehearsal process, so I think that it definitely influences my linear costume design. And how I approach design and collaboration.

KYLA KAZUSCHYK: I think this is something that's new. I don't remember reading about that in books on costume design. I think that the formula that we were taught is yeah work with the director, maybe work with the other designers and then just give it to the performer. That can be so limiting.

FIGURE 8.27 *"Letting Go" rendering by Camilla Morrison for* Nightmares Are Dreams, Too *(photo courtesy of Camilla Morrison)*

FIGURE 8.28 *Caitlin Morrison wearing "Letting Go" in* Nightmares Are Dreams, Too *(photo courtesy of Camilla Morrison)*

CAMILLA MORRISON: Yeah and if the performer really has a strong idea or a different thing that they have been approaching the character with, then I would rather support that and as long as the director supports it as well, then I want to support that through costume design. But you're right, we have been taught that the designs are final and at first rehearsal we share, these are the final designs, this is what you're wearing. And I think that sometimes that's what we're encouraged to teach our students as well, is you know, it's your job to just wear the thing that I designed. And part of that is true, as an actor it's your job to tell the full story on stage for performance and the design elements, but also if given the opportunity to collaborate with the designers in some way, then it can only enhance their performance.

KYLA KAZUSCHYK: And things can be more flexible than we think. That's what I have learned in my experience in devised theatre, like I want things to be rigid and like, from my perspective as a shop manager like, yeah tell me what the final design is and I'll just make it. That is easier in so many ways, but it cuts off so many other possibilities and working in devised theatre where it can be so chaotic and you don't know what it's going to be, but you have to figure something out and you have to be ready to be flexible, then you're ready to be flexible, even if there's a script. Just because there's a script like you're saying like you have your opinion as a costume designer but actors are doing different research and they're doing different work in rehearsals. And they might be going in a different direction or a direction that you can blend with the direction that you're going in. It is possible to be more flexible than we are.

CAMILLA MORRISON: It really is, and when we are stuck to a really short timeline then it's hard to be flexible. But because the designs start in advance of rehearsals, like if the people who are hired to be in those roles are sort of like, if there was a way to talk with them before rehearsal started, you know, then there may be even more possibility for collaboration there.

KYLA KAZUSCHYK: Why not? Okay, so tell me about part two, what are you working on now?

CAMILLA MORRISON: Okay, so right now I'm working on a project called stories of women in North Dakota and that's kind of my working title I think my title or either the title of one piece or the whole thing is going to be *Of the Earth*. I'm very excited about this. So this project is funded by the North Dakota Council on the Arts and individual artist fellowship, which is a grant that I got this year to do this project so I'm really thrilled to be supported by the state of North Dakota to do this project, and this is similar to my thesis *Nightmares are Dreams, Too*, so I've been lovingly calling it *Nightmares are Dreams, Too* Part Two, which I probably still will continue to call it but this piece is going to be so, I submitted a series of questions to the institutional review board here at UND so that I could make an ethical survey where I am interviewing individuals who identify as women from North Dakota and we are having a zoom conversation talking about aging, we're talking about, one of the questions that I'm asking is what, when you think about women in North Dakota, what are some words that come to mind—we're talking about if there were times when they felt that they were treated unfairly because they are a woman. But also what are some of the joys they find of being a woman. So a really large series of ideas that I'm asking about through a series of questions. And I'm taking the sort of collective responses of anybody who is involved, which I've had quite a variety of people, which is really wonderful and some people who identify as being from North Dakota but no longer live in North Dakota so being able to do it over zoom has actually allowed me to expand the type of people that I'm talking with which is exciting. So, taking the process of listening to the stories of women from North Dakota and then I am making those sort of stories and ideas into first poetry and then art and design and then I will be creating costumes from those stories. So my collaborators there are some people who have theatre in their life or in their backgrounds, in some way, and there are some people who have never been involved in theatre. So my sort of collaborators in the initial idea of what these pieces are, are many women from North Dakota which is really interesting and most people I've never met before.

KYLA KAZUSCHYK: This is so creative, it's such a creative idea and it's such a cool idea to start with costumes. Your lens is a costume designer but you're able to see more broadly and see that art impacts more than that, and to see how your viewpoint as a costume designer is going to be able to create art. In contrast to people that are performers directors like, yeah we're going to tell a story and then other things can enhance the story, but like your vision is like what are they going to look like and how is that going to tell the story.

CAMILLA MORRISON: And how do you share an experience and how do you tell about a life, you know we talked about costume design, as there are a lot of things that you can identify someone through. Are they wearing a uniform? Maybe that is part of their job. But how do you talk about, like, have you always known that you want to be a mother? How do you show that through costume design? That's one of the things that we're talking about is, have you ever wanted to be a mother, do you feel called to motherhood? And when did you know? That's one of the things I'm really curious about. So how do you show that through costume design is what I'm exploring now. How can we show these stories more through things that we can wear on our bodies somehow?

KYLA KAZUSCHYK: That's so interesting and how yeah, how do we tell those stories in a way that it's going to resonate with an audience and then what is an audience going to take away from that? Is it your plan to invite the people that you've interviewed to the performance?

CAMILLA MORRISON: Yes, my original desire was to have some of the people who are involved be the models in the pieces. I'm currently in the design process of this project, sort of the creation design process. I still have a few interviews that might happen. But I've started the design process. My original hope was that people in my community could be the models and that still might be possible, we'll see, but right now it's looking like they might be on dress forms for now and then maybe on bodies later, so I will be widely sharing—part of my grant is that I have to share the costumes in multiple regions of North Dakota. And so I'll be sharing them via zoom, probably. But the participants will definitely be invited. The wrap up of the interview is asking them if they want to be acknowledged somehow in any sort of program notes and how do they want to be acknowledged and if they want to be updated on what's happening and so far they've all said yes so I'll share these pieces with them and most of them have expressed they're very curious of how these things are going to become costumes. The first piece that I did was my own stories. I knew that I was showing something that I understood. But now I'm showing something that will make a lot of sense to me, but the people who told me their stories might look at it and they may say what is that? So I want to make sure that I am making my community proud by sharing this piece with them, but also I'm mindful of the fact that not everybody is necessarily going to be familiar with the type of avant garde costuming that I love to do so I'm excited to share more of this with them.

KYLA KAZUSCHYK: It must be like a responsibility.

FIGURE 8.29 *Courtney Davis wearing "Necessary Strength," designed and built by Camilla Morrison for Of the Earth (photo courtesy of Camilla Morrison)*

FIGURE 8.30 *"Necessary Strength" rendering by Camilla Morrison for* Of the Earth *(photo courtesy of Camilla Morrison)*

CAMILLA MORRISON: It does feel like responsibility because people have told me so many wonderful personal stories. I want them to feel heard. I want them to feel represented, and also to know that other people may also identify and understand part of their story just by looking at these pieces.

KYLA KAZUSCHYK: The more you explain this, the more I'm really curious to see if anyone has ever done anything like this. Have you gone back and looked?

CAMILLA MORRISON: Well, good question because I did wind up doing a little bit more research, when I was writing my thesis paper which, some of the research happened before I did this entire project and mostly what I did is I looked at feminist art installations, and so I looked at Judy Chicago. Judy Chicago is one of the people that I looked at and her piece *The Dinner Party* was really interesting. Thinking about historical women and how they are represented through place sitting. So that was one of the things that I looked at. I also was inspired by Marina Abramovic and her piece *The Artist is Present*. So I did a little bit of research about how people have either sort of found a way to have a shared experience or told stories of women through different pieces. And there certainly were other artists that I found inspirational along the way, but I didn't see anybody doing costume design work like this.

KYLA KAZUSCHYK: It's very interesting to me that the avenue that you would think like every artist you mentioned definitely overlaps with what you're doing—performance art and visual art, feminist art for sure—but the first place my brain goes to is applied theatre and playback theatre where like a group of actors will talk to a community and then tell that community's story, sometimes with costume pieces but usually just with their bodies and their voices. And that's what you're doing but with costumes and like with dress at the forefront, instead of just having voices and dialogue and bodies at the forefront.

CAMILLA MORRISON: I've actually specifically taken away any sort of dialogue and any sort of specific one person's story. I really love verbatim theatre. I think that's really interesting,

FIGURE 8.31 *Shelby Hazel wearing "Love and Expectations," designed and built by Camilla Morrison for* Of the Earth *(photo courtesy of Camilla Morrison)*

where they interview people and then say verbatim exactly what they said back. I think that's super interesting. I would love to do something like that, but I have specifically wanted to take away any one individual story and think about it in a more wide scope, so that more individuals, you know, not just in North Dakota, may be able to understand a little bit more of the North Dakota experience. Because a lot of people that I've talked to have had a very different experience. If somebody may have grown up on a reservation or a farm community or maybe a larger city then those are all very different experiences, but they've had some shared experiences because they're women in the world. So there's not going to be any dialogue I'm trying to decide, I will probably decide later if there's going to be a description of the pieces. There probably will be a short description of the pieces and what they're intended to mean. But there again is not going to be any sort of, nobody's going to come out and say any monologues or read anything from any of the interviews—the interviews are all completely anonymous.

KYLA KAZUSCHYK: And they're displayed through the dress. I can't wait to see how this turns out. Another place that I think that it might overlap with is thinking about how you're exploding the idea of storytelling. You mentioned that you spoke to Indigenous people. One way to think of storytelling is storytelling as craft. Thinking about art forms like embroidery and beadwork and how in many Indigenous cultures they are telling stories through their dress.

CAMILLA MORRISON: Yeah absolutely, the specific patterns of star quilts, there's very specific patterns that are associated with families and the different beadwork and the types of beads and like the different types of decoration on clothing is also for different ages. I think that's incredible and part of what I want to do, so this is just one piece of the project. Another piece of the project

FIGURE 8.32 *"Love and Expectations" rendering by Camilla Morrison for Of the Earth (photo courtesy of Camilla Morrison)*

is I'm doing a community workshop where the community is going to be invited. I'm inviting the community to think about what are the stories that they might want to tell through costume. My dream would be to work with young people and to like work with young artists of different cultures in North Dakota to think about how they want to tell their stories and how they might incorporate some of their culture and traditional way of clothes, telling stories through clothing and how they may sort of change that to really serve and tell their own story. That's my dream sort of beyond this.

KYLA KAZUSCHYK: That's so exciting and I bet kids would be so receptive to that. Kids are already doing that, like kids that I know are already like this piece of fabric, this is who I am, this is my cape. Kids are ready for that. And if they just had more tools, if they had the vocabulary that you could work with them on that can be so cool.

CAMILLA MORRISON: I would love that to be something moving forward. Because I know that I will never be able to actually represent everybody's stories through these pieces, which is why they become a little bit more general. So it's not just, you know, three people's stories represented in these six costumes, it's more—it's the wider view. And so I would really love for native artists to be able to honor their family traditions and honor the traditional costume in the community and use that to create their own art and create their own costumes. I'm not going to try to appropriate any of that for my own purposes.

KYLA KAZUSCHYK: Right. But working with people to tell their own stories that's already more exciting, that's already the evolution you're on, like you worked on telling your own stories now you're working at collaborating with other people on their stories—it makes sense that the next progression of your art is helping people to tell their own stories.

CAMILLA MORRISON: Thank you.

KYLA KAZUSCHYK: We've actually gone on so many tangents beyond because I'm so excited about this project. And I think that it definitely ties into devised theatre and it's actually like new forms which I'm super excited about

FIGURE 8.33 *Amaya Grant wearing "Grounding Seeds," designed and built by Camilla Morrison for* Of the Earth *(photo courtesy of Camilla Morrison)*

FIGURE 8.34 *"Grounding Seeds" rendering by Camilla Morrison for* Of the Earth *(photo courtesy of Camilla Morrison)*

too. You're on the next level of principles of devised theatre. So to tie it back to principles of devised theatre do you see parallels between collaboration and devising and what you do in your classroom?

CAMILLA MORRISON: Yeah, absolutely, I think that as theatre artists who work in devised theatre we really have to know and understand everything that's going on, know the whole scope. And so I think that in a lot of my classes, especially in design-focused classes, then the class needs to understand the whole scope of what we're trying to do, like what is the goal of costume design and how can we tell a story. So I think that that certainly plays into it, and then we in costume design class are almost like a little devising community because we don't have the rest of the design team in my classes. Right now, we don't have a director, set designer, lighting designer, or actors. So we really have to think about everything from all of those different perspectives. So I do think that it is a little bit more of a devising mindset. Where we're thinking about all of those different roles and approaching design from that perspective, rather than really staying in only the role of the costume designer. So I think that does connect even though we're not working with all of those different individuals in the class.

KYLA KAZUSCHYK: I think, even in terms of structurally, too, that's a good point—thinking about the design process. But just thinking about how we listen to each other's voices and amplify each other's voices and create space for each other's voices. How does what we do in devising processes connect with other skills we learn through theatre? If we value empathy, we believe that it is important to care about people and to listen to them and it's important to listen to everyone's individual stories and find connections between our stories. It all ties back together.

CAMILLA MORRISON: Yeah, it really does. So, I guess, another way, in thinking about the structure of the class is in my costume design class, every project, each student has to share their project with the class and they have to explain

FIGURE 8.35 RaeAnn Anderson wearing "This Must Be," designed and built by Camilla Morrison for Of the Earth (photo courtesy of Camilla Morrison)

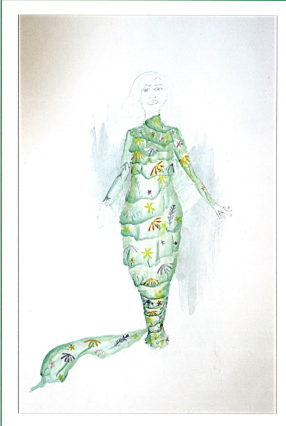

FIGURE 8.36 "This Must Be" rendering by Camilla Morrison for Of the Earth (photo courtesy of Camilla Morrison)

their work, but then the class also needs to respond and ask questions, and you know sort of give the chance to talk more and like, what could that project become if they continued working on it. So in that sense they really are in a more devising mindset because they're listening and giving each other feedback, so that is, yeah that's absolutely true.

KYLA KAZUSCHYK: That's awesome and that's going to help them as they are visualizing stuff and as they're fleshing out their designs and figuring out the whole plan for their design.

CAMILLA MORRISON: Yeah, getting feedback along the way, absolutely.

KYLA KAZUSCHYK: So this idea of feedback is the next thing I want to ask you about that is another thing—you and I have worked on projects before about this idea of circular mentorship, that like the old model of university is like the teacher knows everything the students don't know anything and a lot of people are holding fast to that model. And I think it's got to be thrown out the window. I think that model has got to be destroyed, I feel really passionately about that. And you are an inspiration to me of this too, because you were my student, and I knew stuff that you didn't know, but you knew stuff that I didn't know and I had experiences that you hadn't had and you've had experiences that I didn't have. And if I had just approached you as a graduate student as like, look you don't know anything, I know everything, let me tell you the things I know, you better listen to me, then I would have missed out on everything that I learned from you and all the projects that we were able to collaborate on and really like enhance each other's work by listening to each other. And I'm so grateful that I had that experience with you and I'm always thinking of ways to continue that and how to have that open communication with other students. Is that something that you think about and practice?

CAMILLA MORRISON: I do, yeah absolutely, and I think it is because of the experience that I've had with you, you

FIGURE 8.37 *"Waters We Know" rendering by Camilla Morrison for* Of the Earth *(photo courtesy of Camilla Morrison)*

know there is really something that I learned from you. One of the things that really stands out to me is when we had dye/paint class, and you sort of took it as the perspective of we're going to try these things together, we're going to try things together and we're going to learn about them together. And so that has really influenced how I move forward in my classes and in the costume shop in my designs. So I will often design something I've never done before into the show that I'm working on, so that I am learning something new, the students are learning something new and we're figuring it out together. That's definitely something that I think about a lot. I have a student who's getting ready to graduate, Shelby Hazel, who is I think another great example of this, where we have had weekly conversations on it as a part of her senior project class, we have a weekly meeting where we sort of just talk about about how projects are going, how classes are going, what types of jobs to look for, and also we just talk about what's going on in general. And it's been really helpful to hear her perspective on a lot of things. And sometimes I will say, Hey do you remember this project that we did in class, I'm thinking about changing it. And I really appreciate hearing her direct perspective because you know we get anonymous feedback at the end of every class about generally how things went in class but we don't always get specific feedback on all of the projects that people do. So it's been really helpful having the opportunity to ask her questions and she's willing to share her open opinion with me. So I think that a level of collaboration like that also comes with trust and showing that you're working together, and you are not the person who holds all of the knowledge, because that just doesn't exist—the one person who holds all of the knowledge. I think that as a teacher that's sort of what I thought that I was supposed to be when I was starting, that I'm supposed to know more, I'm supposed to know the most and I was supposed to have answers ready. And now I am not worried at all if somebody asks me a question that I don't know, I will research it and then I get to learn more things and share more things with people. So I agree that this idea that we have to know everything is an unreasonable expectation. To let go of that makes sure that the student knows that what they're interested in is valuable and if they come to the table with more experience then like their experience is valuable too.

KYLA KAZUSCHYK: Yeah absolutely, I think that's so important. And I'm so glad that you have that right now with an undergraduate student that you've been able to establish that relationship where they feel comfortable sharing honest feedback about stuff and that you can develop ideas together. And I think it's so interesting that you bring it back to fabric modification class, because I think I've been transparent with you about this that I was so scared to teach that class. Because I knew that I wasn't the expert on fabric modification, and so I just leveled with everyone in that class, that this is what it is but what I can offer as a teacher, knowing that I don't know everything, I can offer a space and I can facilitate discussions and we can discover stuff together. I think that is the best thing that universities have to offer at this point in the game—a space to discover stuff.

CAMILLA MORRISON: Yeah and because you were willing to be so transparent with us about what was going to happen in that class and that it really was going to be a collaborative environment. I think that I learned so much in that class because I was willing to just try things. I wasn't waiting for somebody to watch if I was doing it perfectly like we tried things we figured things out. Like, here's some things, we're going to try them. I think I learned a lot from that class and

FIGURE 8.38 *Karyn Krause wearing "Waters We Know," designed and built by Camilla Morrison (photo courtesy of Camilla Morrison)*

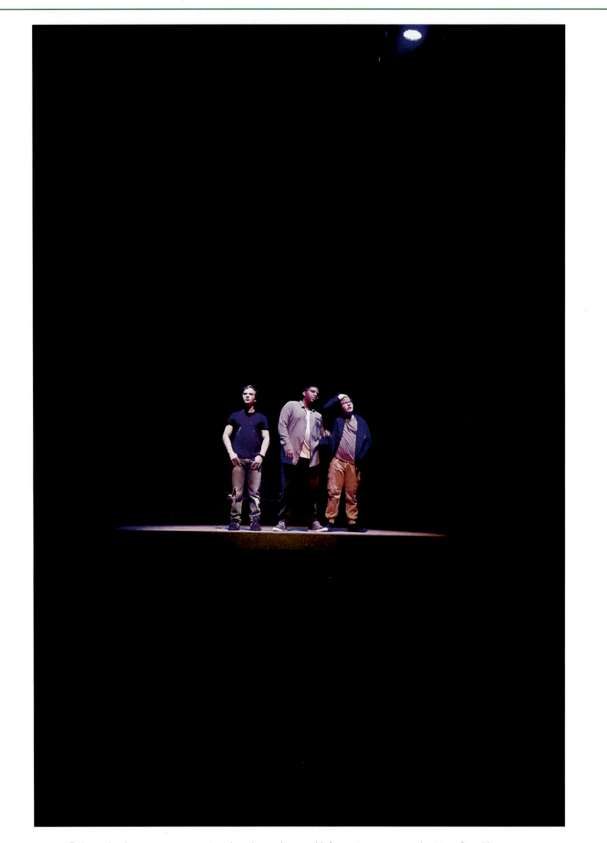

FIGURE 8.39 *Embrace the chaos as you stare out into the unknown.* Love and Information *on stage at Louisiana State University*

that taught me how to not put so much pressure on myself to do something perfectly from the beginning. Because it takes a lot and I think it does take a lot to unlearn that if you aren't doing things perfectly the first time, then you're wasting your time. And I really believe that our design process needs to be especially in our classes really iterative where we are having the chance to revise and think about things, and if we say okay, you have this project and we're not going to have any check-ins or anything it's just due then we're focusing on what is the thing that is done and not the process. Reciprocal mentorship can be a challenge with undergrad students because they do expect so much that you are the bringer of knowledge, but I think that what has allowed me to really have that with Shelby is that number one I'm not really grading her anymore she's not in any of my classes. I'm supervising her senior project but the last class she took with me was last year, and we also have spent more time together because she works in the costume shop so I know her pretty well after working with her for years. And also I'm willing to share things more openly with her, because we spend so much time in the costume shop and she knows that sometimes I know what I'm doing and sometimes I don't.

So I think that's been helpful and now she is going on, this is going to be her second summer as the costume shop manager and designer at Minot summer theatre where they do really big productions and so she's going to be running the costume shop and designing for the second time. So I'm really proud that she's willing to just jump into this thing and try, because we have established that jumping into things and trying is exactly what we should be doing.

KYLA KAZUSCHYK: And that's how you build resilience, that's how you become more resilient is exactly jumping into things and trying.

A lot of people are stuck in that idea, and this goes back to training, like how we're trained to be silos, to be in these roles that like, stay in your lane, you only know your stuff and get your stuff done and then give it to someone else. Instead of, well I have a lot of experience in my lane, but I have ideas about other lanes and I can respect that other people have a bulk of experience in one area or on one thing, but could have ideas about other things too, and then we can shape and develop together.

CAMILLA MORRISON: And that is really the heart of devising.

APPENDIX

RESOURCES

- Quick and Gender Neutral Measurements
- An Efficient Method for Drafting a Sloper
- Handstitching Techniques
- Research Process Possibilities
- Paperwork Examples and Templates

The appendix includes:

- A gender neutral measurement sheet to take and use, along with step by step instructions for how to measure another person or yourself quickly, efficiently, and politely.
- A simple step by step guide for how to draft a sloper using these measurements.
- Clear and reproducible instructions of the most useful handsewing techniques.
- A format for how to conduct research for a devised project.
- Examples of budget worksheets, scene breakdowns for shows without clear scenes, alternative dressing lists, and other paperwork, along with reusable templates.

QUICK AND GENDER NEUTRAL MEASUREMENTS

There are a lot of measurement sheet templates out there. I have used a lot of them as a costume designer looking to pull and purchase, as a cutter/draper looking to draft and build, as a teacher training students, and as a shop manager measuring large amounts of people in small amounts of time. Many existing measurement sheet templates are based on an outdated and unnecessary gender binary. This is easy to edit out. Here is what is important:

- measurements that directly correlate to sizes of garments
- measurements that give the information necessary to create patterns for garments
- measurements that are comprehensive and accurate without being intrusive
- measurements that are listed in a sequence that flows efficiently, can be taken quickly, and require the least amount of physical exertion possible.

A measurement sheet template can be a living document. The format of it does not need to be set in stone. It can change and evolve, like everything. Edit out what is no longer serving you and your community, and add in what you need as new needs arise.

The template in Figure 9.1 is what I am currently using. The measurements go from head to toe, circumference then length, front then back. I invite you to copy this template and use it exactly if that suits you, or use parts of it and make any adjustments you like.

When a performer comes in to be measured, I start by asking them to fill out the top part of the measurement sheet with their information, including commercial sizes if they know them. I let them know that if they don't know any sizes, that is okay too. Knowing what size garments a performer buys for themselves when they shop can give a shortcut to pulling and purchasing garments that need to fit in a contemporary style. Of course, sizes vary greatly by brand, and not everyone knows all their sizes, so it is helpful to take comprehensive measurements too.

Also at the top of this measurement sheet, there is a spot for performers to indicate what pronouns they use. This is important, especially when you are meeting people for the first time, so you can refer to them appropriately and with respect to who they are. Many of the backstage theatre spaces we work in are set up based on an antiquated gender binary, with one dressing room for "women" and one for "men." It takes a bit of creativity to solve this problem, but it is possible. Make sure private changing areas are available for everyone. You can do this by using existing bathroom stalls, or setting up screens or curtains.

Once the performer has finished filling out the top of the measurement sheet, it is on to the measuring. Ideally, have one person measuring and a second person writing the measurements down. If there is not a second person available, that

Costume Shop Measurements   Measured by: _____

Name _____   Date: _____

Show and Character(s): _____

Pronouns: _____

We currently have two dressing rooms backstage. Each large room has bathroom stalls where you may change privately if you wish. There is also one gender neutral neutral hallway bathroom. At tech rehearsal, you may sign up on the list on the door of the room where you would like to have your costumes stored.

Tattoos (size and location): _____

Piercings:		Allergies:	
Height:	Trousers/jeans:	Dress:	Shirt:
Weight:	Suit:	Bra:	Shoe:

Head:		CB nape to shoulder:	
Headband:		to elbow:	
Ear to Ear:		to wrist:	
Neck--Upper:	Base:	Underarm to wrist:	
Shoulder Seam:		Shoulder to bicep:	
Chest:	expanded:	to wrist:	
Ribcage:		Armscye:	
Waist:	expanded:	Bicep:	
High hip:	taken at:	Forearm:	
Low hip:	taken at:	Wrist:	
Front half:		Hand (duck):	
Halter:		Thigh:	
Point to point:		Calf:	
Across Shoulder:	Front: Back:	Above knee:	
Armscye to Armscye:	Front: Back:	Below knee:	
Nape to Waist:	Front: Back:	Ankle:	
Nape to floor:	Front: Back:	Waist to below knee:	
Underarm to waist:		Waist to floor:	
Half girth:		Inseam to floor:	
Full Girth:		Seated rise:	

Trace foot on back of sheeet.

FIGURE 9.1 *Blank measurement sheet*

is okay, just measure and write. It is also possible to measure yourself. This is a bit challenging, but it is possible. An informative video that goes over how to take each measurement step by step on yourself can be shared with performers so they can watch and follow along, measuring themselves.

The first measurement is head, around the circumference of the skull, keeping the tape measure parallel to the floor. Next is headband. This goes around the head following the hairline. Next is ear to ear, which goes from the top of the ear over the head to the top of the other ear. There are two measurements for the neck: top, which is around the neck at the point where the neck connects to the head, and then base, which is around the neck at the point where it connects to the torso.

Shoulder seam is along the top of the shoulder, from the point where the arm connects to the torso, to the point where the neck connects to the torso.

For the next few measurements, if you have someone writing for you, you can keep the tape measure wrapped around the performer's body as you measure all the circumferences. Before you wrap it around, ask the performer to remove anything in their pockets that might add to the hip measurement. Always let them know what you are about to do before you do it. You can say something like, "Excuse me, I am going to wrap the tape measure around your chest."

Chest is around the widest part of the chest, with the tape measure parallel to the floor. While you have the tape measure there, ask the performer to take a deep breath, and then indicate the expanded measurement. Some people expand in their chest when they breathe, others expand in their waist. Taking expanded measurements ensures that you do not make costumes so tight that performers are not able to breathe.

Ribcage is around the skeleton's ribcage, generally below the widest part of the chest. Waist is around the torso between the ribcage and the hip bones, sometimes the narrowest part of the torso. While you have the tape measure around the waist, ask the performer to take another deep breath, and indicate the expanded measurement.

High hip is around the hip bones, usually 4–6 inches below the waist. Measure how far below the waist you took this measurement, and indicate "taken at." Low hip is around the widest part of the hips. To find this, stand so you are looking at the performer in profile, and hold the tape measure at their side.

Front half is from side seam to side seam, around the widest part of the chest.

To take the halter measurement, hold the tape measure at zero, put the tape measure around the back of the performer's neck, and adjust it so that 10 is at approximately the apex of the bust. Look to the other apex of the bust. If it is 35, then the halter measurement is 25. To take the point to point measurement, burn 10 inches in the same way. Hold the tape measure at zero with your arms out, and use the tape measure held against the performer's chest to see how many inches between the apex of the bust to the other apex of the bust.

For the next set of measurements, the most efficient way to do it is to take all the front measurements, then all the back measurements.

Across shoulder is from the tip of the shoulder where the arm connects to the torso across the neck to the other shoulder tip. Armscye to armscye is from the midpoint of the armscye across the pectoral muscles in front and across the scapula in back to the other midpoint of the armscye. Nape to waist is from the center front or center back of the neck base, where the neck connects to the torso, down the center front or back of the body, to the waist. You can indicate that number, then drop the measure from the neck and hold it from the waist to the floor to get the nape to floor measurement.

Underarm to waist is along the side seam of the torso, from where the arm connects to the torso to the waist.

For half girth and full girth, hold the end of the tape measure at the center front of the performer's waist, and then ask them to hold it in place there. Tell them that the tape measure is going to pass between their legs, before you do it, then do it, pulling it so it is snug but not tight, to the center back of the waist. Indicate that number, then while they are still holding it, bring it over their shoulder to find the full girth measurement. Record the number where the tape measure meets the end they are holding at the waist. If a performer comes in to be measured wearing a skirt, just skip the girth measurements. You can always estimate and make corrections later.

For the next set of measurements, ask the performer to hold their arm out with their elbow bent. Demonstrate what you mean. CB nape to shoulder is from the center back of the neck to the point where the arm connects to the torso. Indicate that number, then continue to the elbow, and then to the wrist. If you do not have someone writing for you, take all three of these measurements at once and then write them down.

Underarm to wrist is from the point where the arm connects to the torso under the arm, to the wrist, while the performer is holding their arm at their side naturally. Shoulder to bicep is on the top of the arm, from the point where the arm connects to the torso to the midpoint of the bicep, and then to the wrist.

To take the armscye measurement, ask the performer to lift their arm, then pass the tape measure around their arm. Ask them to put their arm down at their side naturally, and record the number around the circumference of the connection between the arm and the torso.

Ask the performer if they are right- or left-handed. If they say left, ask them to flex their left bicep, and demonstrate with your own arm. For bicep, measure around the widest part of the bicep muscle. While they are still flexing, measure around the bent elbow and then the flexed forearm.

Thank them for flexing and then let them know they can relax their arm. Wrist is around the point where the hand connects to the arm.

Ask them to make a duck with their hand, and demonstrate with your own hand. Measure around the widest part of the knuckles to get the hand measurement. Curious performers may be interested in the purpose of this measurement, which is to determine how small we can make sleeve openings.

Ask the performer to lunge so that their thigh is flexed. Demonstrate by lunging yourself. Measure around the widest part of the thigh, then around the widest part of the calf while they are still lunging. Then ask them to stand up straight. If you have someone writing for you, you can stay kneeling down and measure around the leg above the knee, below the knee, and then around the ankle. For waist to below knee, place the end of the tape measure on the side of their waist and measure along the outseam to below the knee and then to the floor.

To measure the inseam, ask the performer to face away from you, by saying something like, "Could you please turn and face that door?" Look at their legs and note the point where the leg connects to the torso in the inseam. Visualize that point extending horizontally out to the outseam. Place the tape measure on the outseam side of the performer's leg and measure from that point to the floor. There is no need to touch anyone in a way that could make them uncomfortable, and it is also not necessary to ask them to place the tape measure between their legs.

Finally, ask the performer to sit in a chair and measure from the chair to their waist to get the seated rise measurement. While they are sitting down, ask them to slip off a shoe and then step on the back of the measurement sheet so you can trace their foot.

Once you have practiced this measurement method a few times, you can complete it very quickly, saving your time and the performer's time, and still getting all the information you need.

FIGURE 9.2 *Bodice and sleeve sloper*

AN EFFICIENT METHOD FOR DRAFTING A SLOPER

A sloper, or body block, is a close-fitting garment in a basic shape that can be adjusted to create any garment. There are many complex sets of instructions for drafting and draping sloper patterns. Following many different types of instructions will help you develop a method that works for you. The more slopers you create, the stronger your understanding of pattern shapes will be. The more slopers you fit on bodies, the better equipped you will be to create slopers that fit accurately.

Drafting patterns can be daunting when you are new at it. It is like learning a new language, and like anything else, it gets easier with practice. The goal with all types of pattern creation, especially for devised work, is to arrive at an accurate pattern as quickly and efficiently as possible.

A pattern for a sloper is a starting point. The idea is to get into the ballpark, and then you can make adjustments from there. Following is the method I have developed for drafting a sloper.

Start by drawing a thumbnail sketch of the front and back bodice shapes, and then use the performer's measurements to figure out what the pattern measurements need to be. Fill in these numbers on your thumbnail sketch. Essentially you are creating a blueprint for the full size pattern. Once you have all the measurement specifications filled in, get a ruler and a large piece of paper and map out the shapes (Figures 9.3 to 9.6).

FIGURE 9.3 *A way to start. Sketch the shapes of a bodice, sleeve, and skirt sloper*

Appendix

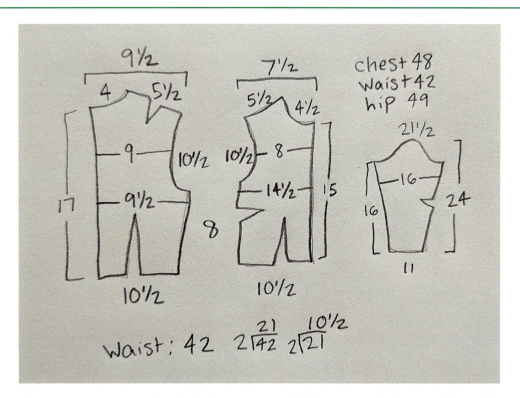

FIGURE 9.4 *Determine pattern measurements based on body measurements and fill them in on your sketch, creating a blueprint before creating the full scale pattern*

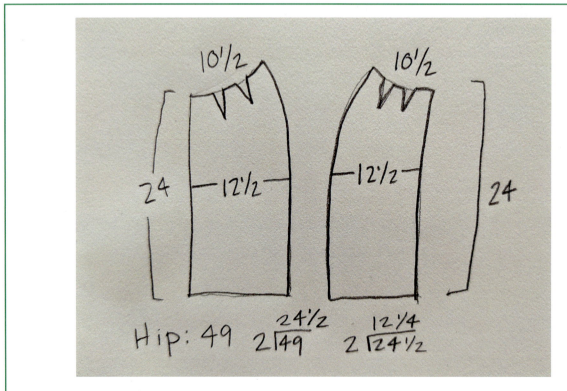

FIGURE 9.5 *Plan a pattern for a skirt by dividing measurements*

Costume Shop Measurements				Measured by:		
Name				Date:		
Show and Character(s):						
Pronouns:						
We currently have two dressing rooms backstage. Each large room has bathroom stalls where you may change privately if you wish. There is also one gender neutral neutral hallway bathroom. At tech rehearsal, you may sign up on the list on the door of the room where you would like to have your costumes stored.						
Tattoos (size and location):						
Piercings:				Allergies:		
Height:		Trousers/jeans:		Dress:		Shirt:
Weight:		Suit:		Bra:		Shoe:
Head:	24.5			CB nape to shoulder: 10		
Headband:	25.5			to elbow: 22		
Ear to Ear:	14			to wrist: 24		
Neck–Upper:	16	Base:	17	Underarm to wrist: 16		
Shoulder Seam:	5.5			Shoulder to bicep: 7		
Chest:	48	expanded:	48	to wrist: 24		
Ribcage:	43			Armscye: 21		
Waist:	42	expanded:	41	Bicep:	15.5	
High hip:	46	taken at:	4	Forearm:	12.5	
Low hip:	49	taken at:	8	Wrist:	8	
Front half:	29			Hand (duck): 11		
Halter:	32			Thigh:	28	
Point to point:	9			Calf:	20	
Across Shoulder:		Front: 15	Back: 19	Above knee: 22		
Armscye to Armscye:		Front: 16	Back: 18	Below knee: 18		
Nape to Waist:		Front: 15	Back: 17	Ankle:		11
Nape to floor:		Front: 58	Back: 61	Waist to below knee: 24		
Underarm to waist: 8				Waist to floor: 42		
Half girth:	33			Inseam to floor: 30		
Full Girth:	70			Seated rise: 10		
Trace foot on back of sheeet.						

FIGURE 9.6 *Measurements used for sloper blueprint examples*

HANDSTITCHING TECHNIQUES

If you have access to a sewing machine, that's great. You can alter and build garments quite quickly. If you do not have access to a sewing machine, it is possible to assemble and alter garments with just needle, thread, and scissors. There are many existing resources that describe how to sew by hand. There is also not necessarily a "right" or "wrong" way to use thread to hold things together. As long as it is secure enough for the task at hand and looks the way you want it to look, you are in good shape. Here, I offer descriptions of handstitching techniques that have been useful in my work. I hope they are helpful to you.

Basting Stitch

Also known as a running stitch—the simplest of all the handsewing stitches. Use this when you want to attach things together temporarily in a way that can be easily removed. Also useful for thread tracing lines on fabric. Thread your needle and don't tie any knots. Pull the thread through the eye of the needle so that one tail is approximately 6–8 inches and the other is about 30 inches. Sink the needle into the fabric and advance half an inch before pulling the needle out. Repeat, following the line where you want to stitch, in and out, in and out. You can vary the stitch length depending on the application. If you are stitching a very wide hem, you may want to make each stitch longer than an inch.

Back Stitch

This is the most secure of all the handsewing stitches. Use this when you want to attach things together in a more permanent way. Start by threading your needle and tying a knot at the end of the longer tail of thread. I tie a knot by making a loop of thread, twirling it around three times, and then pulling the end of the thread through the loop. Any method of tying a knot here is fine, as long as the knot is big enough that it won't get pulled through the fabric. Trim the tail of the thread so that the knot is at the very end. Begin just like the basting stitch: sink your needle in to the fabric and out of the fabric about a quarter-inch beyond where you sunk it in, on your stitching line. Pull the thread all the way through so that the knot at the end is touching the fabric. Then, take the point of your needle BACK to the point where you first sunk it in, where the knot is. Sink the needle in, and then out a quarter-inch beyond the point where your thread is coming out of the fabric. Pull the thread all the way through so that the stitches are taut. For the next stitch, sink the point of the needle in where the first stitch ended, advance beyond it under it, and pull it through. Repeat, consistently going back to your last stitch and advancing forward on the line beyond it. For even more secure backstitches, make the stitch length shorter than a quarter-inch.

To securely finish any line of handstitching, I recommend a French knot, also known as an embroidery knot. Sink your needle in and out of the fabric right under where your thread is coming out of the fabric, as if you are taking a stitch that is one-sixteenth of an inch long, but do not pull your needle all the way through. Take the thread that is coming out of the fabric (not the one that is coming out of the needle) and wrap it around the sharp end of the needle three times. Pull this thread taught, hold it down by pinching the thread and the fabric, and pull the needle through. Before you clip your thread, take another stitch right under the knot so that the tail isn't coming directly out of the knot, which would make it easier to come loose. Always clip your threads close to the fabric.

Whip Stitch

A very secure stitch, useful for attaching one fabric on top of another fabric. In costume shops, this is often used for stitching labels into garments. Begin with your needle threaded and a knot tied at the end of the longer tail. Sink your needle into the fabric above the line (the overlap of the two fabrics), and come out below the line. Pull the thread so that the knot is against the fabric, then take another stitch, sinking your needle in above the line and coming out below. Like all stitches, you can vary the length of your stitches depending on how secure it needs to be. For stitching labels into garments, keep your stitches about one-eighth of an inch to one-quarter of an inch. Finish with a French knot.

At any point in any line of stitching, if you have less than six inches of thread left, tie a French knot wherever you are and finish the rest of the line of stitching with a new thread.

Slip Stitch

Use this any time you want your stitches to be invisible, like when you are stitching trim or applique on top of a garment, or stitching a fold to stay folded. Start by taking a small anchoring stitch next to the fold. Then, sink your needle into the fold and send it through the fold as if the fold were a tunnel for about a quarter inch. Pull the needle out of the fold, then take a tiny anchoring stitch, like a small bit of the fabric, sinking the needle in and out of the base fabric directly next to the fold, right next to where the thread came out. Send your needle for another dive through the tunnel, sinking it into the fold right next to where the last thread came out, advancing for about a quarter inch, and then coming out of the fold. Repeat.

Cross Stitch

Also known as a catch stitch. Useful for stitching up hems because it has circular flexibility and can be invisible from the outside of a garment. In this description, the "line" will be the edge of the hem, folded up in the inside of the garment. If you are right-handed, begin with your needle pointing to your left. Take a small stitch, about one-eighth of an inch, just through the hem allowance, with your needle parallel to the line. Pull the thread through so that the knot is touching the fabric. Advance about half an inch to the right of the stitch you just took, then take a tiny stitch in the fabric above the hem allowance. Keep your needle parallel to the line. Try to grab just one or two threads of the fabric, so that these stitches are not visible on the outside of the garment. Pull the stitch so that it is taught, but be careful to not pull so tightly that you create dimples in the fabric. Advance another half inch to your right, keep the needle pointed toward your left, and take another one-eighth inch long stitch parallel to the line, about one-eighth of an inch below it, just through the hem allowance. Continuing in this manner, you will see Xs of thread form, hence the name cross stitch. Finish with a French knot.

RESEARCH PROCESS POSSIBILITIES

Every devising project is going to be different, so it is impossible to create a template that is truly one size fits all. You will need to make adjustments based on the needs of your specific situation. That is part of what is exciting about devising, yet it can also be what makes it feel frightening. If you are feeling at a loss for where to even begin, hopefully parts of this framework will be helpful to you.

Step 1

Is there a source text? If so, does it hold any information about specific characters? You may be able to begin your process much like you would for a non-devised piece, even if there are still a lot of other moving parts.

If you are starting with a text that does not specify characters, begin by making a list of topics or themes mentioned in the text.

If you are not starting with any text, take notes on early conversations. What ideas are coming up in the group? These conversations might be taking place in rehearsals, in organized production meetings, or in informal discussions among collaborators. Make a list of themes or topics that come up.

Step 2

Gather images. If you have access to books, look through books. If you have access to the internet, search the internet for images related to your list of topics. You can start as simply as entering words from your list into the search bar of search engines. This will give you a surface level assembly of images. Follow your instincts, trust your gut, go down the rabbit holes that pique your curiosity. As much as devising is about listening to others, it can also be an opportunity to practice listening to yourself. The images you compile could be literal representations of the initial ideas, or they could be more abstract.

Another way to gather images is to go outside and take photographs. Observe the world around you and capture anything that connects to the themes of your project. This could include art, architecture, nature, people. If you are working on a piece that might be set in contemporary times, pay attention to what people are wearing and what clothes are available in stores.

Step 3

Organize your collection of images somehow. Use a method that will work for you. This could be saved in files on your computer, stored on a drive online or on a website, like Dropbox or Google Drive or Pinterest. If you found images in books, maybe your collection is a stack of photocopies. If you took photos with a camera or smartphone, organize them in files on a computer, print them from a computer, or get them printed at a drugstore. I highly recommend having a stack of tangible images if possible.

Step 4

Share your images and talk about them! If you have images printed out, you can spread them out over the table as you meet with your team of collaborators. Ask questions about what resonates with the group, what feels like it is working with the direction the piece is heading in. If you have pictures printed out and cut apart, you can move them around and see what patterns emerge and what ideas take shape. Listen to feedback about what images aren't right for the piece and remove those images.

Step 5

Go back and find more images in the vein of the things that are working. Save the things that didn't work this time, maybe they will fit perfectly on a different project.

Continue cycling through steps 1–5 as the piece develops. In a devising process, the research period might not really end, because the direction can change at any moment and you've got to be ready to change with it. So the more efficient you can get at all of these steps, the easier it will be to adjust and be ready to create something new.

PAPERWORK EXAMPLES AND TEMPLATES

Please feel free to copy and use any of these templates exactly as they are, and feel free to take parts of them and adjust them to suit your needs. The first is a version of a statement of necessary intimacy, originally created by costumer Laura Perkins.

LSU THEATRE STATEMENT OF NECESSARY INTIMACY: COSTUME DEPARTMENT

Policy of Necessary Intimacy and Mutual Respect

In costume work, it is necessary for costume personnel to engage in what we refer to as "necessary intimacy." This will be defined as follows:

- Touching performers' bodies (including their hair and faces) and garment and accessories (including wigs) worn by performers in order to measure, mark, fit, and establish fit.
- Discussion of performers' bodies (including hair and faces), undergarments, and garments worn by performers in order to measure, mark, fit, and establish fit.
- Touching garments and undergarments worn by performers in order to launder, alter, and maintain them.

Mutual respect is necessary for costume personnel and performers to work together

Costume personnel will at all times engage in utmost respectful behavior regarding race, ethnicity, gender identity, sexual orientation, age, ability, neurodiversity, and any other performer concern.

General rules of behavior include:

- Costume personnel will always request permission and/or telegraph intention and/or announce intent to touch areas of the body during measurements, fittings, rehearsals, and performances.
- Costume personnel will always ask performer level of comfort with privacy in changing clothing, and will understand that leaving the performer to change privately in the fitting room is the norm unless the performer gives them verbal permission otherwise. Costume personnel are aware and will keep alert that permission may be altered at any time.
- Costume personnel will always speak respectfully of the body, clothing, and accessories (including hair and wig), and performer.
- Costume personnel will promote and acknowledge that all challenges are always with clothing, garments, and accessories—not with bodies.
- Costume personnel will use appropriate pronouns and terminology for all individuals involved in the production, and will accept correction with grace.

Performers are expected to engage in utmost respectful behavior regarding comfort level of costume employees including:

- Wear appropriate undergarments to all fittings (including initial measurements), dress rehearsals, and performances.
- Establish comfort level of undress with costume employee for all fittings and do not assume that the comfort level of undress remains the same.
- Maintain a respectful level of dress while in the dressing room during pre-show, show, and post-show.
- Always speak respectfully of the body, clothing, and accessories (including makeup, hair, and wig), of not only themselves but of all other performers and of the costume personnel.
- With all individuals involved in the production, use appropriate pronouns and terminology and accept correction with grace.

Love and Information Budget

Item	Date	Amount	
Plato's Closet	14-Jan	202.08	
Plato's Closet	21-Jan	454.9	
H and M	21-Jan	408.77	
Plato's Closet	22-Jan	123.2	
Amazon Pacific Coast Treasures	23-Jan	16.87	
Amazon uxcell	23-Jan	28.6	
Amazon uxcell	23-Jan	7.15	
JC Penney	28-Jan	217.58	
H and M	3-Feb	219.96	
Target	4-Feb	222.93	
Plato's Closet	5-Feb	100	
JC Penney	5-Feb	63.35	
Target	5-Feb	127.22	
Amazon	5-Feb	145.14	
DSW	12-Feb	133.2	
Amazon tax credit			13.2
		2470.95	2500

FIGURE 9.7 *Keep track of spending with a budget spreadsheet*

Both performers and costume personnel agree to the following:

- Refrain from wearing strongly scented toiletries, smoking, vaping, or otherwise wearing allergen when scheduled for measurements or fittings, or at any time while wearing a costume.
- Engage in respectful personal device and social media behavior in line with that of professional regional theatres:
    - o   Do not conduct calls or texts during measurements or fittings.
    - o   Do not take pictures of others without their permission.
    - o   Do not share pictures from fittings, backstage, in dressing rooms, or in costume unless it is approved as a marketing technique by the department or as a necessary part of work.
- o   If permitted to take photos as per the department, credit all designers and performers if posting to social media. This requires consent of all parties named and may require departmental approval.

If at any time you feel that this policy has been violated, please immediately notify [include name and contact information of designated responsible person in your organization here]

_____

I have read and accept these responsibilities   Date
(Performer's signature)

_____

Please print name

Scene	Secret	Census	Fan	MOVE	Torture	Lab	Sleep	Remote	MOVE
Section	1	1	1	1	1	1	1	1	
Alex, FA									
Joe, C, K									
Charles, FA, K, C									
Meg, FA, K									
Lee Ann, FA, C, K	black hoodie, grey jeans, grey shirt								
Andres, C									
Chelsea, FA, C, K									
Noah, C									
Kelsie, FA, K, C									
Lucas, FA, C, K									

FIGURE 9.8   *Create a scene breakdown like a grid that you can fill in as you watch rehearsal*

Scene	Secret	Census	Fan	Torture	Lab	Sleep	Scene	Remote
Alex							**Alex**	Blue jeans Grey tee Big brown sweater Black flats
Joe					Khakis Grey/pink tee Hoodie Sneakers		**Joe**	
Charles			Marvel tee shirt Basketball shorts Sneakers				**Charles**	Jeans Green tee Brown hoodie Sneakers
Meg		grey jeans black tank top Light grey sweater Black boots			Black tank top Dress Green jersey cardigan Black boots		**Meg**	
Lee Ann	grey jeans grey shirt black hoodie Black flats			Coveralls			**Lee Ann**	
Andres		Grey jeans Grey tee red sweater Black sneakers					**Andres**	
Chelsea			Black/red tee shirt Jeans Black flats				**Chelsea**	
Noah	Grey jeans Brown tee green jean jacket Black sneakers				Grey jeans Brown tee Button up, sleeves rolled up Black sneakers		**Noah**	
Kelsie					Grey jeans Black tank top Lavender button up Black blazer Black boots	Grey jeans Black tank top Hoodie Sneakers	**Kelsie**	
Lucas						Blue jeans Blue tee Red hoodie Sneakers	**Lucas**	

FIGURE 9.9 *To keep track of changes and of who is on stage at the same time, dressing lists entered into a scene breakdown can be useful*

Lee Ann Hernandez

Scene	Costume
Secret	Grey jeans
Census	Grey shirt
Fan	Black hoodie
	Black flats

Torture	Coveralls
Lab, Sleep, Remote	
Irrational	Grey jeans
Affair	Grey tee
	Black flats

Mother	Grey jeans
Fired	Bird shirt
	Flannel
	Black flats

Santa	Grey jeans
IN LINE	Bird shirt
Message	Black flats
Morse code, Grass, Terminal	
MOVE	Grey jeans
Schizophrenic	White tee
Spies	Denim shirt
Dream	Brown cardigan
Recluse	Black flats
God's Voice	
Child Fear	
Flashlights	
Star	
Wedding Video	Black bike shorts
	White camisole
Savant	Bird shirt
Ex	Beige flats

Memory House	Painters coveralls
	Beige flats
Dinner	
TimeTables	Coveralls
Piano	
Birds Chirping	Coveralls
Flashback	
MOVE	Black bike shorts
Linguist	White camisole
	White graphic tee
	White button up
	Beige flats

Maths	Black bike shorts
Flags	White camisole
	White graphic tee
	White shirt

Sex	Beige flats
God	White camisole
Rash	White graphic tee
Children	Black bike shorts
Magazine	White button up
Shrink	Navy skirt
	Navy blazer
	Scarf

DANCE	Beige flats
	White camisole
	White graphic tee
	Black bike shorts

Child Sorry	Beige flats
Climate	White camisole
	White graphic tee
	Black bike shorts

Censor	Beige flats
Google	White camisole
Wife	White graphic tee
Decision	black bike shorts
	PINK SWEATER!

Child Pain	Black jeans
	Grey longsleeve
	Black flats

Earthquake	Black jeans
	Grey longsleeve
	Black cardigan
	Black flats

WAVING	Coveralls

Chinese Poetry	Black jeans
Manic	Grey longsleeve
Grief	Black flats

Fate	Khakis
	Denim shirt
	Black flats

Stone	Khakis
Virtual	Denim shirt
Small Thing	Grey cardigan
	Black flats

Facts	Khakis

FIGURE 9.10 *The same information, who wears what in each scene, separated by performer, to let them know what to wear in each scene*

Appendix

Alex Abney	8-Feb	9-Feb	10-Feb	11-Feb	12-Feb	14-Feb	15-Feb	16-Feb	17-Feb	####	19-Feb
Blue Jeans	/	/	/	/	/	/	/	/	/	/	/
Grey tee	/	/	/	/	/	/	/	/	/	/	/
Brown Sweater	/	/	/	/	/	/	/	/	/	/	/
Beige Stripe Sweater	/	/	/	/	/	/	/	/	/	/	/
Black Flats	/	/	/	/	/	/	/	/	/	/	/
Pink velvet jacket	/	/	/	/	/	/	/	/	/	/	/
Blue stripe shirt	/	/	/	/	/	/	/	/	/	/	/
Floral Dress	/	/	/	/	/	/	/	/	/	/	/
Black boots	/	/	/	/	/	/	/	/	/	/	/
Leather jacket	/	/	/	/	/	/	/	/	/	/	/
White shirt	/	/	/	/	/	/	/	/	/	/	/
Navy skirt	/	/	/	/	/	/	/	/	/	/	/
Navy blazer with wings	/	/	/	/	/	/	/	/	/	/	/
Red white and blue scarf	/	/	/	/	/	/	/	/	/	/	/
Grey sweater	/	/	/	/	/	/	/	/	/	/	/
Grey lace top	/	/	/	/	/	/	/	/	/	/	/
Black long coat	/	/	/	/	/	/	/	/	/	/	/
Baseball tee	/	/	/	/	/	/	/	/	/	/	/
Joy division hoodie	/	/	/	/	/	/	/	/	/	/	/
Black jeans	/	/	/	/	/	/	/	/	/	/	/
Coveralls	/	/	/	/	/	/	/	/	/	/	/
Green top	/	/	/	/	/	/	/	/	/	/	/
Grey cardigan	/	/	/	/	/	/	/	/	/	/	/

Machine wash cold as needed
Wardrobe spray as needed
PRESS when needed

FIGURE 9.11 *Check-in lists for wardrobe crew, color coded with laundry instructions*

INDEX

Note: Page numbers in italics refer to a figure or a caption

A
ableism 181
Abramovic, Marina 211
accessibility 80, 191–92
acrylic paint *40, 42*
actors: and costume design 83; involving in costume creation 125–26, 129, 131–32; using their own clothes for costumes 32, 67, 73, 133–34
Adair, Amani *165–66*
aerial artistry 9, *126–28*, 189–90
after-school programs 113
ageism 181
Airline Highway: cast changes 10; costume design for 83, 97–8, 103; dress rehearsal *11*; mentioned 84; research images *86*; scenes from *86*; at Swine Palace *98*
alternative storytelling 75
Anderson, RaeAnn *215*
Applause Youth Theatre (Cary, North Carolina) 112–13, *115, 117*
Arbury, Ahmed 169
Around the World in Folk and Fairytales 59
Artist is Present, The (Abramovic) 211
Artist Spotlights: Adanma Barton 157–69; Alan White 51–8; Andrea Morales 78–86; Camilla Morrison 199–219; Carrie Bellew 12–6; Carrigan O'Brian 65–6; Emilio Rodriguez 192–98; Emma Arends Montes 92–103; Gina Sandí Díaz 44–51; Kain Gill 21–8; Lena Sands 151–55; Maggie McGurn 71–8; Mikaela Herrera 59–65; Nathan Ynacay 86–92; Pamela Rodriguez-Montero 169–77; Rachel Baranski 112–18; Rachel Engstrom 139–51; Rowen Haigh 28–33; Sara Osi Scott 107–10; Siouxsie Easter 132–39; Suellen da Costa Coelho 185–91; Tonya Hays 16–21
Association for Theatre in Higher Education (ATHE) 180
As the Ivy Grows 133, *134–35*
audience: engagement of 46; experience of 54, 66, 79–9, 92, 110, 116, 141, 147, 149, 158, 194, 209; feedback from 31, 67, 76; participation 1, *12*, 13, 31, 91, 140, 200, 203–05; surveys from 205; young 75, 115, 174–75, 199
autobiography 55, 63, 73–6, 78
Avery, Nicole "Broadway" *193, 197*

B
Babylon, Journey of the Refugees 52
back stitch 227–28
Baranski, Rachel 112–18
Barton, Adanma Onydike *157–69, 163, 165, 168*
basting stitch 227
Bear Loves Honey, The 29–31, *31*
"Beautifully Emotional" 203
Beckett, Samuel 147
Bellew, Carrie 12–6, *15, 184*
Berea College Theatre *168*
Beydoun, Leyla *198*
Black and Brown Theatre *193–95, 198, 200*
Black Lives Matter 60, 169
Bogart, Anne 186
brainstorming 38, 52, 54, 115, 117, 197, 203
Broe, Jazmine Kuyayki *193, 195*
budgets 25, 56, 116, 122, 230

C
Cajun Christmas on the Bayou 12
Camilla Morrison *212*
"Carrying" 205–07
cast list 9–11
Chakin, Joseph 3
Chapman, Daniel *163, 165, 168*
Chapman University 145
character creation 121–22, 124–25, 133
Chicago, Judy 211
choreography and choreographers 7–8, 38, *40*, 48, 67, 87–8, 93–5, 116, 119, 122, 140–42, 144, 148, 175–76, 188; *see also* dance
Churchill, Carol 3
classism 181
Clinton, Hillary 133
Coelho, Suellen da Costa 185–91; costumes by *188–90*; renderings by *187*
collaboration 2, 21, 28, 29, 45, 52, 82, 92, 101, 106, 112; with actors *86*, *98*, 131, *190*; interdisciplinary 175–76; non-hierarchical 179–80
collaborative art 2, 59, 86, 105, 179, 182
collages 24, 36, 93–4, 112, *112, 114*
collective art 28
collective creation 44, 169
college theatre 26
Collins, Ally *134–35*
communication: with actors 126, *131*; hand signals 181–82; transparency in 182; verbal 38–42; visual 35–8, 67
community theatre 47–8, 149
"Contacting the World" conference 32
Contreras, Fernando 49
Corner of 26 and Lost (McGurn) 72, 73–4, *74*
cosplay 51, 58
Costella, Katelyn 134
costume changes 74, 108, *109*, 129
costumes: and actor agency 85–6; actors' own clothes 32, 67, 73, 133–34; adding and subtracting layers 25, 69–70, 84, 90, 130; base costumes 116; for brides of Dracula 90; for dancers 186–88, *187–89*; on dress forms 67; enough to specify character 181; fittings 131–32, *132*; '50s era 144; "found" sources 33; grey morph suits 131, *133*; keeping stock organized 69; list by performer 233; about love and loss 3, 36, 38, *39–44*; necessary intimacy and mutual respect in fittings 229–31; patterns for 224–27, *225*; photographs of 126, 129–32; as projection surfaces 4, 121–22, *121, 133*; as props 52, 83, 138; pulling 67, 69, 71, 98, 102, 126; in a range of sizes 67–8; renderings 88–9, 93–4, 96, 105, 152–53, 154, 187, 203, 205, 208, 211, 213–16; sketching 24–5, 119–20, 194; that allow movement 134; from thrift/secondhand stores 31, 69, 71, 87
Costume Technician's Handbook, The (Ingham and Covey) 35
Covey, Liz 35
Critical Mass Performance Group *150*
cross stitch 228
cultural humility 42

D
Dali, Salvador 186
dance 3, 28, *39*, 67, 68, 93, 124, *127*, 140–41; costumes for *39–40, 68, 186–88, 187–89*; devised 186, *186–87*; immersive 190; *see also* choreography and choreographers

Dannenfelser, David 132
Davis, Courtney 210
decision making: consensus-based 180–82; non-hierarchical 136–37, 179–80
devised film 21, 27
devised theatre: advantages of 51–2; costume department 2; defined 1–2, 12, 51, 59, 65–6, 71, 86; power and possibility of 3, 5; with and without script 2–3, 122
Diary of Anne Frank 95, 101
Díaz, Gina Sandí 44–51, *49*, 172
Dinner Party, The (Chicago) 211
Double Edged Theater 52
Douglas, Kiana 195
Doyle, Anthony 21, 60, 64
Dracula 87–8, *88–90*, 90–2
dramaturgs 55–6, 60, 62, 92
Dreamland 184
Dream Logos 61–2; aerial artistry 9, *126–28*, 189–90; character changes 128; collaboration for 3; costumes for 122, 124–26, 128–29, 180, 182; dramaturg for 60, 64; at Edinburgh International Fringe Festival 5, 123–24, 128, 130, 134; inspiration for 122; at Louisiana State University 126; notes and rough sketches for 120; rehearsal for 4, 131; scenes from 127–28; snake goddess costumes 129
Dupas, Maja 41

E
Easter, Siouxsie 132–39
Edinburgh International Fringe Festival 10, 43
El Buen Pastor (women's prison) 48–9, *49*
"Elephant Wars" 94, *94*
empathy 81, 90, 195–96
Engstrom, Rachel 139–51, *139*; costumes by *139*, *143–45*
equity 13, 56, 91, 191–92
Erickson, Nick 7, 38, 60, 62, 122
Eugene O'Neil Theater Center 38, 65
Eurydice 96, *96*

F
fabrics: direct dye application 41; dyeable and paintable 9–10, 42, 106; inexpensive for mockups 124; Modcloth 95; modification of 216; painted *39*, 106; photo transfer fabric 40; stretch 122, 124–25, 127; watercolor pencils heat set into 39
feminism 75, 79
fitting room supplies 129
flexibility 7, 10, 22, 45, 79–80, 83–6, 114, 125, 143, 171, 180
Flikkie, Jan 163, 165, 168
Floyd, George 169
Foley, Bryce 197–98
448 Psychosis 65
Frankenstein, After Mary Shelly 151, 153
Fraser, Mikaela 170, 172–74

G
Garcia, Eric Meyer 25
Gargoyles 132
Gill, Kain 21–8
Gloria 96–7, *97*
Grant, Amaya 214
Grimké, Angelina Weld 16
Grits 26
"Grounding Seeds" 214
Gudan, Hannah 206–07
Gulfport High School 184

H
Haigh, Rowen 28–33
hair 11, 14, 24, 49, 96, 174, 191
Hall, Todrick 93
Hamilton 80, 149
HamlEt 139, 143, *143–44*, *143–44*, 145
handstitching 227–28
Hauf, Abby 134
Hays, Tonya 16–21
Hazel, Shelby 201, 212, 216
Herrera, Mikaela 59–65
Hidden Figures 169
Honest Accomplice Theatre 8
Horribly Short (film festival) 27
How to Catch a Karen 154, *154–55*
humility 90, 101; cultural 42
"Hungry Belly, Hungry Body" 204

I
Ilochonwu, Obinna 163
improvisation 1, 47, 59, 77, 79, 81, 84, 86, 116–17, 122, 132, 138, 183
Ingham, Rosemary 35
installation art 3
Is the High Worth the Risk? 184

J
Jesus In Vitro Panthera Onca 43
Johnson, Kendra 42
Johnson, Lincoln 184
Jones-Jones, Kennikki 199
Journey to Congo Square 68
Jsanea, Rio 41

K
Kaufman, Moises 18
Kennesaw State University (Georgia) 170, 172–74
Keystone, Nancy 150
Krause, Karyn 217

L
Las Anates 43
Latinx theatre 46
Lauchle, Luke 134–35
León, Ofir 49
Leon, Ophelia 48
Letters to a Lady 17
"Letting Go" 208
lighting 43, 46, 99, 108, 111, *120*, 126, 140, 142, 149
Link, Malcolm Andrew 168
Little Prince, The 116
LMNOP 86
Lock, Lisa 175, *175–76*
Los Pejor (novel, Contreras) 48
Los Pejor/Las Pejor (stage production) 48–9, *49*
Louisiana State University 3, *39*, 49, 64, 70, 81, *107*, 126, *206*; museum of art 200, *207*; policy of necessary intimacy 229–31
"Love and Expectations" 201, 212–13
Love and Information 35; airport setting 122; budget 230; character changes 69, 120; color scheme for 105; costume design for 3; fitting photos 130–31; at Louisiana State University 3, 70–1; music for 111; paperwork for 157–62; rehearsals for 120; research images 36, 121; scenes from 218

M
Map of Migrations (Murillo) 176
Marenca, Valentina 49
Mariology 152–53, 154, *154*
marketing materials 116
Márquez, Gabriel García 50
masks 146, *175–76*, 190
McAdams, Barbara Pitts 18
McGurn, Maggie 71–8, *72*, 202
measurements 221–24, *224*, 227
mentorship 100, 185, 188–89, 219
Mirror on the Wall 193, 195
misogyny 181
mistakes 14, 27, 100–01
moment work 12, 18, 20, 52, 157
Moment Work, Tectonic Theater Project's Process of Devising Theater (Kaufman and McAdams) 18, 184
monologues 50–1, 79, 137–38, 166, 212
monologue shows 12–3, 15
Monroe, James 163, 165
Montes, Emma Arends 92–103, *98*, *102*, 107, 168; renderings by *93–4*, *96*
Moorman, Ricara 168
Morales, Andrea 78–86
Morgan, Amanda Wansa 170, 172–74
Morrison, Caitlin 208
Morrison, Camilla 105, 199–219, *211*, *213*, 216; costumes by *183*, *201–02*, *206–08*, *210*, *212*, *214–15*, *217*; renderings by *203–05*, *208*, *211*, *213–16*
Murillo, Michelle 176
Muscatello, Lindsey 114
music 54, 86, 115, 139–41, 144, 148, 152
Music Inspired Design 110–11, *111*, 113–14
musicals 48, 86, 115, 136–37, 147, 150

N

Naked Empire Buffon Company *154*
Nasir, Evleen *202*
National Theatre Center *65*
Native Americans *19*
Native Gardens *84*
"Necessary Strength" *210–11*
Neverland *91*
Newcott, Rosemary *170, 172–74*
Nightmares Are Dreams, Too *76, 183, 200, 202–08*
Nunez, Raquel d. Garbanzo *163*

O

O'Brian, Carrigan *38, 65–6*
OC Centric New Play Festival *139*
Of the Earth *201, 209, 210–16, 217*
online theatre *91, 155*
organization *25–6, 157, 167, 229*; costume list *233*; scene breakdown grid *231–32*; spreadsheets *158–62*; wardrobe crew check-in *234*
Our Weddings *32, 32*

P

painted fabric *39*
paper dolls *154*
paperwork *229*; *see also* organization
Peculiar Proximity to Spiritual Mysteries, A *176*
Persley, Nicole Hodges *180–81*
photo transfer fabric *40*
physical theater *3, 186, 190*
pipe cleaners *138*
Plastic Drastic *25*
postmortems *14*
Pradella, Michele *134–35*
printer transfer paper *41*
Private Wars *61*
production management *7–9*; developing a plan *9–11*; need for flexibility *11–2*
props *24, 52, 55–6, 83, 99, 111, 138, 166*
Pukaar *32*
puppets *52–3, 87, 154*

Q

Quiones, Sam *184*

R

race *57–60, 78–9*
Rachel (Grimké) *16*
racism *51, 54, 92, 181*
Rai, Kendra *11*
REDCAT NOW Festival 2017 *150*
reference sketches *see* sketching
rehearsals *69, 106, 117, 131, 153*; dress *11, 106*; importance of *119–20*; recording *66*
renderings *88–9, 93–4, 96, 105, 152–53, 154, 187, 203–05, 208, 211, 213–15*

research images *7, 36, 36, 40, 85, 105–06, 111, 121*
research process *228–29*
resilience *27, 79, 101, 105, 219*
resist dye *41*
Rivera, Daniel Alexander *198*
Rodriguez, Emilio *192–98*
Rodriguez-Montero, Pamela *169–77, 170, 172–75*
Roosevelt, Eleanor *17*
Rosencrantz and Guildenstern Are Dead *144*
Royally Unseen *56, 57*

S

Sandglass Theater *52*
Sands, Lena *151–55, 152*; costumes by *150–51, 154*; renderings by *152–53*
Savage/Love: costume design for *3, 39–40, 43*; costume fittings *131*; costumes inspired by tattoos *106, 108*; at Edinburgh International Fringe Festival *2*; at Louisiana State University *107*; planning for costume design *9–10, 10, 36, 38, 42, 44, 106*; rehearsals for *120*; renderings *37*; research images *111*; scenes from *37–8, 40–1, 43, 43, 70–1*; schedule for *7–8*; warm-up exercises *120*
Say Her Name, Breonna Taylor *158, 163–66, 165, 168*
scheduling *7–8, 22, 136, 164, 203*
Scott, Sara Osi *107–10, 109–10*
sexism *55, 92*
Shakespeare, William *143–45, 147, 195*
Shepard, Sam *3*
shoes *84–5, 94, 126, 136, 142, 207*
shop manager *2–3, 7, 9, 40, 101, 119, 157, 174, 208, 219, 221*
shopper *2, 9*
Shupe, Ami *163, 165, 168*
Siddiqui, Hina *32–3*
Signos Teatro Danza *49*
Silence the Musical *147*
sketching *24–5, 119, 120, 194*
skin color *60*
slip stitch *228*
slopers *224–26, 225, 227*
Small Mouth Sounds *102*
Southeastern Theatre Conference (SETC) *18, 48, 184*
Star Wars *58*
Steinem, Gloria *79*
Stillwell Theatre *170, 72–74*
Stinson, Kaetlyn *134*
storytelling *3, 17, 48, 55, 91, 150, 169, 174–75, 212*; alternative *75*; community *107*; and costumes *183*; theatrical *20*
Sullivan, Rachel *8–9*
summer camps *113, 115, 116*
Superheroes in Disguise *192–93, 197–99*
sustainability *46, 48, 71, 80*
Sweeney, Mat *151*

T

Tales from Ovid *153*
Taylor, Breonna *158, 163–66, 165, 168*
Tectonic theatre *12, 18, 184*
templates *25, 157, 221, 228–34*
theatre: for children *112–18*; college *26*; community *48, 149*; Latinx *46*; online *91, 155*; physical *3, 186, 190*; politically active *150*; site-specific *147*; Tectonic *12, 18, 184*; virtual *55*; zoom *80, 91, 102, 131, 146, 166, 167*
This for That *29, 33, 33*
"This Must Be" *215*
Three Fates, The (Ynacay) *87*
Thumbelina *170, 172–74*
Tiwari, Saawan *193, 195*
"To Be A Woman" *204*
track-out programs *113*
transhumanism *54*
Trojan Women *14, 15*

U

understructure garments/undergarments *11, 60, 126, 229–230*
Untitled Communion *150*
Upgrade (Doyle) *21–4, 61, 64*

V

Valley High School (Louisville) *184*
virtual theatre *55*

W

Waiting for Godot *147*
Wallis, The *151*
wardrobe crew *234*
warm-up exercises *120*
Washington, Tamika *139*
watercolor pencils *39*
"Waters We Know" *216, 217*
Weber, LeAnne *134*
Wells College *133, 134–35*
whip stitch *228*
White, Alan *8, 51–8, 51, 57, 59*
white supremacy *179*
"Who Gets to Be An American?" *18–9*
Wilson, Mercedes *202*
Women in North Dakota *208–12*
women's prison *48–9*

Y

Ynacay, Nathan *86–92, 87–9*
Ypsilanti Elementary school *197–99*

Z

Zambrano, Joshua *193, 195*
zoom theatre *80, 91, 102, 131, 146, 166, 167*
Zukerman Museum of Art *175–76*

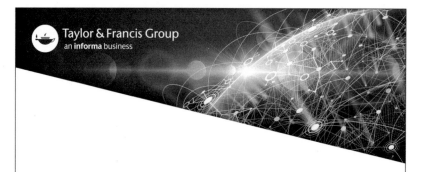